DOUG OWRAM

The Government Generation: Canadian intellectuals and the state 1900–1945

UNIVERSITY OF TORONTO PRESS
Toronto Buffalo London

© University of Toronto Press 1986
Toronto Buffalo London
Printed in Canada

ISBN 0-8020-2581-1 (cloth)
ISBN 0-8020-6604-6 (paper)

Printed on acid-free paper

Canadian Cataloguing in Publication Data

Owram, Douglas, 1947–
    The government generation

    Includes bibliographical references and index.
    ISBN 0-8020-2581-1 (bound). – ISBN 0-8020-6604-6 (pbk.)

    1. Intellectuals – Canada.   2. Canada – Politics
and government – 20th century.   3. Canada – Economic
policy.   I. Title.

    HM213.097 1986   305.5'52'0971   C86-093688-0

This book has been published with the help of a grant from the Social
Science Federation of Canada, using funds provided by the Social Sciences
and Humanities Research Council of Canada. Publication has also been
assisted by block grants from the Canada Council and the Ontario Arts
Council.

THE GOVERNMENT GENERATION:

CANADIAN INTELLECTUALS AND THE STATE 1900-1945

War, depression, secularization, urbanization, and the rise of industry –
between 1900 and 1945 Canada struggled with all these developments, and
from them was born the modern welfare state. New services were created,
along with new taxes to pay for them and expanded bureaucracies to
administer them. Government activity grew enormously; so did government
expenditures. The role of the state in a modern industrialized society
became the focus of a lively and continuing debate for two generations of
intellectual reformers.

Doug Owram looks back at that debate and the academics, civil servants,
and political activists who engaged in it. Adam Shortt, W.L. Grant, Frank
Underhill, W.C. Clark, Harold Innis, and many others exchanged ideas –
sometimes cautiously, sometimes passionately – about the wisdom of
planning and reform, and on practical schemes for their realization. Owram
explores the reforming impulse and its political dimension: the impact
of war and depression on attitudes to the state, the League of Social
Reconstruction and its relations with the CCF, R.B. Bennett's New Deal,
and the various changes of heart experienced over forty years by
Mackenzie King.

The Canada that emerged from the Second World War was very different
from the one that had existed at the turn of the century; relations between
the individual and the state had altered drastically and irrevocably. The
people examined in this book and the social and political movements in
which they believed helped shape Canada's response to powerful forces that
were changing its way of life forever.

DOUG OWRAM is a professor of history, University of Alberta, and the author
of *Promise of Eden: The Canadian Expansionist Movement and the Idea of
the West, 1856-1900.*

To my parents

Contents

Preface

The first half of the twentieth century brought dramatic and irrevocable changes in the role of governments in Canada. The terms *welfare state, positive state, mixed economy,* and *state capitalism* and numerous others have been used to describe the results. Whatever labels are employed, however, the facts are obvious and inescapable. In the years between Laurier's election as prime minister in 1896 and the end of the Second World War there was a dramatic expansion in the responsibilities and size of Canadian government at all levels. We can gain some idea of the extent of these changes by a brief comparison of the Laurier and King governments. In its first year in office the total expenditures of the Laurier government were $36 million. The revenues that supported these expenditures were raised primarily by the indirect taxes provided by customs and excise duties, while spending was directed by 14 ministers presiding over a permanent civil service of approximately 5000 people.[1]

By 1945 the budget had reached nearly $5.25 billion and the end of the war would bring only temporary reductions before the upward trend of expenditures resumed. Government departments and agencies had expanded to include bodies like the Bank of Canada (to protect our money), the Canadian Broadcasting Corporation (to protect our souls), and the Department of Health and Welfare (to protect everything in between). The growth in departments was accompanied by a proportionate increase in the civil service, which now amounted to more than 115,000 individuals. Their wages alone were five times as great as the total Dominion budget in 1896. The range of state activities had also expanded. Old Age Pensions, Unemployment Insurance, Family Allowances, Dominion Assisted Housing, and other social security policies had been implemented. Equally important was the assumption by such traditional departments as Finance that a much more active and interventionist role in economic management was required. Indeed, the very concept of economic management was a product of these years. Major new levies, including direct corporate and income taxes, had supplanted customs and excise taxes as the major sources of revenue. If the 'rugged individualism' of Canada which so many writers trumpeted about in Laurier's time had ever been a part of Canadian society, it was certainly replaced by a more complex web of government support systems by the end of the Second World War. Nothing marked the first half of the twentieth century so much as this change in the nature and role of the state. This work will discuss the evolution of the modern state in Canada by looking at one powerful force that both assessed and urged that development: that community of intellectuals who were not only active in observing and assessing the changing nature of the state in Canada but were also the proponents of, and participants in, that change.[2]

Underlying these activities was a series of changes within the intellectual community itself. The religious values that shaped the society and the church-based universities that articulated Canadian intellectual values were increasingly challenged by the rise of scientific thought, and specific doctrines like Darwinism, by the end of the nineteenth century. As the twentieth century began, these intellectual challenges were compounded by emerging social conditions that demanded new roles for the intellectual and religious communities. The academic in his ivory tower and the clergyman preaching on esoteric points of doctrine were increasingly irrelevant in a society faced with new and dangerous social and economic divisions. Though many academics remained cloistered within their traditional disciplines and many clergymen were never profoundly affected by social concerns, the significant trend of the age was towards a new coalition of activist intellectuals who sought both to assess the needs of modern society and to advocate solutions.

For these intellectuals it was not enough to criticize government and wait for it to respond. Rather, it was their view that modern conditions, in particular the rise of an industrial economy, demanded not only a much enlarged state but also new expertise in running the nation. Politicians, and the businessmen for whom the politicians were often thought to speak, were too caught up in their own vested interests, and too uninformed about the complexities of the modern era, to be left to their own devices, especially as new and frightening voices of discontent seemed to threaten the stability of the nation. The spectre of social polarization required a well-thought-out strategy of change that would avoid either ill-considered experimentation or harsh reaction. For the intellectuals the answer was increasingly clear. As disinterested experts they had to gain sufficient influence to be heard at the highest levels of policy making. Concomitant with the rise of the modern state, therefore, was a concerted drive on the part of a new elite to assert its importance as an agent of reform.

This work does not pretend to provide the whole story behind the rise of the modern state nor does it deal with those reform causes in which the state was not central. Such a task would take more than one volume. There were many other voices for reform that were responding to the same industrial and social conditions discussed in the following pages. Labour unionism, business reformism and reaction, the women's movement, public insecurity, the examples of other nations, and sheer partisan politics all played an important part in the evolution of the modern state. To some degree these factors impinge on this work, but the main theme is the interaction between ideas and social forces and the effect these have had on government. In addition, politics, the legislative and administrative processes, and other factors are important to the understanding of the way in which this interaction worked out, but they are not central to this study. Rather, the focus is on the impulse toward reform by means of state intervention from a particular group of intellectuals. Given these limitations, however, it is the contention of this study that the changing philosophies and the individuals who articulated these changes and sought to act on them were crucial in defining modern Canada.

Throughout this work such terms as *intellectual community*, *intellectual elite*, *brainstrust*, and *intelligentsia* will be employed as a means of describing those intellectuals active in the redefinition of the Canadian state. The exact parameters of this group are defined more fully in the text; but briefly, I am talking only about those specifically interested in and active in promoting discussion or action on the role of the state in Canada. The work most emphatically does not assess the views of all intellectuals in Canada in the years covered.

This limitation raises another difficulty. During the research and writing of this work it became apparent that the term *intellectual* was an elusive one. The easiest definition would be to include only those with either an academic position or, at least, the possession of an advanced degree, because academics, or former academics, predominate throughout the work. To have made the distinction quite so formal would have been to distort the historical process. The 'intellectual community,' especially in the period before the First War, was a product not only of education and profession, but also of social connections and outlook. It was still the age when the amateur expert had not been displaced by the trained professional. Consequently, though academics and ex-academics did have a direct influence on all its members, they never possessed exclusive membership in the elite. Moreover the boundary between intellectual reform and other reform movements was as porous as the definition of the intellectual itself. In the pre-First World War period intellectuals were very much involved with 'middle-class reformism,' which included philanthropists, business reformers, politicians, and, of course, the clergy. Even later, as the university community grew and as the academic asserted his own ideals of reform in a more specific manner, there were always those who fit the mould of intellectual reformer, though they might not possess a doctorate and had never taught in a university. Vincent Massey, one of the last of the gentlemen reformers, provides one obvious example, as do J.S. McLean of Canada Packers and J.M. Macdonnell of National Trust. As Queen's principal W.H. Fyfe once said of the latter, he was 'a damned good imitation of a businessman but right inside he is an academic.'[3] Thus the definition of intellectual reformism is shaped not simply by profession or training, although those are important, but by a shared outlook toward problem solving and analysis, common social values, and close personal connections.

One final qualification should be noted. It is the argument of the first four chapters that there developed in Canada an urban progressive movement that was of some importance in defining the debate in the years up to 1920. This focus is not intended to minimize the importance of rural progressivism which was very strong throughout these years. Rather, it simply reflects the emphasis of the intellectual community, which with very few exceptions was urban, worked and lived in an urban environment, and therefore was involved in urban rather than rural reform. There were several points of cross-over, however, and these will be discussed.

The relation between the intellectual and state reform in this study falls into three overlapping divisions. The first includes the period from 1900 to shortly after the end of the First World War. This was an era in which moral reformism, the social gospel, social uplift, and other approaches mingled in a middle-class effort to come to grips with the new problems of industrialism and urbanization. It was also a time when members of the university community were just beginning to assert their importance as reformers. The second stage begins in the 1920s and matures in the Depression years. Its main characteristics are the assertion of influence by the professional expert, especially the social scientist, and the formation of an elite of young reformers and nationalists who succeeded the pre-war urban progressives. The final part of this work is concerned with the translation of ideas into policy and this new elite's rise to influence in politics and the civil service at the national level.

This book might best be described as a 'mid-range synthesis,' broader in scope than the classic historical monograph but more specifically focused than a general overview. The argument relies in the first instance on primary sources, both printed and manuscript, in order to analyse the evolution of ideas about the state in these years. At the same time a topic as broad in its subject matter as this one would have been impossible without recent studies undertaken by other historians not just in the field of intellectual history but also in such related areas as political, social, and economic history. The argument that follows has been influenced by excellent works related to various aspects of the growth of the modern state and the changing nature of the intellectual community. Recent studies by Richard Allen, Paul Craven, John English, Barry Ferguson, J.L. Granatstein, Michiel Horn, A.B. Mc-Killop, and James Struthers, to name just a few, provided crucial information, and, even more importantly, key hypotheses from which this work could proceed. In addition, histories of universities, which have flourished in the past decade or so, have made it possible to unravel the tremendously complex changes taking place within the academic community itself. These and numerous other sources cited in the notes reveal the tremendous progress that contemporary historians have made in understanding twentieth-century Canada. It is my hope that this work can contribute to that understanding.

Several people were helpful in the production of this work. Carl Berger, Robert Bothwell, David Fransen, David Mills, and Paul Voisey all read parts of it and made valuable suggestions for changes, as did anonymous readers for the University of Toronto Press and the Social Science Federation of Canada. J.L. Granatstein and David Fransen were extremely helpful in providing me with leads resulting from their own work in this area. R.B. Bryce and Irene Spry gave me the benefit of their thoughts on an era in which they were so actively involved. My thanks to Sharon Mackenzie, Eli Brooks, and Lydia Dugbazah who did much of the typing of the manuscript. At the University of Toronto Press John Parry had the thankless job of copy-editing, while Gerry Hallowell did his usual helpful and thorough job as editor. All the above made the research and writing of this manuscript a much easier task than otherwise would have been the case. They, however, must be held blameless for the contents of this work for those remain mine.

THE GOVERNMENT GENERATION

1

'A city of pigs': the intellectual community and social crisis 1895-1914

The years surrounding the turn of the century brought about a fundamental reorientation of the relation between the Canadian academic and the community around him. This period, though one of prosperity, also witnessed social and intellectual crisis. The boom beginning in the last years of the nineteenth century had helped bring about a transformation of the way in which Canadians lived, worked, and thought. In the process traditional institutions, creeds, and solutions became insufficient to deal with the new problems of the twentieth century. Not the least of those affected were those who by training, avocation, and outlook considered themselves members of the intellectual community in Canada. To an increasingly disturbing degree they discovered that they and their ideas were becoming, if not irrelevant, at least marginal to the society around them. It was, as one writer has noted, not 'generally a happy time to be in Canadian academic life.'[1] The result was that these traditional guardians of Canadian values and morals began to search for a new role for themselves in society and for new solutions to the problems confronting Canada. In the process they would begin a transformation both of their own role in society and of that society itself.

As the nineteenth century rolled over into the twentieth, an article in the academic journal *Queen's Quarterly* by a recent law graduate of the university and a future Canadian senator, Andrew Haydon, appeared on the problem of the relation between legislation and morality. On the surface it was a seemingly abstract and rather esoteric issue, yet it obviously struck a chord among other readers of the *Quarterly*. A debate stemming from the piece occupied space in the journal over the next five years.[2] The arguments that were made and the points of consensus that emerged reveal a great deal about the intellectual community's concerns about the direction of Canadian society, possible paths to social improvement, and philosophical ideals at a time when all these things were under challenge.

Haydon's article was inspired by one of the more controversial issues of the day – prohibition. The question of enforced abstinence from alcohol had been an important theme in Canadian political discussion for some time and was, at the time of Haydon's piece, reaching new levels of importance. In Ontario an 1894 plebiscite had indicated widespread support for action against 'the liquor interests,' while in 1898 Wilfrid Laurier had reluctantly fulfilled a campaign promise by holding a Dominion-wide plebiscite. A narrow majority had voted in favour of prohibition, but the large dissenting vote as well as the failure of the prohibition cause in Quebec meant that the issue was far from being decided. Throughout Canada 'wets' and 'drys' took pen in hand to argue their case. Haydon's presentation was, therefore, an attempt to debate some of the basic legal and moral principles behind one of the major social issues of the day.[3]

According to Haydon, the attempt to legislate morality arose out of the insecurity of the age. 'Settled social establishments' were being broken down by increased mobility, industrial circumstances, and technological innovation. This situation led the often confused and bewildered 'ordinary man' to seek panaceas. This search for simple answers and quick cures was what motivated the social reformer who would impose prohibition on the community. The problem with this was, according to Haydon, that legislation must be the final expression of a process that began with the civilizing voice of the reformer, developed into new community values, and was ultimately expressed in law. Any attempt to shortcircuit the process by imposing a law to enforce morality was not only likely to fail but was itself morally wrong. Any 'undue interference' on the part of the state 'may prevent individual action, which is the condition for having any morality at all.' In such areas, then, law had a very limited utility. 'Its true relation to morality is to promote by endorsation and not by attempting to aggressively enforce moral observances.'[4]

In the various replies to Haydon there was a great deal of enthusiastic argument as to the specific role of the courts, the church, the legislator, and the community. Agonized discussion tried to differentiate between laws on gambling and those on liquor, while others sought to prove that protection of the sabbath was somewhat different than prohibition. What is striking about the debate, however, is the fundamental agreement that obviously bound together this community of academics and university graduates at the turn of the century. All accepted Haydon's basic premise that as reform was an internal rather than an external matter it must derive from an individual act of will rather than from external enforcement. As Queen's political economy professor Adam Shortt put it, 'There must be a possibility of acting wrongly if acting rightly is to be a moral act.' The proper role for the reformer, therefore, was not as lawmaker but as educator. 'The great moral progress which has been made in temperance,' argued the Reverend G.M. Macdonnell, 'is the result not so much of legislation as of the effects of the moral reformers in teaching and inspiring self-control.' Legislation could not assist in this area. Indeed, it could actually have a negative effect in that 'it destroys the appeal to the spirit of self-restraint.' As the action of the state must 'always partake of the nature of force' and as the use of legislation by the moral reformer was 'a kind of lash for whipping an unwilling people into line,' the role of the state was limited in its usefulness. It could, it was true, prompt virtue and discourage vice by licensing systems, regulations, and other measures, but ultimately individuals must be the arbiters of their own actions, for only in this way was personal and social progress possible.[5]

There was nothing very startling in these conclusions. The degree of consensus that existed indicates that the authors were explicating well-worn themes rather than breaking any significant new ground. It is, however, the fact that the themes were common among the late-Victorian intellectual community that makes the debate important. Two of the streams of thought that run through the debate both reflect very powerful intellectual beliefs of the period and point to the limitations of the intellectual community's ability to deal with a rapidly changing world.

The first stream emphasized the reform of the inner spirit as a means, and the only means, by which real and lasting improvement in civilization might be achieved. 'Man is a self-conscious and self-determined being, ever seeking to realize himself in the ends which he pursues. In this effort for self-realization he soon discovers that he can only find complete satisfaction in and through Society; in other words the moral good must include the good of others.' Such expressions were scattered throughout the articles and revealed, in greater and lesser degrees of sophistication, an attachment to the philosophic school of post-Hegelian idealism. That philosophic creed, which had been imported into Canada via Scotland, had become the centre-piece of academic philosophy by the end of the century. Queen's University had been one of the centres of the movement, and the fact that all the participants in the debate had probably learned their philosophy in the classroom of the great Queen's idealist, John Watson, may have explained some of the agreement they expressed.[6]

If the idealist orientation is clear, however, the sources cited by the various writers indicate a second stream of thought that influenced the intellectual outlook in this period. For aside from citing traditional idealists like Bernard Bosanquet, the various writers felt free to bring the prestige and ideas of mid-Victorian liberalism into their arguments. Men such as John Stuart Mill and Jeremy Bentham were freely quoted alongside the idealists. This second stream of thought emphasized an attachment to individualism. 'The individual freedom of man ever striving to actively assert himself,' Haydon wrote, 'will not be hedged around by conditions that unnecessarily restrain its free exercise.' Minority rights are thus accentuated to the point where one author argues that 'so long as one individual has failed to attain this moral virtue' the state should not legislate in such a way as to force that individual to comply with the majority viewpoint.[7]

The two streams of thought reflect both the complexity of Canadian philosophic values in these years and hint at some of the tensions that had to be resolved as the nation moved into the twentieth century. In part, of course, individualism was compatible with idealism. That philosophy's emphasis on the inner conscience and the importance of enlightened reason put a tremendous burden on the individual to seek out his own course in the world. It was not that simple, however, for as the citations to Bentham and Mill indicate, there was also a strong attachment in Canada to British constitutional traditions, which emphasized the naturally harmonious relation between individual free will and social well-being. There was, however, a substantial possibility of conflict between idealist philosophy and British constitutionalism. Idealism tended to stress man's role in society and his obligations to that society. It was a viewpoint that in many writings subordinated the individual to the community. In contrast, the British constitutional tradition had elevated the individual above the bonds of state or class over the last century. It was not easy for the two traditions to exist side by side within the Canadian intellectual community. The possible conflicts that existed depended on a specifically Canadian relationship drawn between an individualism that drew on classical economics and utilitarian philosophy and the idealism that stressed that the individual 'can find realization only through society.'[8]

In the realm of legislation and social action, individualism seemed paramount. Canadian, British, and American political and philosophical systems in the nineteenth century had worked toward the removal of artificial class restraints on action. Man, so the myth went, had become free to decide his own fate and was not bound in as had been his ancestors. The problem was that with the possibility of success went the possibility of failure. In an open society the individual could blame nobody but himself. Arnold Haultain, classical liberal and secretary to Goldwin Smith, summed it up when he warned those who would demand new systems to 'see that your tools are sharp and go about your business.' While Canadians never subscribed to the extreme individualism of a Herbert Spencer, this was still an age that reflected the glorious optimism of a world in which nineteenth-century liberalism was a very powerful force.[9]

This mixture of idealism and individualism thus posited a world in which the free will of man was untrammelled by the institutions around him. His moral sense and social leanings would, if properly directed, make that individual effort work toward the benefit of society. Allowing these forces to work themselves out was thus seen as the best means of achieving social improvement. Within this context there was a natural conservatism about action on the part of the state. As the arguments in the *Queen's Quarterly* pointed out, the removal of the decision from the individual was, in itself, an act that seemed to endanger moral improvement. Only the most pressing social need, therefore, would justify such an action. The difference between the prohibitionist and anti-prohibitionist intellectuals was not so much the principles they espoused as the question of whether suppressing the liquor trade was just such a pressing social need.

Yet the idealist strain within the individualism makes the debate a particularly Canadian one. South of the border, in that 'misguided democracy,' the question of state action often turned on matters of principle in which liberty, seen as freedom from restraint, was set up as an absolute principle against which other actions must be judged. Liberty was thus desirable in its own right, and anything that restrained it came in for close scrutiny. In Canada, few within the intellectual community, aside from Goldwin Smith and Arnold Haultain, defended the concept of liberty in the American sense. Individual choice was not so much an absolute principle as it was a means to other more social ends. As the various writings in the *Queen's Quarterly* concluded, the free will of the individual was the best way of achieving the end purpose, the uplifting of society to a more moral level. 'The test of a policy,' wrote Liberal prohibitionist and reformer Newton Rowell, 'must be its efficiency in accomplishing the purpose aimed at.'[10] Individual autonomy was thus employed because it was, in modern terminology, efficient, not because it was a moral purpose in itself. The emphasis of the late nineteenth century on the individual was thus restrained; certain social needs could override individual rights in the name of the community. The line between prohibitionist and anti-prohibitionist was not as great as might have been thought. This is not to say that 'freedom' as a concept in Canada was unimportant, but it was, in the idealist tradition of the late nineteenth century, muted. There was a delicate and complex balance between spirit and environment, and the issue was whether this balance was more likely to be put into disarray than helped by state intervention.

The limited role assigned to the state thus did not imply that individuals should be left to find their own way in society. Such an idea would have been looked upon with horror by those same people who argued against state intervention. Guidance was essential, for man had to understand both his duty to society and the proper way in which to analyse his own actions. Only by emphasizing the positive in society while condemning the evil could men of good will work toward the improvement of civilization. This was not an age that believed in ethical relativism. As Adam Shortt said, the direction must always be 'eternal progress with perfection as its goal.'[11] Those who pointed the way thus assumed a central role in society. In particular, the two guardians of higher culture, the school and the church, had as their central role the provision of intellectual and moral guidance for the nation. The central institutions for social improvement thus became not the state, which could at best minister only to external matters, but the classroom and the pulpit.

Historically in Canada the classroom and the pulpit had merged in the university. With a couple of exceptions, religious and denominational forces had been a major factor in shaping the direction of higher education in the nineteenth century. The training of clerics for the church and the preservation of doctrinal purity among the flock had led various denominations to form their own institutions even at the cost of a

fragmented and financially starved college system. Two major institutions, Toronto and Manitoba, did, it was true, have a non-denomi-
national structure, but only at the university level. The real heart of
the institutions was the numerous colleges, most of them religiously
affiliated. Only McGill University in Montreal stood somewhat above
narrow denominationalism, representing instead the educational voice
of the Anglo-Protestant business class in a Roman Catholic province.[12]

By the end of the nineteenth century the chaotic formation, refor-
mation, and affiliation process that had marked earlier university development in Canada had slowed somewhat. Smaller and financially
strapped institutions had either collapsed or had affiliated with others.
Those that remained now had a degree of permanence in spite of continuing financial precariousness. The most striking contrast with more
recent times is the small size of the Canadian system. The entire enrolment of 6,500 in 1901 was less than that of one medium-sized university today. Less than a dozen institutions – Dalhousie, New Brunswick,
Laval, Bishop's, McGill, Queen's, Toronto, Western, and Manitoba –
were large enough, sometimes barely so, to call themselves universities.
Faculties were equally small, and staff members were thus expected
to teach an incredible range of fields and courses. For example, the
total Arts and Science Faculty of the University of New Brunswick in
1891 was a mere six individuals, and they taught everything from chemistry to classics.[13] Nevertheless, the institutional structure of Canadian
universities for the first half of the twentieth century was taking shape.
Once the new western Canadian universities were founded in the first
decade of the twentieth century there would be few new institutions
developed until after the Second World War.

Within the universities the major debate of the nineteenth century
had been over the proper relation between science and religion. The
Darwinian revolution had accelerated the rise of scientific thought and
thereby the challenge to the supremacy of religion within the university system. By the end of the century, scientific study had largely freed
itself from religious tutelage in most institutions. This was an event
of some importance for it involved not just the courses taught or the
faculty employed but the very way in which the university approached
knowledge. The scientific method, with what has been termed its emphasis on the 'brute fact,' had gained autonomy within the university
structure. Idealism had allowed religious thought to reach a temporary
accommodation with scientific knowledge, but in the process so much
had been ceded that the next generation would see the complete triumph

of the scientific method. The anti-denominationalist movement that existed at the turn of the century was, in fact, a harbinger of a movement toward widespread secularization of higher education in most English-Canadian universities.[14]

That process of secularization was, in 1900, still largely in the future. Denominational affiliation may have been under challenge in a number of institutions, but few would have argued that the university was other than a Christian institution. Stories of agnostics or atheists openly teaching their godless systems in American universities could still bring cries of righteous horror from Canadian educators. Reflecting this continued religious orientation was the predominance of clerics within university faculties, especially in Arts. The religious affiliations of many institutions meant, as well, that chief administrators were also often clerics. George Munro Grant, the principal of Queen's, was, by 1900, the elder statesman of this group. He would be followed in the principalship by his protégé, the Reverend Daniel Gordon. James Loudon, president of the University of Toronto, was not a cleric, but the colleges were headed by churchmen for the most part, and the choice of the Reverend Robert Falconer as his successor meant that after 1907 Canada's largest university was also headed by an ordained minister.

There were various historical reasons for the high profile of clergymen in university teaching, including the denominational orientation of so many institutions and the earlier close relation between the intellectual elite of the nation and the church. However, their role within the institution flowed naturally from the understanding of the purpose of the institution. Who was better trained than the educated clergyman to direct the moral development of a student and to encourage the development of his intellectual faculties toward the moral improvement of society? So long as social reform was couched in moral terms, as it was in idealist thought, the clerical role would remain important.

Another and smaller group of faculty represented a somewhat different perspective, at least potentially, on the future of university training. These were the social scientists who had gained a foothold on Canadian campuses. Adam Shortt, an alumnus of Queen's, returned to his university in 1888, after graduate training in Edinburgh. Born in 1859 in the small Ontario town of Kilworth, Shortt was a product of the intense belief of many Scots Presbyterians in the value of education. Struggling from a basic primary education through high school, Shortt found his grades had improved enough by 1879 to win him a scholarship to Queen's. As with many others of his generation, his original assumption was that higher education prepared the way for a clerical career. If Shortt had retained his conviction, it is unlikely he would have played the part he did in Canadian intellectual history. As it was, he drifted from religion to philosophy and from philosophy to political economy. Thus he was, whether consciously or not, turning his back on the academic traditions of the nineteenth century for those that would increasingly characterize the twentieth. After his appointment at Queen's, Shortt continued to search for a new role for the academic, and for himself. As he explained in 1903, he was tired of being 'merely a voice from the wilderness.'[15] Both in his choice of specialization, therefore, and in his search for a meaningful role for the academic, Adam Shortt reflected the rise of a new strain of thought within intellectual circles. That he had not yet fully defined that role as of 1903 simply indicates that the questions posed by the new era had not yet yielded answers.

In 1889 A.W. Flux was appointed to a similar position at McGill. Much more significant to the social sciences at that university, however, was the appointment a few years later of Stephen Leacock. Leacock provided a sharp contrast to his earnest Presbyterian counterpart at Queen's. Born of a well-to-do English family, and with a somewhat ne'er-do-well father, Leacock was born into the class that Shortt would come to know only after he went to university. His father, it was true, took the Leacock family to Canada to farm, and Stephen grew up in the sort of small-town atmosphere that typified Shortt's own background. The circumstances were, nevertheless, quite different. The Leacocks, it is fair to say, were declassed English gentility and Stephen was always expected to acquire an education and escape the farm. Attending school in Toronto, including the elite Upper Canada College, Leacock went on to the University of Toronto and then attended Strathroy Collegiate Institute to become a teacher. As he commented later, 'My education has fitted me for nothing but to pass it on to other people.' A short time later he was able to return to Upper Canada College, this time as a master, and to work towards his degree at Toronto, which he completed in 1891. Upper Canada College was only a stepping-stone to the ambitious Leacock, however. He went on to earn a doctorate from the University of Chicago and, at the age of 33, became a permanent member of the McGill Faculty. The Englishman from the faded genteel background with the irreverent sense of humour, for which he is best known today, joined the earnest Presbyterian, Adam Shortt, as one of a new breed of academics in Canada.[16]

The third centre for the new social sciences was at Toronto. That university had appointed William Ashley to teach both history and political economy in 1888. In 1892 Ashley left for Harvard and was replaced by James Mavor, who would remain there until his retirement in 1923. Mavor's experience and personality were distinct, to say the least, and he was as different from Shortt and Leacock as they were from each other. He was the only one of the three who was not raised in Canada. He was also the only one of the three without any university degree, having dropped out of Glasgow University. Mavor's claim to expertise in political economy came from his involvement in the idealistic radical movements of the 1870s and 1880s. His ability to land a professorship on the basis of this experience and some writing reveals the continuing force of the 'gentleman scholar' in political economy and the concept that political economy was a generalist subject dealing with social problems rather than a technical 'science' in the modern sense. Whereas Shortt exemplified the Queen's tradition and Leacock despised McGill, Mavor seems to have been somewhat oblivious to Toronto. Described as a man of 'magisterial if eccentric demeanour' with 'bohemian behaviour, odd dress, stutter and excessively sophisticated lectures,' Mavor seemed to fit the popular stereotype of the academic even if he had not obtained a degree.[17]

Shortt, Leacock, and Mavor, with their individualistic personalities and isolated appointments, thus marked the beginning of political economy as an academic discipline in Canada. For other, smaller universities, political economy also made an appearance by this time but was often taught by faculty members whose primary responsibility lay elsewhere. W.C. Kierstead, who taught political economy at the University of New Brunswick, is a good example. His graduate work was in philosophy at the universities of New Brunswick and Chicago. His philosophic orientation was idealist, but he spent his career teaching political economy in various forms. The result was concern with social and economic policy, but with a philosophic bent.[18]

While the social sciences thus existed within the Canadian university system at the turn of the century, their role was still minor and the standards of teaching were unsophisticated. This situation is in sharp contrast with both Britain and the United States, where, by the 1890s, a high degree of professionalization had been achieved. Specialized journals, national organizations, and high academic prestige had been successfully nurtured by a generation of academic social scientists who regarded both themselves and their discipline as a distinct profession.[19] In Canada, a scattered minority of individuals, largely trained in other disciplines, existed without any organization or professional connection.

Various factors, including the small size of Canadian universities, the lack of funding, and the absence of specialized graduate training within Canada, help explain the relative weakness of the social sciences within Canada. Most important, however, neither of two necessary preconditions to the acceptance of social science was firmly established in Canada. First, it would have had to be accepted that the scientific technique was valid as a means of assessing social problems. In spite of the dominance of the scientific method within the natural sciences and the acceptance of 'reason' by idealist philosophers like John Watson, this was not really the case in Canada. When even political economists like Adam Shortt retained a strong belief that inner spiritual reform was more important than reform of the environment in which man lived, it was apparent that the social sciences were not completely autonomous.

The second precondition was also absent. Historically the social sciences have developed in response to industrialism. Thus in Great Britain a well-established cadre of political economists from Adam Smith to Alfred Marshall had made that nation the centre of economic thought. On the European continent and in the United States, where industrialization was more recent, economic thought became firmly established only in the late nineteenth century.[20] In Canada, however, the currents of political economy were made less relevant by the rural and agrarian state of Canadian society. Studies of scarcity, the marketplace, industry, and other matters were all considered valid but remote in a land that was but an observer on the fringes of the industrial giants.

The absence of each precondition was related to the absence of the other. Philosophic values interacted with social environment to produce particular beliefs about the nature of social improvement. Many Canadians believed that such improvement depended on the individual, because circumstances in Canada gave man the ability to shape his own fate. That fate, moreover, should rest not on the mere improvement of external conditions but on the uplifting of the inner spirit. This was achieved, in turn, by good moral training and by a sense that man was a member of a community rather than an atom in a universe of individuals. In this balance between autonomous individualism and an organic sense of community, the crucial issue was not the shaping of policies to respond to environment but the shaping of the spirit to respond to human need. Moral guidance, not social scientific assessment, was thus the key to a better world.

This complex of ideas depended on the belief that Canadians were in a position, through their own experience and training, to act both as autonomous and moral individuals. If individual autonomy were seen either as an inefficient way to achieve social improvement or as seriously inequitable, then the whole structure of relations would change, both inside and outside the university. Within a few years of the debate on legislation and morality in the *Queen's Quarterly*, the basic assumptions on which this generation acted would be obsolete. Complex social changes would force dramatic shifts in man's assessment of himself and his environment.

Ideas do not exist independently of the environment in which they are espoused. This is particularly so when those ideas are held up as a code of values for social action. Thus it was with the philosophic system of idealism in Canada. The system gained ascendancy in Canadian universities not because it was more consistent or more sophisticated than alternate approaches. What it did do was blend the demands of changing scientific theory with a conservative social-religious outlook that dominated the Dominion in the last quarter of the nineteenth century. Most importantly, it preserved the so-called moral imperative that shaped so much of the Canadian ethical system while facilitating at the same time an abandonment of literal acceptance of the Bible.[21]

While there were certain inherent instabilities in the structure of idealism, especially in the relation between religion and reason, idealism was ultimately to fall from its prominent position more because of the world it attempted to explain. Canadian society was changing so rapidly by the early twentieth century that the tenets of idealism seemed less and less plausible as an answer to the problems confronting man. As a rule, this weakening of previous ways of looking at the world was reflected in an increased unease within the academic community about Canadian society. There was a certain irony in this. For years Canadians, including intellectuals, had awaited the long-sought 'boom' as a necessary step in the country's progress. Now, at the turn of the century, when that boom finally materialized, academics, journalists, educators, and clerics lamented that the great vision of the nineteenth century was fading and, indeed, may always have been illusory. Arnold Haultain's well-known 1904 comment that 'the nineteenth century seems to have brought us to the edge of a precipice' reflected the anguish of a community attempting to adjust philosophical and methodological systems in a changing world.[22]

For the person who wished to be pessimistic there were ominous signs in the two decades before the First World War. Canada's relations with the mother country remained a source of debate and of growing division as imperialism began to take on increasingly concrete and militaristic forms. French-English questions, made sensitive by Louis Riel's execution in 1885, were further inflamed by a series of arguments over schools, religion, and language. In particular, the western provinces were the scene of serious religious controversies as both Protestants and Catholics sought to assert their own vision of the future on Canada's frontier. The problems of the West were compounded as large-scale immigration raised increasing fears of 'the foreign element' and the future of Canada.[23] All of these issues were favourite topics of discussion and debate. None, however, seemed so threatening as the possibility that Canada had lost its sense of purpose and that Canadians were losing their spiritual values.

Something of this concern can be seen in the later writings of the country's leading moral and intellectual figure. George Munro Grant had been very much a spokesman throughout his life for the mission of Canada. In his enthusiasms for idealistic imperialism, educational reform, western expansion, and the nation itself, Grant had typified the hopes of the Confederation generation. It may have been somewhat of a shock, therefore, to those who were present in Convocation Hall in 1901 to hear one of his last addresses to his beloved Queen's. It was not an optimistic portrait of a future that he knew he would not live to see.

Canada, he said, had accomplished much. It was territorially complete, and economically it was finally making rapid progress. Grant, however, felt that the most important problem remained unanswered. 'What kind of nation is it to be? Is it to be a huge "city of pigs," to use Plato's phrase; or is it to be a land of high-souled men and women?' He was not optimistic: 'Judging by the tone of the public press, I for one am often saddened beyond the power of words to express. The ideals presented to us are increase of population – no matter what its quality or what the general standard of living and thinking, and increase in wealth – no matter how obtained whether by sponging on the Mother Country or grovelling at the feet of the multi-millionaires.' The problem was a 'vulgar and insolent materialism of thought and life.'[24] If Canada were not yet a nation of pigs, it certainly had its share of people at the trough. Material prosperity, having lost its moral purpose, threatened to destroy Canada rather than allow it to achieve its destiny.

Grant's pessimism should not be mistaken for the grumblings of an elderly and ill man toward a younger generation. Among Canadian intellectuals in this period there was a surprising lack of enthusiasm for the way in which the nation was moving into what Prime Minister Laurier had termed 'Canada's century.' Though there were exceptions, the writings of this period force the conclusion that Grant's lament was that not of a generation but of a social class toward an increasingly materialistic and anti-intellectual world.

Some criticism of the modern world was straightforward and explicit. Alfred Cambray, Catholic and member of the Action catholique de la jeunesse canadienne-française, blamed 'l'amour de l'argent' and, as with many of those who worried about the decline of faith, saw the world as sinking into a 'néopaganisme.' Given the French Canadians' tradition that their morality and faith were what distinguished them from English North Americans, it is not surprising that a good many other French-Canadian intellectuals and nationalists echoed Cambray's sentiments to one degree or another. In English Canada the tone was almost as conservative. Canon H.J. Cody, a Toronto Anglican and future president of the University of Toronto, warned in 1913 that the nation was in danger of destroying itself unless it turned away from shallow materialism and sought new 'reverence for personality.' Arnold Haultain had echoed the same concern about self-destruction when he warned that 'the happiness of a nation is not necessarily the outcome of its material prosperity.' Indeed, as Greece and Rome showed, material prosperity often came with decadence and decline. The Reverend G.M. Macdonnell saw this neo-paganism expressed in the form of 'the new economic man' who would ride over all moral considerations in the name of profit. O.C.S. Wallace, the chancellor of McMaster College, saw a decline in the personal sense of responsibility and warned of modern 'dangers in respect to conscience.'[25]

Among the most doubtful about the state of Canadian values was the first generation of Canadian political economists. The bitterest satire on the age came from the pen of Stephen Leacock, whose 1914 work *Arcadian Adventures of the Idle Rich* parodied modern society. It is a world in which there are 'brilliant flashes of wit and repartee about the rise in Wabash and the fall in Cement,' where both religion and university professors have adopted the mannerisms and morals of the material world around them. The minister who 'had spent fifty years in trying to reconcile Hegel with St. Paul' was outdated and 'a failure, and all his congregation knew it.' Old values and the search for truth itself had become irrelevant in a world dedicated to material pleasure.[26]

Adam Shortt and James Mavor lacked Leacock's ability to satirize, but their view of society was similar to that of their McGill colleague. Mavor, as recent studies have shown, exhibited an unhappy combination of ardent reformer and 'disappointed skeptic.' Shortt, strongly influenced by the idealism of Queen's University, followed his mentor, George Grant, in decrying the lack of attention in Canada to the quality as well as the quantity of development. What Canadian society failed to understand was that 'the starvation of the spiritual man is really more distressing than the starvation of the physical man.' The problem for Shortt was not that some men were becoming wealthy during the economic boom. That was inevitable. His real concern was whether those men of new power and influence would have 'the sense of responsibility' that would permit them 'to exercise their rights and fulfill their obligations.'[27]

Such righteous anti-materialism only hints at the problem of the age. It is unlikely that Canadians were more materialistic, less moral, or more shallow culturally or philosophically than they had been fifty years earlier. The behaviour of the participants in the great railway boom of the 1850s was, after all, hardly a good example for the youth of the nation to follow. The problem for the intellectual community was twofold. First, the drive to material improvement was taking on new and more industrialized forms. The economic boom that hit Canada between the later 1890s and 1912 allowed tremendous growth in machine technology, the scale of industrial plant, and primary resource production. The number of individuals employed in manufacturing increased some 350 percent between 1890 and 1910, while the scale industries increased, especially in the years immediately preceding the First World War.[28] It is difficult to talk of an industrial revolution when discussing a growth that rested to a large degree on primary resource export. However, the experience of the country – especially of central Canada – in the years 1898 to 1912 had many of the social characteristics of just such a revolution.

Second, while becoming more materialistic, the world was also becoming more complex. In particular, an ever greater percentage of Canadians was becoming dependent for its material well-being not on its own efforts but on large industrial employers who had no direct contact with or knowledge of the worker. As has been argued with regard to the United States a generation earlier, the process of industrialization and the impingement of technology led to an increasingly complex interdependence: that state 'of social integration and consolidation whereby one part of society is transmitted in the form of direct or indirect consequences to other parts of society with accelerating rapidity, widening scope, and increasing intensity. A society is interdependent to the extent that its component members or parts are influenced by each other.' This tendency challenged the very basis of the traditional role of the intellectual as guardian of social values. Turn-of-the-century writings posited a relatively stable community in which the individual as an 'autonomous creator,' when properly directed, would serve as a constructive part of a stable community.[29] Only on this basis was the crucial function of the church and the educational system possible, at least in their existing form. What concerned many intellectuals was that the world that they knew, and their place in it, was being threatened by economic growth and material prosperity.

It is in this context that the nature of the commentaries on the changing society of the era become understandable. In particular, there was a growing concern over the shifting demographic base of Canada. In the hundreds of individual decisions made around kitchen tables on the farms of the country the intellectual community saw realized its fears concerning the dislocation of Canadian society. As farm owners, or their sons and daughters, responded to the economic opportunities around them, there was, beginning in the 1880s and peaking immediately before the war, a growing movement from the country to the city. The movement was greatest in southern Ontario, where the growth of manufacturing was more directly felt than elsewhere. Between 1901 and 1911, for example, between 125,000 and 200,000 individuals left rural areas. Twenty-four Ontario counties saw an absolute decrease in population. In Quebec the story was much the same, as thousands left marginal plots of land to take their chances in the new industries of Montreal or in New England factory towns. As the Reverend John Macdougall noted, Boston, not Winnipeg, was the country's third-largest city in terms of resident Canadians. The temptation to abandon the farm for the New England mill towns expressed in the romantic novel of old Quebec, *Maria Chapdelaine*, was simply a reflection of a mood that existed throughout the province. In the Maritimes the situation was the much same, except that the absence of local industry meant that those who abandoned the farm also tended to leave the region. During this period of boom and population expansion for Canada as a whole, Nova Scotia and New Brunswick's population barely increased. Prince Edward Island's actually declined. Only in the West did a still open frontier allow a significant growth in rural population after 1900.[30]

As the countryside declined, the cities grew. Between 1891 and 1911 the urban population of Canada grew from 31.8 to 45.2 per cent. Ontario and British Columbia were both more urban than rural by the latter date, and Quebec was nearly so. Equally significant was the tendency toward concentration of the urban population in a few large centres. Many medium-sized towns and cities saw little or no growth in this period, as industrial concentration tended to favour larger communities. Between 1891 and 1911 Montreal grew from just over 200,000 to more than half a million people, while Toronto increased from 180,000 to nearly 400,000. Winnipeg, with a population of 130,000 in 1911, was larger than any Canadian city had been forty years earlier.[31]

While writings on rural depopulation are relatively common after 1890, it is not until the final few years before the war that they reached a peak. Growing social problems in the cities, housing and sanitation difficulties, and the 1911 census, which revealed the trend toward urbanization, all made the 'rural problem' a major subject of investigation and discussion. Both the Methodist and Presbyterian churches commissioned detailed studies. The Social Services Congress in Ottawa in 1914 devoted considerable attention to the issue; farm leader and future Ontario premier E.C. Drury argued that the session on rural depopulation 'was the most important being held.' Former federal minister of labour and social reformer William Lyon Mackenzie King agreed with this sentiment, terming 'the decline of the rural population in Ontario ... in some respects the most serious in its consequences of all the economic changes the past two decades have witnessed.'[32]

What made the problem all the more difficult for those who confronted it was the fact that they, for the most part, recognized the underlying economic forces that were contributing to rural decline. Urbanization was a result of machine technology and the necessity, therefore, of larger units of production. Moreover, as Adam Shortt pointed out, machine technology also meant that there was simply less need for manpower in rural areas. Farm labourers, and for that matter farmers, were being replaced by more efficient methods of crop production. 'The idea that you can keep people on the farm by persuading them to stay there is not true, because under new conditions a piece of land cultivated in the proper way requires fewer and fewer people.'[33]

This understanding of the economic forces at work did not in any way lessen the concern. Not surprisingly, the campaign against rural depopulation was led by farm spokesmen and organizations. Newspapers like the *Canadian Countryman*, the *Farmers' Magazine*, and the *Farmer's Sun* urged farmers to resist the temptations of urban life and condemned the drift to the cities. Underpinning their arguments was the propagation of a view, no doubt sincerely believed, that a healthy farm community was the basis of a healthy Canadian society. As one writer argued, 'a prosperous God-fearing rural population is the tap-root of national progress. As the farmer is so is the nation.' Drury agreed and warned that the solution of the rural problem involved 'the preservation of the springs of our civilization, of the fountain-head on which the whole depends.'[34]

The worries of those directly concerned with the rural community are easily understood. Very practical considerations were at stake. A relative decline in rural population meant less political power in elections. This, in turn, implied policies in the future oriented more toward urban than rural interests and the further deterioration of the farmer's position. Rural depopulation and the concentration of industry also caused a deterioration in country life in another way. As the Reverend John Macdougall observed in his study for the Presbyterian church, village-based services were declining as tasks undertaken by local artisans became a part of the general manufacturing process. Village population and services thus decreased, leaving the farmer more isolated than ever.[35] Overall those who remained on the farm had very good reasons for emphasizing the virtues of rural life.

What is revealing is the degree to which the myth of rural virtue was adopted by those writing from the cities. It was a controller of the city of Toronto, not a farm spokesman, who condemned the city in the most extreme tones at the 1914 Social Services Congress. To J.O. McCarthy the city was little more than a parasite, drawing the life blood from the country and the moral integrity from the nation: 'For half a century and more in Ontario, the rural districts have poured into our cities a constant stream of healthy vigorous, clean lived people. The standard of our citizenship in physique and morals has been largely influenced, if not controlled by our country life. But with the comparatively faster growth of our cities, conditions are changing, and the change has but begun.' Sir George Ross, the former premier of Ontario, argued in almost the same terms that with the drain of people to the cities the 'physical and material stamina which is universally admitted pertains to life on the farm must be seriously affected and the dynamic force of the whole country affected.' The Reverend James Robertson of the Presbyterian Missions Board condemned policies that meant that a new generation of urban children 'have no chance to play on the grass and pick flowers and drink in the enriching vigor of good air.' In *La Revue canadienne*, J.C. Chapais condemned the shallow attractions of 'le luxe, l'ivrognerie, l'amour de plaisir' that drew people to the cities and was thus affecting the moral and material progress of the nation. Henri Bourassa warned that in the cities youth would lose 'leur santé, leur robuste simplicité, souvent même leur honneur.' Even Adam Shortt complained that the 'great problem of Canada, as of other progressive cities, is the country.' His distrust of the city led him to advocate a series of idyllic, and unrealistic, garden suburbs which would allow industrial workers to get 'far enough back in the country for them to get back on the land on which they can devote some of their spare time.'[36]

Given the outpouring of articles and speeches on the topic, such examples could continue indefinitely. The point to be made, however, is that urban as well as rural observers deplored the shift to the cities. There was a certain irony in many of these comments as well as an understandable psychology. The flight from the rural areas and the previous dominance of rural population in Canada meant that a good many of those writing from the cities on the evils of rural depopulation were themselves from rural backgrounds. Of those mentioned above, for example, none came from an urban background. In this light their comments on the vigour of the countryside renewing the cities takes on new meaning.[37]

Whatever the psychology of the observers, however, the fact remains that the society in which this generation had grown up in, was undergoing dramatic and seemingly uncontrolled change. As early as the Royal Commission on Labour and Capital in 1886 there had been a growing concern about the development of an urban working class. The publication of works like Sir Herbert Ames's *City below the Hill* in 1897 and of Mackenzie King's pieces on sweated labour seemed only to confirm the worst. Urbanization in Canada threatened to bring about the misery, social strife, and class antagonism that Canadians associated with other nations. 'Slum life,' a former mayor of Lethbridge warned, 'is starting to get a hold in this country.'[38]

While there was genuine concern about the plight of the individuals caught in tenements and in underpaid industries, there was also the very real concern that such misery was a threat to the nation as a whole. The rejection rate of British youth by the military during the Boer War, one magazine noted, revealed what urban life did to the defences of a nation. Even democracy itself might be at stake, for, as other nations showed, 'great cities furnish the natural conditions for the creation of despotic government, the despotisms of organized selfish interests as in New York or the personal despotisms in some European countries.'[39]

The strong, even apocalyptic, comments of those writing at the turn of the century appear excessive from today's perspective. It must be remembered, however, that to later generations existence within an urban and industrial society would be considered normal. For those born in the nineteenth century, however, the assumption had been that agrarian development was the key to national success. Settlement of the West, not the expansion of the cities, was depicted as the wave of the future. It was unfamiliarity with large-scale urbanization that made people so concerned with what was happening. Even on the international scene, the sort of urbanization that accompanied industrialization was a relatively new phenomenon. In Britain urban domination at the expense of the countryside had been apparent only for a little more than half a century. In the United States the great period of industrialization had taken place within the living memory of many of those currently writing. Moreover, both nations had been faced with social and political problems that Canadians had heard of in often lurid and condemnatory tones. The prospect of a rapid transformation of the structure of the Canadian economy and of Canadian society was thus viewed with considerable trepidation. Society seemed to be, as the phrase of the time went, in an 'unstable stage,' and the consequences of that instability were as yet uncertain. The nineteenth-century vision of a utopian future based on technology and open land was becoming for many, including Adam Shortt, a twentieth-century nightmare of industrial blight and social strife: 'The skies of our towns and cities would be obscured with smoke, while soot and cinders would begrime our streets and dwellings. Goodly numbers of us, with all our latent spiritual capacities, would be sent to find realization by burrowing in the earth, there to disembowel the hills and strew the surface of the land with their entrails.' Need we, he concluded, 'ask what would be the effect on our higher natures while engaged in such work?'[40]

With such visions many feared the worst. Trusts on the one side and militant unions on the other directly challenged the ideal of man working out his destiny on an individual basis. If, as the rural myth would have it, modern freedom and democracy were a product of the freehold farmer's and small shopkeeper's proprietary sense and independence, then the decline of these groups in the face of large businessmen and working-class employees might pose very real problems for Canadian social stability. There was a growing fear that the political, constitutional, and social system that Canada had known in the nineteenth century was doomed to extinction. Businessmen who glorified the current state and many union leaders who condemned it freely predicted, or warned, that the system was about to be replaced by a new socialist order. Mass urban democracy was a relatively new phenomenon, and there was no certainty that it was compatible with democracy. The British constitutional system might prove as unsuited for modern society as feudalism had for the earlier stages of commercial and industrial development. The concept that socialism was a radical and destabilizing force thus had an immediacy foreign to post-Second World War North America.

Such attitudes were undoubtedly reinforced by the movement of some within that traditional guardian of social values, the church, to redefine its social role in a way that included the advocacy of a socialist society. This, in turn, was a more radical expression of the deep-seated effort within church circles to deal with modern problems of society. This movement, known as the social gospel, was not necessarily socialist. For many church leaders, however, the idea seemed a plausible extension of the values preached by Christianity. 'The great trouble with our social order is that our ruling ideas are wrong ideas,' wrote one intellectual supporter of the social gospel. 'We have been trying to build up a civilization on individualism.' For some it seemed the only response in a world that daily proved the impossibility of looking to individual action amid industrial environments so complex that the average citizen was helpless.[41]

This radical version of the social gospel movement was a natural and significant response to the perceived crisis. It sought to preserve the dictates of the moral imperative and the idealistic notion of an organic and improving civilization by jettisoning the other nineteenth-century ideals of autonomous individualism and, not incidentally, the constitutional and political systems this implied. Three points need to be made about this movement, however. First, even within the social gospel movement the radical espousal of socialism came from a minority. Second, however much the social gospel might represent a bridge between the religious-rural world of the nineteenth century and the urban-secular one of the twentieth, the concept of reform as a question of moral improvement that typified the social gospel was very much a product of nineteenth-century thought. Ultimately the spirit of man, whether acting alone in the face of a complex industrial society or collectively in altering that society, remained the underpinning of the movement. Socialism, as viewed here, was more a moral ideal than a program of economic management.[42] Third, whether from a minority or not, the espousals of socialism from church figures made the threat of socialism seem all the more real to others.

It is perhaps indicative of the uncertainty that existed within the ranks of Canadian intellectuals that, for the most part, their pre-1914 critique of socialism tended to be emotional rather than a product of reasoned logic. Of course, the emotionalism of the intellectual community was a relative thing and looked tame compared to the apocalyptic warnings of much of the press or the near-hysteria of men like the American James Emery in his speech before the Empire Club in 1906. In comparison, the rambling arguments of University of Toronto professor E.J. Kylie before the same group seemed a model of lucidity. Kylie reflected the academic sympathy for social uplift in his expressed support of 'intellectual socialism' while condemning 'socialism of the street.' It was, it would seem, acceptable to want to overturn the current system by reforming the spirit of the people and not by forcing the issue.[43]

For most writers, Kylie's distinctions were needlessly esoteric. For them, the problem with socialism was simple. It, as with so much else in that age, was a product of the 'city of pigs.' Socialism, in its obsession with material well-being and its class selfishness, denied both the importance of the human spirit and the concept of an organic community. This argument was more explicitly expressed, perhaps, in French Canada, where materialist socialism was viewed as a direct challenge to church and culture. Socialism, argued Alfred Cambray, took one back to the days of Spartacus and Roman rebellions, an era before Christianity had worked its influence on the world. 'Le socialisme, se vantant d'employer les mêmes moyens que le paganisme, ne pourra donc que le menes de nouveau la ruine et la sauvagerie.'[44]

For English Canadians the same point was made by arguing not that socialism was anti-Christian but that it was anti-community. The problem with socialism, Adam Shortt concluded, was that it was too individualistic: 'The really practical aspect of socialism and its real danger to modern society lies not in its sentimental or strictly socialistic features, but in its individualistic basis. The strength of that basis is the appeal to personal and material self-interest of men who, in their ignorance, have been led to believe that they are being unjustly deprived of a great part of the wealth which properly belongs to them by a tyrannous and selfish upper class.' A combination of this 'narrow and individualistic basis' with its 'blind, crude and incalculable force' was what made the movement so dangerous. Materialist greed, the same flaw that pervaded all of society, had infected those who would change it. The 'sure and early promise of the coming millennium,' the same quick panacea that attracted the prohibitionist, attracted the socialist.[45]

For these critics of socialism, then, the movement represented not the answer to the problems of the new order but a symptom. As surely as the exodus from the country and the growth of slums marked industrialism, so socialism proved the growing selfishness of society. The critics feared that the greed that seemed to overshadow the 'new economic man' of the twentieth century made socialism inevitable.[46]

The perceived 'social crisis' in the first years of the twentieth century challenged the concept of social improvement as something best achieved through voluntary moral reform directed toward community benefit. The belief that social well-being could be improved by such a process had always been dependent on certain fundamental concepts. First, as has already been argued, the individual had to have a certain degree of control over his own destiny. Second, society and its agencies had to be set up in such a way as to ensure the proper transmission of moral values to the individual. Otherwise personal effort would be directed toward selfish ends and the concept of an organically knit community would collapse. In the impersonal cauldron of the urban and industrial world, however, these concepts seemed increasingly unrealistic. Industrialism had thus created a paradox. On the one hand, the social and economic conditions which confronted society more than ever demanded the presence of the 'moral imperative' within the community. It would take selfless effort to confront the challenges of slums, disease, bad working conditions, and poverty. On the other hand, those very conditions undermined the sense of duty that was needed. The class orientation of socialism was, as surely as the greed of the trust, proof to the majority of middle-class intellectuals of the degeneration of the spirit of the community. The spirit of idealism remained alive in the intellectual community, but there was increasing doubt whether society as a whole could be made to accept its values. Some new approach would be necessary to face the problems of the new century.

One attempt to deal with this whole question came from William Caldwell, the Scottish-educated Sir William Macdonald Professor of moral philosophy at McGill. Sensing the crisis both in religion and in idealism, Caldwell became interested in the new pragmatic philosophy that had developed in the United States. Bringing it north of the border, he attempted to incorporate aspects of American pragmatism and Canadian idealism. He hoped thereby to reconcile the importance of the work of people like William James and John Dewey with the deeply imbedded values of the Canadian intellectual community. In the process he was faced with many of the same problems that confronted his colleagues. Would a new set of philosophical values free Canadian thinkers from their own doubts and provide a means of facing modern society? It was a difficult challenge for a man brought up firmly within the ranks of the idealists.[47]

The starting point for Caldwell was religion. He expressed sympathy with the belief of many churchmen that their institution must adapt to the modern world. At the same time he was concerned that such adaptation would destroy the real function of the church. We must never 'go so far as to maintain that the chief business of religion is merely a better adjustment of the social conditions of our present life.' To do so would be to lower the church to the same material concerns that so many condemned. No matter how successful the social policies of the church might seem, they would ultimately fail, for man's mortality would leave him discontented even 'in the most socialistically arranged state possible.' The social gospel movement was thus a misdirection of religious effort. Caldwell's might have been simply another conservative religious voice arguing that the things of Caesar be left to Caesar except for his recognition of the need for the modernization of a dying institution. Religion was becoming increasingly irrelevant to modern man. Citing Maeterlinck, he noted that the real significance of the modern world was that for the first time man was leaving one religion not for another but for no religion. 'Men,' he wrote, 'simply do not believe, and it is not true, that the parish priest and the church of to-day are still the focus or the centre of illumination, or civilization, or inspiration that they used to be.' Religion was largely finished as the guardian of society. In education, for example, Caldwell saw both financial and educational forces that would lead to the withdrawal of the churches. Society thus had to face the reality of a world in which religion was no longer a central force.[48]

Having dismantled the old relation between society and religion, the modern world was left with the task of constructing a new order. It was this dilemma that led Caldwell to turn to the American pragmatists, who seemed to face the modern world without illusion. Pragmatism, he said, represented 'the discontent of a dying century with the weight of its own creations in the realm of science and theory along with the newer and fresher consciousness of the fact that there can be no rigid separation of philosophy from the general thought of mankind.' At the same time, however, it presented Caldwell with a great problem. Pragmatism hovered on the edge of an ethical relativism in which any doctrine of morality and good threatened to dissolve into a series of expedients. 'There is doubtless,' he noted, 'a great danger here in this repudiation of all semi-exact, or the cut-and-dry, theories of the theologies and of the natural science as principles or rules of conduct.' Taking this sort of position to its logical conclusion led to a posture that, as was the case with some of Dewey's work, was 'like surrendering philosophy altogether.'[49]

What hemmed Caldwell in and what forced him to remain irresolute between pragmatism and idealism was his desire to find an absolute ideal on the one hand while confronting social and religious realities on the other. Could either philosophy or society withstand a world in which religion was collapsing while new pressures confronted man? 'The moral instinct, therefore, being in our day weakened by pseudo-science and commercialism, certainly stands in need of the support of philosophy, at least in the case of the thoughtful who would face life without illusions and also with no fear of knowledge.' It was questionable, however, whether philosophy could reach beyond the study to the man in the larger world: 'Our various theories about the rise and fall of religious and scientific philosophies and social policies have had, as yet, very little hold or effect upon the heart or the will of the people ... The people, therefore, and mankind generally, are in the main, just as moral and just as immoral as they have ever been. And, all things considered, they are, on the whole, more likely to become more moral rather than less moral.'[50] The crisis was not so much in the decline of man: he was the same as he had always been. It was a crisis of those who sought to respond to social change. The admission of philosophy's impotence, and of religion's, did not resolve the problem, but it was probably the frankest statement of its nature.

Caldwell's major work, *Pragmatism and Idealism*, was buried under an assault by John Watson who, as Canada's leading idealist, obviously resented the challenge to his beliefs.[51] His work thus never received either the attention or the following it otherwise might have. It is nevertheless one of the more important efforts of a Canadian philosopher to deal with new currents of thought in the early twentieth century. Caldwell did not create a new philosophical synthesis; this he signally failed to accomplish. The importance of his work is that he articulated the dilemma facing Canadian educators and intellectuals. Philosophic ideals of the nineteenth century seemed increasingly powerless and irrelevant, while religion, faced with the same threat of irrelevance, was abandoning the saving of souls in favour of social reform. The brave values expounded by the writers in the Queen's Quarterly seemed impractical in the face of the massive social problems that confronted the nation. Both the educator and the church would have to reassess their roles and their beliefs. Perhaps a new type of adviser to society was needed to replace churchman and philosopher? Perhaps the state was the only agency powerful enough to deal with the major issues that confronted society? Could new advisers be found? Was the state either able or ready to assume its new role?

2

The intellectual and the state
1900-14

Canada had never shown itself as committed to the doctrine of the 'laissez-faire' state as either the United States or Great Britain. That doctrine, though always more a statement of an ideal than a reflection of policy, had had a tremendous influence on both of Canada's major trading partners in the nineteenth century. Politically it reflected the assertion of power by a commercial middle class and its demand for a chance to shape its own destiny. Economically it was reinforced by the theories of the classical economists who followed in the footsteps of Adam Smith and his arguments concerning the potential for growth in the free play of market forces. It received philosophical justification in the writings of English utilitarians like Jeremy Bentham and John Stuart Mill. It received a sociological basis and further philosophical reinforcement, especially in the United States, with the popularization and occasional vulgarization of the views of Herbert Spencer.[1] Canadians were very much aware of these currents of thought and vigorously debated the various points presented by the advocates of laissez-faire. For them, however, it was a debate in which the issues seemed rather remote. The Canadian historical experience pointed in a somewhat different direction.

The laissez-faire state, it has been pointed out, rose to challenge the mercantilism that preceded it.[2] It is thus of some significance that Canada never truly rejected mercantilism. Rather, it was forced, over its vigorous protests, into the cold world of classical economics by Great Britain's abandonment of mercantilism in the 1840s. Moreover, Canadians soon found the new order unsuited to their tastes. First they adopted a 'preferentialist' substitute for mercantilism by means of the 1854 Reciprocity Treaty with the United States while simultaneously toying with protectionism in the 1859 Galt-Cayley tariff. When the United States abrogated the Reciprocity Treaty in 1866, Canada first sought a renewal of the agreement and then moved toward a strong protectionist system in the National Policy of the later 1870s. The Liberals soon learned the danger of challenging that policy and, assuming office under Wilfrid Laurier, donned the protectionist cloak themselves. Even more important was the active role the state had always taken directly in the developmental policies of the nation. From the early nineteenth century, as export markets developed for British North American resources, the colonies had been forced to confront the problems of a vast geography, small population, and even smaller pool of investment capital by becoming directly involved in various projects. Beginning with canals after the War of 1812, this involvement had grown as the more expensive railway technology developed in the mid-nineteenth century. Land grants, subsidies, and, with Confederation, the direct ownership of railways followed. In the famous monopoly clause of the Canadian Pacific Railway Company there was even a lesser incarnation of the traditional mercantilist device of a state-sanctioned monopoly. The practice continued at the turn of the century, with Laurier's government becoming involved in schemes to add to the transcontinental railway network.

There was thus never any ironclad principle of non-involvement by the Canadian government in economic matters. The challenge now for reformers was to convince the government and citizenry that the enthusiasm that had always been shown for developmental projects should also be shown in responding to the social and economic problems emanating from the new age of industrialism. Developmental assistance was no longer sufficient, because the individual was increasingly buffeted by environmental forces that swamped the moral efforts of church and school. The state was the only body, after all, that had sufficient resources and power to shape the evolution of society in the face of the dramatic and powerful changes that were taking place. The tradition of state interventionism in Canada had to be broadened.

Typical of the appeals that were made in the first years of the twentieth century was the one made by Montreal economist Eduoard Montpetit. Born in 1882, educated at Montreal and Paris, he was appointed to the faculty of the University of Montreal in 1910 as a professor of political science. Montpetit felt that he had a dual mission, to convince French Canadians of the importance both of his discipline and of the need for the state to undertake rational social and economic planning. The two goals were related. In a series of articles he traced the history of economic thought and connected it to the various ages of economic activity. There was, he admitted, for the economist, a certain appeal to the age of the industrial revolution in Great Britain and continental Europe, when economic law had been left to rule unhindered by the interference of government. 'Mais il a aussi abandonée les hommes à leurs propres forces, c'est-a-dire condamné les faibles à la defaite, en rejetant l'intervention de l'Etat.' The result was an unfortunate social warfare in which wealth became the guiding principle of society. 'La lutte n'est pas égale que sontiennent, au sein de la liberté, les hommes à la poursuite de la richesse. La force libérée triomphe plus facile encore. Les faibles, les dépourvus, les moins favorisés, subiront la défaite, pour un temps.'[3]

For Canada the lesson was clear. So far it had escaped the social and political consequences flowing from this laissez-faire philosophy. This was its great advantage in Montpetit's eyes. 'Nous possedons ce que Le Play appelle la paix sociale.' Recent occurrences, however, gave warning that this would not last unless Canadians in general and French Canadians in particular recognized that the active intervention of the state was 'une nécessité sociale.' The laissez-faire system had always presented problems. In current circumstances to continue it was to court disaster.[4]

Montpetit's views were widespread within the intellectual community in the years before the war. Within the religious community, for example, there were emotional appeals for increased government action on social and economic matters. Given the strong 'moral imperative' within church circles and the social gospel movement's dismay at the way in which unrestrained capitalism had warped social values, such cries are hardly surprising. Thus the Social Services Congress of 1914 saw numerous calls for large-scale government action in the face of the social crisis. Unemployment insurance, old age pensions, mothers' pensions, and other schemes were all presented as necessary moral responses to inhumane conditions. Proposals for such measures, which could come only from government, indicate the degree to which the churches sensed that their own role in the community was increasingly inadequate. Only the state had the power to deal with the problem, and the state, therefore, had to take responsibility. 'Does anyone challenge that the State has failed?' asked the Reverend John Macdougall. 'The great evils of society are the indictment of the State.' S.W.

Dean, the superintendent of the Methodist Church of Toronto, echoed Macdougall. 'The Church must demand the parenthood of the State be asserted in providing for and protecting the weak.'[5]

The religious passion of the social gospel movement gave the cries for government intervention a special fervour. In less dramatic language, however, other segments of the intellectual community were expressing similar thoughts. These sentiments grew in strength as the first years of the century passed. Conservative McGill economist Stephen Leacock, for example, essentially agreed with Montpetit, commenting that in spite of the material progress of the revolution the 'liberation from all forms of governmental restraint' of the economy 'was open to serious objection for the effect it had on the labouring classes, women and children.' Other writers, with good reason, began to look abroad to investigate the response of other governments to social problems. In nations like Germany, Belgium, and Britain, as well as in fellow dominions Australia and New Zealand, the state had been much more active in its response to the impact of industrialization. Old age pensions, health measures, workmen's compensation, and other schemes had been experimented with to varying degrees. For Canadian commentators the question was whether such schemes worked and why Canada was so far behind other jurisdictions. The fact that many of the examples were within the British Empire simply made the debate that much more relevant; so too did the presence within the group of that supposed model of efficiency, Germany. This is not to say that the commentators were enthusiastically supportive of all the experiments tried elsewhere. There was, however, a general sense that Canada was being far too reticent, even if other governments were going too quickly.[6]

Those advocating such changes had to be sensitive to the accusation that all this talk of the state was simply another sort of woolly-headed socialism. Even if those proposing such schemes did not think of themselves as socialists, the schemes might, in the long run, lead to a socialist society. Queen's political economist O.D. Skelton asked rhetorically, whether 'certain tendencies in state action, certain policies widely championed by parties and by individuals not in sympathy with the organized socialist movement, are not really socialism on the instalment plan.'[7]

For Skelton the answer was unequivocally not. Those who argued otherwise had, in his opinion, no real appreciation of the conditions that bred socialism and of the acute problems that existed as a result of industrial growth. For, Skelton argued, socialism developed not from the foolishness of the worker or the plots of conspiratorial agitators but from the social and political environment. 'The excesses of unregulated capitalism ... were making the counter-forces of socialism inevitable.' A dialectic process was at work in which abuse bred reaction. In this light, state intervention was not automatically to be considered socialist. Much depended on the nature of that intervention, its motivation, and its economic soundness. Those who clung to an outmoded vision of the state might be the real promoters of socialism, for their rigid insistence on unregulated capitalism would, sooner or later, encourage a socialist response: 'Where industrialism dominates, where the door of economic opportunity is shut, where autocratic repression is the policy of the state, where the parliamentary group prevails, a strong socialist movement is possible.' What Canadians had to recognize was that progressive reforms initiated by the state were not only 'not necessarily socialistic; they are the best bulwark against socialism. They are homeopathic cures, vaccination against its growth.' Capitalism had no 'heaven born sanction' and would survive only if it could prove itself a useful vehicle of economic sufficiency and social improvement on a mass scale. Only action by the state to ensure the efficiency and humanity of capitalism would offer the possibility of long-run social stability and a continued immunity from the class hatreds and social convulsions of European society.[8]

Skelton's argument that state intervention could be viewed as a safety valve, relieving the worst points of pressure on the existing social system, was an important one. It stood in contrast to the sort of apocalyptic rhetoric so common in these years. That rhetoric had pictured two contrasting societies. One, nurtured in agrarian freedom and a Christian education, emphasized the individual's moral responsibility toward society for his or her acts. The other, brewed in the industrial ghettoes and grinding poverty of the new age, seemed to deny the possibility of both individual freedom and moral standards in the face of complex environmental decay. As in the Marxist tradition, this latter stark depiction of the modern world theorized that industrialism forced an inevitable response. Only collectivism was suited for such a secular and urbanized world. In Skelton's argument, the danger did not disappear, but, with a flexible response, it could be lessened. The alternative that he presented was one not of apocalypse but of an older order adapting as necessary in order to preserve what was worth preserving while changing what needed to be changed. How the new standards were to be defined was left unanswered by Skelton and would prove a difficult problem to resolve in future years. His argument remains, nevertheless, an important statement on behalf of a pragmatic, even expedient, approach to government action that called for the supersession of ideological categories by the search for solutions.

In spite of the widespread calls for a more active state, such changes were neither easily nor automatically obtained. Though the Canadian intellectual community looked more to Carlyle, the British Tory historian, or to Caird, the Scottish idealist, than to men like Mill or Bentham, the nineteenth-century British constitutional tradition was deeply entrenched in Canada, especially within the ruling Liberal party. That political tradition, moreover, tended to be seen by the Laurier administration in more anti-statist terms than by any other government in Canadian history. The result was a gap in the dominant philosophical beliefs between the political leadership of the nation and that portion of the intellectual community that was becoming increasingly concerned about the future of the nation. Part of this gap between the intellectual community and the political leadership was generational. The three men in the Laurier administration most responsible for determining government economic and social policies were Laurier himself, his minister of finance, William Fielding, and his minister of trade and commerce, Richard Cartwright. By the time the government began its last Parliament, in 1908, Cartwright was 73, Laurier 67, and Fielding 58. None of the three had had his political and economic views of the role of the state shaped by industrialization or ubanization. Their experiences came from a very different era, when constitutional issues predominated. Confederation, schools questions, the aftermath of the introduction of responsible government, and other similar themes had dominated their early years in politics. Economic issues were important, of course, but tended to be framed in terms of one major issue – the tariff. The 1911 election would reveal just how important an issue it still could be. The fact remained, however, that Laurier's senior advisers maintained a very limited concept of the proper role of the state in the modern world. Hard-won constitutional freedoms for the individual seemed to dictate a resistance to government encroachments into new areas.

Laurier was perhaps the most unequivocal in this attitude. As critics and admirers in his own time were aware, his liberalism had been defined in the momentous struggle of the *rouge*-Liberal Party in Quebec to free itself from the hostility of the church. Laurier, in his attempt to resolve this problem, had in 1877 laid out a definition of liberalism in Canada that had disavowed the radical and republican anti-clerical liberalism of continental Europe in favour of the British mid-Victorian ideals of constitutional reform. Repeal of the Corn Laws, disestablishment of the church, and extension of the franchise were the sorts of programs Laurier saw as flowing from the ideology of liberalism.[9] The role of government was thus not to force action in any one direction but to remove barriers to man's own efforts to undertake personal and social improvement. In Laurier's viewpoint there was, in other words, a political counterpart to the philosophical debate carried on in the *Queen's Quarterly* over prohibition. Man must be free to seek his own improvement and be responsible for his own destiny.

Given these attitudes, Laurier believed any government intervention in social or economic matters beyond those well established in Canadian tradition had to be approached with the greatest of caution. The delicate balance between the individual's own efforts and societal well-being was easily upset, and newly privileged classes could emerge to replace the old ones. It was for this reason, for example, that in spite of an expressed sympathy with the needs of the elderly he showed an obvious lack of enthusiasm for proposals to bring in old age pensions in Canada. As for the social programs of New Zealand and Australia, he rejected them out of hand. 'If you remove the incentive of ambition and emulation from public enterprises,' he warned in 1907, 'you suppress progress, you condemn the community to stagnation and immobility.'[10]

Laurier's caution was matched by that of Cartwright and Fielding. Their response to the growing demand for some sort of action was to develop not an old age pension, with government contributions, but an annuity system, in which the money paid out would be the result of money paid in. It was also to be voluntary. In essence, the annuity plan, as Fielding noted, was similar to the sort of thing an insurance company could undertake. The only differences were that the government was a more secure investment and that it would subsidize the scheme to the extent of absorbing the administrative costs. Fielding was careful to stress in his presentation of the plan that there was 'nothing novel, nothing unusual' in its contents. His comment sums up the orthodoxy that characterized the Laurier government on such matters.[11]

This belief in the importance of individual responsibility was reflected, as has been pointed out elsewhere, in two general principles.

One, inherited from the British tradition, argued that no government program should be so generous as to encourage otherwise self-supporting people to fall into a position where they sought support. Known as the doctrine of 'less eligibility,' this principle would rule government attitudes towards social programs for many years to come. The second principle followed from the first. It held that the government should become involved in the support of the needy only where all other avenues failed. Individual effort, family support, and private charity were seen as the backbone of the welfare system in Canada. Social security from the government, to the extent it was accepted at all, was seen in 'residual' terms. In normal circumstances the role of the government, especially the Dominion government, in matters of social welfare was an extremely limited one. Once again the analogy with the debate over prohibition holds. The Cartwright-Fielding annuity scheme was designed to encourage individuals to make the right choice, but it did not attempt to alter the basic principle that it was up to the individual, or the family, to provide for old age.[12]

There were forces working on the party that countered this nineteenth-century attitude to some extent and forced Laurier's government to undertake some innovative new activities. O.D. Skelton's pragmatic arguments for change represented one possibility for the adjustment of nineteenth-century liberalism to twentieth-century conditions. Such views would not be accepted, however, for some years to come. A more immediate source of change came in the field of labour relations. The volatile confrontations of the early twentieth century resulted from rapid shifts in the economic structure of the nation. These outstripped the societal and legal institutions designed to provide guidelines in relations between employees and management. The subsequent frustration often spilled over into violence or other activity which the public regarded as both senseless and dangerous. In response to this increasingly dangerous regulatory vacuum, the government began to move into the field of labour policy. The growing danger to social order as well as the disruptions to the economic system led to the establishment, between 1900 and 1910, of the basic principles of collective bargaining in Canadian law. Many of these principles remain intact to the present day.[13]

The man most responsible for the development of these principles was William Lyon Mackenzie King. His personal abilities and his less-than-modest ambition allowed him to carve out a position for himself in a new post, deputy minister of labour in 1900. He was only 26 years old at the time. By 1909 he had moved into the Liberal party and the cabinet as minister of labour, also a newly created post. The government's relations with labour in these years, and its approach to labour problems, were very much a reflection of King's attitudes. As there is already in existence a detailed study of King's labour relation policies, there is little point in restating them here. Two important points should be made, however. First, by training and inclination Mackenzie King was a member of the same intellectual community that was at this time so concerned about the direction of Canadian society. Trained in political economy, King attended the universities of Toronto, Chicago, and Harvard. There he was exposed to various theories on government and society as well as to the practical social problems of the era. He was also, in his religion and his outlook, a man in whom the 'moral imperative' was extremely strong. The desire to help the socially un-derprivileged led King to work in Jane Addams's famous Hull House in Chicago for a period and to focus his political ambitions on the cause of labour. Thus when the earnest young reformer first met patronage boss and minister of railways and canals George Graham, he com-mented in disgust on the absence of purpose in the partisan politician. 'Graham to my mind is a man without ideals or much principle. There is a streak of blasphemy in him, a want of reverence, and a low level which makes him a poor leader of men.' There was more than a touch of sanctimonious arrogance in such a comment, and King would show himself well able to employ patronage in the future. King did believe, however, that he was different from politicians like Graham because he had a moral mission to fulfil in government. This purpose was grounded in a strong post-Hegelian idealism derived from his education and re-ligious beliefs and meant that he saw the importance of the individual as inseparable from that individual's relation to the community. To King 'social control ... was essential to the protection of the well being of the many.' Such social control was best achieved through voluntary moral reform, but if that was impossible then the well-being of the community dictated state action.[14]

Both the desire to use moral injunctions and the willingness to use state control were reflected in King's actions in the Department of Labour. The former predominated in the early years in such measures as the Conciliation Act of 1900 and the formation of the *Labour Gazette* under King's editorship. In both cases the role of government was pic-tured as one of publicity and fact gathering. With access to the facts, parties would have a common information base on which to make judgments. Publicity would embarrass, that is, exert moral pressure, on recalcitrant parties to modify their position. King's personal work on conciliation boards over the next few years further embodied this attitude and, equally significant, did not involve the government in areas that raised basic questions of principle. As the machinery was, by and large, voluntary rather than compulsory, it was acceptable to even the most laissez-faire of Laurier's Liberal party.[15]

Not all men were as rational or as easily embarrassed as King would have liked, however, and the danger to vital links in the Canadian economic system soon forced more direct involvement on the part of the state. In 1903 the passage of the Railway Labour Disputes Act introduced, in King's words, 'the principle of compulsory arbitration,' which 'is a new one in this country.' Later years saw the government become increasingly involved in forcing action simply because the new relations of an industrial society were so interdependent that massive disruptions in key sectors became intolerable. With the passage of the Industrial Disputes Investigation Act in 1907, King moved the government a step further away from persuasion and toward control. As minister of labour he fathered the Combines Investigation Act of 1910. Though weak enough that few companies would actually be threatened by it, the act represented the acceptance in principle of the necessity of government moving in to curb the free flow of market forces.[16]

By later standards, few of King's actions appear very radical. In the context of the time and in the government of the day, however, King was probably the most reformist of Laurier's senior civil servants and, after 1909, cabinet ministers. Nor was this always a comfortable position. King found himself on occasion taking positions that other Liberals found somewhat heretical. During the bitter Lethbridge coal miners' strike of 1906, for example, Laurier rejected state intervention to force an end to the strike on the grounds that the government had no right to interfere with private property. As deputy minister of labour, Mackenzie King wrote: 'In any civilized community private rights should cease when they become public wrongs.' Later, in 1909, when King was minister and moving the Combines Investigation Act through cabinet, he met resistance from both Fielding and Cartwright. The bill was delayed several weeks until they could be brought to accept the idea as inevitable. Nor was the resistance from his own party finished when he cleared cabinet and presented the bill to the Commons. There he came in for public chiding by a member of his own party. 'As a Liberal of the old school,' said Alberta Liberal Michael Clark, 'I approach the question of state control with very considerable suspicion.' The Combines Investigation Act and especially King's mildly radical rhetoric in defending it struck Clark as diverging from the basic principles of liberalism: 'I regret very much, on my hon. friends account, to hear a young Liberal approach the subject of state control in so light hearted a manner because I recollect the fact that the progress of true Liberalism has been associated in the history of England with the diminution of state control.' Publicity and the public's power in the marketplace, Clark felt, were better answers to industrial problems and monopolization. All that was needed was the simple expedient of 'freedom of commerce' and an informed public.[17]

At about the same time King faced similar resistance from the same individuals on the question of establishing a Royal Commission on Technical Education. Beginning in the late nineteenth century, Canadian educators had become increasingly concerned about the structure of Canadian schools in the face of growing urbanization and industrialization. This general debate had increasingly focused in the early twentieth century on the training of youth for the developing industrial occupations. In Ontario, as early as 1905, Premier Whitney declared industrial training to be central to both high employment and continued economic growth. At the Dominion level, King saw the issue as so important that it was imperative for the national government to investigate this issue which, constitutionally, fell within provincial jurisdiction. 'Our whole industrial system,' he argued before Parliament in 1909, 'renders it absolutely necessary that a nation which is going to progress and keep abreast of the times must equip its workers along modern lines, must provide its workers with a practical training to enable them to deal with the new conditions under which they are obliged to work.' What the opposition listening to the speech did not realize, however, was that King made this speech not so much to convince them as to convince his cabinet colleagues, who, he felt, were dragging their feet on the idea.[18]

On at least one occasion King's attitudes brought him into disagreement with his political hero, Wilfrid Laurier. The incident occurred in the wake of a nasty strike on the Grand Trunk Railway in 1910. King had been directly involved, on the government's behalf, in an attempt to bring about a resolution to the strike, and after a great deal of frustrating negotiations a tentative settlement had been reached.[19] The Grand Trunk, however, was balking at various issues concerning the rights of the former strikers. Most important were the questions of reinstatement and pension rights. King, in his effort to bring about a settlement, engaged in a series of promises and threats that would have seen the government become directly involved either in forcing the Grand Trunk to take action by introducing legislation or by guaranteeing the workers' positions at government expense, for at least a period of time.

Laurier was not pleased with King's activism. 'Your suggestion to secure the men by legislation would seem to me to be a very unfortunate and dangerous precedent ... I certainly regret the action which the Government took as embodied in your confidential letter to Hays, but I will not put my judgement against your own and against the rest of Council.' Of course, Laurier probably knew that in spite of his disclaimer the letter would have an effect. King looked to Laurier as a political father figure and, not incidentally, as the man on whom his future career depended. He replied to Laurier: 'You cannot regret more deeply than I the confidential letter sent Mr. Hays.' The ideas therein, he intimated, would not be pursued. At the same time he outlined, in conciliatory tones, the fundamental difference between himself and Laurier. 'There was,' he said, 'a third party to consider, namely, the public was in the light of what any other course might mean so far as the public was concerned and in this light alone, that I felt the course taken was the only one which would serve the situation.'[20] In the end no government action was taken to protect the workers, and the men involved in the strike suffered accordingly. King, nevertheless, had clearly expressed his personal inclination to use state power if needed. Laurier, for his part, had reflected the concern with which he viewed this rapid expansion of governmental responsibility in the face of growing problems related to industrial development.

A note of caution must be introduced into this discussion of relations between Laurier and King. Mackenzie King was a loyal Laurier Liberal, and though there was a perceptible difference in their attitudes toward the role of the state, it would be an overstatement to portray King as being continually frustrated by Laurier's cautious approach to such matters. King, after all, retained his belief in the preferability of leaving the individual alone to work out his own destiny, wherever possible. Later commentators would accuse King of the same sort of laissez-faire outlook that was currently being used to describe Laurier. Equally, Laurier, Fielding, and Cartwright should not be dismissed as anachronistic political dinosaurs rapidly losing touch with the wishes of the people. The political dominance of the party in the period from 1896 to 1911 makes such an idea dubious at best. Individualism remained a part of the Canadian ethos, even though it was becoming increasingly difficult to adhere to it. Rather than view Laurier, or King, or Skelton, or any particular segment of the intellectual community as either anachronistic or representative of the public mood, it is more useful to think in terms of a society in a state of intellectual ferment as a result of social and economic change. The various positions represent a series of points of coalesced opinion that, in varying ways, sought to respond to the social and economic pressures of the period.

One of the difficulties for those who advocated a change in the role of state was a widespread belief that Canadian governments at all levels were incapable of expanding their activities in any sort of efficient or competent manner. In part this was a reflection of the small budgets and limited expertise available to governments in this period. The Dominion government, for example, had a tax base that rested almost exclusively on tariff and excise duties. Revenues were thus both inflexible and relatively low. The total revenue of the government of Canada reached only $100 million in the final year of the Laurier administration. The low revenue was matched by a small civil service. At the beginning of the century the federal civil service was less than 5,000 strong, and even after a decade of growth it had reached only about 9,000. Such a body was unlikely to be able to take on much more than it was currently handling. The provinces, within the jurisdiction of which many social welfare matters lay, were even more limited in their budgets. The total current account expenditure of all the provinces combined in the last year before the war was less than $50 million. Given such limited fiscal resources, the sort of initiatives that had led the Ontario government into the field of hydro-electric development would remain rare. The financial capacity simply did not exist, and the public would not tolerate massive increases in taxation.[21]

The problem was not just one of fiscal capacity. It was also one of trust. An interesting paradox appears in the writings in the years leading up to the First World War. On the one hand, the intellectual community seemed generally to encourage an increased role for the state. On the other hand, there was a very real disdain among these same writers for government, political and official. This created a dilemma. If the government was as bad as they seemed to argue, then it was questionable whether it could be used as an agent of social or economic reform. Therefore, before adequate social and economic reform was possible, reform of government was imperative.

The first charge levelled against the state of government in Canada was that the level of morality in public life was dangerously low. This accusation was hardly surprising, given the scandals that dotted the political life of the country in the latter part of the nineteenth century. At the Dominion level, the infamous Pacific scandal of the 1870s and the Langevin-McGreevy scandal of the early 1890s had been complemented by other, less famous incidents. At the provincial level, the Baie de Chaleur scandal in Quebec saw a provincial premier forced out of office, accused of bribery and corruption. Other provinces and other premiers or their colleagues seemed circumspect only by comparison. Nothing in the first years of the twentieth century indicated that things were about to change. The Laurier government was marred by a number of indiscretions and minor incidents of corruption.

So far as commentators were concerned, the cause of this low public morality was not hard to find. The general materialism of society had elevated the shallow and selfish principles of commercial greed to such an important place that they soon infested the political world. A series of investigations on insurance frauds prompted *Canadian Magazine* editor John Cooper to complain in 1906 that 'all these investigations show that the selfishness of the capitalists and the self-seeking of the politicians are almost criminal. The people are robbed and cheated and burdened. The average citizen has no chance when the politicians and the capitalist combine against him.' McGill professor Andrew Macphail warned that the only way in which matters would improve was if businessmen and politicians were separated and the public treasury closed 'against speculators who, under the guise of developing the country by the imposition of taxes, are concerned only to exploit it, and quickly assume the successive roles of confidence man, gambler, beggar, blackmailer.'[22]

In a more humorous but no less pointed vein, Stephen Leacock wrote satirically of the horror of a group of businessmen when they began to realize that city hall was corrupt. ' "The thing is a scandal," said Mr. Lucullus Fyshe. "Why these fellows down at city hall are simply a pack of rogues. I had occasion to do some business there the other day ... and do you know I actually found these people take money" ... "They take money. I took the assistant treasurer aside and I said I want such and such done, and I slipped a fifty dollar bill into his hand. And the fellow took it, like a shot." ' Such corruption was too much for the indignant businessmen of Plutoria Avenue, especially when key city contracts were coming due. They organized a reform slate, won the election, and introduced clean government: 'And as they talked, the good news spread from group to group that it was already known that the new franchise of the Citizen's Light was to be made for two centuries so as to give the Company a fair chance to see what it could do. At the word of it the grave faces of the manly bondholders flushed with pride, and the soft eyes of listening shareholders laughed back in joy. For they had no doubt or fear, now that clean government had come. They know what the Company could do.'[23]

The problems of government did not always involve corruption. The dominance of political and partisan concerns at the expense of the public interest was also a matter of criticism. The Liberals' abandonment of their traditional adherence to free trade was a primary example of the sort of expedient policies that seemed to rule both parties. What seemed to matter was the well-being not of the nation but the party. 'There are now in Canada two pseudo-Conservative parties,' wrote Andrew Macphail after the 1908 election, 'both standing for the same privileges and for the interests of the same class. It is little wonder that the voters neglected to exchange the one for the other.'[24]

The disturbing question was why the Canadian public tolerated this state of affairs. The search for a satisfactory answer returned the commentators to the shallow materialism that pervaded Canadian society. The voters were willing to be bought off, financially with promises of money and emotionally with the flags, hoopla, and superficial appeals of the politicians. 'It is probably true,' wrote a disgusted Queen's economist W.W. Swanson in 1911, 'that eighty-five or ninety voters out of a hundred can be relied upon by party bosses to follow out the course indicated by the caucus and the convention.' The Reverend A.W. Andrews warned that political corruption was possible only because the electorate was morally weak. 'Let the moral quality of the electorate grow weak, then corrupt corporations may buy both legislators and electors.'[25]

These sorts of arguments pointed toward the uncomfortable conclusion that democracy had failed and that the ignorance of the people on issues and their weak morality simply proved the fallibility of the common man. That this sort of conclusion should hover on the periphery of turn-of-the-century writings on government is not hard to understand. Until the late nineteenth century, democracy had been viewed in a negative light by most Canadian writers as symbolizing the tragic flaw of the American system. Recently the term had been accepted as descriptive of Canadian government, but neither the word nor the ideal behind it had been embraced by all segments of the intellectual community. Among more conservative intellectuals this criticism of democracy could be made explicit. Both Andrew Macphail of McGill and Maurice Hutton, the Toronto classicist, for example, saw democracy as a decidedly mixed blessing, in which many of the best elements of society were being dominated by the worst. In politics, Macphail argued, a sort of Gresham's law had come into play, driving out the intelligent politician in favour of those 'who are both ignorant and poor.'[26]

Not all were so explicitly critical as Macphail and Hutton, but the tone of disdain for the 'lower elements' that both expressed was fairly common in intellectual circles and would remain a recurring theme in future years. Adam Shortt commented bitterly on one occasion that 'it is not enough to make me despair of democracy to observe how elementary is the stupidity which the common man exhibits when acting in bulk.' Even the generally democratic O.D. Skelton lamented to his friend W.L. Grant in 1904 over the cultural and political dominance of 'farmers and shopkeepers.' A few years later he denied the usefulness and the practicality of the populist idea of the referendum on the grounds that issues were too complex for the average man to become informed upon.[27]

These complaints should not be taken to mean that there was a dominantly anti-democratic tone to the thinking of Canadian intellectuals. It was more that as a class they were were disappointed that the public did not perceive what they perceived. For example, in the election of 1911 a real choice existed for the first time in years. The Liberal party had negotiated a reciprocity agreement with the United States, and the issue of protectionism versus free trade again had some meaning. It was a perfect time for a rational debate as to the future economic directions of the nation. The course of the election campaign seemed, however, only to confirm the complaints of the intellectual community. Rather than seeing a rational debate, the public was treated to emotional anti-Americanism and to the self-interested machinations of renegade Liberal Clifford Sifton and his manufacturing allies. Naturally those intellectuals who supported the Liberals were the most disappointed with the Conservative election victory. Even those sympathetic to the Conservative position, however, disliked the way in which the campaign had been conducted. As W.L. Grant wrote after the results were known, 'I felt very strongly that this limited Reciprocity was a matter which should have been decided by Business and Trade experts, whereas it had largely been decided by appeals to the spirit of Canadian Nationalism.'[28]

Competent leadership of Canada in a time of social turmoil thus seemed to be coming neither from the top, the elected representatives of the people, nor from the bottom, the people themselves. The politicians were viewed as mired in the wallow of corruption or fierce partisanship, while the public possessed no sense of direction in a world where traditional ethical and religious values were under challenge. Only one potential source of advice remained. Within the governmental system the Canadian civil service provided a core of advisers to the government who might be able to rise above partisan politics and to chart the policy responses necessary for the future. If anything, however, there was greater disdain exhibited both by the intellectual community and by the public toward the civil service than toward the politicians.

There were several reasons for this general belief that the civil service could not provide the necessary advice. The concept of a competent advisory body on policy depended on two preconditions. First, there had to exist a body of professional experts who, by training and experience, were more able than politicians to frame policy alternatives. Second, the government had to be willing to accept the advice of that body. Increasingly, as will be argued, certain groups of intellectuals were beginning to view themselves as just those experts so badly needed by government. The problem was that the concept of the professional expert had not fully developed in Canada by the turn of the century. Only slowly and with some difficulty did the areas of science and engineering establish themselves within the public service as areas of professional expertise. The establishment of the Geological Survey in the 1840s, the growth of railway engineering after Confederation, and the engineers' own increased sense of professional standards all gradually brought acceptance of the fact that specific technical areas needed professionally trained experts. Even there, however, the standards remained uncertain as partisanship and favouritism intruded upon the principle.

Outside these technical areas the concept of the expert adviser did not really exist. Public servants of long experience or high repute might bring wisdom or common sense to the discussion of matters and thereby have considerable influence. For the most part, however, the distinction between the framers of policy and its adminstrators was much sharper in the pre-First World War period than it would be in later years. Ministers devised policy, and civil servants administered it. Nor did this mean merely that the ministers shaped general directions for policy while allowing their staff to eliminate options and create specific policy proposals. Departments individually and the government generally were run to a very large degree from the political level. Ministers became directly involved in the shaping of policy and, very often, involved in its details as well. The machinery became increasingly inefficient and onerous as the size of government grew, but, as a 1912 report to government indicated, it remained the system nevertheless. Even the senior public servant remained much more of an administrator than a policy adviser.[29] The historical role of the public service was changing, forced in part by the new concerns of the community, but it did not yet have the expertise outside of technical areas to act as a core of advisers to the government on policy formation.

The problem to many observers was that expertise could never be developed so long as one of the great practices of the nineteenth century – patronage – remained. In theory the Canadian civil service had evolved along the lines of the non-partisan British civil service, and patronage was thus supposed not to exist to any significant degree. In fact, however, patronage was as much a Canadian tradition as responsible government, and the two had arrived together in the 1840s. In the highly partisan attitude of the post-Confederation period even the myth of a non-partisan service collapsed in the face of explicit defences of the patronage system by various cabinet ministers. Clifford Sifton's boast to newspaperman and Liberal reformer J.S. Willison that 'I fired a Tory whenever I wanted to and never explained or apologized' summed up the approach toward the civil service that had become customary by the turn of the century.[30]

The increasing power of patronage had long been noted and condemned by intellectuals in Canada. One of the few issues on which George Munro Grant and Goldwin Smith had agreed was the evil of the patronage system. It was hardly remarkable, therefore, that complaints continued into the twentieth century. The sense of concern behind these complaints was, however, becoming much more urgent. Earlier writers had usually concentrated on the impact of the patronage system on the morality of the nation and its political leaders. Patronage was wrong, in other words, because it was not fair and because it contradicted the belief that man must have the opportunity to succeed or fail according to his abilities. By the twentieth century, however, the emphasis shifted. Patronage was not only unfair, it was inefficient. How were governments staffed by placemen and hacks, and municipalities run by political machines, to deal with the complex and important policy issues of the day? Virtue was no longer its only reward. Efficiency was as well. 'The reform is demanded in the interest of the service, in the interest of public morals, and in the interest of efficiency,' wrote J.S. Willison.[31]

A closely related concern involved the allocation of new functions to government so long as the patronage system survived. Presumably any such new function could, and very likely would, be used to serve partisan ends and be run by partisan appointments. Much public and opposition resistance to the growth of government, indeed, was predicated on the fear that party manipulation rather than public interest dictated the acquisition of new government powers. This raised questions as to whether the operation of such new activities would be in the public interest and forced elaborate proposals for quasi-independent boards or unwieldy commissions to remove the danger of patronage. Growth would be achieved much more simply and public resistance to the concept lessened if patronage could be brought under control. As Adam Shortt wrote in 1906, 'It is impossible to secure an efficient civil service, or to prevent it from being the victim of party manipulation until the whole system is taken out of politics and placed upon an independent basis of merit and capacity.'[32]

This pessimistic dirge against things governmental arose from a group that was profoundly concerned about the direction of social development, worried about the future role of education and religion, and moving toward a new vision of the intellectual's role in society. The conclusions as to the current state of affairs reached by these intellectuals helped define that new role, at least in their own mind. The individual, it appeared, was enmeshed in an increasingly complex social and economic web and was thus no longer capable of determining his own fate. Government, with the power of law and extensive resources at its command, seemed a logical agency to intervene on behalf of the individual in the face of this newly complex society. Government, however, did not seem capable in its current state of undertaking this new and enlarged role. Somebody had to provide guidance, both to the people and to government, through the maze of problems and issues that the twentieth century presented. 'The task of legislation grows more perplexing every year,' wrote O.D. Skelton in 1913. 'The scope of law-making widens, the complexity of each subject increases with the growing complexity of the industrial community, the need of expert guidance through the maze of statutes becomes cumulatively greater.' In Quebec, Errol Bouchette agreed with Skelton and pointed out to his fellow francophones that expert guidance of economic development was necessary as well if French Canada were to keep pace with English Canada. Social and economic stagnation threatened unless new expert strategies could be brought to bear on the problems at hand.[33]

The calls for greater employment of expert advice reflected the emergence in at least a portion of the intellectual community of a new perception of its proper function within Canadian life. The disengaged intellectual, the moral arbiter of the nineteenth century, had to become more directly involved in specific policy issues in the twentieth century. The expertise already existed, they believed, but it was not sufficiently recognized by the community. Part of the blame for this fact had to be laid at the doorstep of the intellectual community itself. As William Swanson argued, the aloof pose that the intellectual had taken towards politics and the civil service was understandable, given the record of both. At the same time such an attitude ensured the continuance of the very problems that were so strongly condemned: 'There is a second, somewhat larger class, which plumes itself upon being independent of any party whatsoever; but which presumes to play a judicial role, holding the balance between the contending parties. Most of the members of this class pose as belonging to the so-called "intellectuals". Their influence is necessarily very slight, as they merely decide one way or another upon a plan mapped out by others. This, of course, is regrettable; for many of these men, by education or wealth, are fitted to play an important part in shaping the political life and thought of the people.' Andrew Macphail thought it was more than unfortunate. His pessimism about the abilities of both politicians and an untutored people made him believe that it was imperative for a new intellectual elite to replace the obsolete elites of the predemocratic era. 'Democracy has never succeeded, or monarchy either,' he warned, 'where the "best men" followed their own pleasures and allowed the worst men to seize the reins of government.' Politicians and the public would have to learn, and sooner rather than later, that universities were not merely places 'from which abstractions may be uttered to boys' and that the professor is not 'necessarily a fool.'[34]

This concern with social activism provides a parallel with those other moral guardians of nineteenth-century wisdom, the clergy. Just as many in the church began to fear that their institution was becoming irrelevant because of its failure to deal with modern issues, so there were elements within the university community, and among those associated with it, that felt the traditional role of the intellectual as educator and writer insufficient. Both groups, and of course they were closely interconnected, felt beleaguered by a society that in its commercial orientation, secularism, and materialism seemed alien to the values they represented. Both feared the decline of the central institutions of social order – church and school – and both began to sense that the declining importance of these institutions was not merely a sign of public moral decay but was more deeply rooted in the changing nature of Canadian society. New intellectual values would have to be developed as would a new role for the intellectual community in order to assist society and to reassert the importance of intellectual leadership in Canada.

This search was most clearly expressed by members of disciplines that were most oriented to the new environmental and multi-causal orientation that seemed an essential condition in the modern world. If experts were needed to assess social issues, then, it followed, the social sciences were disciplines best suited to the task. The arguments of O.D. Skelton and Errol Bouchette were very much at the centre of the intellectual's search for a new role in society. As was the case with earlier generations in Great Britain and the United States, these intellectuals claimed, in the 'intellectual quicksand of an increasingly interdependent social universe,' to be able to plot the way to the future.[35] Did anyone think that they were worth listening to?

3

The social sciences and
the search for authority
1906-16

On 25 October 1906 James Emery of the Citizens' Industrial Association of America came to Toronto to speak to the Empire Club. An accomplished speaker and militant anti-unionist, Emery probably felt comfortable as he stepped up to talk to this affluent and business-oriented audience about the evils of modern radicalism. To ensure a warm reception, however, he followed the practice of many speakers and introduced his topic in a light-hearted manner. He had no intention, he said, of approaching the problem 'from the mere dry standpoint of the political economist.' His audience deserved better, for not only was the political economist boring but what he had to say was of little relevance. It was a discipline that could be defined as what happens 'when a man who knows nothing on any subject talks to one who knows less than he does on something which they both know nothing about.'[1]

Emery's sarcasm is not surprising. Academics and businessmen have, more often than not, lived in an atmosphere of mutual disdain bordering on outright contempt. Emery's attack, however, was not just on the practitioners of political economy but on the discipline itself. The social sciences in Canada, of which political economy was by far the most advanced, were not yet widely accepted as practical means for dealing with social problems. Nor, it followed, were political economists yet established as professional experts who had a special ability to understand contemporary problems. Even among political economists there was a degree of defensiveness concerning the nature of their profession. 'When I sit and warm my hands, as best I may,' wrote Stephen Leacock, 'at the little heap of embers which is now Political Economy, I cannot but contrast its dying glow with the generous blaze of the vainglorious and triumphant science it once was.' The discipline seemed to have lost its sense of direction. Few political economists before the First World War challenged the perception that businessmen were the true experts on economic development. A knowledge of economics might, of course, round out the businessman and give him an additional tool in assessing economic trends, but no economic theory learned in a musty classroom was thought comparable to the experience of business itself. As A.W. Flux, McGill economist, wrote in 1902, 'The study of economic principles is no substitute for native capacity in qualifying a man to do well as a banker.' Ten years later Queen's economist W.W. Swanson made essentially the same point by arguing that only banks possessed and could be expected to possess the expertise required to handle a complex matter like bank inspection. Any attempt at outside regulation that did not accept this fact would be futile.[2]

This lack of authority on the part of the social sciences created an obvious problem for those who wished to see these disciplines directly involved in modern social problems. There was also another handicap: the tradition that saw the academic, social scientist or not, as being properly somewhat removed from the press of immediate issues in favour of more detached contemplation. James Mavor, in his inaugural address at the University of Toronto, summed up this view when he argued that if the political economist was to make good his claim as a reputable scientist he must relinquish any expectation of playing the politician. 'The region of science is the region of thought, of action too, no doubt, in the sense of experiment and observation, but still essentially the region of thought, of logical continuity, of guarded progress from one proof to another, of careful employment of theory and hypotheses.' In contrast stood what he termed art, including the art of politics, which concentrated on doing rather than thinking. 'The science of political economy is the province of the economist, the art of political economy is the province of the statesman, or the practical administrator in civic, national or international affairs.' They operated in separate spheres, and while the statesman should read what the economists wrote and the economists watch the statesmen, there was little connection between them. 'It was as unreasonable to demand of the economist administrative ability as to demand of the statesman intimate knowledge and grasp of economic principles.'[3]

By the later part of the 1900-14 period Mavor's attitude was increasingly unacceptable to social scientists. Two forces were leading them toward a repudiation of this traditional view of the academic. First, as Montpetit had argued, their assessment of the nature of the social crisis affecting Canada and the apparent inability of government to deal with the crisis led them to conclude that their expertise was necessary, not merely as theorists, but as part of a practical solution to pressing problems. Second, and related, it was increasingly apparent that their own position as reputable and important 'scientists' would be firmly established in Canada only when they could demonstrate that Emery was wrong and that they had something to offer the public. Both their own reputations and the improvement of society thus seemed to demand, in their view, that they establish their authority as experts able to deal with practical problems.

It was not all that easy, however. The concept of the academic expert as applied social reformer was new to Canada, and it would take some time before it was accepted. The result in the pre-war years was that the great majority of reform movements were broadly based, depending on the businessman reformer, the church philanthropist, and the amateur enthusiast who had 'studied' the issue of the day much more than the academic. At the same time a trend is noticeable. Once the academic community, or portions of it, decided that they had to become involved in immediate social issues, they consciously sought to assert their authority as the ones best equipped to deal with the complex issues of the day.

The relation between the intellectual, the amateur reformer, and others in the pre-war period was complex and ever shifting. Some idea can be gained, however, of the sorts of patterns that did occur by looking at the evolution of one of the most potent of the pre-war reform movements, the effort to improve the quality of urban life. Urban reform movements had been developing in Canada with increasing force since the 1880s and by the early twentieth century they were perhaps the most important arena of Canadian efforts at reform.[4] This followed naturally from the concerns of the day. Urbanization, in its effects on both country and city, was often seen as the single most important factor underlying the so-called social crisis. It followed, therefore, that a decent urban environment was an absolute necessity if Canadian social standards were to be preserved in the future. Also, in a world in which a belief in environmental causation was challenging older assumptions about individual responsibility, the realities of urban life reinforced the environmental viewpoint. Unlike the farmer, the city dweller found the basics of life beyond his individual control. Electricity, water, transportation, and other necessities rested on community decisions or in the hands of distant politicians and remote corporations. 'Complex interdependence' was, to those assessing the problems of urban life, a very real fact of twentieth-century life.

The earliest writers on Canadian urban reform concentrated on the miseries and immoralities of city life. Prostitution, child neglect, slums, and criminal activity were graphically portrayed by writers of the late nineteenth century. In response, a series of loosely related reform movements developed in major Canadian cities. Initially, as befitted the age, these movements followed a narrow line between environmental and individual reform. In effect two themes were apparent. One looked to 'moral uplift' and, its mirror image, the prevention of moral decline, by encouraging a more moral environment for the individual. Prohibition and sabbatarianism provide examples of this, as do many aspects of the child welfare movement of the late nineteenth century.[5]

The other side of the urban reform movement stressed efficiency. This concern often developed from a growing middle-class recognition that the services on which they as well as the poor depended were being run either ineffectively or in corporate rather than the public interest. Street railways, electric power, and other essentials were too important to allow control to be vested in selfish or corrupt individuals who put private gain ahead of public service. This basic human reaction is hardly surprising or revolutionary, but it did lead to a growing willingness on the part of many otherwise-conservative citizens to abandon the doctrine of laissez-faire in such areas in favour of increased municipal regulation and perhaps even public ownership. 'Where shall we obtain the power to compel the carrying on of these undertakings in a manner not antagonistic to the interests of the general public?' asked one reformer as early as 1891. 'There can be but one answer, viz. in the power of control vested in the municipal or central authorities. The only question that can arise is, how far shall public control extend, and how large a domain may be left to private enterprise?'[6]

As the urban reform movement evolved in the years approaching the First World War, issues of efficiency and moral improvement became increasingly intertwined. No single reform or approach seemed sufficient to deal with the myriad problems. Thus, as the movement evolved it implied the necessity of an increased role for government through regulation in the public interest, planning for future development, and the possibility of municipal ownership of various public services. Expenditures and policies would inevitably increase in size and complexity. For the social scientist, urban issues seemed a ready-made set of problems awaiting advisers.

Among those political economists who did take an active role in urban reform, none was more important before the First World War than Samuel Morley Wickett of Toronto. Born in 1872 at Brooklin, Ontario, Wickett was one of those many intellectuals whose roots lay in the rural areas of Canada but whose career depended on the city. First exposed to the social sciences as an undergraduate at the University of Toronto in the 1890s, Wickett became a protégé of James Mavor. Upon graduation, and with Mavor's encouragement, he studied in Austria, where he was exposed to more interventionist ideas about state planning. Returning to Toronto where he became a lecturer, Wickett soon became involved in the various questions of urban reform and by the early 1900s was publishing regularly on that subject.[7]

To this point Wickett was assuming a traditional academic role in teaching, doing research, and publishing on a particular area of interest. Wickett, however, was as much attached to the practical problems of reform as he was to the university. Moreover, he found his attentions further divided by the demands of an inherited family business. The fact that in 1905, when the various demands became too great, he chose to relinquish his university post while remaining active in business and in public affairs indicates a much more interventionist approach than that traditionally associated with the university. It is also revealing that the man who was by this time Canada's foremost expert on municipal affairs did not feel the need to attach himself to a university to bolster his authority. Instead of using the university, Wickett used public speaking engagements to develop his ideas on the problems of the city. In addresses to women's associations, and Canadian and Empire clubs in various locations, as well as in continued publications, Wickett continued to press for solutions to specific urban problems. This approach was taken a step further in 1913 when he entered city politics in Toronto as an alderman. The academic social scientist had followed the imperative of relevance to its logical conclusion. Unfortunately his early death in 1915 cut short a career that demonstrated the new links that were forming between the academic community and social reform.[8]

From the time he began writing on urban problems, Wickett concentrated on a few basic themes. The first was simply to argue that city government was going to be a crucial area of policy formation in the future. Urban questions had, until recently, 'never violently agitated the Canadian public,' but growing urban populations, and with them urban expenditures, would soon change that. 'The increasing concentration of population that has caused such changes in economic and political conditions in various countries of the world,' he wrote in 1900, 'is not absent in Canada.' Those who thought city government was, because of its limited constitutional powers, not very important were out of touch with current trends. Moreover, for Wickett those who looked wistfully back to the rural communities were wasting their time. The future of Canada lay with the cities, and current problems would have to be addressed on that basis: 'We have no traditions of organization. The key to the success of the old world, in its governmental affairs, has undoubtedly been the professional responsibility of its departmental officials. We have had no such traditions.' The transformation of the politicians and the people at large was, in Wickett's mind, less immediately crucial than the transformation of the civil service that advised municipal government. An efficient and expert administration would decrease the load on elected officials while simultaneously providing a comprehensive and systematic approach to the solution of problems that the pressures of elected office did not permit.[9]

Wickett's belief that civic affairs could be improved through more efficient administration struck a chord among Canadian social scientists and intellectual commentators, and throughout the heyday of municipal reform the great bulk of their writings supported his basic arguments. The first step toward effective municipal reform was the recognition that the 'modern city is not merely an agent of the state or province for the more convenient making of ordinances or by-laws,' wrote W.B. Munro, 'but a factor in economic life – a purveyor of water, gas, electricity, a builder of streets and public structures, a large employer of daily labour and a promoter of private industrial development.' A young graduate of the University of Toronto, Frank Underhill, agreed, arguing that 'the supreme need of our cities is a conscious and deliberate plan for the future' and that this, in turn, demanded an expert body of administrators.[10]

The strong belief in the need for expert administration at city hall also led to discussions of the concept of commission government for Canadian cities. This notion sought to bring expertise to city administration while removing certain important city activities from the temptations of political life. The difficulty was that it also raised some fundamental questions about the relation between political power and responsibility. If a permanent and autonomous set of bureaucrats was given control of city affairs, then the corresponding control of elected officials would be diminished. However, advocates of commission government argued that tying the experts too closely to the politicians would defeat the very purpose of the reforms. The question of finding a way to make the administration efficient yet accountable raised a basic problem of modern bureaucracy.

There was no consensus among academics on the necessity or desirability of this American concept. Wickett himself wavered on the question. In much of his writing he seemed in a general sort of way to favour the concept, though the detailed structure of commission government was always less important to him than the development of an administration with sufficient expertise 'under whatever name, whether called Commissioners or controllers.' Wickett's caution was not to be seen in the enthusiasm of Frank Underhill, who saw commission government as a major step towards the solution of modern urban problems. 'There is then a two-fold fault in our municipal machinery as it works at present: it lacks all systematic organization among its parts; and we cannot induce good men to step in and work it, because the general disorder makes constructive effort almost hopeless.' The way to bring order out of the existing chaos was to institute a powerful commission government which, because city government 'is mostly, almost entirely, administrative,' could grapple with problems while setting aside the irrelevancies that politics brought to the fore. Underhill's faith in the potential of expert planning as a source of social betterment was to reappear.[11]

In contrast to Underhill and even to Wickett were those who expressed very serious doubts about commission government. O.D. Skelton, for example, anticipated Underhill's arguments when he wrote in 1909 that excessive faith in non-elected and non-responsible experts was dangerous. 'There is serious danger that permanence in policy may degenerate into stagnation and red-tapeism and over-conservatism, danger that exemption from political pressure should also mean exemption from public responsibility and disregard or resentment of public criticism.' W.B. Munro supported Skelton's opposition to commission government with the argument that it was un-British and unnecessary. Indeed, it was the attempt to escape from particularly American problems, such as party slates at the municipal level, that led to the popularity of commission government in that country. As Canada drew upon a different and better tradition, no such system was needed.[12]

The issues raised by the debate over commission government were fundamental and would echo through later decades as Canadians grappled with the relation between the expert adviser and political control. It would be a mistake, however, to assume from the above citations that political economists dominated urban reform in Canada. The specialized expert was beginning to assert a role for himself in dealing with the complex problems that such reform raised, but the very concept of expertise remained loosely defined and reform was still very much the property of the eclectic generalist. In fact, if one looks at the major organizations involved in urban problems it becomes apparent that the professional remained on the periphery.

This is well illustrated by the history of the most ambitious attempt in this period to institutionalize the study of urban issues, the formation of the Civic Improvement League of Canada. The origins of the League, established in 1915, rest with two earlier organizations concerned with contemporary problems. The first was the Commission of Conservation appointed by Laurier in 1909 and headed by his former minister of the interior, Clifford Sifton. The commission's creation was the result of growing concern for the conservation of natural resources in Canada. The depletion of natural resources by export-oriented firms had raised serious questions beginning in the late 1890s as to the future of Canada's natural heritage. The commission was formed to plan for the future and, drawing its inspiration from parallel groups in the United States, concentrated on matters such as water management, reforestation, and lands. In all cases the concern was not so much conservation in the modern sense of wilderness preservation as resource management.[13]

The Commission of Conservation was given a fair degree of autonomy in order to free it from the dangers of patronage politics. This autonomy also provided the means for those within the commission to widen the mandate of the organization beyond issues of conservation and move into problems directly connected to the major social issues of the day. The section of the commission charged with studying issues related to land soon moved beyond preservation of the soil to the preservation of farmers on that soil.[14] The mirror side of the same concern, urban life, would be developed by the section charged with matters of public health.

Public health was closely linked to urban reform. Bad sanitation, poor housing, and unsafe water, when combined with the crowded living conditions in poorer parts of cities, created substantial hazards to health. The 'primitive public health structure' that had evolved in the late nineteenth century soon proved inadequate to these changing conditions. The health of the city population could not be separated from the overall urban environment. It was thus natural that when the commission established a section concerned with public health it soon became involved with the general issues of urban reform. Thus, for example, in 1910, P.H. Bryce, medical officer of the Department of the Interior, urged a series of social measures, such as school lunches, as matters directly related to the health of the community. From this it was a short step to his conclusion that governments had to become directly involved in all aspects of the urban problem, for cities and towns could no longer be developed 'with our *laissez-faire* American methods.'[15]

This orientation was made even more explicit the year after Bryce's article appeared when the commission was host to a conference on public health and urban problems under the chairmanship of the well-known physician E.B. Osler. At this conference public health and other issues of the physical urban environment merged into an overall concern for the quality of life in the city. C.A. Hodgetts, medical adviser to the Public Health section, summarized a popular theme of the conference when he called, as Bryce had the year before, for greater government involvement in reform and social welfare: 'It is somewhat farcical that a state should decline to accept any responsibility, financial or otherwise, to provide the means whereby crime and disease may be immunized, if not prevented, by bettering the housing conditions. Yet the same state will plan and devise the most approved and up-to-date house for a man after he has become a criminal.'

Enthusiasts like Bryce and Hodgetts soon made purely public health issues subordinate to a more general concern about the future development of city life. By 1914 the shift had been made explicit when G. Frank Beer of the Toronto Housing Company addressed the section with the cry that 'slums produce inefficiency; inefficiency begets poverty; and poverty of their character results in disease and degradation.' A new organization was necessary, Beer concluded, to draw together the various bodies interested in urban problems in order to co-ordinate the attack on the most serious issue confronting modern society.[16]

By the time Beer addressed the commission he was, with Wickett, one of Toronto's best-known urban reformers. His prominence was also an indication of the eclectic nature of modern reformism. A businessman and former president of the Canadian Manufacturers' Association, Beer was an enthusiastic philanthropist and anything but a stereotyp-

ical capitalist. Having made sufficient money to give him independence, Beer became less and less interested in work and increasingly
oriented toward social reform. Issues like immigration, tax reform, and
unemployment all attracted his attention. Of most interest to him,
however, were questions involving town planning and public housing,
and his enthusiasm led him into a scheme of co-partnership housing
designed for the 'decent working class.' The result was the Toronto
Housing Company, with Beer as its president. Aside from his efforts at
public housing he used his position as a platform to convince Canadians
of the importance of urban planning.[17]

One of those who needed little convincing was Sir John Willison,
newspaperman and prominent renegade Liberal. Willison had been
involved in various reform causes through the early 1900s and the
Toronto Civic Guild, of which he was a member, had been instrumental
in developing the concept that led to the Toronto Housing Company.
Thus, when Beer sought him out as an ally in the cause of urban reform
and town planning, Willison responded with enthusiasm. 'We will be
guilty of criminal negligence,' he wrote Beer in early 1913, 'if we allow
to be reproduced in Canada such conditions as have developed in old
world cities and from which multitudes have been glad to escape to
this continent.'[18]

Their enthusiasm and their connections within business, social, and
political elites made Beer and Willison a formidable combination. Willison was a political ally and supporter of Clifford Sifton and was thus
able to provide Beer with access to the head of the Commission of
Conservation. Beer used that access to urge Sifton to support the cause
of town planning. With the support that already existed from within
the Public Health section of the commission, it is therefore not surprising that in 1914 Sifton endorsed the growing orientation towards
urban problems. 'Our cities are not so large,' he commented to a commission Conference on City Planning that year, 'that they are out of
control, and it is still possible within the next ten or twelve years to
relieve any evil conditions which exist at the present time.' Sifton
followed this rhetoric with concrete action when, in 1914, he hired
well-known British town planner Thomas Adams. The Commission of
Conservation had now made its commitment to town planning and
urban reform explicit.[19]

Adams was even more of an enthusiast for town planning than Beer,
and before long he was in contact with both Beer and Willison urging
their support for the formation of a national organization under the

auspices of the commission. The three of them were soon actively involved in preparations for what was to become the Civic Improvement League. Interested parties were contacted, funds were extracted from the commission, and by late 1915, in spite of all the difficulties posed by the wartime situation, the three were able to mount a preliminary conference in Ottawa.[20]

When the preliminary conference gathered in November, those in attendance represented a cross-section of the various groups interested in social reform and public policy from across the nation. The alliance that had formed between middle-class reform, town planning, and public health was well represented by people like Adams, P.H. Bryce, and Beer. Willison presided over the conference as chairman. The others in attendance were amazingly diverse. J.J. Kelso, the child welfare worker from Toronto, was there, and so was author and urban reformer W.D. Lighthall from Montreal. Social gospeller J.S. Woodsworth was there from the Canadian Welfare League as well. There were also a number of prominent social scientists present, including Adam Shortt, Bryce Stewart, and, of course, Morley Wickett.[21]

In January 1916 and May 1917, two further conferences of the League were held, and complex structures of national, provincial, and local councils were established. The war gradually eroded the League, however, and by 1918 the organization was moribund.[22] By that time other causes were gaining the attention of the nation, and the commission itself was soon to disappear. The Civic Improvement League was never revived. The League is thus significant not for what it accomplished but because it represented an effort on the part of a government body to expand interest in a major area of social reform and to lobby for better and more active government intervention in a series of modern problems. Moreover, if the League is judged not by its longevity but by the interest in it at the early meetings, then it was an important organization indeed. The 1916 meeting of the League had a body of delegates whose credentials as reformers were every bit as impressive as the famous Social Services Congress of 1914. The League, however, pointed with greater accuracy towards the changes that were taking place in the nature of reform in Canada. The earlier conference, though eclectic, leaned towards religiously rooted moral reform based on the imperatives of the social gospel, while the 1915 conference, though also eclectic, favoured a more secularly oriented, urban middle-class reformism. The two movements are not completely separable of course, and many individuals were at both meetings, but if it is possible to talk of an urban progressivism in Canada, it was present in those rooms in Ottawa in 1915.

Among these urban progressives, if the meeting of the League can be taken as representative, there was a strong tendency to discuss issues in terms not of morality but efficiency. The actual term *efficiency* was central to anumber of talks at the conference, especially to key addresses by Adams, Beer, and Sifton. 'We must work with our heads more and our hearts less,' said Beer. 'It is because of our recognition of the necessity for wise leadership, deeper study and effective organization that we are here to-day.' The existence of the war reinforced the necessity for efficiency. 'If we leave effective organization for the forces that hinder progress,' in other words to the Germans, 'we are guilty of social treason.'[23] Social engineering and technocratic reform dominated this conference, and to the degree that this emphasis diverged from that of the moral reformers of the Social Services Congress, the 1915 sessions represented at least a potential for divergence in the approach to government involvement and social reform in Canada.

These efficiency-oriented urban reformers were still limited in their willingness to employ the powers of the state. With a core of businessmen and professionals, the group was strongly anti-socialist, and every reform involving compulsion by the state created concern. Government could become involved, as the very origins of the Civic Improvement League implied, but its natural role was seen as one of co-ordination and guidance for individuals or oganizations from outside government. As Thomas Adams wrote to Willison regarding a proposed land settlement scheme, 'I hope you agree that the more proper function of government is to find the right conditions in the first place by the way of planning ... and that it enters dangerous fields when it tampers unduly with the later social development.'[24] Laissez-faire was not a guiding principle for these reformers, but voluntarism was.

It is also important to note the disparate nature of urban progressivism in Canada as represented by the League. For all the talk of efficient planning and in spite of the presence of professional town planners like Adams, the Civic Improvement League was not an organization of experts. Lighthall summed up much when he referred to it as an organization of 'idealists and enthusiasts,' composed of men who were there because they were interested in the issues rather than because they were especially trained in those issues.[25] Commitment to 'good causes' as much as professionalism was essential in the eyes of the League. Urban reform remained an extension of middle-class philanthropy.

The outlook and membership of the League make it roughly analogous to the late-nineteenth-century umbrella organization in the United States known as the American Social Science Association. Both bodies were animated by concerns over the evolution of society, and both mark an attempt to define the direction and the structure of the reform movement, not on the basis of professional training, but in terms of involvement with and commitment to the organization. Within the sort of structures developed by both organizations, the professional social scientist was not a central figure. Men like Shortt and E.J. Kylie of Toronto did, it was true, participate in the Civic Improvement League, but only in minor capacities. The reform movement had not yet completely accepted the social sciences as having a special claim to recognition for the expertise that they could bring to bear. If there were accepted experts, they rested in the sciences and in the professions. Medical men like Bryce were much more important to the movement than were social scientists. The Civic Improvement League was thus in many ways a transitional organization. Its concerns with efficiency forewarned of an increasingly technocratic future, and its support for government involvement in planning the urban environment repudiated laissez-faire individualism. It was, nevertheless, an organization that believed in voluntarism where the state was involved and was dominated by the genteel reform tradition of the middle class rather than by the rising professional groups associated with modern social issues.[26]

While reform movements before the First World War were eclectic mixtures of middle-class reformers of various types, the social scientific community was, in this same period, beginning to develop structures that would allow its disciplines to achieve greater relevance in the world of social assessment and reform. Both within the universities and within the professional organizations that were developed in these years, Canadian academics interested in public policy showed a conscious desire to assert their own relevance to a changing world.

One means of responding to those who criticized academics and their work was to restructure the university in order to make it more relevant to modern issues. Faculty members wondered whether they were meeting the needs of their students or society with programs that often

seemed far distant from the commercial orientation of modern industrial life. This concern was most apparent among social scientists, who,
in many instances, believed that the arts faculty should put itself on
the same 'scientific' basis that had been the practice in science and
professional faculties for some time. This approach included a belief
in the desirability of applied courses for arts students, analogous to
engineering in science. In response to this attitude, courses in banking
and other business-related themes developed between 1910 and 1920.
Though Dalhousie was perhaps the first Canadian university to offer
a diploma program in commerce, the development of a degree in commerce at the University of Toronto in 1909 marks the beginning of the
integration of such programs within traditional offerings. Others followed rapidly. Queen's University, for example, began extension courses
in banking in 1913 and by the end of the war had developed a full
commerce program under the guidance of the young economist William
Clifford Clark. In Quebec the establishment of the Ecole des hautes
études commerciales and its affiliation with Laval in 1915 provided
business training for francophone students, while in English Canada,
McGill and Alberta both developed commerce programs during the war.
By the 1920s, commerce or business courses had become standard fare
at major Canadian universities.[27]

Those who promoted such programs used two basic arguments to do
so, both summarized in an early argument by Morley Wickett. First,
said Wickett, the development of such programs would not fundamentally alter existing social science courses. These disciplines already had
a natural orientation towards the practical, and 'businessmen can already find much of interest to them in the curricula of our larger
universities.' All that had to be done was to restructure and regroup
existing courses in an appropriate fashion. Second, it was a matter of
self-defence. The presence across the border of inferior 'business' colleges gave warning to Canadian academics that if nothing were done,
students with an interest in business would be siphoned off to narrow
commercial programs, where all attempts at general education were
abandoned in favour of technical training. By retaining future businessmen within the university system, both the university and society
would benefit. The university would develop better contacts with, and
understanding, from the business class, while society would be improved because the businessman's university education would allow
him 'to look upon business from a higher standpoint.'[28]

Such attitudes did not go unchallenged. As has been indicated, the

Canadian intellectual community was generally critical of the shallow materialism that it saw as pervading modern society. Proposals for business courses seemed designed to turn the universities into the conscious agents of that very materialism. Stephen Leacock of McGill, perhaps sensitive to his university's close ties to the Montreal business community, looked with dismay upon the evolution of practical programs. Reciting a parable about demands by business tycoons that practical courses be instituted for their sons, Leacock commented that while earlier generations had despised the businessman and even reduced that class by having one 'occasionally boiled in oil,' the modern age had 'enthroned the despised trader in triumph on the debris of broken autocracies.' Universities had been scrambling to serve the new overlords of their society ever since: 'The result was that a great number of tin-pot institutions and two penny departments began to turn out a new kind of graduate, who spelt Caesar with a G and thought that Edmund Burke was the name of a brewer. Over the surface of the graduate's mind was spread a thin layer of practical knowledge brittle as ginger bread.'[29] For Leacock and for others the triumph of practical training in the arts faculty was not so much a victory for social science as it was a defeat for the true educational function of the university. Yet even Leacock recognized that such programs were inevitable if the university was to maintain a central place in the Canadian educational system.

The introduction of new programs was only one means by which the social sciences could assert their relevance to modern Canada. It was also important for them to gain recognition as disciplines apart from the older philosophical and theological areas with which they had been tied in their founding years. In the pre-war years this separation had been achieved to the extent that an ever-increasing number of social scientists were trained in their own disciplines, usually at graduate schools in the United States and Great Britain. There were still serious weaknesses in the community's sense of identity and ability to exchange ideas. No journal existed as a forum for its ideas, and no organizational structure provided a forum for the development of research and professional standards. In 1913 Adam Shortt, by then civil service commissioner in Ottawa, and his successor at Queen's sought to remedy this with the formation of the Canadian Political Science Association (CPSA).

The timing of the formation of the CPSA was not the best. Its first meeting was held in September 1913. Before the next meeting was held, war had broken out. By 1915 the organization was moribund, and the association would not be revived until after the eve of another great disaster, the Depression. Even with its brief initial existence, however, the CPSA is important. It provided for the first time a distinct structure that attempted to unite the various strands of social scientific thought under one umbrella organization. Previously, when those who considered themselves social scientists or political economists (the two terms were practically interchangeable in Canada at this time) ventured into public policy discussions, they had been involved in organizations according to their particular interests – civil service reform movements, urban reform bodies, or whatever. In such organizations they were but one element, and often a minority, of a large group of church reformers, enthusiastic amateurs, single-cause reformers, and politicians. In the CPSA, however, the approach to the problem, rather than the problem itself, was taken to define the parameters. Thus at the first meeting there were papers presented on a range of issues, from municipal government to housing policy. What united the disparate papers was a belief that a series of complex, environmentally based concerns demanded a dedicated and careful assessment aimed towards policy development.[30]

The initial membership of the CPSA emphasizes this same point. Though university membership or, for that matter, academic degrees remained less important than a certain attitude towards problem-solving, the 1913 CPSA was very much dominated by professionally trained social scientists. Adam Shortt was the first president, and O.D. Skelton the first vice-president. The executive included men like Stewart Bryce, an expert on labour exchanges, who was a graduate of Queen's and Columbia. Other members of the executive included Mavor from Toronto and W.B. Munro.

At the same time, the CPSA's membership revealed a realization on the part of social scientists that they still needed the assistance of others interested in social issues if they were to be credible. Thus O.D. Skelton solicited the involvement of people like Frank Beer, whose interests made him a likely candidate for the asssociation, in spite of his lack of connection with any university. When Beer queried Skelton as to the membership of the new body, Skelton replied not by listing other academics but by referring to reformers from the community like Willison, and Joseph Atkinson of the Toronto *Star*. Likewise, Montreal reformer Herbert Ames had long ago established his credentials as a serious observer of social conditions and was made a member of the executive. Even Sidney Fisher, a former minister of agriculture in the Laurier government, was made a member of that same executive.[31]

The CPSA is also significant because it provided an occasion for an explicit statement of the view that social expertise had a special role to play in modern society. As President Adam Shortt noted in his founding address, the association was intended not for the average citizen but for those 'reflective and public spirited citizens with whom, in their respective lives, as Goethe says, "All great and good things lie." ' It was a club designed to draw the intellectual elite of the nation into studies of the problems of society. 'One does not try to do fine work through the instrumentality of the mob. It is through a select, active minority that the most effective and progressive ideas as to the political and social welfare must be attained.' Shortt's elitism remained intact. It was not a question merely of forming an elite discussion group, however. In Shortt's view, the CPSA was a staging ground for the development of policy ideas that would have a direct impact on government. Using the analogy of the innoculating needle, he talked of the infusion of new ideas into the 'tissues of the body politic. If the operation is skilfully performed, the serum will diffuse itself by way of the proper channels throughout the whole system.' The vision was one of a new class of professionals who would act as the protectors of society even as doctors protected against illness. In another analogy Shortt referred to architects, the men who designed the shape of society for others to build. In either case the direction mapped out for political economists was the same. Their discipline had an important and practical role to play, not only in studies within the university, but also in the outside world. Shortt was stating in explicit fashion the claim of political economy to recognition within Canadian society at large.[32]

Shortt's arguments in 1913 must have pleased Quebec's Edouard Montpetit, himself a member of the new association, who, the year before, had made many of the same arguments in an article with the revealing title, 'Le mouvement économique. L'économic politique est elle une science ennuyeuse et abstrait?' Far too often, he said, the general public associated economics with the theorizing of men like British economist W.S. Jevons or the 'Lausanne school' of L. Walras and V. Pareto. For Montpetit, however, theory was not the heart of political economy, and such work constituted only a small part of the economist's activities. Generally 'la science a continué de s'attacher à la réalité.' Political economy was anything but boring or abstract: 'Comment l'économiste poura-t-il embrasser dans son ensemble et scruter jusque dans ses recoins cette formidable vie? Par l'observation continue, attentive, avertie, méthodique. Il étudiera, s'il peut, en prenant part au mouvement industriel, commercial et financier; en aidant les initiatives sociales.'

This vision of the political economist as an expert closely tied to social policy drew its inspiration, in part, from experiences in the United States. In the early twentieth century American reform developed increasingly close ties with segments of the intellectual community. Academics became involved in public policy, and the connections between intellectual 'experts' on social and economic reform and elected politicians developed accordingly. In 1912, a university president, Woodrow Wilson, was elected president of the United States. The struggling and often ignored Canadian community of political economists naturally saw in American developments a model for their own future.[33]

This model was often capsulized by the phrase, 'the Wisconsin idea.' There were many aspects to the Wisconsin idea, but the one of most interest to the Canadian intellectual community was the alliance that had developed between the University of Wisconsin and progressive reformers in the state government. The whole state had become, in the eyes of supporters of the movement, 'an experiment station in politics, in social and industrial legislation, in democratization of science and higher education.' Within this laboratory the social scientists were given an important role in directing and advising on the future direction of experiments under way. Though the close ties between the government and university raised questions about the autonomy of the university, the general image of the 'Wisconsin idea' in intellectual circles was positive. It was also well known. A laudatory book on the subject was published in 1912, and in 1913 Richard Van Hise, president of the University of Wisconsin, visited Canada to explain the important function his institution had assumed. In their assertions of a greater role for political economy, Shortt and Montpetit were thus merely reflecting a natural belief that American use of the intellectual community marked the inevitable course of future development.[34]

This early interest in public policy raises an interesting point. Later generations of economists have occasionally complained that the movement of political economists into public service seduced them away from the basic theoretical research that underlay the discipline.[35] These early writings indicate, however, that seduction is hardly the appropriate term. It was the political economic community that sought to seduce the public sector, and, as Montpetit's views indicate, theory was never considered the primary service the social scientific community could render in Canada. Canadian conditions and the American experiment seemed to demand a more direct role.

Reform of the universities and establishment of bodies like the Canadian Political Science Association were all very well. If, however, the profession were to acquire power and influence it had to become a force within government. Accordingly, as concern with social issues increased, social scientists sought to establish closer contacts with various levels of government on a direct basis. This was facilitated by the narrow base of the Canadian elite. Academics were rare enough and politicians available enough that before the Second World War even the prime minister was available to those professors who wished to see him or correspond with him on matters of public concern. Certainly prime ministers Laurier and Borden, as well as provincial premiers, cabinet ministers, and other politicians, corresponded with varying degrees of regularity with intellectuals concerned about public issues. By far the strongest connections between a major political figure and the academic community, however, involved that intellectual idealist in the world of politics, William Lyon Mackenzie King.

It was natural for the intellectual community to look to King for some recognition. He was, after all, one of them. Moreover, his success in the civil service and then in political circles served as an example of the practical role that the professional could play in government. At the same time, in a pattern that was to hold through the years, King's ample ego and his distinctive personality were viewed with some dismay in intellectual circles. His personality, however, was less important than the fact that he seemed to represent the potential for more scientific, humane, and interventionist government under the guidance of knowledgable and rational men. W.L. Grant, the son of the late principal of Queen's and an intellectual figure in his own right, wrote King in 1910: 'Now that Sir Wilfrid is growing old, there is no one to whom I look with such confidence as I do yourself to keep the party both clean and progressive.' A year later, when King lost his seat in the general election, Skelton wrote to commiserate with him and to say that whatever King did in the future, 'the country will receive from you the same progressive and effective service given in the precedent making years of the Ministry of Labour.'[36]

King was not only a model of intellectual progressivism; he was also a useful contact. The labour conciliation boards that resulted from his legislation and that were under the control of the Department of Labour created an opportunity for several political economists to play a role in the public arena. In addition, King accepted the importance of adequate research into important areas of government interest, and men like Skelton and future Dominion statistician R.H. Coats obtained commissions from him to study various Canadian economic problems. For a discipline that was anxious to become directly involved in practical issues, such work provided an opportunity both to investigate new areas and to assert the relevance of political economy in the modern world.[37]

Next to Mackenzie King, the individual who was most important in forging early links between the university and government, was Adam Shortt. As early as 1905 Shortt had argued that the political economist should apply his expertise to government problems: 'I have felt that the time was coming in Canada as in other countries, and especially in the United States, when the Government would avail itself of the training and research of its university professors in various departments, thereby aiding their research and enabling them to bring back to their students some of the freshness and reality of concrete problems. In a sense this is what the Government has done in placing Mr. King at the head of the Department of Labour.' When King heard of these comments, he got together with Shortt to discuss 'certain general relationships between Governments and university professors in other countries.' Before long Shortt had become one of King's most active labour conciliators, sitting on some eleven different boards over the next few years. These contracts may also have paved the way for Shortt's transfer of allegiance from the university to the government when, in September 1908, he accepted appointment as civil service commissioner.[38]

Shortt's appointment to this position was significant: it expanded the role of the academic within government and aided the related process of civil service reform. As was discussed earlier, Shortt had long been critical of the way in which patronage had undermined the effectiveness of the Canadian civil service. As an active proponent of reform, he had hastened to the support of such organizations as the Civil Service Reform League and to individuals who spoke out in favour of reform, as well as writing on the issue himself.[39] There was never any doubt that he would accept Laurier's offer.

Shortt was brought to Ottawa as one of two commissioners charged with the administration of the new 1908 Civil Service Act. This act sought to make classifications within the service more rational as well as to ensure that merit became the primary criterion for hiring and promotion. There were, however, limitations on the effectiveness of this first step towards reform. Most importantly the act applied only to the 'inside service,' roughly those involved in headquarters positions as well as a few key officials in other locations. The great majority of civil servants remained under the older and much more arbitrary procedures that dated back to the era of Confederation. As the outside service had always been the focus of most patronage activity, critics of the 1908 act argued with some reason that little, if anything, was being changed.[40]

The deficiencies of the act revealed the ambivalence of the government towards reform. On the one hand, old practices died hard, and many of Laurier's supporters were nervous about tampering with a system that they had used to great effect in recent years. On the other hand, patronage was, to put it simply, a nuisance for politicians. Members of Parliament on the government benches were under continual siege by faithful followers who demanded rewards. Since everyone knew that patronage was commonly practised, it was difficult for the politician to refuse too many requests lest crucial contributions and support dwindle. The dependence of politicians on patronage was thus countered by the recurrent desire to free themselves of the albatross. A new Civil Service Act and a commission to which requests might be referred thus had certain benefits. Also important was the apparent acceptance of the principle long argued by many intellectuals, that the changing role of the government demanded new standards of efficiency within the civil service. At the very least, the growing storm of complaints about patronage may have led the Laurier government to feel that some compromise was necessary to appease civil service reformers.

Whatever the reasons for the bill and no matter how limited its application, Shortt had great hopes for its success. He immediately set about designing competitive applications for prospective civil servants, and with his co-commissioner, Michel LaRochelle, he began to investigate other ways in which the civil service might be streamlined. He was even able to bring about the further involvement of the university community in government by hiring various university professors to administer the new examinations. Shortt's concept of his role involved much more than bringing a degree of honesty to the civil service system. Civil service reform, guided by an expert like himself, provided an opportunity to reorient government away from the highly partisan and ad hoc procedures characteristic of the nineteenth century and towards a model of planning and public service adapted to dealing with the emerging problems of a new era. 'Freed of the profligate-spending and patronage-management of the existing "independent" departmental system, the government could get down to determining long-term and coherent policies which the nation's contemporary problems warranted.'[41]

Shortt's actual experience fell far below his expectations. The problem of civil service reform was massive and involved not only the restriction of patronage but also the restructuring of the civil service itself and the redefinition of relation between the permanent adviser and the politician. To achieve these goals would take decades, and Shortt was naive to think that they could be accomplished quickly under governments that were less than fully committed to the principle of reform in the first place. Thus, for example, in 1912, the new Conservative government of Robert Borden appointed A.B. Morine and two other commissioners to investigate the state of the civil service with an eye to further reform. The commission soon bogged down, however, and stories of scandal surrounding Morine soon destroyed its credibility. Shortt had never been enthusiastic about the Morine Commission, as it possessed none of the expert and detached personnel that he saw as essential. He was, therefore, quick to suggest that Borden replace it with a one-man investigation under the direction of British treasury expert Sir George Murray. Murray was duly appointed and before long issued a telling report that went beyond issues of classification and patronage to the whole complex question of the relation between the minister and his advisers. His suggestions for greater efficiency through wider delegation of responsibility and a more clearly designed structure of civil service appointments and promotions reflected many of Shortt's own ideas. The problem was that the report, as Borden later wrote, 'went considerably beyond the scope of the proposed inquiry.'[42] Little immediate came of the flurry of investigations that followed Shortt's appointment.

The unwillingness of the government to respond to either Shortt or Murray was followed by an even greater failure for the concept of civil service reform. Shortt, unable to gain rapid changes in the system, increasingly reverted to his earlier role as critic of the existing system – except this time from within. Going before various public forums, he argued that the demands of a modern nation and, with 1914, the demands of war made a system based on merit and ability imperative. The 1908 act had to be extended.[43] The fact that Shortt's activities were tolerated by Borden indicates the prime minister's continued interest in reform. Not all party members were so enthusiastic, however, and Shortt found himself confronting one of the party's major dispensers of patronage, Minister of Public Works Robert Rogers.

On one of his speaking forays, Shortt attacked Rogers as a particularly odious purveyor of patronage. Rogers, in turn, launched into a vigorous criticism of the commissioner in the House of Commons. For Shortt's former colleagues it was a clear-cut case of the guilty party complaining that he had been found out, and they rallied to Shortt's defence. 'To win the condemnation of the worst of influences in Canadian life is a real distinction,' wrote W.L. Grant, when he heard of the incident. Standing as a champion of the right did not automatically bring triumph, however. Shortt's accusations had been sloppy in their details if not in their general argument, and he was thus left uncomfortably vulnerable. Borden was becoming increasingly unhappy with his civil service commissioner and later would comment that the man he had inherited from Laurier was not 'altogether suited, either by his previous academic experience, or his temperament, for the duties of Civil Service Commissioner.' Thus in 1917, when the government created a Board of Historical Publications, Borden, and ostensibly Shortt, were pleased to see the latter assume its chairmanship. One academic's experiment as a government reformer ultimately led him back into scholarly activities, albeit under government auspices.[44]

Shortt's activities as civil service commissioner were an important precedent in changing the nature of government in Canada. He, as much as Mackenzie King, helped pave the way for future employment of expert academics by government. In the case of both men, however, the pre-war role of the social scientist in government needs clarification. Mackenzie King, after all, had obtained his position as much through influence as through training.[45] Shortt, it was true, was hired because of his academic reputation as a man knowledgeable about civil service reform, but even this fact must be qualified. The attitudes of both Laurier and Borden towards his position stressed its quasi-judicial function, as laid out under the 1908 act. Its key ingredient was integrity rather than expertise. A reputable academic, above party politics, was admirably suited for this post, and Shortt was hired as a man above reproach rather than as an expert. He was to be the theologan and conscience of the government, though in twentieth century-garb.

Needless to say, Adam Shortt would not have accepted this interpretation. His view of the place of the intellectual in government was more exalted. Integrity was important, of course, and the ability to avoid petty partisanship and narrow ambition was a part of that necessary integrity. For Shortt and many others, however, any system that saw the academic of value only because of his integrity and a general sort of undifferentiated wisdom was missing the real opportunities that the intellectual community offered to government. As Shortt made clear in his CPSA address, the existence within that community of a group of social scientists who by training and inclination were especially well equipped to deal with complex social and economic issues provided the key to efficient government policy formation in the future. The interests of society demanded that government recognize the legitimacy of political economy as a discipline with special relevance to its needs. 'This is an age of experts,' he commented in 1912. 'Efficiency of government cannot be given unless the person placed in office has information and the faculty of using his judgement.'[46]

Shortt's concept of the role of the expert came closest to realization in these years not at the Dominion but at the provincial level. The complexities of the modern economy were brought home to Canada in 1912-13 when, after years of steady growth, recession hit. Immigration, agricultural settlement, and, most importantly, capital investment from abroad declined precipitously, causing bankruptcies to rise and unemployment to increase. Such downturns were not new to Canada, of course. Periodic recessions had been well known throughout the nineteenth century, and Finance Minister Thomas White commented of the economic problems facing the country in 1912 that there was 'nothing exceptional or peculiar about the ... situation' and that it was simply 'history repeating itself.' The nature of the downturn, however, and the effect it had on the industrial work-force made many feel that this recession was different. The character of the modern industrial state, with the economic dependence of an employee class that it implied, seemed to make the social consequences of recession greater than in the past, when agriculture had dominated to a greater degree. As the recession deepened, various reformers called for some sort of government action. In 1914, for example, Willison wrote Borden urging him 'to appoint Sir Clifford Sifton, or some other man of ability and organizing capacity, to head an unpaid voluntary commission which would devote its whole time not to the ordinary measures of relief but to finding new employment and making homes say amongst farmers for those who will not be able to find work.' In the end, however, it was not Ottawa but the Ontario government that acted. Frank Beer had been in correspondence with reform politician W.J. Hanna urging a full investigation of the industrial situation in Ontario. Hanna supported the idea and along with fellow politician and reform-minded colleague Newton Rowell appointed the Ontario Commission on Unemployment in early 1915. Willison became its chairman.[47]

The commission contained other familiar faces besides Willison's. Beer was a member, as were such noted Toronto reformers and philanthropists as W.K. McNaught, Canon H.J. Cody, and the Reverend Neil McNeil. What made the commission especially interesting, however, was the relatively high profile assumed by political economists. Professor Gilbert Jackson of the University of Toronto was a member of the commission, while W.W. Swanson of Queen's, R.H. Coats and Stewart Bryce of Ottawa, and E.J. Kylie of the University of Toronto all provided assistance at various points in the commission's studies, as did a number of American economists. Jackson and Swanson had an especially strong influence on the commission. The former acted, with physician and reformer Helen MacMurchy, as secretary to the commission and with Beer drafted much of its report. Swanson seems to have assumed a staff role for the commission and was also involved in writing various sections of the final report. Their influence significantly affected the conclusions that were reached and demonstrated the sort of key position in policy advice that men like Shortt had been advocating for political economists.[48]

The recession was tailor-made for those political economists who wished to assert their relevance. The business cycle was a complex manifestation well beyond the understanding of even astute businessmen. The reminder of its costs that the 1912 recession brought was all the more bewildering because, if one discounts a modest 1907 slump, it had been so long since the economy had experienced a serious downturn. This was the first time that a serious recession had developed in Canada since political economy had become a recognized university discipline in the nation. Moreover, economists seemed to be able to assert a particular expertise on questions of the cycle. That subject had been the primary theme of a number of investigations by top British and continental European writers in recent years. Such investigations gave at least the hope that modern political economy would prove Finance Minister White's fatalism incorrect. Perhaps greater understanding of the relation between trade, the level of employment, and the nature of the business cycle would allow a degree of control. Gilbert Jackson's own appointment to the commission was probably not un-related to his conviction that such control was indeed possible with some planning and government intervention. 'Forty years ago, depressions in trade could be regarded as the act of God; the distress that followed them was pitiable, but no man knew how it could be avoided ... To-day conditions are altogether different. A number of governments, as far apart as Austria and Wisconsin, are demonstrating that they can do something for their unemployed. The plain inference is that in Canada we can do something for our own.'[49]

The report of the commission reflected both this general premiss and an economic method. There were, it was true, references to the evils of individual laziness and the alcohol problem (this latter point being essential, given the men who sponsored the commission), but the main thrust of the commission was to see unemployment in social and economic rather than in individual terms. 'Personal causes of unemployment have received, heretofore, a disproportionate amount of attention.' Unemployment was a part of the problem of industrialization. 'The result of their enquiries,' concluded the report, 'has impressed on your Commissioners most forcibly the fact that the depression, which occurred in 1914 and 1915, was but a phase of a movement alternating between inflation and depression, which is a characteristic of modern industry.' The acceptance of the fact that the individual was not primarily to blame, at least in times of recession, marked a major step towards an environmental analysis of social concerns. Equally important, if unemployment was not primarily the fault of the unemployed, neither was it a problem that concerned them alone. 'Inaction on unemployment involves the physical, and often the moral deterioration of many workers. It encourages indiscriminate begging and is responsible for the growth of a parasitic class. It compels mothers with young children to neglect their domestic duties, in order to secure a livelihood.'[50]

The conclusions concerning the nature of unemployment in the modern world pointed toward greater intervention by government. If the economic structure of the nation rather than the personal habits of the individual underlay large-scale unemployment, and if that unemployment affected the general well-being and efficiency of society, then it followed that society at large had to deal with the problem. As the commission commented, 'It is difficult to believe that any form of organized relief, which does not directly pauperize, can be more costly to society than the refusal to take action.' Moreover, 'if the state wishes to secure the fullest loyalty and efficiency of its citizens must it not assume a larger measure of leadership than in the past?'[51]

The logic of the commission pointed toward state intervention, but its recommendations were quite modest. The idea of unemployment insurance was raised but only as a voluntary scheme for certain trades. The main suggestion for government action was to pre-plan public works in such a way that they could be stepped up in times of recession. Immigration, the report argued, should also be regulated more carefully to ensure that Canadian economic needs were being met. The main emphasis, however, was on the provision of a series of labour bureaux which provincial governments and perhaps eventually the Dominion could provide to assist the worker to find employment.[52] Modest though these recommendations were, they did call on government to become a deliberate, if relatively small, balance wheel in the economy through public works expenditures. They also urged it to assume the expense and responsibility of acting as an employment agency and possibly as the intermediary in an unemployment insurance scheme.

The recommendations were hardly radical, but they were indicative of the way in which a changing social structure and a new approach to social and economic problems were leading toward the idea of greater government intervention. To have expected anything more radical from the commission would have been unrealistic. First, the understanding of macro-economic manipulation of the economy was still relatively basic. In spite of Jackson's brave words in 1914, actual control of the business cycle as opposed to amelioration of its effects was still beyond the horizons of most economists. The proposal for preplanned public works remained an isolated recommendation rather than becoming part of a wider conception of government involvement in the market-place.[53] The concept of monetary adjustments through interest rate changes or manipulation of the money supply had not yet evolved even at the theoretical level. Government, moreover, was still relatively limited in size and thus could have only so much effect on the economy. The realities of the age, in other words, imposed restraints on the possible recommendations of the commission.

Second, there was an attitudinal factor of some importance as well. The commission accepted the social costs of unemployment and, there-fore, the appropriateness of involvement by government in attempting to deal with the situation. As in other areas, however, an acceptance of the importance of co-ordination, as in the labour bureaux, and amelioration, as in pre-planned public works, did not mean support for compulsion by government. Thus, for example, the commission rejected compulsory unemployment insurance. Any measure that used the power of the state to force an individual to participate in a program, even if for the individual's good, was seen as a dangerous infringement of the basic principle that the individual had to work out his own destiny – even if that meant failure. Laissez-faire individualism was crumbling in the face of modern complexity, but voluntarism remained a potent force.

While the Ontario Commission on Unemployment was perhaps more influenced by social scientific method than any other government study to that date, it was but one of many projects in which social scientists were beginning to be more active outside the university. Wickett, Shortt, Skelton, and, to a lesser extent, Mackenzie King all sought to bring social scientific method and analysis to bear on the problems of government. They, like Swanson and Jackson, approached their problems from certain common presumptions about the nature of causation and the role of environment. Social and economic problems were to them complex issues that could not be resolved by the individual acting alone. The state, guided by expert advice, was seen as a necessary agent in dealing with modern social problems and in preventing rapid change from destroying social well-being and economic efficiency. This first generation of social scientists was thus reformist in outlook and anti-laissez-faire in temperament. Unlike its nineteenth-century counterparts in the United States, it never called on the laws of its disciplines to condemn government intervention.[54] On the contrary, it took its wares to government to illustrate how important a tool the social sciences could be in asserting the function of government.

The emergence of the Canadian social scientific community in these years must also be set in the wider context of reform in the country. Even as the few activities touched on above indicate, reform in urban Canada was based on a series of related movements that sprang from concerns over issues like urbanization, government efficiency, social dislocation, and industrialization.[55] The movements were based on middle-class values and varied from moral reformism to the sort of social engineering that many political economists found compatible with their own perspective. Underlying the movement was a series of complex motivations that mixed a sense of sincere concern, social snobbery, and a sense of self-preservation. General to them all, however, seems to have been some variation on the theme raised by Skelton, that inadequate responses to modern conditions would only encourage radicalism.

Borrowing from parallel American reform, Canadian historians have often employed the term *progressivism* to describe the variety of social reform movements that sprang up from within the middle class and intellectual community in this period. Given the flow of ideas back and forth across the border and the exposure of men like King and Skelton to American reform ideals while in graduate school, the term is appropriate to describe the emergent intellectual activism. It is applicable to Canada, however, only with some qualification. The difference in timing must be kept in mind. By the early 1890s American writers had clearly identified the existence of a 'social crisis' resulting from industrialization and urbanization. By 1900 earlier populist and socialist crusades had begun to evolve into a middle-class progressivism typified by the rambunctious presidency of Theodore Roosevelt and the numerous social reform groups, writings, and causes of the same era. In Canada, though similar structural changes in the economic and social order began in the 1880s and 1890s, the effects were not significant enough to gain widespread public attention until after 1900. Responses to the perceived social crisis also emerged later. Though there were nineteenth-century precedents in such areas as public health, it was not until about 1910 that the social gospel movement, urban reform, and other progressive causes developed strong organizations or gained widespread attention. Not until 1914, with the Social Services Congress, and 1915, with the Civic Reform League, did the various loose strands of progressivism in Canada begin to develop into a national force.[56]

In other words, there was a lag in Canadian reform relative to the United States. The reason was straightforward: Canada underwent rapid industrialization and urbanization later than the United States. Though the analogy should not be carried too far, the effect of the Canadian boom of 1898-1912 on social conditions resembled that of the post-Civil War American boom. In both cases new challenges were posed to a community that had previously looked at itself in agrarian and rural terms. Only then did progressivism begin to make sense, and as a result Canadians were just beginning to urge serious reform of government at a time when American progressivism had already become mature and, some would say, decadent. In the normal course of events, the lag would not have lasted. Once Canadians perceived the existence of a parallel social crisis, they could look across the border, or to European reform movements, for appropriate responses and thereby formulate reforms borrowed or altered from the experience of other countries. By 1914 this was already beginning. The 'normal' course of events was not to be, however, for the war would force a whole new set of questions forward about the relation between the individual and the state just as new views were beginning to develop on the issue. And if the relatively late and minor part played by the United States in the First World War brought a major crisis to progressivism there, as has been asserted, then it is hardly surprising that urban progressivism in Canada underwent an even greater crisis.[57] The difference was that in Canada war and its aftermath shattered urban progressivism before it had had time to reach maturity.

4

Statism and democracy
1914-18

The Canadian intellectual community reacted to the declaration of war in much the same way as did the politicians and general populace. The complex elite of academics, university administrators, social gospellers, and businessmen reformers, the various combinations of which had formed the ranks of Canadian progressivism, saw the war as an extension of the spirit of their movement. Historian G.M. Wrong of the University of Toronto was typical. Speaking in October 1914, he scorned those who would spend their time in 'vain regrets' over the outbreak of war. 'It is magnificent that humanity ... should learn to stand together on broad human interests,' he pointed out. 'The victory for justice will place our humanity on a higher level than it was before.'[1]

To a degree the expectations of the reformers were met. As John English points out in his study of the First World War, there emerged an 'ideology of service.' In both political parties, he argues, the war altered political perceptions and forced politicians to subordinate traditional local issues and partisan politics and to concentrate instead on the fundamental national questions raised by the war. As a result, traditional loyalties proved insufficient to hold the parties together, and new alignments were formed on the basis of war-related issues. He also notes that reform politicians had been advocating such an ideology of service well before the conflict.[2] For years, reform writings had been preaching a doctrine of service to the larger good and duty to society while condemning selfish materialism. As Adam Shortt's mixed experiences as civil service commissioner indicate, reformist values had at best been only partly realized. The coming of the war provided an opportunity for such views to gain momentum. Over the next three years such views assumed an increasingly important position, finally becoming explicit in the Union government of 1917.

The very forces that led to the triumph of this ideology, however, created new doubts within the intellectual community. By the time the devastating and soul-wrenching conflict in Europe came to an end, many of those who had most enthusiastically supported the war looked with dismay at what it had wrought. The future seemed to point toward chaos. Unity had become fragmentation, and optimism crumbled in the face of seemingly insuperable difficulties. Four years of war, said Stephen Leacock, had brought Canadians to a point approaching 'social panic': 'The state as we know it, threatens to dissolve into labour unions, conventions, boards of conciliation and conferences. Society, shaken to its base, hurls itself into the industrial suicide of the general strike, refusing to feed itself, denying its wants.'[3] As with so much else that occurred between 1914 and 1918, the shift in perception came about as a result of the grinding destruction of the war itself. In the process those intellectual reformers who had been concerned with the role of the state before the war found their perceptions of government and society irrevocably altered.

The initial enthusiasm for the war effort was reflected in the strong support given to it by Canadian universities. Administrators, faculty, and the public at large all made it abundantly clear to the student body that the war took precedence over studies. Moral persuasion to enlist was reinforced at several universities, including Toronto, McGill, Queen's, Winnipeg, and Alberta, through a system of academic credits for time spent in the forces. The results were dramatic. By 1916 more than half of the University of Alberta's male students had enlisted. Toronto saw its Arts Faculty enrolment drop by some 600 by the 1915 session, while at McGill some 850 students joined the military through the war. Some 300 were killed. The small Wesley College in Winnipeg saw more than 300 undergraduates enlist, the president announcing proudly in 1917 that 'every man in the [theology] class [had] sought admission to the army.'[4]

Not only students were affected. A good many graduates postponed or interrupted further studies or teaching careers and went off to war. W.L. Grant, son of the former principal of Queen's, is a good example. Grant had joined the Queen's faculty after completing graduate work at Harvard. His abilities and his Queen's connections meant that he was soon well established on campus. Through the columns of the *Queen's Quarterly* he quickly became involved in questions of reform. When war came, however, he saw it as taking precedence and enlisted in spite of his age of 41 years. He served in France, was wounded, and returned to Canada in 1917. No romantic, he recognized the war to be a symbol of the failure of civilization. At the same time he had no doubts about the justness of the cause.[5]

W.L. Grant's course of action was paralleled by men like the 30-year-old J.M. Macdonnell, Queen's graduate and trustee, and man of many public interests; by 25-year-old Frank Underhill, the young enthusiast from Toronto; and by University of Toronto faculty member Edward Kylie, who was killed in training. Nor was Grant the oldest faculty member to serve. Fifty-year-old Andrew Macphail of McGill joined the service as a physician and spent much of the next four years in France. For those who, for reasons of age, physical ability, or conscience, felt that they could not get directly involved in military action there were alternatives. Many of the best-educated and best-known of Canadian clerics served as military chaplains or in the Young Men's Christian Association (YMCA) in Europe. Social gospeller Charles Gordon transferred his desire for social service to the front and became one of Canada's most famous military chaplains. Under his pen name Ralph Connor he would later employ his talent as a novelist to portray the experience of the Canadian soldier. For those who stayed at home there was a great deal of war work to be accomplished in fund raising, the writing of pro-war literature, and the organization of voluntary work.[6]

In assessing the high level of support within the intellectual community for the war, the emotionalism of the months after August 1914 must be kept in mind. Canadian intellectuals were as swept up in the early war fever as was the general public. For those who were predisposed to an imperial outlook, as many were, the emotional reaction was all that much stronger. Automatic and deep-seated reactions were triggered by the presence of the Empire in the conflict. 'Fair dealing, justice and righteousness' were supposedly the foundations of British society, and no detailed argument or explanations were needed to convince these Canadians that the war was just. In speeches, editorials, and sermons, a great many of those associated with progressive reformism before the war became advocates of a strong prosecution of the war after August 1914. Those who remained unaffected by such emotionalism at the beginning would have needed a strong sense of independence and a certain callousness to remain detached in the emotional cauldron that developed amid growing casualties and public anger as the years passed.[7]

The specific and immediate cause for Britain's entry into the war had been the violation of Belgian neutrality by Germany. Questions of national honour and of the protection of small nations were employed to underpin Canadian support for the war. As the war went on, however, the emotional demands placed upon society required higher principles. As the costs mounted, Germany's image grew proportionately darker. Horror stories of atrocities in Belgium, yellow journalism, and official government propaganda combined to create an image of anti-Christ suitable for Armageddon. It was not just the sanctity of British treaties that was at stake, but the British way of life. The issue, said Newton Rowell in 1917, was 'whether Prussian military autocracy, cold, brutal and ruthless, is to prevail, or whether free democracy and the principle that "Right is greater than might" are to have a place in the world.' A professor of philosophy at Dalhousie recoiled in horror at his realization that in German conduct 'no dishonesty is too gross, no purpose is too malignant, no atrocity is too savage to be glossed over.'[8]

A nation that, like Germany, had become so insanely bent on world domination needed explanation, and Canadian intellectuals were ready and willing to provide one. The assessment of the German psyche and the ethics of German society became a matter of fascination for Canadian writers. The answers they offered were straightforward. German actions in 1914, they argued, were not some aberration in behaviour but the culmination of more than a generation of the deliberate development of a statist and militarist philosophy. Generally Canadians looked to two factors to explain the success of this philosophy. The first was the extreme nationalism that resulted from the long history of disunity in Germany and from the drive to nationhood that culminated in 1870. The second was that nationalism had been given unwarranted legitimacy and had been converted into blind worship of the state by philosophers like Nietzsche, Fichte, and Treitschke, those 'apostles of frightfulness,' as one McGill faculty member termed them. The net result was a collective mental and moral flaw in the German people, which led to 'an uncritical devotion to the will of the highest authority, slavish acceptance of official policy, and mechanical adulation of the sovereign.'[9]

A mood that in truth sprung from the passions of war was thus given an intellectual rationale, and as the killing went on intellectuals found even the most hyperbolic language insufficient. By the time Principal J.O. Miller of Ridley College wrote in 1917 that the conflict was 'the most titanic of all struggles in the history of the human race,' he was only stating the obvious, and when he argued that the war was 'a conflict between two eternally warring spirits: Autocracy and Democracy,' he was uttering an argument so often repeated that it had become the real issue of the war in the minds of most Canadians.[10] It is all too easy to view the First War through the filter of the cynical post-war reaction to it. That reaction, however, should not obscure the mixture of enthusiasm, desperation, and belief that characterized the years of the conflict itself. For that mood shaped Canadian support for the cause among intellectuals and reformers.

There was another reason for support of the war. At least in the first years of the conflict it was generally believed by progressives that the war effort was congruent with their domestic aims. Canadians would finally be forced to face the realities of the twentieth century. Specifically, middle-class reform before 1914 had been increasingly concerned that urbanization and industrialization had fragmented Canadian society into antagonistic class units and condemned much of the population to live a life of anonymous misery in the growing slums of large cities. Unless the necessary reform measures were begun, these developments would threaten not only the poor but all Canadians, as high unemployment and widespread poverty would encourage the growth of crime and social violence. Locked in their materialistic search for wealth, however, Canadians seemed unaware of the dangers to their democracy and their society that the reformers sensed. The war, horrible though it might be, seemed at last to provide the sense of community necessary to deal with the social crisis. This was the significance of George Wrong's October 1914 comment, and it was implicit in Robert Borden's statement a couple of months later that the war 'has brought us together in co-operation and mutual helpfulness divergent interests, differing beliefs and dissonant ideals.'[11] From the trial of fire a new sense of the interdependence of society might create a new dedication to social improvement as opposed to personal aggrandizement.

The progressive impulse was thought directly applicable to the wartime experience in another way: the encouragement of efficiency. Efficiency would be promoted because, of course, it was necessary if the allied resources of men and material were to be as effective as possible in winning the war. The wasteful pursuit of economic luxuries that so predominated in peacetime was not tolerable now that war had come. 'We are not thrifty people,' Adam Shortt lamented in 1915. 'We waste immense amounts, millions and millions in our daily production' and 'are making very few economic sacrifices in connection with this war.' Two years later Stephen Leacock used stronger language to make the same point. 'Thousands, tens of thousands, millions of our men and women are engaged in silly or idle services or in production that is for mere luxuries and comforts and that helps nothing in the conduct of the war.' Marjory MacMurchy, author, reformer, and supporter of women's causes, extended the principle to the housewife and the mother, arguing that the running of their household and the raising of children in an efficient manner was essential to the strength of the nation.[12]

The efficiency necessary to win the war was available in the precepts of the progressive movement. Three different applications of the concept of efficiency from peacetime seemed to be relevant to both the war and the post-war period. The first concept concentrated on government and implied the absence of such activities as patronage, corruption, and extreme partisanship. The pre-war demands for civil service reform took on new significance in wartime. When men were dying for their country the idea that politicians or civil servants might employ their powers for their own purposes became increasingly intolerable. Resources devoted to patronage that might have been devoted to the war effort were powerful arguments in favour of efficiency. Pre-war politicians of many reform causes such as Willison, Rowell, Charles Magrath, and even a man who was no stranger to patronage himself, Clifford Sifton, now carried their campaign for such reforms into the fight for a government that would rise above partisanship and self-interest in the name of the efficient prosecution of the war. The fact that they had 'passed through the thickets of wartime politics to a common meeting place' was not surprising.[13] Their pre-war involvement in progressive causes had indicated certain common presuppositions about the necessary direction for Canada. The concept of an honest, well-run, and principled government embodying the national will had been a part of their creed for some time. The war simply made the moral imperative underlying the demand for efficiency in government all the greater.

The second application of efficiency implied the effective use of the men, resources, and industries of the nation. Once again the war simply made more urgent a series of ideas that had been in vogue before 1914. The concepts of scientific management and industrial training and the formation of the Commission of Conservation had all reflected the desire to use available resources efficiently. The massive destruction of warfare accentuated the motivation behind such movements and raised questions about the post-war world. 'It is patent to the most impracticable,' wrote one observer, 'that the future of the race is inseparably bound up with making the most of what we have.'[14]

Indeed, the word efficiency was so powerful that it had yet a third implication. It became a code word for the concept of a society in which orderliness prevailed, with individuals dedicating themselves to personal moral and social improvement. This was a matter not so much of applying some specific technique as of an improvement in attitude on the part of the public. It was really another way of condemning the shallow materialism that had been the target of so much criticism from intellectual circles in recent years. War, of course, supplanted material self-interest with a nobler cause and demanded social discipline in the efficient prosecution of that cause. 'We have had immense attention paid in our educational institutions to training people for the production of life, but very little attention paid to the training of people for consumption of life,' wrote Adam Shortt in 1915. 'We must face the melancholy fact that a great deal of our so-called civilization is mere barbarism.'[15] The intellectual community in Canada could not resist revealing its dismay that the rest of the populace could not live so cultured and noble a life as it.

There was a certain irony in this increased interest in efficiency during the war. In the English-speaking world there had for several years been a strong admiration for the efficiency and order of Germany. The spectacular rise of German military and industrial strength in the late nineteenth and early twentieth centuries was well known in the Empire, because it was that growth that made Germany such a strong rival to Great Britain. The perceived dedication of the average German to doing his work well and playing his part in society had evoked jealous concern from those who feared that the British Empire, too long concerned with luxury, had become decadent. 'The flower of the rural population of Britain left long ago for the colonies and the United States,' argued one pre-war article. 'A goodly proportion of what remained gravitated to the industrial centres and contributed its quota to the "submerged tenth." The hysterics of the English over the German danger are perhaps not indications of a decadent race. Yet there are also signs of a decaying people, the "submerged tenth" just mentioned for instance.'[16]

With the outbreak of the war, the idea that Germany was the paragon of modern efficiency was somewhat disquieting. There were thus attempts to argue that German efficiency had received too much attention. Germans were ordered, it was true, but they were not innovative. Such explanations weren't all that comforting, however, for there was a very real worry that efficiency was the product of a hierarchical society and sgovernment. Robert Falconer, president of the University of Toronto, summed up the concern in a rhetorial question.

'Monarchical absolutism has proved its ability to regulate outward conditions. Democracy has to prove it can regulate the conditions of its people no less efficiently. Can villages, towns, cities, provinces, a Dominion be as well governed by those whom the electorate puts into power as by a paternal dynasty?'[17]

Not only was it necessary to prove that efficiency could be attained by a democracy; it had also to be shown that democracy could survive efficiency. One way to do this was to ensure that the movement toward efficiency remained coupled with reform. Progressives had always, at least in theory, seen efficiency as a means toward the end of a better society. The two were thus closely related in the writings of the period. The war, of course, diverted immediate concerns toward victory and thus might have seemed deleterious to reform. In fact, however, most writers saw it as ultimately beneficial to the currents of reform in the nation. If they did nothing else, the tremendous social stresses placed on a nation by war made some changes inevitable. The very quest for efficiency in the name of the war effort would open the eyes of many to the wasteful aspects of the older system. Citing the comment of the British chancellor of the Exchequer to the effect that one duke cost as much as three dreadnoughts, Toronto reformer S.T. Wood applied to Canada: 'In Canada the people have not undertaken the creation of dukes, but they have created several millionaires who are quite as costly and burdensome.' Measures to redistribute income that were called for in the name of justice before 1914 could now be demanded in the name of the war effort. Queen's political economist O.D. Skelton made essentially the same point when he commented on the imposition of an income tax in 1917: 'Necessity has brought now what justice might have called for in vain some years longer.'[18]

Indeed, among those like Skelton whose commitment to the imperial idea was less than enthusiastic, this perceived congruence between war and reform may have been especially important in creating support for the war. Skelton had before the war such a strong anti-British attitude that his friends saw it as an eccentric quirk in an otherwise brilliant man. Nor, when war came, did Skelton become caught up in the rhetoric of the Canadian fight for civilization. Instead, as he wrote to W.L. Grant at one point, imperialism was the reason for Canadian involvement. 'We went into the war wholly from racial sympathy with England, and would have been in it equally (though perhaps not as whole heartedly) had Belgium been out of the question and Morocco in it.' Yet Skelton looked to the Canadian involvement in the war with some optimism. 'The consciousness of effort and sacrifice and honour shared in common has quickened a national spirit that will not die.' Regional barriers and parochial interests were being eroded by the war. This new sense of unity, moreover, would provide the impetus to allow the achievement of the long-sought reforms of government and society. 'The ambition to make Canada the land of widest opportunity, of leanest government, of most united community spirit, of fullest realization of the deeper realities of life, will give ample opportunity for the men of the east and the men of the west to work shoulder to shoulder.'[19] When a cold rationalist and anti-imperialist like O.D. Skelton could become slightly misty-eyed about the possibilities of warfare, it is not surprising that so many other English-Canadian intellectuals were oblivious in the first years of the war to the complexity of the relation between war and social change.

By 1917 events seemed to be bearing out the expectations of people like Skelton. In addition to levying income and business profits taxes in that year, the Dominion government implemented further civil service reform, assumed burdens previously left to private charity, moved on nationalization of the Canadian Northern and Grand Trunk railways, and took the first step towards female suffrage. Several provinces had already adopted female suffrage, and that great crusade of moral reform, prohibition, had made tremendous headway. All the Canadian provinces enacted some sort of prohibitory legislation during the war. It was one thing to argue for the necessity of internal spiritual reform in peacetime. It was quite another to hold such a position when prohibitionists tied it to the efficient prosecution of the war. Many reformers, of course, were not prohibitionists, but the general trend of events seemed to indicate that the earlier hopes were justified.[20]

The aftermath of war seemed likely to encourage even more reforms. Though the interest of the Canadian government in post-war reconstruction was vague and superficial compared to its efforts in the Second World War, there was more discussion of the problem than has often been recognized. Initially these talks focused on the problem of the returning veteran. The creation of a Military Hospitals Commission in 1915 and of a Board of Pension Commissioners the next year marked an ever-widening acceptance of the necessity for ongoing government involvement in veteran care. By 1917, questions began to be asked about what would happen when the war was over and the hundreds of thousands in the Canadian Expeditionary Force were returned to civilian life. The government seemed to have only two choices: plan now or

pay later. 'If employment is not awaiting our returned soldiers,' warned
Frank Beer in 1917, 'there will arise a demand for public assistance,
and no government will refuse such a demand.' The only alternative
was to plan for reconstruction in industry 'which inevitably must come
soon.'[21]

Change was not only inevitable as a result of forces unleashed and
practical as a means of preventing unrest, it was also a moral necessity.
The sacrifices that were being made at the front demanded justification
in the shape of a better post-war society. Prime Minister Lloyd George
employed the most apt expression of this feeling when he talked of
making Britain a land fit for heroes. Stephen Leacock made the same
point but put it in more contractual terms when he noted that the
state had assumed new powers in war including, in 1917, that of conscription. To Leacock conscription was justifiable, and he termed it
'the crowning pride of democracy.' It did, however, create an irrevocable obligation for the state that imposed it. The more that was
demanded of the citizenry, the more the citizenry could expect of the
state. 'The obligation to die must carry with it the right to live. If
every citizen owes it to society that he must fight for it in the case of
need, then society owes to every citizen the opportunity of a livelihood.
"Unemployment" in the case of the willing and the able becomes
henceforth a social crime.'[22]

These concerns for unity and efficiency were exhibited across a broad
ideological spectrum, from conservative imperialists like Stephen Leacock through liberal nationalists like O.D. Skelton to radical social
gospellers like J.S. Woodsworth and Salem Bland. Such agreement among
men so diverse in other ways emphasizes what was apparent before
the war. There was a sense of unity within the reform community.
There were differences as to exact remedies, of course, but all saw basic
problems with the materialistic, individualistic, and problem-laden
society of the pre-war years. This dissatisfaction, in turn, meant that
they entered the war years both with the hope that the war would
force change and with a continued degree of unity in the desire for
that change. Those who understood the necessities of the age stood
against those who seemed willing to drift along without comprehension. In some ways Stephen Leacock in 1914 had more in common with
Salem Bland than he did with the businessmen on the board of governors at McGill.

One of the forces binding the reform community together was the presence of a common series of presuppositions about society and the purpose of change. The language of moral reform had not yet been replaced by the technocracy of the modern social sciences or the economic determinism of radical Marxism. The rhetoric of the war itself was that of good against evil. Canadians were fighting for the 'final triumph of truth and righteousness' both on the battlefields and on the domestic front.[23] The Christian tradition that had so dominated education until recently provided a common or nearly common attitude as to what reform was about. Efficiency was a means rather than an end, and the goal was spiritual and moral improvement of society.

Specifically, the language of the intellectual community during the war continued to be couched largely in the language of post-Helegian Christian idealism. This was expressed at times in formal logical constructs and ethical arguments and at other times in casual rhetoric depicting the spiritual nature of well-being, the relation between duty and freedom, and man's organic relation to the society around him. For some, like President Robert Falconer of the University of Toronto and Henry Marshall Tory of the University of Alberta, this attachment was explicit, as it was for Salem Bland. For others, the influence remained in spite of countervailing philosophies. Both Adam Shortt and Stephen Leacock, for example, mixed the empirical training of their discipline of economics with the idealism of their general educational and religious backgrounds.[24]

By far the most sophisticated and erudite presentation of the idealist case came at the end of the war. John Watson, Canada's senior idealist philosopher, found that the war experience compelled him to write a study of the relation between the individual and the state. Following the history of the philosophy of the state from Greece through the present, it was an ambitious effort for a man of 71 years. And though he argued in his introduction that he deliberately avoided all reference to the war, both his title, the *The State in Peace and War*, and the contents of the work indicate that the current conflict was very much on his mind. Indeed, as he wrote the year before, 'I confess this dreadful war has almost paralyzed any initiative I possess. I find it hard to get my mind away from Flanders and Italy and Macedonia and Mesopotamia and Jerusalem.'[25] At a time when nations seemed to have gone mad and when people were dying for the abstraction of the state, Watson obviously felt that the need existed for a close assessment of state power from a philosophical and ethical basis.

For Watson, the starting point was his long-standing argument that man is a social animal and cannot be considered apart from the society in which he lives. The 'consciousness of self as a spiritual being cannot be separated from consciousness of self as a member of society.' This was fundamental to idealism. Man without society was meaningless, and so too therefore were concepts like freedom, happiness, and morality. Man's fulfilment is inextricably tied, in Watson's writings, to the society around him. Even freedom exists only in relation to the community's well-being. Tracing this concept back to both Plato and Aristotle, Watson makes it the basis for the relation between man and the state. Man had certain rights and freedoms, but they were inseparable from the existence of the state: 'The citizen should not consider that he is any chartered libertine, free to do whatever seems good in his eyes. There must indeed be freedom to live the higher life without interference from either neighbour or state; such freedom, however, does not mean licence, but subordination of all personal motives and conduct to the laws of the community. In such subordination there is no loss of real freedom, but on the contrary the realisation of the common will, which is on the whole a rational will.'[26] Man was truly made free only when he abandoned the state of nature and accepted the concept of the wider commitment to society.

This sense that the state was a natural part of social evolution still had to be translated into some sort of formal justification for assumption of power by the state. Watson was obviously uncomfortable with those who emphasized force and power as the basic relation between the state and its citizenry. Hobbes is dismissed in a few paragraphs, while Machiavelli's pragmatic and amoral view of governing is condemned. 'The State could not be absolved,' as Machiavelli implied, 'from all moral law and employ fraud, deceit, treachery and violence under all circumstances and as a regular principle of action.' Rather, as the Greeks sensed, the state 'ought to be the embodiment of the best mind of the community.' It was, in essence, a moral extension of the community, and its moral failure, therefore, implied the moral failure of the people. Sheer force, having no moral content, was therefore not an acceptable basis for state power. Rather, the justification for the assumption of power by the state lay in its very morality, in its ability to secure for man the social animal the best life possible. That 'best life,' however, was not to be interpreted as meaning merely personal pleasure. Looking at the individualism of John Stuart Mill, for example, Watson finds it incomprehensible that Mill intended 'that a man is to be left to act in accordance with the promptings of unregulated desire.'[27]

As a social being, man's actions were justifiable only insofar as they were in harmony with the larger interests of the community. The state, therefore, was justified to the degree it acted to harmonize the individual's desires and the community's well-being.

This created a dilemma. As the embodiment of the moral will of the community the state became a very powerful instrument that had the right to assume unlimited control over citizens in the name of the higher good. 'There is a compulsion which is in harmony with freedom,' Watson argued. The idealist, in contrast to the individualist, held that 'the good of the individual is identical with the good of the community. It is held to be man's nature that he cannot find permanent satisfaction except in identifying his personal good with the good of the community ... That being so, in his best mind he has no objection to State interference which is not in harmony with his private or particular desires, but is in harmony with his own explicit or implicit ideal of himself.'[28] It is in concepts like this that the relation between idealism and the rhetoric of the war becomes apparent. Man's duty was defined for Watson by his natural relation to the society around him. The problem remained, however, within this context of duty and state interference, of how to define the basis of state action. Who or what was to be the basis for defining the higher well-being of the community and the state actions necessary to bring that higher well-being to fruition?

Watson attempted to find an answer to this most difficult problem by extending the concept of the general will designed by Rousseau. The definition of this term was as difficult for Watson as it was for Rousseau. It could not be a function of mere numbers. To define the 'right' course of action in mere numerical terms would have led to extreme relativism. What was the 'right' course of action one day would become wrong the next. 'A thing is not made right because it is in consonance with public sentiment.' Even if this opinion was expressed not just by a majority but by an overwhelming public sentiment, things did not change. 'The fact, for example, that the German people are unanimous in believing that world-conquest is the mission of Germany does not prove that their will coincides with the interests of humanity. We cannot assume that the agreement of all is the same as the good of all.'[29]

Watson attempted to resolve the problem of defining the 'general will' by employing a philosophical version of that peculiar Canadian concept of the double majority. He looked to an institutionalized procedure to make the voice of society important in decision-making. 'In all the institutions, voluntary or involuntary, which form the very complex web of modern society,' he saw agencies for the evolving of the general will. More than that, however, is the necessity that they are morally correct in their decisions. The will must be expressed and must be morally correct before the state is justified in acting. Watson's assumption was that proper religious scruples and educational background would make the two complementary. The people would understand naturally the moral course of action. The state thus truly becomes a moral agency embodying the 'common will of the community.'[30] The demands of the state in time of war, therefore, so long as it was a just war, were simply another expression of the common will of the community. True freedom and happiness lay in adapting one's own wishes to the service of that common will. The ideology of service rested on a philosophic base.

There was a problem, however. Watson, like others, had to deal with the fact that Germany was the original source of Canadian idealism. Hegel and Kant, as transmitted through a Scottish prism, were the men who had laid the basis for Watson's own philosophic views. Given the amount of time Canadians were spending denouncing the philosophic basis of German militarism and autocracy, any defender of idealism thus had to disassociate himself from current German values. The answer to this dilemma was straightforward. Canadian idealists argued that though German philosophy was the birthplace of idealism, it had long since abandoned the philosophy. The association of Germany in the minds of many Canadians with small university towns 'beautifully situated and still enjoying the quaintness and charm of the days of German idealism' was false, said Robert Falconer. Neither the university town atmosphere nor the idealist philosophy was Germany any longer. According to Watson, Germany had forsaken the idealism of Hegel by the end of the nineteenth century. 'The doctrine that the State has no limits but its own selfish interests ... is really due to a reaction against the idealist philosophy.' Materialism, as both Watson and Falconer noted, had then assumed the dominant role in German philosophy. It was this that had helped forge 'the aggressive and ambitious spirit which since 1870 has characterised the German people.' Philosopher statists like Fichte, Moleschott, and Buchner provided the philosophy that helped bring the 'decay of morality and religion which has attacked the German people themselves. They have become indoctrinated with a false philosophy of the State.' There was no doubt, Falconer concluded, that 'the old German idealism is almost extinct.'[31]

Current German thinking on the state, according to this argument, thus ran in a straight line back through the materialists to the expediency of a Machiavelli or the acceptance of raw force of someone like Hobbes. The British system, with a certain twist, stretched through Hegel and Kant back towards the Greek philosophers. It was not the nationality of the philosopher or the people generally that mattered but the spirit of morality that was cultivated within a given society at a given time. Germany's current status as an international outlaw was explainable 'in the character of the people who ruled, of the scientists who taught, and of the historians who prophesied. The wrong kind of people have been ruling and teaching and preaching. Their ideas were not sufficiently human to train a nation to play her part in the civilised world. Wherefore we have again,' concluded Falconer, 'a justification of the view that the highest aim of education is to produce a thoroughly disciplined character directed by spiritual conceptions. The pursuit of the ideal was once Germany's aim also, but the ideal was lost when she became absorbed in a method directed for material ends by leaders without humanity.'[32] The true lesson of German history, therefore, was not the danger of idealism to Canadian values but the importance of adhering to the creed. Had Germany not abandoned this ethical base the war might not have begun. Certainly only idealism provided Canadians with the sense of values to persevere now that the contest was under way.

Idealism provided the philosophic underpinnings that bound together various arguments in support of the war. The belief in the justness of the war, in the potential for far-reaching reforms, and in the acceptance of widespread changes that war was likely to bring contained a common theme that stressed that society as a whole was entering a new phase in its development and that the individual had a duty to work towards the fulfilment of that social promise. The result of a populace that understood this would be a unity that bound all Canadians together in a common mission. Compulsion would be irrelevant, or at least peripheral, because society would voluntarily take the necessary actions to achieve success. Finance Minister Thomas White, employing the ebullient language of politics, expressed this sentiment in a 1917 speech to the Ottawa branch of the Canadian Patriotic Fund: 'A nation of mixed race, of diverse nationalities, with a heterogeneous population of eight millions scattered over a territory as large as Europe, as large as the United States, we have recruited, organized, equipped and trained an army of 425,000 men ... We have imposed upon ourselves heavy taxation, pledged the national credit, subscribed the loans to amounts which before the outbreak of the war we would have regarded as beyond the utmost of our power; and it has all been done voluntarily, without compulsion, without constraint, without even persuasion on the part of any external authority.'[33] Even as White spoke, however, the voluntarist image was becoming obsolete. The state was beginning to move into an ever wider area of direct compulsion to ensure maximum effort to win the war. Nor could all those areas of new use of authority be construed by even the most optimistic reformer as directed towards the post-war shaping of a better society. State power was growing tremendously by 1917, and the problems of the unleashed power of the state that the combination of idealism and war allowed began to raise troublesome questions.

John English has noted that as the war went on the 'individual was lost in the overwhelming magnitude of the war effort and in the complex organic conception of the state which it created.' What made the individual all the more powerless was the deep-rooted philosophic basis for that organic conception of the state. The arguments for sacrificing personal liberty to state imperatives were implicit in the writings of idealism. All that was needed was a clear situation where state action on a large scale seemed necessary for the benefit of the community. The war provided the situation, and the Canadian state was immediately given the necessary powers to prosecute the war in the name of the community. The War Measures Act of 1914, passed with the support of the opposition, provided the government with a tremendous range of powers and effectively suspended individual rights. As time went on and as the crisis of the war deepened, the government found itself, often reluctantly, using that act and others to take on even greater control over the life of the nation. Food controllers, fuel controllers, censorship, order-in-council government, detention, and other strong actions meant that by 1917 the unleashing of the state had brought many measures far removed from the reform aspirations of the progressive community. Thomas White's glowing description of a united and voluntary effort saw its counterpoint in the latter part of the war in a growing concern that freedom was being eroded in the name of the fight for democracy. Even democracy itself might be destroyed by the conflict. 'All we can do is select our dictators,' wrote O.D. Skelton in 1918.[34]

The assessment of this changing mood in Canada in the last two years of the war has to begin in the trenches. For the altered outlook was as much a reaction to the horror of the war as it was to any specific government action. The greater the costs of the war the more people questioned the impact it was having, and by 1917 the costs had become staggering. More and more men were dying for ill-defined tactical advantages. For those who were there, the optimistic idealism had long since been replaced by a grim numbing of the spirit. The mood was caught perfectly in a macabre 1916 passage from the war diary of Andrew Macphail. 'It is impossible to give an accurate impression of the situation here. One might relate incident after incident, each one as it occurred, and yet the total would be false to one who had not seen the life with one's own eyes. In walking up the trenches one sees men digging a drain. They come upon a buried body, and they cut the limbs aways as if they were the roots of a tree ... A man will build a comfortable dug-out for himself, and find when the work is nearly done that a part of a body is protruding from the floor. He sprinkles lime on it ...'[35]

The war in the trenches also had its effect at home. While not exposed to the immediate horrors of the war, those at home had experienced month after month of the numbing and wearing effects of awaiting the next casualty lists. Few remained untouched as those lists continued to grow. The nation that had marched off to war with such enthusiasm and high hopes in 1914 was, by 1917, collectively traumatized by three years of mass slaughter. Even in the speeches of the supposedly inspiring individuals brought before various clubs in Canada, something of this despair occasionally slipped through. The Reverend John MacNeill, recently returned from France, spoke to those at home of the bravery of the boys. Their trials were such, however, that his sense of determined hope collapsed briefly. 'Do you wonder that the hardest fight for these men is not to hold their trenches, but to hold their visions? It is a sordid, sodden business. It is difficult for idealism to survive in wallow and slaughter and vermin, and stable floors for beds, and crouching dugouts for billets.'[36]

The problem was that the war was a means to an end. For various reasons, it had been said, Germany had to be defeated in order for British civilization to survive and develop. As the horror and the cost in human lives increased, however, it became increasingly difficult to remember that the end was worth it. Even the most patriotic occasionally found themselves hovering on a precipice of doubt. Robert Falconer, for example, began a series of inspirational sermons to the students at the University of Toronto with the proud fact that 'the finest product of our civilisation is being rushed to the front.' But here was a paradox. If the finest were being sent to the front to die, then who were they dying for? How, in the idealist scheme of things, could society be improved by the killing of its finest members? 'To make an impossible supposition, imagine that all the noble Britons were to volunteer and to perish, leaving as survivors only those who were unwilling to undergo the discomfort, to endure the danger of defending their country, a remnant composed of such as were callous to criticism and willing to profit by the disaster of others, selfish beneficiaries of their vicarious sacrifice. Would a state composed of these parasites be worth being wounded and dying for?' The answer was clearly 'no,' but in this line of argument lay intolerable conclusions, and Falconer quickly shifted themes. Yet the haunted fear remained that, indeed, 'the human race had gone mad.'[37]

John Watson also had problems in justifying the carnage of this war. The state, it was true, had the right to use its power over the citizenry to pursue the highest good. As the war went on, however, it became increasingly difficult to be certain that this war would bring man to a higher plane. 'The only case in which war can be held to set aside temporarily the claim to life and freedom is when it is necessary to save the nation from destruction.' Yet it was difficult to argue that Britain, much less Canada, had actually been in danger of destruction. The Empire had entered the war on behalf of Belgium. Watson is, therefore, forced to add to national survival another reason for war. 'It is the function of the State to defend the conditions under which the best life is possible. Manifestly, therefore, nothing short of threatened extinction of the State, or a violation of the national honour implied in the observance of its Treaty obligations, can justify the temporary abolition of the right of all men to life as a necessary condition of their contribution to the highest good.'[38] It seemed a very high price to pay for national honour and treaty obligations.

By 1917 the war seemed to be destroying not only the soldier in the trenches but the social fabric of Canada as well. As compulsion replaced voluntarism the already thin façade of national unity collapsed. Coercion was used to bring reluctant minorities to support the war effort further. The passage of the Wartime Elections Act, which disfranchised thousands of recent immigrants because the government feared lukewarm support of the war; the formation of the Union government, which isolated French Canada in the rump of the old Liberal party; and the introduction of conscription, which made it clear that the state would use its power to force men into the war effort, raised serious questions about authoritarianism. How could a war that was fought on the basis of the compulsive power of the state fulfil the idealist vision of an awakened people acting together to improve the state of society?

In attempting to answer this question, the loose complex of groups that made up progressivism began to show rifts. For some groups, this use of state power did not alter the fact that the great majority of Canadians were making the maximum effort on a voluntary basis. The use of law against recalcitrant minorities was simply a necessity in a time of trial. 'The final triumph of democracy can only be assured by the willing subordination of the individual to the State,' and if the few that were unwilling threatened the good of the whole then action was necessary. This attitude was especially common among the political and business wings of progressivism. Willison, Rowell, Sifton, and, for that matter, Robert Borden himself all saw such measures to be necessary. They certainly did not see the actions of 1917 as an abandonment of reform ideals. Instead, as has been pointed out elsewhere, many of the leaders of the Union government saw their political coalition as the culmination of the drive for reform. First the war would be won, and then reform would follow. 'We are at the end of an era in Canada,' Willison wrote Borden in July 1917. 'The Canadian manufacturers, who have developed all the selfishness and arrogance of a privileged class, must have less power at Ottawa in the future.'[39]

Others were less certain. The earlier assumptions about the relation between prosecution of the war and social improvement seemed increasingly questionable given government actions. Authoritarianism rather than progressivism seemed to many to be the underlying purpose of the Union government. This concern surfaced most explosively in the government's implementation of conscription, and historians since have made it the focus of attention in writing of the controversies of the First World War. Certainly this was also the case with some contemporaries. For O.D. Skelton, for example, the decision to introduce conscription was the final indication that the war was weakening rather than strengthening the Canadian social fabric. 'Abstractly,' Skelton did think that conscription was the 'fairest solution to our military tasks,' but he recoiled at its use in the Canadian situation. Several factors lay behind this conclusion. First, Skelton had for some time been a supporter of the Liberal party and by 1917 was a personal friend and admirer of Laurier, whose biography he was writing. No doubt Laurier's personal opposition to conscription affected Skelton. More important, however, Skelton saw conscription as destroying the spirit of unity that was a necessary precondition to meaningful reform. Skelton was not opposed to the war, but as he saw the war as one part of a greater task facing Canada, he was opposed to policies that pursued victory at any price.[40]

Important though conscription was, it should not be taken as the only cause of the crisis that developed in 1917-18. Conscription was a symbol, albeit an important one, of the changing relation between the state and the intellectual community. Among English Canadians, after all, conscription was supported by the majority, and men like Skelton were in a definite minority even within intellectual circles. Even he, perhaps sensing the public mood, avoided any public opposition to conscription during the crisis. The real fear was that the statism and militarism against which Canadians were supposedly fighting was becoming embedded in their own national character. One author, writing in the *University Magazine* at the end of the war, brought the contradiction out in his discussion of the relation between the individual and the state. Given the tremendous costs of the war, he began, it was important that the victorious nations make 'the clearest and simplest statement of the principle they fought to preserve.' That principle, he continued, was to destroy the worship of the 'state ideal' that was at the basis of German militarism. Opposing such statism was individualistic democracy. Thus, with the victory over Germany and its allies, 'in this war the conception of individual freedom has triumphed over the conception of State supremacy.' Or had it? 'But let there be no mistake; it has triumphed at the expense of sacrifices that unconsciously and insensibly have undermined the basic idea of democracy. In defending itself democracy is in danger of destroying its own foundation.'[41]

By 1917-18, this ironic analysis of the war was common. Andrew Macphail summed it up in terse form in his diary when he commented at New Year 1917 that 'we took up arms against the "Prussian spirit." Now that spirit is entering our hearts.' W.L. Grant warned as early as 1915 that the returning soldier would have another campaign after he finished with the one in France. 'At the end of the war a tremendous obligation will be laid upon those of us who are left to continue the battle against militarism for victory will be seen by a large number of shortsighted people to have justified militarism, and there will be a tremendous confusion in the minds of many between the means and the end.'[42]

This sort of concern was not confined to any one part of the political spectrum. For those who thought that Canada's future lay with the free enterprise system, the fear was that statism in war would lead to statism in peace. As the editor of the *Canadian Banker* warned in 1919, the state's overweening role might not end simply because the war was over: 'There is on every hand a tendency to exalt the state. Men appeal to the Government to cure every ill, to solve every tangle, to regulate every field of human endeavour. It is urged that the state should take over and operate the mines and the railroads, build houses and lend money, sell goods and fix prices ... The all-wise and all-powerful state is to order all our ways.' On the left, the fear was that a powerful state was emerging that was oriented towards not socialism but militarism. The outlawing of strikes in war industries and the free use of emergency powers against radicals augured poorly for meaningful reform after the war. Social gospel radical and pacifist J.S. Woodsworth struck this note in his letter of resignation to the Methodist church: 'The devil of militarism cannot be driven out by the power of militarism without the successful nations themselves becoming militarized.'[43]

All these writers raised essentially the same point. The means employed to make the world safe for democracy had led to such horrendous results that the end was in danger of being destroyed. This is an obvious comment, but it emphasizes the old adage that the ends could not be discussed apart from the means. The process of change itself, as opposed to the purpose of that change, became relatively more important. In a society where the internal spiritual motivation and the existence of an absolute morality had been matters of deepest faith, this was a shift of some significance. It paralleled the rise of the social scientific concern with method and its emphasis on external and quantifiable results as opposed to internal and metaphysical concerns.

The growing concern over the impact of the war created a degree of pessimism and disarray within the Canadian intellectual community. The earlier optimism that the war would act as a catalyst for necessary changes now seemed in doubt. That optimism had rested on the belief that the conflict was galvanizing Canadian society into a unified whole. This new unity was, it was further assumed, easily going to be harnessed to pursue reforms in the interests of social well-being. The tremendous costs of the war, the evolving policies of the Canadian government, and the domestic crises within Canada challenged all these assumptions.

Contributing to this sense of pessimism was the simple fact that Canadian intellectual reformers found themselves with little influence in the conduct of the war. There was no stream of academics to Ottawa to deal with the new complex issues arising from the war. Indeed, the advice that they proffered in their speeches and articles seemed to have little or no effect on the supposedly progressive Borden government. The only elements of the so-called progressive community that did become involved in government in wartime were those who already had strong political connections, like Sifton, or major business figures like Sir Joseph Flavelle, a man who was at best on the periphery of progressivism.[44] Moreover, this group became somewhat estranged from other progressive elements with its seeming willingness to accept without protest the authoritarian measures of the Borden government during the 1917 crisis. The simple and galling fact was that the intellectual reform groups had simply not gained enough acceptance in government circles to make their opinion really count. As things began to wrong toward the end of the war they naturally felt frustrated and impotent at their inability to make their ideas heard.

There was, it was true, the Civic Improvement League, which was formed during the war, and Willison's Unemployment Commission in Ontario, which sat through the first part of the conflict. In both instances, however, the impetus behind these organizations antedated the war. In general, the war hurt progressivism rather than helped it. The Civic Improvement League collapsed as the demands of the war took precedence among public-spirited individuals. The same fate awaited the newly formed Canadian Political Science Association. Created to allow for highly informed discussions of public matters, the association disintegrated in the face of the competing demands of war. The social gospel movement, so much a wing of progressivism before the war, found itself factionalized by internal divisions over ideology, pacifism, and theology.[45]

Reform remained a major issue. The problem was that as the end of the war approached the reform impulse seemed to many to be scattered into meaningless and even destructive directions. 'No doubt there is a new ideal of social justice in the making in it all,' James Cappon wrote to W.L. Grant in 1919. 'But what the world will have to go through before it is made! Quite a half of the legislation and movements we think progressive or reform – because they are new – are merely the convulsive movements of a sick man tossing in his bed.' Nor could the problem be said to be peculiar to Canada. Revolution in Russia made communism something more than a spectre haunting Europe, while rebellion at war's end in Germany and Austria added to the widespread concern over international anarchy. Even Great Britain, the model for so many Canadians, was thought by imperialists, or ex-imperialist – Andrew Macphail, to be sinking into the morass. 'The old England is gone as completely as the old Russia,' he commented in the spring of 1918. 'Income tax and death duties have accomplished their appointed tasks ... Social trouble was met by political device without regard to political principle.' Expediency now dominated in the mother of parliaments. 'Rebellion in Ireland was appeased by a convention assembled to grant to the rebels what they were powerless to achieve by force of arms. For no reason at all a radical professor was engaged in framing a new education, and another radical professor was engaged to uprear a new fabric upon the ruins of the House of Lords. The heart of our soldiers will be destroyed. They have seen the sullen workers on the Clyde and in the mines appeased with praise, that the youngest rivetter or the meanest had equal honour with the soldier in the trench.'[46]

Men like Cappon and Macphail might be dismissed as unrepresentative both because they were aging and because their sort of conservative reform had always put a high premium on order. Among radical social gospellers there was a much more ready acceptance of the importance of reform, even if it necessitated social conflict in the process. As one correspondent commented to J.S. Woodsworth, 'It may be that the very upheaval holds in store good beyond all our conception. Systems are tried in the balance and found wanting. Systems are disintegrating before our eyes, things that can be shaken are being shaken.'[47] The vision of the redeeming fires of the apocalypse hinted at a millennial conception of reform and a continued belief that the violent state of the world was but a necessary means to a positive end.

It is thus in the realm of radical thought that there is a degree of continuity with pre-war progressivism. Radicals saw social upheaval as all progressives had earlier seen the war, as a force for positive social change. Now, however, their increasingly militant stance was acceptable to ever fewer Canadian reformers. Not only the conservatives like Macphail or Cappon balked at such revolutionary rhetoric, but so too did the bulk of moderate reformers. In an age when instability seemed so rampant, social reformers began to be concerned once again that continued chaos would increase injustice rather than diminish it. The real post-war danger to Canada seemed to be 'civil conflicts begotten of class hatred,' as Mackenzie King phrased it in 1918. Before the war such concerns had led to a greater demand for reform, as a means of preventing class conflict. Now, however, it seemed as if reform was essentially a class measure. 'Class interests predominate,' lamented Swanson in 1918. It was thus necessary to search again for the unity that the war had seemed to promise but had ultimately failed to develop. Unity, social order, and stability became increasingly the concerns of the intellectual 'progressives' at the end of the war. Richard Allen has developed the picture of a pre-war social gospel movement becoming fragmented by the war into three distinct strains – conservative, moderate, and radical. Secular reform experienced the same fate. The cross-currents of progressive concern over social chaos on the one hand and authoritarianism on the other caused that broad range of reformers, which had existed within a common framework of presuppositions and been involved in numerous overlapping organizations, to fragment into their constituent elements by war's end.[48]

For these intellectuals, of whatever political leaning, the assessment of the relation between state and society was made all that much more difficult to rationalize by the fact that their intellectual world seemed to be fragmenting along with their society. The polarization of groups within society, the seeming disintegration of the social fabric, domestically and internationally, the growing revulsion against militarism, and the long agony of the war, which towered over other concerns, brought into question many of the basic assumptions of philosophic idealism. The very basis of Canadian social thought over the past generation seemed to be eroding.

It was not that idealism had been replaced with an alternative philosophical basis of thought, or that idealism was dead in Canada. The writings at the end of the war reveal that it was still present in the lexicon of Canadian social reform. To give three examples, conservative Stephen Leacock's Unsolved Riddle of Social Justice (1920), Liberal reformer Mackenzie King's Industry and Humanity (1918), and radical Salem Bland's The New Christianity (1918) all remained firmly within the idealist school of thought. Though written from quite different points on the political spectrum, the various works are linked by three common themes. First, they all envisage reform in terms of a spiritual renewal of the will of the Canadian people to seek the higher good. Second, this sense of spiritual renewal is portrayed in terms of an organic conception of society. For Bland this organicism is given the language of evangelical Christianity, as the sweep of destiny and the greater social will bring about the Kingdom of God on earth. 'By an action as cosmic and irresistible as the movement of a great river, democracy is invading the industrial world.' King portrays it in similar terms, though because the reforms he seeks are less radical, so too is his concept of the social will. For Leacock, the social will involves voluntary acceptance of the spirit of discipline revealed in the war through the 'force of organization.' Finally, and connected to the spiritual renewal of society and its organic nature, all three reject, at least in theory, the older individualism that was already being mythified as the prominent feature of pre-war life in Canada. 'The old laissez faire attitude of non-interference with personal rights and private property was based on the self-interest of a privileged few,' commented King. Leacock agreed, referring to the war to make the point that 'our fortunes are not in our individual keeping' and that 'the welfare of each' has to be regarded as contributory to the welfare of all.[49]

For all the idealism inherent in these writings, the philosophic base of Canadian thought had been eroding over the previous generation. The events of the war and the social concerns at the end of it challenged the world of John Watson on several counts. First, the war had been portrayed as an idealist crusade, and the reaction against it naturally raised questions about a system of values that allowed such slaughter. As even Falconer and Watson found, there were uncomfortable problems in using idealist ethics to justify the war. This is not surprising. Few philosophic systems could have succeeded in explaining the horror of 1914-18. The problem was that idealism was tied to the war and to the generation that sent Canadians to war at a time when the ideals posited were coming under question. Second, the idealist's organicism seemed to exalt the state at a time when statism called for tremendous sacrifice and raised serious doubts. Hegel could not be disassociated from Fichte so easily. Third and finally, the idealist assumption that man in society could work on the basis of reason and commitment to social betterment seemed challenged by the events of the past four years. Neither the reasonable human being, the reasonable society, nor the certainty of the justness of social goals was as accepted as previously. Society could act both in an irrational way and with means that, even with noble ends before it, led to self-destruction. The always-elusive 'reasonable' action and just 'general will' seemed phantoms in a world that had hinted at madness.

The implications of this new and less innocent perspective were revealed in a paper presented by University of Toronto philosopher George Sidney Brett on the occasion of his induction into the Royal Society of Canada in May 1919. Though Brett was as yet less known than an idealist like Watson, it was he who pointed the way to the

future of Canadian thought. At first glance Brett was an unlikely candidate for this task. Educated at Oxford at the turn of the century, he
was exposed to the idealist greats, Bosanquet, Bradley, and Green.[50]
Then or later, however, he became interested in psychology, and his
philosophy owed much to that emerging social science. By the time he
presented his paper to the Royal Society, he was prepared to argue that
no philosophic system would succeed that did not take into account
the way in which man can act in unreasoning and irrational ways.

Brett began his argument by noting aspects of the philosophy of
Descartes evolving from that philosopher's supposition that animals
could be viewed as machines. Implicit in this position, Brett argued,
was a picture of man as unique in the universe, both in his ability to
reason and in his superior moral sensibilities. The problem was that
the distinction proved not to be that clear. Animals have instincts,
which machines do not, while many of man's activities 'are reflex
activities' and thus similar to those of animals. Over the next centuries
this overlap between man and the animals continued to be explored.
By the end of the nineteenth century, man's moral and reasoning supremacy was under challenge, largely from the new applications of
Darwinianism. 'The soul which Descartes never openly repudiated but
kept in splendid isolation as a fragment of the Divine lodged in an
animal organism, now seemed threatened with final extinction.'[51]

In the place of the image of the human spirit as divine, said Brett,
came an idolization of science. Facts, reason, and proof soon became
the tests of reason, and those who opposed the new world of the sciences
were fighting a 'lost cause.' However, nothing in science seems able to
penetrate beyond the automatic and reflexive side of mankind. Scientists make man more powerful, and more destructive, but have not
assisted him in defining his goals. Those goals 'arise in a world of desires
and purposes which neither physics nor chemistry nor even psychology
can so much as pretend to resolve into atoms or mind-stuff.' There was
the danger that man now faced the worst of both worlds. The exaltation
of his animal instincts and the downgrading of reason had left a moral
vacuum that science could not fill while handing him ever more potent
technologies. Man had been freed from the philosophical and technological constraints of the past, but the war clearly demonstrated that
this was anything but cause for celebration. 'Their can be little doubt
that this deliverance has been mistaken for a proclamation of
lawlessness.'[52]

Brett's worried commentary on the modern world was not new. His arguments drew on Bergson, Freud, and others well established. But in the quiet pre-war period, Canadian philosophy had seemed largely impervious to these images of irrational man and a chaotic universe. By 1919, however, Canadian society had cause to doubt the supremacy of rationality *and* reason, as well as to question the nature of motivation. It seemed more and more unlikely that society could pretend to understand the 'black box' of the human mind. External actions rather than spiritual ends had to be the basis of judgment, because the motivation behind those ends was ultimately unknowable and because too much faith that those ends were justified had proved far too costly to the world: 'Philosophy did not cause the recent war, nor has it caused the subsequent anarchy; but it must of necessity be an active power in war, and revolution and peace, because men love to justify their actions and the justification becomes the philosophical creed in which the spirit of action is embodied. Marxism, syndicalism, Bolshevism and the other modern developments are all rooted in a scheme of ideas which is as truly philosophy as Platonism, Hegelianism or the new realism. This we must sooner or later face, and first of all we must be clear about our original question – is life essentially rational or irrational?'[53] Epistemology and metaphysics were being challenged by political economy.

5

The social sciences and the service state 1919-29

A casual observer of the Canadian scene in the years immediately after the First World War might have concluded that the pessimistic talk of the collapse of progressivism was the misplaced lament of a small minority. Reform seemed alive and well in Canada. Society seemed to be preparing to transform itself and to employ the powers of the state to redistribute both power and wealth. Perhaps the war had, as one writer suggested, caused men and women to be 'shocked into the consciousness that the principle of brotherhood must be set up as the foundation of civilized society if it is to endure.' In the militancy of the Winnipeg General Strike, the formation of the One Big Union, and the gradual coalescing of the various agrarian movements, radical social gospel leaders foresaw the emergence of a moral power and a political will that would forever transform the Canadian state. 'Pre-war days are not good enough for us to-day,' warned the president of the Manitoba Grain Growers' Association, R.C. Henders; 'we have gone through a baptism of blood that ought to fit us for a bigger and nobler service than was ever rendered by any man at any time previous to this present war.'[1]

A similar if less ideological idealism was expressed by other reformers in the renewed campaign for moral uplift. At the centre of this movement was, of course, the grand issue of prohibition. The years 1919-20 saw the peak of the movement's power in Canada. A series of measures on prohibition, 'ban the bar,' prevention of import, and temperance went before the public in most provinces. The trend, as the anti-liquor crusaders liked to point out, was toward abolition of the liquor trade in Canada. They now awaited, with a degree of naïveté, the inevitable reduction of major social problems in a sober world. In the mean time other moral issues called for attention, from race-track gambling, through sabbatarianism, to censorship.[2]

Moreover, the state appeared to be responding to the currents of reform. In addition to bringing about prohibition measures, public pressure and the wartime precedents of state involvement led to a number of potentially significant social programs. In 1916 Manitoba passed a Mothers' Pensions Act to assist single women in bringing up their children. Such legislation would have been thought beyond the legitimate activities of government even fifteen years earlier yet by 1920 five of the nine Canadian provinces had some similar program on the books.[3] Such measures as this, coupled with the spread of Workmen's Compensation Acts, veterans' benefits, public child welfare systems, and other examples of state involvement, indicate that Canada no longer even pretended to be a true laissez-faire state by 1920. The growing reform movements of the era made it appear as if the changes were just beginning.

It was against this backdrop that urban middle-class progressivism, including the reform-oriented intellectual community, sought to reconstitute itself. It was a difficult process in spite of the numerous reform measures that called for attention. Issues had become more sharply defined and the nation more polarized. There was uncertainty as to how to find the cause or even the ideology that could reunite reform in Canada. Prohibition, so popular among many middle-class Protestants, could not provide that unity. Canadian intellectuals were extremely divided on the issue, with many regarding such a measure as Prussian in spirit. Others, of course, advocated prohibition. Still others, like Mackenzie King, seemed divided within themselves. 'This morning I voted against the importation of liquor into the Province of Ontario,' he recorded in his diary in April 1921. 'By a coincidence the two boxes of whisky I had asked Lemieux to purchase for me in Montreal came today.' As he pointed out, he believed in freedom of choice personally but did not feel people capable of exercising such freedom wisely. It is a capsule illustration both of the reason why prohibition could not act as a unifying cause and why it failed. By the middle of the decade it was apparent that the great experiment had largely been abandoned.[4]

Another great cause also proved disappointing. Before and during the war women's movements had rallied to seek female suffrage as a means of bringing the virtues of womanhood to the world of politics. The drive of 'maternal feminism' to ensure that women would gain a say in running society had never been a cause close to the heart of the predominantly male middle-class reformism with which the intellectual community was associated. Nevertheless, had the expectations espoused by supporters of women's suffrage been fulfilled, it would have done much to provide direction for post-war reformism. Though an obvious step forward, however, the vote for women, which was achieved in all provinces but Quebec and in federal elections by the end of the war, proved a disappointment. Rather than marking the opening of an era of higher values, it seemed to suggest the dying of a great cause. As with male reformers after the war, women found themselves 'divided by region, race and class.' They could not provide the lead for their uncertain male counterparts.[5]

There were other possibilities, of course. Sir John Willison and a group of businessmen associated with various progressive causes formed the Canadian Reconstruction Association (the CRA) in 1918. Designed to bring rational and scientific assessment to bear on government policy, the organization declared itself dedicated to a pantheon of progressive causes. In particular, it looked to the cause of the veteran and dedicated itself 'to consider problems affecting the soldiers. To assist in their re-establishment in civil life, whether on land or in the factories, in the shops or in the professions. To co-operate with soldiers' organizations in all well-considered measures to ensure the permanent comfort and welfare of those among them who have been partly or wholly disabled for any self-sustaining occupation.'[6] The Women's Committee, headed by Marjorie MacMurchy, extended this general statement of principle into consideration of problems in a number of social areas.

The CRA could not provide a rallying point for reform as had such bodies as the Civic Improvement League. It was too much of a businessman's organization. Concerned with the industrial competitiveness of Canada after the war, much of the association's energy went into promotion of protective, though 'scientific' tariffs, and the regulation of industry by government. The association, however, seemed unable to distinguish between the interests of business and the wider concerns of reform. Whatever its original intentions, the groups's primary effort seemed limited to the interests of one class within Canadian society. Concern with industrial and technological development tended to divert too much attention from reform and social justice to be acceptable to many Canadian progressives. There is no indication that the CRA ever developed a strong following outside the business community.[7] Its goals were too compromised by class interests. Within three years it had collapsed.

Similar problems and contradictions plagued the Dominion government's efforts to move into business regulation. The establishment of a Board of Commerce in 1919 in order to try and control prices was a direct assertion of the new, more activist role sought by many for the state in the interests of the public. As with the CRA, however, the board seemed caught between the older 'developmental' concept of state intervention in the name of the business community and the newer concern with public welfare proposals. In the end, the former seemed to predominate, and the board never became the vehicle it might have. It was effectively moribund within a year of its appointment.[8]

Most significant of all, perhaps, was the failure of the more ideologically charged farm and labour movements to gain the adherence of the urban and intellectual progressives. The reason for this failure was straightforward and was summed up by political economist Robert MacIver of Toronto. 'You cannot establish a new order unless you are willing to pull down the old system,' he warned in the spring of 1919. 'Are we willing to pull down the old systems? If not there is no use in talking about building new ones.' The answer was clearly that much of the Canadian intellectual community was not willing to pull down the old systems, at least not to the degree envisaged in the more radical rhetoric of the era. The militancy of 1919 frightened a good many who considered themselves advocates of social reform. Willison, for example, was dismayed at the revolutionary rhetoric that abounded at the end of the war and at the implications that such rhetoric carried of class conflict.[9]

Canadian social scientists were somewhat more intrigued by some of the reform ideas around than were businessmen. There was considerable sympathy among Canadian political economists, for example, with the efforts of the farmers to establish a co-operative system as a means of preserving their well-being. O.D. Skelton was so sympathetic to the possibilities of agrarian reform that he even drafted a program of reform for the Canadian Council of Agriculture. With few exceptions, however, sympathy for the problems of the farmers and support of some of their goals did not translate into support for direct political action on their part. In a nation already strained by social cleavage and economic division, the entry of a special interest party like the Progressives was seen more as a reflection of the problem than as a possible solution. For the militant labour unions there was a great deal less sympathy and practically no support.[10]

Contributing to the divisions between these major reform movements and the Canadian intellectual community was the post-war paranoia about all things that even hinted of 'Bolshevism.' The Russian revolution of 1917, that country's subsequent withdrawal from the war, and internal chaos within the new Soviet Union raised the fear among many that the contagion would spread to North America. Though more virulent in the United States than in Canada, this 'Red scare' was felt north of the border. Any reformers who appeared at all radical were in danger of being branded what one visiting American speaker termed 'a mob of unwashed, bewhiskered nobodies who do not know their right hand from their left.' This is not to argue that many Canadian intellectuals participated in this sort of anti-communism. On the contrary, there were articles dismissing such emotional rhetoric as irrational. The very emotionalism, however, served as a further illustration of the way in which reform, if not tempered, could further split a divided society.[11]

Such opposition to radical reform is hardly surprising. Socialism, or rather the fear of socialism, had proven a major impetus to the reform movement before the war. As has been argued above, progressivism looked to a better use of the facilities of the state to prevent the growth of 'old world' evils that would cause class-conscious socialism. The problem was that, for some people, events in the post-war world indicated that the spectre had not been exorcised. 'We are moving towards socialism,' Stephen Leacock lamented in 1924. 'We are moving through the mist; nearer and nearer with every bit of government regulation, nearer and nearer through the mist to the edge of the abyss over which civilization may be precipitated to its final catastrophe.' For a pessimistic Leacock, things had obviously gone too far already. By the mid-1920s John Willison seemed to be in agreement. High levels of government taxation and 'too much reform' caused him to look back with fondness on an earlier era of individualism. Likewise, Clifford Sifton lamented all those current theories that were subversive to the idea 'that a man's virtue is founded on his own integrity.'[12]

To take such comments as an indication of a pervasive neo-conservatism among Canadian intellectuals and former urban reformers would be to misconstrue what was happening. Leacock, Willison, and Sifton were typical in their concern that socialism not develop but were unusual in their pessimistic conclusion that the movement to socialism was already well under way. Rather, there was a continued belief in the necessity of reform but, that was coupled with a belief that any movement that thought in terms of class, whether of the right or left, was dangerous to Canadian society. As William Lyon Mackenzie King argued in 1919, reform continued to be necessary in order to prevent both the injustices of rampant individualism and the reaction against it, socialism. 'Single control, whether by Capital, Labor or the State, sooner or later is certain to mean autocratic control.'[13]

All in all, urban middle-class reform was in disarray in the early 1920s. Part of it had galloped off to the single cause of prohibition and moral reform while other parts became increasingly disenchanted with reform altogether. Those Canadian intellectuals, especially the social scientists, who remained interested in a wide range of public issues stood somewhat apart. They did not, with a few exceptions, turn back to a celebration of laissez-faire, continuing to believe that direct state involvement in social and economic problems was necessary in the modern age. Neither did they wholeheartedly embrace the crusade of agrarian reform or labour. Rather, their approach seems to have been deliberately cautious and unemotional. There was little of the 'social passion' that drove the social gospel movement and that, before 1914, had set the tone of Canadian progressivism. Impassioned calls for one or another social program were met with careful questions about details and costs.[14]

This caution was yet another legacy of the war. The war had raised passions to new heights in the quest for victory, and the consequences of the unleashed emotions lay on the battlefields of Europe. New crusades, even in peacetime, in the name of great causes were not likely to appeal to an intellectual community that had always looked to social stability as the other aspect of reform. MacIver's question had been answered by at least his peers. The Canadian social sciences did not want to pull down the existing system. The problem was how to ensure that the modern state was sufficiently effective in meeting social demands to stop others from tearing it down out of anger. In a sense the pessimists had been right after all. Canadian progressivism was badly divided. In a myriad of voices, no clear direction could be found, and before long the great reform tide of 1919 ebbed. Canadians as a whole generally appeared no more ready than the progressive movement to undertake a drastic restructuring of their society.[15]

The fragmentation of progressivism in the post-war world was also attributable to the collapse of the once-powerful Union government. With men like Rowell and Borden in it and with Willison, Sifton, and Dafoe supporting it, it had claimed as its twin missions the winning of the war and the reform of the nation. The former had predominated

over the latter, however, and by war's end much of its natural constituency was lost. Nor was its handling of the post-war situation helpful in regaining support. The belated establishment of a Committee on
Repatriation and Employment under Minister of Immigration J.A. Calder
did little to reassure those concerned with careful planning of the post-
war world. Calder's organization was put together too late and too
hastily to be effective. It was thus understandable that he warned
Canadians that 'this problem of repatriation of the soldiers and the
caring for thousands of dependents who are to come home, will never
in the world be solved by any government.' As MacIver noted, the fact
that 'even a cabinet minister [was] saying that perhaps reconstruction
is not necessary' indicated how far short the Union government had
fallen in the minds of many. As the Union coalition fell apart through
1919 and 1920, few felt there was much worth saving.[16]

Of course there was an emerging alternative. The Liberal party,
which under Laurier had been perceived by many reformers as clinging
to an outmoded laissez-faire view of the state, got a new leader soon
after the war. William Lyon Mackenzie King, who had returned to
Canada and at war's end settled in at Kingsmere writing *Industry and
Humanity*, had carefully prepared for the inevitable change. Observing
the party at close range in the last months of Laurier's leadership, King
had come to the conclusion that it had to be reshaped into an instrument for reform and, not incidentally, that he was the one to do so.
'I confess at times I feel Sir Wilfrid lacks a sense of honour in many
things and that he is just playing the game to suit himself and is now
more or less indifferent to real reform and the country's needs ... Certainly the Liberal party in Canada is at a low ebb.'[17] By August 1919
King's opportunity had come. Laurier was dead, and his era was finally
over. The King era was about to begin.

In assuming the leadership, King was still perceived by much of the
country as a reformer. His pre-war work in the Department of Labour
had provided Laurier's government with its most interventionist portfolio. During the war he had worked with Joseph Atkinson of the
Toronto *Star* to develop a social reform policy for the party, often in
the face of a reluctant Laurier. The program they developed emphasized
such social welfare measures as old age pensions, widows' allowances,
and unemployment insurance. Nor did the publication of *Industry and
Humanity* hurt King's reputation. Horribly written and at times con-
fusingly vague, the work possessed sufficient practical commentary and
a general enough progressive tone to earn it plaudits from the academic

community in both Canada and the United States. Thus when King assumed the leadership of the party, many within the academic community accepted with hope, if not with the same enthusiasm, O.D. Skelton's faith that 'All who know you will have new hope of a vigorous and progressive Liberal party.'[18]

The expectations were not fulfilled. In order to gain the leadership of a party with a strongly protectionist and conservative Quebec wing, King took a compromise position both on questions of policy and in the general tenor of his leadership. The result was a studied vagueness, interspersed with occasional bouts of reform rhetoric, that continued through his time as opposition leader. Even if King was a reformer, his party was not yet the vehicle for that reform. Historians C.B. Sissons, editor of the *Canadian Forum*, summed up the problem when he wrote to King that he had supported the Progressives in 1921 not because of King but because of King's supporters.[19] When the Liberals assumed power in 1921, they seemed almost as fragmented as progressivism: torn between a newer, interventionist ideal with wide support among King's social science colleagues and an older laissez-faire view that those same individuals viewed as irrelevant to modern problems and unjust in its consequences.

The differences that existed between advocates of reform as a 'social passion' and reform as a 'social science' were thus compounded by the absence of a coherent reform party. The progressive movement scattered in different directions politically as it had intellectually. Men like Leacock, Willison, and Beer remained loyal to the Union-Conservative cause through the 1921 election. Radical social gospellers and farm leaders turned to new parties such as the Progressives or one of the splinter Labour parties. The social scientific community showed little cohesion. A general hope that Mackenzie King might transform the Liberal party and bring a new intellectual style of leadership to Ottawa was not deeply enough rooted to overcome traditional party loyalties or to remove doubts about those in the party ranks. The 1921 election which brought about the first minority government in Canadian history reflected the uncertainty abroad in the land as to the future direction of policy.

The problems faced by reformers in this period reflected more than a temporary post-war readjustment and the problems of a recessionary period. The 'new era' demanded a major intellectual reorientation in Canadian thought on the role of the state and the relation between individuals and the society of which they were a part. The war had raised serious questions for many intellectuals about the appropriateness of philosophic idealism as a basis for social action. This created a dilemma, however. Canadian progressivism had rested to a large degree on just that philosophic basis, and if idealism were rejected then much of the reformist impulse was in danger of being jettisoned as well. The idealist perception of man as a social animal and of society as something more than the sum of its parts had provided the counter-argument to extreme individualism, which called for the fettering of the state in the name of liberty. In the theory of state action there was thus a dilemma that mirrored the uncertainty of post-war politics. The Unionists had been rejected partly because the demands they put on the nation had been too great and because their idealism had been translated all too often into authoritarian policies. The radical wing of the Progressives seemed an unrealistic alternative. Its moral certainty and enthusiasms threatened to divide society rather than bring it together. Yet the Liberal party, the obvious alternative, had no clear direction or philosophy. In this sense its leader summed up the problem of the 1920s. Trained in the empirical sciences, Mackenzie King talked the language of idealism while practising the politics of individualism. Some coherent expression had to be given to the views of people who saw state intervention as a necessary instrument in the modern world; yet that very group was afraid of those enthusiasts who would look to the state, either from the extreme left or militant right, as a semi-mystical embodiment of the people.

The dilemma was represented in the two competing fears of the era. One focused on the dangers of 'Kaiserism' in Canada, if an aggressive state were to pursue wartime practices during peace. This image, of course, grew from wartime experience. After the war it broadened to include other types of authoritarianism, including the autocracy of 'Red revolution' and Bolshevism. In both cases, left and right, the image of evil was cast in terms of a state assuming supremacy to the exclusion of all else. As Mackenzie King argued, Germany was an object lesson on the authoritarian and statist nature of socialism! The other fear was expressed in a powerful myth that had been seen before the war and that continued to flourish afterwards. Images of the heartless days of industrial revolution were conjured up to remind people not to hark back to a false utopia in their reaction against the modern world: 'It was in this century [the nineteenth] that one could have found women working on all fours in the coal mines of Northern England. It was the

early part of this period that witnessed the beginning of child labour
and of sweated workshops, which later became a menace to society
and to human existence.'[20]

A variant of this myth accepted the benefits of the industrial revolution. The changes had, on the whole, aided mankind by increasing
productivity. Mackenzie King, for example, pointed to the loss of jobs
brought by new weaving technology in the nineteenth century but
noted that 'for the tens and hundreds whose loss of employment was
temporary, thousands secured permanent employment later on.' Circumstances had changed, however, as the industrial revolution reached
maturity. Adam Smith's view of the world, even if relevant for an
earlier era, could no longer be seen as realistic in an economy where
large-scale industrialization had decreased individual autonomy. 'It
seems inevitable,' wrote University of Toronto professor T.R. Robinson,
'that in the complex condition of a modern industrial society the individual cannot be left to take care of himself to the extent that he
was under more primitive or simpler conditions. His health, his security
against accidents, his opportunity to earn his daily bread, his welfare
in many respects, is dependent upon conditions that are not within his
exclusive control.' The fate of the individual affected the well-being
of society at large in such an interdependent world, 'so that it is necessary to act collectively rather than individually.' The fear of statism
and the crumbling edifice of idealism did not, therefore, cause Canadian social scientists to turn their backs on the necessity of intervention.[21]

The attempts to find a path between the shoals of state tyranny and
the rocks of heartless individualism tended to create contradictions in
many of the social scientific writings of the era. The whole impulse of
the discipline as well as its assessment of modern conditions called for
a high degree of organization and planning. Yet organization and planning recalled the war and the problems of excessive government control. For all the inconsistencies, there did emerge in the 1920s a new
concept of the role of the state from within the social scientific community. It borrowed eclectically from idealism, from such nineteenth
century schools as utilitarianism, and from more modern pragmatism
to build an intellectual rationale for a modernist, secular, and interventionist state. It was an instance where the intellectual community
in Canada scrambled to catch up to the practical demands of modern
thought and modern society. Its key elements involved what social
worker F.N. Stapleford described as 'socialized individualism' and a
perception of the role of the state that allowed for state intervention

in society not in the name of some collective social goal but for the sake of the potential of the individual on whose behalf the intervention was taking place.[22]

By far the most complete expression of this view of the state came from head of the Political Economy Department at the University of Toronto, R.M. MacIver. MacIver's academic credentials were impeccably Canadian: which is to say that like so many other academics, including the leading idealists, he had been born in Scotland, educated first at the University of Edinburgh and then at Oxford, and had assumed a junior post in Scotland before being brought to the University of Toronto as an associate professor in 1915. A prodigious writer, MacIver had already produced several articles and two major works on sociology by the mid-1920s. None compared in ambition, length, or importance, in his own view, however, to his attempt to synthesize a theory of the state for the post-war era, published in 1926. His *Modern State*, though published only eight years after Watson's *State in War and Peace*, was in many ways the product of a different age.[23]

For MacIver the first step in the reassessment of the nature of the state was to change the terms of discussion. He self-consciously assumed the perspective of a social scientist rather than that of a philosopher and warned at the beginning of his work that he would examine the state 'in no attitude of worship, as did Hegel, and in no attitude of belittlement, as did Spencer, but in the spirit of "scientific exactitude." ' This scientific exactitude involved a frontal attack on the general boundaries of philosophic discussion of the state and particularly on the metaphysical aspects of state theory, which had played such an important part in Canadian writings. For many years MacIver had been making the argument that 'only conscious beings can have value in themselves, can be viewed as an end' and that 'ultimate value can attach to persons alone.' Given this premise, it was impossible to endow either the state or society with metaphysical attributes. Neither could, in themselves, become the 'end' of public policy. The mystical vision of the state was untenable to this believer in scientific exactitude.[24]

Of course, idealists like Watson had also denied the extreme mysticism that some German philosophers had attributed to the state. Nevertheless, Watson's claims that the state was an embodiment of the striving of society's general will towards a higher moral plane created an organic link that MacIver could not accept. Long uncomfortable with idealism, MacIver took occasion to make several critical comments on Hegelianism during the course of his work. The state could not be assumed to embody the general will of the community, as men like Watson contended. 'In general the whole of that living culture which is the expression of the spirit of the people or of an age is beyond the competence of the state. The state reflects it, and does little more. The state orders life, but does not create it.' The concept of the general will, he argued, is untenable, except if seen 'not so much as the will *of* the state as the will *for* the state.' Except in this most general way, it remained unformulated and impossible to tap.[25]

The dismissal of the 'general will' tended to downgrade the idea of sovereignty. For MacIver, sovereignty was not a mystical concept that endowed the state with special qualities. Sovereignty became 'as elusive and inconstant as the wind, an unstable equilibrium of will reacting to a thousand conscious and unconscious influences.'[26] The state, it was true, had a monopoly of coercive power, but that did not change the fact that decisions as to the application of that power – to the employment of sovereignty, in other words – rested on the practical and often grubby base of public moods, power broking, and propaganda. The state could not be assumed to represent any meaningful expression of the 'general will' and thus, even by extension, could not assume any supra-personal aspects. In short, it was neither organic itself nor the mirror of an organic society.

Having demystified the state, MacIver used an analogy from the modern world to describe what remained. The state, he argued, is reminiscent of a business corporation. 'The "general will" is similar to the will of the shareholders that the corporation do well. Government is the management which has the responsibility of translating that sentiment into concrete policies.' This image of the state as a business implied that, like corporate management, a government had only certain valid areas of activity. The state, he continued, is a 'social superstructure' that could no more undertake all social activities or responsibilities than could business. It has an important but limited role to play as but one of many associations formed between men. As a superstructure or association, moreover, its lack of a conscious personality is once again emphasized. The state has purpose and value only in the service it provides: like an association, to the degree it serves its membership, and like a corporation, to the degree it pleases its shareholders. There was, in other, words only one possible reason for the state to exist – the service of its individual citizens. 'In our search for unity we come at last to the individual. We find that unity where many have discovered only its opposite, disharmony and strife, in the will of each to be himself and achieve the objects that are dear to him. We find it not in the surrender but in the fulfilment of person-ality ... Social order must be adjudged not only good but enduring in proportion as it expresses and is created by free personality. This liberty is the very condition of social development.'[27]

In his assertions that the state was a 'superstructure' and in his attacks on idealism, MacIver was, not surprisingly, very much influ-enced by the memory of the war. False doctrines of the state, among the allies as among the Germans, had permitted the state to make such a horrendous claim upon its citizens. Moreover, it was an unjust claim. 'In declaring war the state puts a particular political object above the general ends of family, of the cultural life, of the economic order ... Here we may well ask, Does the end justify the means? ... Citizenship is not the whole life or duty of man.' War was as anachronistic as the divine rights of kings and could be prevented for the most part if man accepted the 'limited character' of the state.[28]

Having repudiated Hegel, MacIver still had to deny Spencer. The sorts of arguments he had developed had been used in the past not just by Spencer but also by the utilitarians and others to limit strictly state interference in many areas of society and the economy. Indeed, MacIver's doctrine of the state did have aspects reminiscent of utilitarianism and especially of the notion that decisions should be based on the greatest good for the greatest number. Experience in the nineteenth century and the social changes of the early twentieth century, however, had proved to MacIver's satisfaction that while the basic instincts of util-itarianism were sound, the extremely individualistic policy implica-tions developed from them were not. MacIver showed his own adherence to the popular image of the industrial revolution by relating various horror stories of that era. Laissez-faire, he warned, gave 'to the name of freedom a sinister as well as an unreal sound.' Extreme individualism was not the proper route to take in protecting the individual. Policy had to be grounded in the circumstances of the age and express a pragmatic approach to the needs of the populace.[29]

In the twentieth century there was no doubt that these needs implied greater state activity. From the time of ancient Greece, observed MacIver, urban life had demanded 'more intense, more complex and more con-tinuous regulation' than rural life. The urbanization of Canada in the wake of industrialization, with the concomitant interdependence of society, meant that the state had to meet the requirements of its clien-tele with new policies. 'It is becoming recognized that men are so bound up in families and groups that the whole suffers from the privation or degradation of any, and that the state can act as a great ministry of social assurance without destroying the initiative and responsibility of its members.' Such measures as health protection, unemployment insurance, minimum wages, and other measures were therefore both a reasonable set of responses to the needs of the public and a means of ensuring that there continued to be enough general acceptance of the existing society to prevent social upheaval.[30]

Many of the arguments presented by MacIver were long familiar to the social scientific community in Canada. The position he argued in the 500 pages of his book had been the subject of discussions for several years. MacIver differed from many of his peers only in the thoroughness with which he worked through the problem. It is this, rather than any claim to originality, that makes it an important piece of work. It marked the emergence of a clear theoretical position for a group of thinkers that had been struggling since at least the war's end to distinguish themselves from proponents of the radical social gospel and paternal-conservatism while maintaining a belief in the importance of the state as a vehicle for social improvement. By formulating the concept of the state as a service agency of the individual, while maintaining that individual's supremacy over the collectivity, the rationale for state action had been defined.

Also important in MacIver's definition was the shift in emphasis that took place between means and ends. Idealism and the other earlier, more religious orderings of social values had stressed the importance of ethical absolutes. For MacIver, and those who thought like him, policy-making had no final end. The state could not hope to replicate the kingdom of God on earth, nor should it try. Ends would be adjusted as public demands shifted. 'The state has no finality, can have no perfected form. What we name democracy is a beginning and not an end.' The process of governing well became, in a sense, an end in itself. It was a managerial concept of the state that fitted well into the idea that the state was analogous to a business.[31]

At this point it is worth examining a tentative hypothesis concerning this new social scientific interpretation of the state. In its orientation towards individualism and pragmatism it marked the emergence of a new variety of liberalism into Canadian political thought.[32] The older idealism, for its part, still existed but was fragmented into a left-reform social gospel wing and a paternalistic conservatism that stressed social stability and government authority. Also present, of course, was traditional individualistic liberalism, increasingly touted by the business community as a defence of capitalist freedom. For the most part the intellectual reform community was turning away from such a view as outmoded, though there were obvious exceptions.[33] Two notes of caution are necessary, however. First, there are complex overlaps in the philosophies of the pre- and post-war eras. Even those social scientists like MacIver and Skelton who were relatively far removed from the tenets of idealism owed a debt to idealist teachings. It is possible to talk only of the relative influence of philosophical constructs rather than of a single philosophic school as a mainspring of the intellectual community, or of any portion of it. Second, these are intellectual, not political, streams in Canadian life. As the well-developed political historiography of the 1920s reveals, one cannot identify conservatism with the Conservative party or liberalism with the Liberal party. The multiple tendencies of thought in Mackenzie King, which have already been noted, are indicative of the way in which varied opinions were contained within the Canadian brokerage system of parties. All the major parties, even the Progressives, gave expression to a wide variety of views on the state and on specific policy matters. Any identification with one stream of thought was, at best, a matter of degree only.

If the state was to be defined in terms of the service it provided, then two questions remained to be answered. First, how was it to be decided what services were necessary? Second, who was to take responsibility for the design and administration of these? It was not sufficient to assume, in populist fashion, that the public would make the right choices and define what was needed in the way of policy. Canadian social scientists thought of themselves as democrats, but few acted as populists. They simply did not believe that the the complexities of the modern state could be entrusted to the ill-informed and indifferent citizenry at large. As MacIver commented, the attitude 'that democracy en masse can legislate or make executive decisions' was naïve, 'confined to Rousseau's mind and the people of the United States of America.' There was no reason for Canadians to be deluded by either model. Any realistic assessment of the modern state would conclude that the public must relinquish any pretence that it could define specific policies or handle them once they came into being. 'Democracy,' as one writer put it, 'spells essentially government by experts.' Having described the state as machine, the social scientific community sought to become its mechanics.[34]

This belief in the importance of expertise marks a degree of continuity between social scientists in the 1920s and their pre-war brethren. In the 1920s the social sciences were stronger and the organizational impulse was much more deeply rooted. Those making a claim to special recognition due to expertise were accordingly more successful in the 1920s than in earlier years. Before the war, the social sciences had struggled for recognition in a university community and a reform movement dominated by the church and by the amateur enthusiast. By the end of the 1920s the social scientists and others with a claim to special expertise in matters of public affairs had largely displaced the amateur while loudly proclaiming their secular nature. When the University of Toronto publication *Contributions to Canadian Economics* editorialized in 1929 that 'the welfare of the nation for the future must depend to an increasing extent on the economist,' it was making a comment not only on man's perceptions of modern problems but on the success of the profession in its drive for recognition.[35]

The drive for organization, distinctiveness, and recognition was revealed in various ways through the decade. The formation in 1922 of the Canadian Historical Association and the founding of the *Canadian Historical Review* provided a forum which, for many years, remained at the centre of social scientific discussion. In 1929 the efforts of D.A. MacGibbon and others led to the revival of the Canadian Political Science Association. New journals sprang up to house the increasing number of writings by social scientists in Canada. Aside from such academic publications as the annual *Contributions to Canadian Economics* emanating from the University of Toronto, there were professional journals like *Social Welfare*, founded in 1918, and the intellectually oriented magazine, *Canadian Forum*, founded in 1920. More than forty monographs were published in political economy alone through the decade, more than had been published in the previous century![36]

The growth of organizations and journals was possible because of the increasing role of the social sciences within universities. By the 1920s political economy, defined variously as economics, political science, sociology, or a combination of all three, had become a mature discipline and a standard offering in most Canadian universities. The University of Toronto, with a faculty of fourteen in political economy as well as various colleagues in commerce and social work, had by far the most impressive collection of social scientists. The Université de Montréal, McGill, Queen's, Saskatchewan, and the University of British Columbia had also seen recent impressive gains made by political economy. The staff was increasingly well trained, with a graduate degree in the discipline becoming a prerequisite for employment and the doctorate becoming increasingly common. The older generalist was disappearing, to be replaced by men and women who thought of themselves as specialists in their discipline rather than as deviant historians, philosophers, or theologians. Though far from fully established, the differences among the various social sciences were also beginning to develop. Several universities made the distinction between economists, political scientists, and sociologists, and certainly the members of the profession were increasingly aware of the differences. MacIver at Toronto and C.A. Dawson at McGill felt themselves to be not just political economists but also sociologists. It was symbolic of the changing discipline that when James Mavor, the idealist whose only degree was honorary, retired from the chairmanship of political economy at Toronto, he was succeeded by the thoroughly professional MacIver.[37]

Equally important in the growth of social sciences in Canada was the course of social work over the decade. Social work had traditionally been centred in such religiously oriented and voluntary organizations as the YMCA as well as the various church bodies. It had begun to develop as a government function with the growth of child welfare toward the end of the nineteenth century. It was the 1920s that brought the most spectacular growth, however, with social workers becoming involved not only in child welfare but in all aspects of urban poverty and family problems. Moreover, the social worker was increasingly likely, at least in the larger cities, to be a paid professional on the public payroll. Even in the case of voluntary organizations there was an increasing use of a core of full-time paid, professionally trained workers.[38]

The members of this new group were determined to assert their status as professional social science experts. As the decade went on, numerous bodies sprang into existence to testify to their sense of distinctiveness. The older, church-based Social Services Council no longer seemed sufficient, and bodies like the National Committee for Mental Hygiene, the Canadian Association of Child Protection Officers, the Canadian Social Hygiene Council, and others formed so rapidly that it must have been difficult even for the social workers to keep track. The biggest step came, however, in 1926, when Canadian social workers, no longer content to operate within the United States-based National Association of Social and Health Work, formed a separate Canadian body, the Canadian Association of Social and Health Work. By 1928 McGill sociologist C.A. Dawson, who had been instrumental in the organizational drives of the decade, could observe with some satisfaction that 'back of you are the resources of this national institution as you face your local work. You are thus part of something infinitely stronger and larger than yourself as an individual.'[39]

Social workers in the 1920s felt that they required two attributes besides organization to be accepted as professionals. First, it was necessary to document their claim that the profession possessed a range of skills that went beyond mere philanthropic good will. This was done in various ways. Attachments to universities were accentuated. Even amateur and part-time workers were 'made over' into professional social workers by exposure at seminars to the latest social science techniques.[40] Though Canadian universities were as yet barely able to begin full-scale programs of social work, there were efforts at large universities like Toronto and McGill to develop such programs. Finally, the presence of trained academics like Dawson and MacIver in social service circles helped provide a sense of professionalism by linking social work with the more developed social sciences.

The second attribute required was a belief, at least among social workers, that their craft indeed constituted a science. Great attention was paid to the development of the 'case-work' method as proof that the profession was infused with a proper methodology that demanded rigorous collection of 'facts' and the objective use of 'evidence' in making decisions. Such a scientific and professional approach also meant that the discipline had to assert its distinctiveness from the amateur philanthropist and volunteers who were so intertwined with the evolution of social work. Here the key argument was based not merely on expertise but also on purpose. Social work writers prided themselves on maintaining a professional objectivity toward the misery they faced. They were social engineers, concerned not only with the individual sufferings of their clients – though there was nothing wrong with concern – but also with the effects of poverty, disease, and other ills on society as a whole. 'At one time,' said social worker Peter Bryce, 'Child Welfare had its source in the ministering spirit inculcated by religion, then in the natural impulses of human sympathy. Now it is part of the defensive foresight of citizens who would protect the future of the state.'[41]

The result of this sense of professional distinctiveness was a growing distance between the ranks of those attached to that new professional, secular, and social scientific approach to welfare and religiously based volunteer movements. The evolution of the journal Social Welfare clearly illustrates this growing separation. Begun in 1918 to appeal to all types of social workers, it had initially a strong element of the social gospel it, with its stated purpose being to 'undertake to fight the battles of the poor, the oppressed, the exploited, the victimized of every class and kind.' In its first years it maintained this tone with an eclectic mixture of articles by social gospellers, prohibitionists, moral uplifters, town planners, and professional social workers. By the early 1920s, however, an increasing percentage of the articles were written by social scientists, either in applied social work or in the universities. Though the journal retained an element of moral uplift through the decade, the dominant theme by the mid-1920s was the call for greater professionalism. The degree of change in both the journal and in the social work community was revealed in a debate in the columns of *Social Welfare* soon after the formation of the Canadian Association of Social and Health Work. There was some doubt as to whether the YMCA should be eligible for affiliation. It was, after all, a mere voluntarist organization based on religious and humanitarian enthusiasm. It was admitted, but only because it had some professionals on staff! 'If at any time,' concluded Peter Bryce, 'the social worker was untrained, uneducated, sentimental, theoretical, that day is gone ... It is now recognized that the field of Social Sciences calls for master minds, highly trained, and more and more each year we are finding men and women of ability and character attracted to it.' As ideology and sympathy yielded to science and professionalism the results were expected to be dramatic: 'From a depressing period it seems to me that we are entering the most exhilarating and challenging time the world has known. The next fifty years will see the most determined, intelligent and concrete effort made to free mankind from ignorance, disease, disabling conditions of all kinds, and enable the individual to live up to the fullness of his stature.'[42]

The growth of social work affected mainly municipal and provincial jurisdictions. At the federal level, active intervention in social and economic matters was more limited despite the precedents of the war. In the decade after 1918 a number of reformers argued that this federal caution was regrettable and that the time had come to encourage more active participation by the Dominion government. Willison's pessimistic views at the end of the war were countered by men like W.L. Grant, who argued that 'state action on a big scale is now as possible as municipal action was fifty years ago.'[43] There was a catch, however.

The modern pragmatic state, if it was to assume new duties and extend its services to the degree possible and desirable, had to obtain the best advice available. The administrative structure and staff had to be equal to the task. Thus the older progressive concerns about efficiency in the civil service and elimination of patronage continued to be an issue in the 1920s. Inseparable from these concerns was the belief that the trained social scientist was the means by which that efficiency could be achieved.

The immediate post-war concerns about the federal civil service were essentially defensive. With the war over, much of the urgency that had shaped the reforms of 1917 dissipated. Civil service efficiency was no longer part and parcel of the great national fight for survival. There was thus an understandable concern on the part of reformers that the gains of the past few years not be eroded. In order to preserve those advances, a number of concerned individuals banded together in a series of loose coalitions to lobby on behalf of the Civil Service Commission and to prevent raids on the system. John Willison, Newton Rowell, and George Wrong, all long-time public figures, were joined by younger men like Vincent Massey and Horace Britain in writing and speaking on behalf of the merit principle. The central figure through much of the decade, however, was W.L. Grant, by this time principal of Upper Canada College in Toronto. For Grant, the gains of the previous few years were important, but they would prove transitory without 'a healthy public opinion or a healthy publicity' to keep the government honest.[44] His intention was to ensure that such sound opinion existed.

Grant and his allies used various means in their battle for the merit system. Formal organizations came into being under names like the Civil Service Research Committee and the Civil Service Reorganization Association. Speeches by civil service commissioners before influential bodies like the Canadian Club and Empire Club were encouraged. Grant and others interested in the topic also did a fair amount of lecturing and speaking on their own in behalf of civil service reform. This lobby of interested citizens also employed more direct methods. When, for example, a series of civil service exemptions created concerns about patronage, it was suggested that Grant write to leaders of the federal parties to bring the issue to their attention. 'Meighen might be advised that it is a contrivance to fill these offices with party servitors to despoil the Merit System. Forke should be reminded of the platform of the Progressives on el[iminating] patronage.' The prime minister was more of a problem. 'God knows what you can say to King.'[45]

Perhaps the most interesting feature of Grant's efforts was the close attachment he developed with successive civil service commissioners and their staff. William Foran, long-time secretary of the commission, was especially important in this regard. Restrained, as the commissioners were, by their position within the civil service, they had to find some indirect means to complain of government policy in public. W.L. Grant and the various reform associations provided the answer. Foran and others regularly informed Grant of matters that should be raised with the government or trumpeted to the public. In turn, Grant regularly received inside information on government intentions and emerging policy. The bureaucracy was becoming more skilled in defending its interests, while intellectual reformers discovered that allies inside government could provide valuable support against wayward politicians. It was a pattern that was to be extremely important in the future.[46]

In many ways the civil service reform movement continued the arguments and concerns of the pre-war era. There were also differences, however, as those involved began to see that the issue was more complex than their earlier counterparts had thought. In particular, reformers had to be concerned not only with the elimination of patronage but also with the complex question of classification. A major investigation and classification of the Dominion civil service had taken place in 1919. Undertaken by E.O. Griffenhagen and Fred Telford of Arthur Young and Co of Chicago, its aim was admirably progressive. Efficiency, equity, and merit were all expected to be promoted by the reorganization of the civil service. All in all, it should have been viewed positively by Canadian intellectuals and social scientists as a victory for rationality in government. It was not. 'A lot of d----d Yankee experts have practically bedevilled the whole thing,' complained W.L. Grant. Squabbles, complaints of inequitable treatment, and confusion over an excessively complex classification system mired the new system in unpleasant controversy from the beginning.[47]

Eventually the necessary modifications were made to the system, and both civil servants and politicians accommodated themselves to the new structures, though often with reluctance.[48] The whole issue, however, was somewhat of a shock to civil service reformers in Canada. Before 1918 they had tended to assume that the elimination of patronage would automatically lead to efficiency and equity. Merit was thought to be the only essential prerequisite to an able civil service; the law of competition would take care of the rest. The debate on reclassification, however, revealed that the elimination of patronage had not ended problems of efficiency and equity. In fact, the regulations pouring out of the civil service commission concerning reclassification and promotion were having an undesirable effect. Thus for Saskatchewan political scientist R.M. Dawson, writing in 1929, the history of the civil service in Canada was not a happy tale of progress up from the depths of patronage. On the contrary, many of his arguments challenged the major thrust of civil service reform as ineffective and misdirected. Fear, not efficiency, seemed to be the result of two decades of fighting for a patronage-free civil service.

The present organization of the Canadian service is built upon fear – fear that party supporters will be appointed, fear that they will be promoted even if they obtain office legitimately, fear that they will be transferred from a poor position to a good one, fear that the deputy minister may be open to unworthy suggestions from the minister ... The result of this attitude has been a search for objective tests and the Commission whose thankless task it is to administer such tests. An attempt has been made to measure objectively things which by their very nature cannot be satisfactorily gauged by mechanical methods, and the Commission is given functions to perform for which it has neither the aptitude, nor the facilities, nor the necessary information.[49]

The elimination of patronage, long the primary goal of reformers, proved to be but the first step, perhaps even an obstacle, in the reform of the public service. Increasingly, the intellectual community began to feel that significant improvement would come only when men with expertise and ability sufficient to meet modern problems gained influence within the civil service. 'Men of little ability and ordinary intelligence,' commented Dawson, 'are unequal to the task.' The civil service had to be designed in such a way so as to eliminate not only the political hangers-on but the mediocre. 'The growth of a complex civilization and a new conception of the state's place in that civilization' made guidance of government by experts absolutely essential.[50]

One group of experts that considered itself especially well suited to modern governance was the social scientific community in Canada. More and more through the 1920s it began to assert its presence in Ottawa. The curbing of patronage did provide a greater opportunity for well-educated men of talent in the civil service. It would also seem that the progressive movement's long years of calls for a better quality of civil servant had an effect in political circles. Robert Borden, Arthur Meighen, and Mackenzie King, though far from uninterested in patronage, all seem to have accepted to some degree the arguments that experts were needed in Ottawa. Though the 'mandarin class' of civil-servant technocrats and advisers was not to develop until later, the 1920s did see the emergence in the nation's capital of a new class of civil servants. Highly educated, certain of their own abilities and of the need for efficient government, these men were the heirs of men like Adam Shortt. Before long they began to bring social scientific training and a pragmatic interventionism into discussions of government policy. In their drive for efficiency and organization they were reminiscent of the movement for urban reform of earlier years.

When Mackenzie King became leader of the Liberal party and then prime minister, the hope among Canadian intellectuals that he would initiate reform was probably complemented by the hope that he would see the value of a modern, scientific training in social issues for men in the government service. King, after all, was one of their own, and in his years as leader of the opposition he had kept in contact with men like Skelton and others interested in the potential of liberalism in Canada.[51] As prime minister, he hardly made the flood of appointments that would have signalled the capture of power by the social sciences, but there were, over the years, a number of significant changes. The social sciences, barely represented in Ottawa before 1921, became a major source of senior government officials in certain areas by the end of the decade.

The most dramatic example of the rise of the newer breed of civil servant came in the Department of External Affairs. The transformation began when King, after hearing his old acquaintance Skelton at a Canadian Club meeting in Ottawa, called on him to act as an adviser in foreign affairs for the upcoming 1923 Imperial Conference.[52] Skelton's advice proved so valuable and his ideas so much in tune with those of King that when Joseph Pope retired as under-secretary of state for external affairs in 1925, Skelton was appointed to succeed him.[53] O.D. Skelton, doctor in political economy, advocate of tax reform and Canadian national autonomy, and a man who believed in an active role for the state, followed in the tradition of his own mentor Adam Shortt in attempting to make the transition from critical observer to participant. Unlike Shortt, Skelton's experience was to be generally successful. The power he achieved made it much easier for others to follow.

As Skelton asserted his presence in External Affairs and as increasing national autonomy caused the department to take on new responsibilities, other academics were brought into the service. In 1929 Norman

Robertson, a Rhodes scholar with advanced training at the Brookings Institute, joined. In 1928 history lecturer Lester B. Pearson gained the senior appointment through competitive examinations, followed by H.L. Keenleyside, who had studied at the University of British Columbia and Clark University before teaching in various American institutions. Though still only a small corner of the civil service, External Affairs had been restructured and restaffed in these years in such a way as to make it the shining example in the minds of many intellectuals of what government service should entail.[54]

Another means of being heard by government also drew from Skelton's example – the temporary assignment of the expert to a particular problem. Again, there were precedents from before the war in the work of various individuals like Shortt and Skelton in conciliation boards. In the 1920s the use of social scientists increased. Aside from Skelton's appointment to give foreign policy advice in 1922, there was the use of D.A. MacGibbon of the University of Alberta as a royal commissioner on the grain trade. Norman Rogers, a political economist teaching at Acadia, was appointed secretary to the Royal Commission on the Maritime Provinces in 1926. When the Meighen government assumed power shortly afterwards and cancelled the appointment, Rogers was not forgotten. The next year, with King safely back in power, Rogers became his private secretary in the Prime Minister's Office.[55]

One of the most promising areas for academics seeking temporary appointments lay in international affairs. In the search for a better civilization after the war, the allies formed a number of bodies, attached to the League of Nations and International Labour Organisation, to investigate modern social and economic problems. The assertion of national status demanded that Canada send its quota of delegates, and the result was a steady opportunity for social scientists to use government time to investigate current issues. Charlotte Whitton, for example, a former assistant editor of *Social Welfare* and secretary to a cabinet minister, was made an assessor of the Child Protection Committee of the League of Nations. Eduoard Montpetit received an appointment from King to an economic conference in Genoa in 1922.[56] P.E. Corbett, law professor at McGill and active reformer, served as an adviser to the International Labour Organisation.

These temporary appointments raise an interesting question. While they did not entail patronage in the sense that appointees were being rewarded for effort on behalf of the party, there was an element of partisanship involved. Skelton, Montpetit, and Rogers were all active

Liberals. Whitton, though a Conservative at heart, was temporarily affiliated with the Liberal party because of her appointment as secretary to a cabinet minister. There were few objections from interested social scientists, however, and the various civil service reform groups never did protest any of these appointments. Partisanship was thought less important than the appointment of well-qualified individuals. Men like Skelton or Rogers, no matter how affiliated with the party in power, could not be identified in the minds of their peers with the grubby and sordid image of the party hanger-on. It does bring home the point often seen in crusades, however. No matter how sincere the cause of a group, there is also often an element of a struggle for a place in the sun.

It is also instructive that none of these appointments was involved with domestic economic policy advice. Among the social sciences, economics was by far the most established in Canada, and it was an area where the Dominion government had clear responsibility. In the 1920s, however, government was just beginning to think of economic planning, in the largest sense, as a distinct area, separate from such specifics as transportation planning and export forecasts. There was some use of economists *as* economists in the 1920s. R.H. Coats, dominion statistician and a former assistant editor of the *Labour Gazette*, saw his role expand beyond the mere recording of data to the provision of material for government policy-makers. Also, both Bryce Stewart and W.C. Clark were involved in the post-war period in experimentation with labour exchanges for the Dominion government. Finally, on at least one occasion, King borrowed the services of former Toronto professor and current editor of the *Canada Year Book*, S.A. Cudmore, to assist the government in obtaining 'comprehensiveness of outlook in integrating current economic trends.'[57]

There were, however, severe limitations on the role assumed by social scientists in the Dominion government in the 1920s. It is significant, for example, that the centre of professional economic expertise in Ottawa remained in the Dominion Bureau of Statistics rather than in such line agencies as the Department of Finance. To an extent this reflected the traditional view, often expressed before the war, that the 'scientific' nature of the social sciences demanded a strong orientation towards the collection and organization of data. The absence of adequate facts, it had often been argued, was what really stood between Canadians and the ability to make the right choices. Indeed, for many the collection of the data was the essence of social science. Once collected and organized in a comprehensible way, the data would permit any intelligent layman to decide what to do.[58] The fact that the government was consulting economists by the 1920s must therefore be qualified not only by the irregular nature of that consultation but also by the continuing tendency to see the role of the adviser in limited terms. Mainstream federal departments concerned with the economy had neither the staff nor apparently the inclination to present the sort of complex economic forecasting that Canadian economists saw as within their abilities. The discipline, as with the other social sciences, was increasingly seen as useful, but the vision of the pragmatic and interventionist state had not yet been integrated with the concept of a coterie of expert advisers determining the ways and means of that intervention.

The phrase 'period of transition' is so overworked by historians that one hesitates to use it. Nevertheless, both in terms of the perception of the proper function of the state and the place of social scientists in defining that role, it is difficult to avoid the term for the period 1918-29. The professionalization of areas of endeavour that had previously been voluntary and handled by the man of general education or by the theologian marks one key aspect of the transition. So too does the emergence of the highly educated intellectual in the service of the federal government. Largely confined to External Affairs and the Dominion Bureau of Statistics in these years, the tendency nevertheless began a major reorientation of the Canadian public service in which university training and connections within the academic network became as important as political ties. Finally, the 1920s also sees the transition of social service, broadly defined, from a religious profession to a secular one. Though the churches were still important in such areas, this secularization was part of a general shift in orientation within Canadian society. Formal religion was simply not as central in many areas as it had been a generation before.

These changes were accelerated by yet another. The 1920s marked the passing or withdrawal from active life of many of the founding figures of turn-of-the-century reform. That first group of progressives, urban planners, and political economists ceded to a younger generation. Morley Wickett had died in 1915, and James Mavor retired in 1923 and died in 1925. Adam Shortt, having moved to the Dominion Archives after his unhappy experiences in the Civil Service Commission, retreated into more purely historical research in the post-war period. Long before his death in 1931, he had ceased to be a major figure in public policy discussion in Canada. Other intellectuals, men like Cappon and MacPhail, found that their advancing age and growing disillusionment with the direction of society made their comments less relevant than they had been. Business reform also saw the passing of a generation. Sir John Willison, as has been pointed out, became increasingly conservative in the post-war years. Whether the initial enthusiasm of the Canadian Reconstruction Association was an indication of anything more than a protectionist impulse is a matter of debate, but certainly as the decade went on both Beer and Willison became disillusioned with the possibilities of reform. 'Is it not true that age brings indifference,' asked Beer in 1924. 'I damn with a growing vocabulary all "politicians", "partizans" and make-believe liberals.' Concern over taxes, social upheaval, and government intervention led them to emphasize the importance of free enterprise and individual opportunity unhampered by government regulation. Still others, like Newton Rowell, found the great panacea, prohibition, to be delusory. The peak of moral uplift was dying with the passing of this generation of men raised, in the immediate post-Confederation era, according to the doctrines of strict Protestantism. For the newer generation, and certainly for many of the social scientists, such moral uplift was unscientific and excessively puritanical. [59]

Voluntary reform was still important, of course, and the sense of dedication it implied was very much present in a still powerful social gospel movement. However, even among the church reformers and agrarian movements, where the language of the social gospel reigned, there was a growing recognition of the importance of professional expertise. For the mercurial farm leader E.A. Partridge, one of the problems of farm and labour movements in the 1920s was their failure to attract the white collar, university-educated professional who would provide both the proper image and expert administration: 'While the farmers and wage workers combined give the numerical strength neither they, in the mass, nor their leaders, speaking generally, supply the knowledge, technical and historical, the culture, the self-control, the vision, the passionate good-will that must be in the ascendant in planning that new social order we are planning. We must enlist the professional element, the efficients of all sorts, to organize and officer the movement.'

Historian and self-proclaimed radical Frank Underhill made the same argument at the end of the decade, complaining that 'the lack of intellectual leadership' had crippled radicalism in Canada. He also summed up the limitations in the influence of intellectuals in policy-making and politics when he commented on the differences between the place accorded planners and reformers of all ideological stripes in the United Kingdom. There, with problems of unemployment and class tensions, intelligent investigation of social and economic programs was an absolute necessity. In the bucolic and prosperous society of Canada, however, 'we have no such incentive to think.' Economic conditions were simply not harsh enough to force the public and politicians to accept the necessity of planning and organization. Underhill wrote his column in May 1929, and the supposed prerequisite, hard conditions, was just months away.[60]

6

The formation of a
new reform elite
1930-5

In October 1935 the Dominion election campaign was coming to a close
in the midst of the worst depression in Canadian history. To Brooke
Claxton, lawyer, McGill professor, and man of many causes, the campaign was a great disappointment. Neither major party had come to
grips with the important issues, and neither leader seemed to be able
to provide the nation with a sense of direction. King's speeches bored
him, and Bennett's left him incredulous. The Liberal party, which
seemed on the eve of victory, he described as 'devoid of imagination,
ideas, organizing ability and drive.' And Claxton was a Liberal supporter! 'I think any three of our sort of group,' he continued, 'would
put on a better stunt in six months.' His use of the phrase 'our sort of
group' as well as the assertion of its superior abilities was far from
casual. He was implying the existence by 1935 of an identifiable network of individuals interested in public affairs that could be clearly
distinguished from the population as a whole as well as from other
groups in society. This network, which he saw as based on intellectual
ability and public concern, was later described by him as 'the people
who attend conferences of the national organizations in Canada and
who form part of the inner council of the political parties.' He was
asserting, in other words, the existence in Canada of an intellectual
elite, politically affiliated and active but tied to no one party, with
both the ability and, presumably, the influence to affect policy.[1]

Any evaluation of the evolving function of the state in social and
economic thought in the 1930s ought to begin with an assessment of
Claxton's assertion. The five and a half years since Underhill's acerbic
comments in the *Forum* about the absence of intellectual leadership

in Canada had been a time of crisis. The collapse of the Canadian economy which began in the fall of 1929 brought reform to the forefront once again. Building on the long-standing concerns of the old progressive movement and on the newer status of professionalism in the social sciences, a group of individuals, tied together by mutual concerns and personal connections, coalesced in the early part of the 1930s into an identifiable and influential elite. This was Claxton's 'group,' and it was to have a profound influence on the direction of social and economic planning.

The precise definition of any elite is a difficult matter. When that elite is described by the equally problematic adjective 'intellectual' and by the phrase 'interested in public policy,' the definition is not made any easier. Yet Canadian historians have long sensed the influence of this elite in the Depression years. Writers have noted the presence of highly educated experts in key areas of politics and public policy. Thus, for example, recent studies have fully developed the importance of the Co-operative Commonwealth Federation's (CCF) 'brain trust' – the League for Social Reconstruction (LSR) – and of the powerful mandarin class of civil servants that developed in Ottawa in this decade.[2] Both groups helped Canadians rethink policies on social and economic matters. Yet it is the argument of this and subsequent chapters that the LSR and the mandarinate are not, in themselves, sufficient to comprehend the intellectual revolution of the 1930s. Too many important and influential figures within the intellectual community, Brooke Claxton among them, belonged to neither group. Rather, both the LSR and the mandarins are best seen as formalized aspects of a larger intellectual network in Canada. This group, once estimated by one of its most ardent members, Graham Spry, at between 40 and 100 individuals, was strongly interconnected, aware of its own status, and vitally concerned with the sorts of issues that had provided the basis of much of the progressive writings of previous years.[3] There were, of course, no membership cards proclaiming one to be in good standing as part of this elite, nor would any two historians agree on an exact list of who should or should not be included. Those involved in the LSR and the new mandarinate in Ottawa are obvious candidates, but generally, as Claxton was aware, the group was not tied to any single base. It was a network of individuals of intellectual outlook, bound together by a number of personal ties, professional relationships, and similar attitudes. The multiplicity of connections and the general belief in the importance of public issues, rather than any single characteristic, defined membership in the elite. With this basic definition in mind, we can determine a number of factors linking the community recognized by both Spry and Claxton.

The most basic characteristic of those who came to form the elite was education. Possession of a university degree would seem to have been so common that it might almost be considered mandatory. Moreover, multiple degrees were probably more common than single ones. Typical were men like Claxton himself, arts graduate and lawyer, or Graham Spry, with an undergraduate degree from Manitoba and postgraduate work at Oxford. In the bureaucracy the tone was set early by Adam Shortt and O.D. Skelton, both with doctorates. The tradition would be carried on by the new civil servants of the 1930s and 1940s. In a society where the vast majority of pupils left school before finishing Grade 12 and only a small percentage of those who did finish went on to complete university, the group was an intellectual elite, at least in its educational attainments.[4]

It was not merely a matter of the amount of education, however. Continued involvement with 'intellectual life' was important, even central, in the self-perception of the great majority of those who might be included in Claxton's elite. Connected with this was a strong sense of affiliation to the university as an institution and focus of activity. The majority of the elite were academics during part or all of their careers. The LSR has accurately been described as having a 'donnish flavour,' with five of six presidents and four of six vice-presidents being academics. The connection between the civil service and the universities was also growing closer. Once again the precedents were set by former professors Shortt and Skelton. As the Depression approached, they were joined by other ex-academics like Pearson and Keenleyside. Norman Rogers moved in both directions, leaving the university in 1927 and returning to it in 1930. He would leave it again in 1935.[5]

The ties to the universities were also shown in other ways. Brooke Claxton saw teaching as a vital part of his law career. W.L. Grant, though away from university by the 1930s, had earlier taught at Queen's and was, as headmaster of Upper Canada College, involved in pedagogy. B.K. Sandwell, editor of *Saturday Night* in the 1930s, had taught at McGill and Queen's in earlier years. Another figure to whom the university was important was J.M. Macdonnell, vice-president of National Trust. He was one of the relatively few businessmen involved in this elite. He was also a man once described by Principal Fyfe of Queen's as a 'damned good imitation of a businessman but right inside he is an academic.' Associated closely with Queen's throughout his life, he would become chairman of its board of governors. J.S. McLean of Canada Packers, another businessman intimately involved with various intellectual causes and public issues, was on the board of governors of the University of Toronto. Education and the university thus provided the elite with a sense of exclusivity and accomplishment that distinguished members from the public at large and from other groups involved in public affairs, such as those based on business and centred in bodies like the Chamber of Commerce.[6]

This sense of exclusivity was reinforced through the decade by the controversial debate as to whether the university community was the appropriate place, or the academic the appropriate person, to become actively involved in public affairs. Differences of opinion between active academics, concerned administrators, and outraged politicians led to dismissals or, more commonly, the threat of dismissal. Such tensions were hardly surprising. Academics were becoming increasingly vocal and political in a decade when financial strains made reduction in staff desirable and occasionally imperative. It was a volatile combination. Suspicions existed on both sides of the debate. The public and the politicians who often received the brunt of academic scorn looked askance at a pampered class of intellectuals living off tax revenue that seemed determined to destroy the system that allowed them such a privileged position. The academics involved in the controversies saw fundamental university traditions of academic freedom being eroded and, more importantly, their duty as concerned citizens being thwarted by politicians and administrators. There was also a touch of paranoia on both sides. Every statement by a faculty member on political matters became controversial, and every dismissal or suspicious retirement could be viewed as the result of political pressure.[7]

The tensions of the age helped maintain a sense of unity among men of otherwise divergent views against threats from those outside the university system. When, for example, the outspoken Frank Underhill ran into trouble with the board of governors and president of the University of Toronto, he could count on widespread support from within the intellectual elite. This was not because Underhill's views were always popular. Most often they were not. What was important, if the elite were to have influence, was the right to speak out without fear of reprisal. Outbursts such as those by Ontario Conservative George Drew against 'parlour pinks who preach Empire disunity from the cloistered protection of jobs which give them all too much time' were a threat to the basic principles of the intellectual community. Thus the somewhat notorious LSR founder, CCF supporter, isolationist, and continentalist received support in his fight with the university from Liberals like R.A. MacKay, Conservatives like Harold Innis, and civil servants like D.A. MacGibbon. Men like diplomat H.L. Keenleyside not only supported him but brought the matter to the attention of O.D. Skelton and Prime Minister Mackenzie King. Most important, businessmen like Maclean and Macdonnell used their positions as members of the board of governors to support the controversial historian in his conflicts with the administration and the provincial government. The ability of the elite to function and its sense of coherence as a group rested in the first instance on a common view of the importance of the university and the intellectual in Canadian life.[8]

Educational background hints at a second identifying characteristic of this elite. Most of its members belonged to the middle or upper class. Thewere a few exceptions, of course. Frank Underhill's artisan family hovered somewhere between the middle and the working classes. A later recruit, economist J.J. Deutsch, came from a poor farm family. Deutsch was the exception, however, and for every example of such impoverishment there were several examples of men with affluent backgrounds, like Claxton and Macdonnell, and those who were truly wealthy, like Vincent Massey. Education, not wealth, was the key attainment necessary to join the elite, but as few from the poorer families attended university, these individuals tended to be without any significant representation from the working class. This fact affected the intellectual network's view of reform and the state throughout its career.

Affluent exceptions notwithstanding, neither wealth nor poverty marked the background of the group. Instead, as might perhaps be expected, much of the emerging intellectual elite of the new generation was drawn from the educated of the previous one. The classroom and the parsonage had provided many of its parents with a livelihood. Thus, for example, both Norman Robertson and Hume Wrong of the Department of External Affairs had fathers who taught in university. Wrong's father was G.M. Wrong of the history department of the University of Toronto. Robertson's was Lemuel Robertson of the Classics Department at the University of British Columbia. J.M. Macdonnell's father had been solicitor for Queen's University. Lester Pearson of External and A.D.P. Heeney, who would become clerk of the Privy Council, both had fathers who were clergymen, as did Frank Scott, Eugene Forsey, and Percy Corbett, all teaching at McGill and members of the LSR. W.L. Grant, of course, had a father who was both a clergyman and an academic, as did economist B.S. Kierstead, son of W.C. Kierstead.[9]

While the influence of the university on this group is both important and straightforward, the influence of religion is ambiguous and complex. Most, though not all, members of the elite were self-consciously secular in their approach to social problems. There were exceptions, however. The left wing of the intellectual elite, such as the LSR, had a greater percentage of explicitly religious individuals than did the elite as a whole. To the degree that the social gospel remained active it did so on the left. Even there, however, the intellectual community of the 1930s tolerated and even embraced a non-religious and on occasion anti-religious tone that would have been unthinkable in Canada twenty years earlier. Frank Underhill's blunt comment when asked to speak before the YMCA that he was 'neither young nor Christian' typified the new style. 'Pete' McQueen, an Alberta-born 'son of the manse,' economist at the University of Saskatchewan, and future director of the Bank of Canada, took it to an extreme, developing an irreverent and profane style that was said to be a reaction against his strict religious upbringing.[10]

Yet the secularism and even conscious anti-religious, anti-puritanical streak that runs through the writings of men like Underhill and the others cannot completely obscure the continued importance of religion within the group. In some cases the connections are relatively direct and obvious. Carl Dawson, McGill sociologist and social work theorist, for example, had been a Baptist minister before he went to the University of Chicago. At Chicago his studies blended religion and sociology, and he obtained degrees in both areas. Vincent Bladen, University of Toronto political economist and future civil servant, had been actively involved in the Student Christian Movement while at Oxford, and as a young social worker, Charlotte Whitton made religious duty a prime theme in her evocations of the need for improved child welfare. Even where the religious ties are not explicit, however, it is reasonable to ask whether a generation that was for the most part schooled in religious duty could completely escape its upbringing. The sense of social concern and the belief that social obligations had to be met that run through the writings of the members of this generation cannot be divorced from their religious background. As Lower later reminisced, he rejected the pietistic and supernatural side of religion but remained 'a natural Protestant,' with all the moral and social implications that conveyed. Equally, D.A. MacGibbon's comment about McQueen, that 'he carried something of the moral urgency of his Presbyterian upbringing into his economic convictions,' might be applied to several intellectuals of the supposedly secular 1930s. Though the elite had to a large degree shed the rhetoric and explicit Christianity of the social gospel, it was in many ways its heir.[11]

The relation between the religiosity of the parents and the growing secularism of the children raises another crucial point. The emerging intellectual elite was given identity not only by its high level of education but also by a common generational experience. Most of those who could be considered a member of this informal network were close enough in age to be considered a single generation. There were, of course, the 'elder' statesmen. Men like O.D. Skelton, W.L. Grant, B.K. Sandwell, and Eduoard Montpetit had all been born in the 1870s and were well into their fifties by the beginning of the Depression. Their continued influence through the 1930s provided a link between the reform generation of the First World War and that of the Depression. At the same time they were the exceptions that proved the rule, for the great majority of members were younger. Indeed, much of the political activism of the decade, especially that emanating from the universities, might have been determined not just by the Depression but by occupational demographics. In the years after the First World War, university enrolment had increased dramatically, from a 1911 level of a little under 13,000 to more than 56,000 by the latter half of the 1920s. This led to a proportionate increase in staff and a relative increase in younger academics. Almost half of those listed in the 1931 census as professors and college principals were under the age of 35.[12]

Most of the elite were about 35 years old. On the older side were historians Arthur Lower of Manitoba and Frank Underhill, as well as the Queen's economist who would become deputy minister of finance in 1932, W.C. Clark. All were born in 1889. Norman Rogers, Hume Wrong, and University of Toronto economist Harold Innis were born in 1894, while the years between their birth and the turn of the century saw the arrival of Lester Pearson, Brooke Claxton, Charlotte Whitton, Pete McQueen, Vincent Bladen, Frank Scott, and, in 1900, Graham Spry; all were destined to be actively involved in state activity during the 1930s and 1940s. They had grown up in similar times and had shared a similar historical experience. Such a background helped reinforce the shared views of the crisis that Canada faced.

The most important common experience of this generation was, of course, the war. All but the youngest and the oldest had been eligible for military service, and most of those who would become the intellectual and bureaucratic leaders of the 1930s and 1940s had served overseas. Underhill, Macdonnell, Claxton, Rogers, Pearson, Grant, Lower, and Innis, to name a few, saw military action in the war. For those who did not serve there were the anxieties of the home front, of relatives or friends wounded or dead. It was for most of them disillusioning. 'We spent hours trying to get some understanding of what we were being asked to do; to bring some reason to the senseless slaughter,' remembered Pearson. 'For what? King and country? Freedom and democracy? These words sounded hollow now in 1918 and we increasingly rebelled against their hypocrisy.' The martial enthusiasm and militarism that had disturbed so many of the established intellectual and reform communities also struck many of these young men in the army. Despite all the propaganda, concluded 22-year-old Brooke Claxton in 1920, complete victory was needlessly costly. 'To have continued thesecond more than the political situation demanded of the military would be a terrible crime against humanity': 'To unnecessarily lose a single life, to waste a dollar, would be a vindication of the masses of the world's charge of the incompetency of government and staff; of profiteer prolongation of the war; of prolongation by those in high places, in all countries, naturally unwilling to retire to the comparative oblivion of civilian life; or of the strong existence of those old subterranean passages, with sliding panels and secret doors, along which the diplomats (not statesmen) of Europe used to crawl after dark.' All in all, he concluded, the war had gone on too long as it was. A reasonable peace could have been concluded in 1917. He was far from alone in his views.[13]

Also common to this generation was the fact that it matured when, as has been argued, urbanization and industrialization were issues of major concern in Canada. The Laurier years and the war-fed boom of 1915-19 had transformed the economy. They had also helped alter the university system. The rise of the social sciences to legitimacy and then, after the war, to prominence has already been noted. This meant that the generation that emerged in the 1930s was the first to have gone through an educational system in which the social sciences were prominent. For the previous generation, religious and philosophically based instruction had provided the staple of undergraduate work. Only in a few exceptional cases, as in Skelton's work under Shortt, were those who attended university before 1900 given much instruction in the social sciences. Thereafter, however, it became increasingly common, and, young though the discipline was, most of those in the intellectual community of activists in the Depression had been exposed to the social scientific approach to problem-solving as undergraduates.

Many had concentrated in the area and thus approached social problems from a perspective that made material and environmental factors more important for them than moral or metaphysical ones in assessing social needs. For better or worse, the scientific revolution of the nineteenth century had expanded beyond the physical sciences in the early twentieth, and these people were the children of philosophical and educational shift.

Combined with this change was the exposure of this generation as students to another facet of the early-twentieth-century university. As has been noted, there was a strong movement from within the academic community to assume its proper role as the leaders of society in a time of crisis. For many professors of the pre-war period, therefore, formal studies were a preparation for the assumption of leadership upon graduation. The views of men like Adam Shortt and George Munro Grant of Queen's, or of George Wrong of Toronto, as to the necessity of public service were bound to affect the views of the next generation. The influence of particular instructors may help explain the public orientation of the emerging elite of the 1930s and many who became active in that group were indeed the students of that earlier generation of progressive activists.

The intellectuals of the 1930s were thus set apart from their countrymen in two ways. First, their formal education and their connections to the world of the university made them a distinct elite within Canadian life. Second, their generational ties, including the devastating experience of the war and exposure to the shifting currents of modern education, distinguished them from the intellectual elites that preceded them. For an earlier generation the tone had been set by the clergy and philosophers; for the new one it was set by political economy.

The ties that linked the elite become all the more meaningful given the nature of Canada in the 1930s. It was a country with a small population and a minuscule university establishment. Throughout the decade the number of university and college teachers hovered somewhere between 2,500 and 3,000. Of these, less than 150 were social scientists, while the great majority, of whatever discipline, did not become actively involved in public affairs. Equally, while there were some 1,200 social workers in Canada by 1931, few possessed either the abilities or the interests to move beyond their own cases to become involved on the larger national stage.[14] Many who took the lead as the voices of social work, like Carl Dawson at McGill and Harry Cassidy of the University of British Columbia, were also academics and social scientists.[15] A social worker like Charlotte Whitton, who remained unattached to the university while assuming leadership in the field and a degree of national prominence, was so rare as to be practically unique. As a result, the number of Canadians who had experienced post-secondary education, usually beyond the undergraduate level, who were of similar age, and who had interests in social and economic policy was so small that the professional ties would almost inevitably be reinforced by personal connections. It was hard not to know each other in such a small group. The elite was bound together by a complex series of friendships, mutual acquaintances, and common experiences.

The connections began at school. Those Canadians who attended graduate school in the humanities and social sciences between 1910 and 1930 tended to select a small number of universities in the United States and England. By far the favourite places for graduate training were Chicago, Oxford, and Harvard, though the occasional Cambridge or Brookings degree was to be found. By the 1920s there were clear distinctions to be made even among the three top universities. Chicago had once been a predominant favourite of Canadian political economists. Skelton, Leacock, and Mackenzie King had all gone there. By the 1920s, however, it was less popular. Of the well-known social scientists of the 1930s, Harold Innis and Carl Dawson, who obtained their doctorates there in 1920 and 1922, were two of the few to continue the tradition. Harvard, for its part, was largely the Queen's political economy graduate school. W.A. Mackintosh, Queen's leading economist after Skelton left in 1923, had a Harvard degree. W.C. Clark, another Skelton protégé also went there, as did R. MacGregor Dawson, the Saskatchewan political scientist and expert on bureaucracy. After a delay of some years, Arthur Lower would attend the institution in the early 1930s.[16]

For most of this generation the centre of the intellectual world lay overseas at Oxford. Whether one looks at the senior civil service, the 'inner circles,' as Claxton would say, of political parties or the leaders of the social scientific disciplines within the university, Oxford dominates. Among the rising elite of External Affairs, men like Pearson and Robertson attended Oxford, as did the first Canadian minister to the United States, Vincent Massey. The LSR was established by Oxford men like Frank Underhill, F.R. Scott, and Graham Spry. The civil service of the 1930s would be staffed by Oxford men like A.D.P. Heeney, Alex Skelton, and J.W. Pickersgill. To this list one must add such figures as Norman Rogers, W.L. Grant, and J.M. Macdonnell.

The exact reasons for the dominance of Oxford graduates are somewhat obscure. Records of Oxonian life in these years surrounding the First War portray a rather dissolute society that seems a long way from the earnest Protestantism that characterized a large number of these staid colonials from Canada. For many it was an uncomfortable experience as they were brought abruptly into a society that treated them with what all too often was a mixture of disdain and indifference. Nor is it possible to explain that the social tensions were compensated for by the excellent education. In the social sciences the quality of instruction was, at best, uneven. Vincent Bladen, who attended Oxford before joining the Department of Political Economy at Toronto in 1921, recounted a warning he received from his tutor. 'I remember well him telling me that I must read Marshall's *Principles* and not just Mill's; but I should remember that the examiners might not have read Marshall so that I must be careful in criticizing Mill. What a sad light this throws on the state of economics at Oxford.' While many Oxford colleges had good tutors and professors, there is little doubt, if one judges by the staff available in the 1910s and 1920s, that the social sciences at either Harvard or Cambridge were better than at Oxford.[17]

Two factors do help account for the tendency of this generation to flock to Oxford. The first was an imperial mystique that lured to the centre of Empire those who sought to be the intellectual leaders of the Dominion. This argument is difficult to document, but it is hard to discount. For many it was not so much the education they received, but the exposure to a particular culture and way of thought that counted. Graham Spry, for example, steeped himself without reservation in the new community, participating in the famous debating clubs, joining the rowing team, and investigating the heady political discussions that circulated through this university of the English elite. The result was that for Spry, Oxford was everything it was supposed to be. As he wrote to classmate Arnold Heeney in 1923, 'There is not a world like the Oxford world. It is the clearing house of intelligence, the whole knowledge of man is concentrated, invisible, but ever present to the view.'[18]

The second factor was less romantic. There were more financial resources available for those Canadians who wished to attend Oxford than there were for other universities. In particular, the Rhodes scholarship provided the means whereby much of the intellectual elite of the 1930s could attend graduate school. A.D.P. Heeney, Norman Robertson, F.R. Scott, Eugene Forsey, and Graham Spry were all Rhodes scholars, as was a young Saskatchewan lawyer named J.A. Corry. The very possession of a Rhodes scholarship tended to facilitate acceptance by others in this able and ambitious group. Scholarships from the Masseys, the Flavelles, and the Imperial Order Daughters of the Empire (IODE) also provided access to the centre of graduate training.[19]

The concentration by Canadians on a small number of graduate schools, especially Oxford, had three effects on the elite that later formed. First, many of its attitudes and enthusiasms can be traced back to university days. Ambitions and ideals first discussed in an Oxford common room remained a thread linking a generation of scholars who had been in a similar educational environment. In some instances these experiences were directly shared. The Canadians at Oxford often congregated together, bound by their status as colonials at the centre of the Empire. The result was a series of acquaintances and friendships that would become important over the next years. Thus, for example, businessman-reformer E.J. Tarr was a friend of Graham Spry's at the University of Manitoba and would renew his friendship when the latter returned from Oxford. Norman Robertson, Spry, Arnold Heeney, and others who would be important political voices a decade later all knew each other at Oxford. So, too, did Hume Wrong, Vincent Massey, and Frank Underhill, as, a little later, did two future mandarins, Alex Skelton and J.W. Pickersgill. Even for those who were not personally acquainted from their university days, overlapping circles of friends facilitated the creation of a distinctive elite.[20]

Second, the universities provided important contacts that allowed these intelligent and able Canadians to move in new circles. Domestically, the mixing of the scholarly middle class with the sons of affluent Canadians gave increased access to power and funds in future years. For all the discomfort that the class-consciousness of Oxford or, to a lesser degree, Harvard created among some of these middle-class Canadians, they gained an entry into the world of the wealthy that otherwise would have been more difficult. The new circles that developed also meant strong international contacts. As the Canadians finished their education and returned to take up teaching positions, civil service careers, or political causes, so too did theirEnglish and American counterparts. The result was an increasingly well-developed international network in universities and government that both prevented parochialism and allowed international exchanges of ideas and policies.

The well-known international contacts were also a reinforcement to the prestige and self-image of this small group of intellectuals that was still trying to assert the value of its ideas at home. It was heady stuff to be invited, as was then associate professor Harold Innis, to dine in 1933 with the famous Keynes.[21] Yet indications of familiarity with some of the Western world's top social scientists appear routinely throughout the decade. It was a testimony to the genuine abilities of this group that it was integrated not only into a national but into an international elite of scholars and policy-makers. A certain transatlantic flavour thus pervaded the elite and separated it still further from the average Canadian.

The tight social and educational ties that developed also shaped the forming elite in two other, negative, ways. It was, even more than its progressive predecessor, overwhelmingly anglophone and male. For the relative absence of both francophones and women, the primary cause would appear to educational. French-Canadian intellectuals did not attend either the same undergraduate or graduate institutions as their anglophone counterparts. The personal connections thus simply did not exist. Nor were these earlier differences overcome in later careers. The reason for this might include different orientation within the Quebec university system, different social views, and a focus on Quebec issues among francophones. Any definitive answer must await further study of the Quebec university community in these years. What is clear, however, is the surprising absence of ties among professionals. There is practically no personal or professional correspondence between English-Canadian reformers and francophones in the 1930s. The Canadian Political Science Association was overwhelmingly anglophone in membership, and those few francophones who were active were either of an earlier generation, as in the case of Montpetit, or were politicians rather than academics.[22] This separation of French and English Canada into the traditional 'two solitudes' was to have disturbing implications as the elite achieved greater influence over the civil service and policy formation in the future.

The emphasis on education, both as a formal part of the expertise of the new elite and as a basis for professional and personal contact, also meant that few women were active within the community. There were, it was true, more women going to university in the 1920s than ever before. In proportionate terms, however, the universities remained overwhelmingly male, and the social sciences even more so. Indeed, one of the concerns with the development of commerce courses was that such social science areas were luring men away from the humanities and thus leaving them to women. Even so, 61 per cent of arts graduates in 1921 were male.[23] Thus relatively few women attended university, fewer still focused on the social sciences, and only the rare exception went on to graduate studies in these areas. Social discrimination and custom thus left women without the qualifications to join the forming elite.

Education, however, does not provide the whole answer to the absence of women within the emerging reform elite. An additional complication comes in the relation between the older and newer eras of reform. The older generation, with its strongly ameliorative and spiritual overtones, had a considerable female presence. General reform causes mingled with the social gospel and with the particular concerns of maternal feminism in a way that reflected the eclectic nature of pre-war reformism.[24] As with other areas of reform, however, the women's movement was weakened in the fragmentation that took place after the First World War. The older exponents of reform had difficulty translating the great causes of prohibition, which had proven delusive as a cure for social ills, and suffrage, which was accomplished by 1918, to a new generation. In Canada, as in the United States, 'young middle class women appeared to have little interest in organized feminism.'[25] Moreover, the 'scientific professionalism' and secularism that characterized the new generation of male reformers made them suspicious of an earlier women's movement that was associated with moral righteousness and even Victorian priggishness.

Of course, women would continue to have an impact on reform, as their presence within various farm movements indicates. They would also continue to press their concerns with female equality, as the famous 'Persons Case' showed. Nevertheless, one of the factors that distinguished post-war reform from its earlier counterpart was the absence of a powerful women's reform movement operating in tandem with male reformers in the effort to change society. To the degree that a women's movement continued, it remained distinct. The women who became a part of the emerging intellectual community, such as political economist Irene Biss or social worker Charlotte Whitton, did so as individuals and not as representatives of women. They were also the exception within a group that was not only predominantly middle class and anglophone, but male.

The basis for a cohesive elite that began at the university level continued in the various scholarly and public associations that these individuals joined after returning to Canada. In particular, two types of associations were important. The first type comprised those associations oriented toward the academic world and defined by professional expertise. The Canadian Historical Association provided common meeting places for those interested in scholarly debate and specialized study. Moreover, the relative newness of the social sciences in Canadian universities and the lack of definition within the disciplines meant that the barriers separating them were less formidable than they would later become. As each developed its own argot and as quantification and specialization within disciplines became more common, it would be increasingly difficult for historians to speak to political scientists and political scientists to speak to economists on specialized topics. This was not the case in the 1920s and early 1930s. Journals and associations tended to have broad representation from all those involved in the study of what might best be described as political economy in its broadest sense. Thus, for example, through the 1920s the *Canadian Historical Review* included men like W.L. Grant and R.M. MacIver on its editorial board.

The professional associations also acted to link the academic practitioner and the broader public, or at least that segment interested in current issues. This was especially true of the Canadian Political Science Association, which had strong representation from the university, the civil service, and interested businessmen. It was typical of the association that D.A. MacGibbon, the man credited with its revival in 1929, combined impeccable professional qualifications, a PhD from Chicago, and a teaching post at Alberta with a strong orientation toward public service. In 1931 he left the university to become chairman of the Board of Grain Commissioners. With Adam Shortt and O.D. Skelton as the first two presidents of the new association, the civil service obviously was seen as a vital part of the Canadian intellectual elite. Indeed, membership figures from the early 1930s indicate that the civil service was vital to the success of the organization. More than 40 per cent of the personal memberships of this national organization came from Ottawa residents. Moreover, businessmen like J.S. McLean and bankers like C.E. Neil served on the executive in the early years. The membership of the association and its stated objective, the 'encouragement of the investigation and study of Political, Economic and Social Problems,' made it possible to attract those interested in political economy, whether from inside or outside the university.[26]

The professional associations of the 1920s and 1930s thus performed a dual role. On the one hand, their existence as well as the scholarly effort they encouraged were a vital component in the assertion by social scientists of professional expertise. These associations provided a common meeting place for academics and a publishing outlet for their papers. The formation of the *Canadian Journal of Economics and Political Science (CJEPS)* in 1935 marked the new possibilities for social science publication that had developed since the First World War. There was also a fair degree of prestige associated with these professional organizations. Meetings of the professional associations received newspaper coverage, and when the CPSA met in Ottawin 1931 it was even asked to have lunch with Prime Minister R.B. Bennett.[27]

On the other hand, these associations, especially the CPSA, were more than scholarly organizations in these years. They were, to a degree, vehicles of the forming elite, and their meetings and discussions had to have a degree of immediate interest to the general public. Scholarly concerns mixed with policy matters in sessions on unemployment and other relevant matters. Thus the 1931 session included papers by McGill professor Leon Marsh, 'The mobility of Labour in Relation to Unemployment,' Bryce Stewart, 'Some Aspects of Unemployment Insurance,' and O.D. Skelton, 'Is Our Economic System Bankrupt?' Where relevance seemed to have been forgotten there were protests. When a session was proposed on the gerrymander of 1882, Frank Scott wrote to protest that 'in these days when vitally important problems are crying out for analysis' such topics should be left off the program. Through the early years of the Depression, however, those concerned with relevance had little to complain about. The CPSA was, if anything, in danger of ignoring theory for application and setting aside issues of scholarly interest for those with policy implications. At the same time this concern for relevance did allow the association to broaden its base of members to include all those intellectuals concerned with public policy. Adam Shortt's 1913 vision of a coterie of interested experts, meeting to discuss social issues and to influence events through rational analysis and public debate, was much closer to reality in 1930 than it had been on the eve of the First World War.[28]

Also important after the war was a new journal that, while not a professional organ, was certainly intellectual. In 1917 a group of University of Toronto students founded a magazine of reformist thought entitled *The Rebel*. Before long it became a journal for the thoughts not only of students but also of such key figures as R.M. MacIver and G.S. Brett. By 1920 the small publication had matured to the degree that it was restructured as the *Canadian Forum*, specifically to present the public with the intelligent opinions of the educated on topics of relevance. With men like Gilbert Jackson, H. King Gordon, and H.R.

Kemp on the editorial board in its first years and with people like MacIver, Mavor, Kemp, and other social scientists prominent in its first issues, it was from the beginning a focus and an outlet for the intellectual community that attempted to bridge the gap between the truly academic journal and the public issues that were increasingly a matter of concern. With its 'liberal-reformist and secularist account of civil society' it was supported primarily by intellectuals concerned with reform and remained a crucial link in the intellectual network throughout the inter-war period.[29]

The professional associations and journals were not the only vehicle for the publicly oriented intellectuals of the post-war period. The 1920s were an era of clubs and associations. Whether because of the anonymity of urbanization, the traditions of camaraderie established in the services, the decline of traditional focal points like the church, or simply greater affluence and a growing middle class, the generation of the 1920s was made up of joiners. From the Canadian Legion and Navy League through the Boy Scouts and Canadian Prisoner Welfare Committee to service clubs like the Rotary and Kinsmen and societies like the Masons, Oddfellows, and IODE, groups thrived in these years. As Brooke Claxton later noted, it was an age of enthusiasm. 'Every kind of organization, national and local, cultural and religious, political and commercial was at a peak of activity hardly equalled since.' Claxton should have known, for he was one of the most enthusiastic of all in his involvement in public activities. 'I have a meeting of the Executive of the League of Nations society,' he wrote to a friend on one occasion, 'and a speech on Ethiopia to the Montreal branch tomorrow, a speech on Monday to the Young Men's Canadian Club, on Tuesday to the St. Lambert High School, on Wedensday to the YMCA, on Thursday to the Faculty of Law, on Friday two speeches to the Baron Byng High School which will have to be put off to some other day as I will have to go to Ottawa, on Sunday a speech to the Emmanuel Church, on Monday a speech to a mass meeting here, on Tuesday a speech to the Temple Emmanuel, on Wednesday a speech to the Canadian Club of Shawinigan Falls.'[30]

As Claxton's own activities indicate, the intellectual community was not immune from the enthusiasm for public activities and associations. For it, however, the boosterism of the local chambers of commerce and the philanthropic activities and middle-class virtues of the Rotary Clubs had little appeal. As intellectuals they tended to denigrate such fund-raising and business support as aimed merely at the physical side of Canadian life. Theirs was the intellectual and educational. It is the difference, wrote Graham Spry, 'between the concrete that may be seen and touched and reproduced by the camera in a newspaper, and the unseen, immeasurable educational work that is done in a school house.'[31] In the 1920s that educational work focused on two related themes, both connected to the wartime experience of this generation.

The first theme involved international relations. In 1914 Canadians had been largely uninformed and uninterested in events beyond the Empire. That had not prevented them becoming involved in four years of war. The generation that had fought in that war wanted to ensure that whatever happened in the future, Canadians would be able to see it coming and deal with it intelligently. For some this implied an isolationist position, to ensure that the war was not repeated. For others the same concern led to support of the League of Nations as the only body able to prevent war in the future. Whatever the exact position taken, there was a consistent concern with events in the outside world. The result was the formation of bodies like the Canadian Institute of International Affairs (CIIA) and the League of Nations Society.[32] The same men who traced their education to similar schools and whose paths crossed at scholarly meetings found themselves involved in these organizations. The web of connections was thus drawn that much closer.

The second and related concern was with Canadian nationalism. Indeed, the writings of the 1920s give indications that until the economic crisis of the Depression altered the focus, nationalism was more important to many of these young intellectuals than was state planning or social reform. The nationalism had two aspects. The first, especially important in the years immediately after the war, was concerned with constitutional relations within the Empire-Commonwealth. Memories of the entanglement in the war and left-over problems of imperial centralization versus Dominion autonomy shaped attitudes and meant that the efforts of King and Skelton to achieve greater autonomy were generally popular. Also present, however, and assuming greater importance as the threat of imperial centralization diminished, was a concern with the state of Canadian nationalism at home. The war, for all its horrors, left a legacy of Canadian self-awareness that contributed to an outpouring of Canadian 'national' literature, painting, and culture generally. Another result of the war, the rift between French and English Canada, prompted concerns for the state of relations between Canada's two main language groups, while in the west the question of immigration and assimilation remained topical. The intellectual elite first took definite form around questions of nationalism.[33]

The clearest example of this came in the activities of the revived Canadian Club network in the years immediately preceding the depression. The Canadian Clubs had begun in the late nineteenth century and had quickly become a forum for fairly high-quality addresses on matters of topical concern. More reformist than the Empire Club, the Canadian Clubs had attracted over the years several members of the progressive movement. In the active Toronto branch, for example, individuals like Newton Rowell, J.S. Willison, Frank Beer, H.P. Plumptre, and W.L. Grant had held positions or been regular participants in the years surrounding the First World War. By the 1920s, however, the Canadian Club network was in decline. For a younger generation of intellectuals, concerned with promoting discussion on issues of importance and in creating a national identity, the collapse of such an institutution was not to be allowed. Before long steps were taken to bring the association back to life.[34]

Though efforts at revival began in 1924, real improvement in the national association came in 1926 with the appointment of 26-year-old Graham Spry as secretary. Spry's energy and the executive's commitment to the national association created an upsurge in membership, the revival of near-defunct branches, and, in 1928, the establishment of a magazine, *The Canadian Nation*. The revival was such that before long the new journal could publish with pride the comment of *Maclean's Magazine* that the Canadian Clubs were 'the greatest intellectual force in Canada, today, next to the Universities.'[35]

The activities of the clubs are beyond the scope of this study. Two points are important, however, in understanding the nature of the developing intellectual elite. First, the objectives of the national association as it developed in the late 1920s reflected a belief in the crucial role of public opinion in a democracy. Drawing on the writings of Walter Lippman and Norman Angell, Spry and others felt a tension between the obvious importance of an informed public in a democracy and the actual low quality of public awareness. 'The fact is that the methods of forming public opinion are inadequately public, and too adequately propagandist,' he wrote in 1929. 'When adequate information is available and sound and disinterested, it is too adequate in quantity and too deficient in clarity, ease of understanding, and has too high a point of solution for the average man.' Only with intelligent leadership disinterestedly bringing issues before the public in an understandable manner would the masses be able to deal with the complex issues of the modern age. That understanding was essential to the functioning of modern democracy. The purpose of the intellectual elite thus became all the more important in the age of the common man. It had to bring sound information to the public and thus prevent the crude propaganda of the salesman, politician, or vested interest group from working unchecked. 'That is our work,' said Spry, 'the creation of an intelligent public opinion': 'The problem of public opinion, indeed, is the problem of democracy and our work has led us to see that problem in four aspects. We would state it thus: first the need of public opinion is accurate information impartially collected; second, the issuing of that information in a form which is clear to the busy man on the street, the busy woman in the home; third, the guarantee by an impartial authority that this information has been scientifically collected and, fourth, the dissemination of that information in a popular form through channels that already exist.' The Canadian Clubs were conceived as much more than a debating society for the already informed. Rather, their purpose reflected the intellectual elite's belief in its own leadership qualities and in the necessity of expert guidance in a modern democracy. The facts, if properly analysed and properly interpreted, would point toward the proper policies and attitudes.[36]

The second point of relevance is the way in which the activities of the Canadian Clubs helped broaden and define the developing network of intellectuals. For people like Spry and Claxton, membership brought them into contact with numerous individuals of similar age, education, and outlook. Moreover, the Canadian Clubs reinforced the personal contacts that already existed within this group of intellectuals. Thus, for example, Monarch Life president Edgar J. Tarr of Winnipeg was an important figure in the revival of the national association, serving as president in 1926. He was also a leading figure behind the CIIA and, when not president of the National Association of Canadian Clubs, led the Winnipeg branch. In Montreal, Brooke Claxton and Frank Scott played important roles in the activities of that branch of the Canadian Club. Their work brought them into contact with Tarr and Spry. In addition, J.M. Macdonnell, closely tied with both Queen's and Toronto, served as president of the Montreal Canadian Club and head of the national association in the late 1920s. S.J. Maclean was vice-chairman of the executive committee the year Macdonnell was president. The association thus attracted those men with the education and interest to devote time and energy to such an enthusiasm. It is not surprising, perhaps, that they tended to be the same men who showed up in other causes in the late 1920s. One group of associations facilitated others. Common causes provided friendships and contacts that might be relied upon in the future.[37]

A brief notation in the *Canadian Nation* of April 1929 pointed to one way in which the network of Canadian Clubs would provide a basis for further consolidation of the elite. Noting the work of the Royal Commission on Broadcasting in Canada, the journal maintained that it 'needs the support of a public opinion that appreciates the issues and makes itself felt.[38] The issue that would transform the general educative function practised by the Canadian Clubs into a more tightly knit, single-cause-oriented lobby had appeared. It was in the work of the soon-to-be-formed Canadian Radio League that the true abilities and the rising influence of the emerging intellectual elite began to be apparent.

The Canadian Radio League was a direct response on the part of this generation of nationalist reformers to the Royal Commission on Radio Broadcasting, or the Aird Commission, which Mackenzie King had appointed in 1928. The commission had been set up to investigate various technical and policy problems emanating from the rapid development of radio broadcasting in the 1920s. In particular, the receivers of the day permitted only so many channels if a clear, interference-free signal was to be made available. Moreover, Canada was under extra pressure because of the large number of American channels that flooded over the border. The regulation of the scarce commodity of radio frequencies and Canadian nationalism were thus both crucial issues before the commission. By the fall of 1929 it had reported, arguing in favour of direct government participation in radio broadcasting as a means of providing high-quality programming and assuring a Canadian presence in radio.[39]

Such proposals were bound to commend themselves to men like Spry. What was better suited to the nationalist intellectual than a series of recommendations that supported Canadian nationalism and that, because of the association of American broadcasting with crass commercialism, seemed to support the concept of intellectual leadership? There was opposition, however. Not surprisingly, private radio broadcasters lobbied to prevent such government intrusion into the marketplace. Vested interest was the determining factor in these cases. Also important, however, was opposition derived at least in part from principle. To the *Financial Post*, for example, the proposals looked like a step towards socialism. 'If we insist on the government entertaining us, we may get into the frame of mind when we shall look to it for bread as well.'[40] Edward Beatty of the Canadian Pacific Railway (CPR) also came out against the system, on grounds of both corporate interest – the CPR was thinking of establishing radio stations – and principle.

As the opposition lobby mounted, Mackenzie King did nothing. Then, just as it appeared that Parliament was going to take up the question, the 1930 election intervened. King's government was replaced by that of R.B. Bennett. There was nothing to indicate that Bennett was opposed to the recommendations of the Aird Commission, but for those who favoured a publicly owned radio network it was not comforting to think that Bennett had been a solicitor for the CPR. At the very least, men like Beatty seemed to have an inside track in convincing the new prime minister on the radio question. It was for this reason that the Canadian Radio League was formed in the fall of 1930.

The activities of the League have been well documented elsewhere. It is sufficient to note here that a well-organized publicity campaign led eventually, and after a good many battles, to the passage of the Canadian Radio Broadcasting Act of 1932 and, after more struggle, to the development of what was to evolve into the modern Canadian Broadcasting Corporation. As with the Canadian Clubs, what is interesting is the personnel involved. At the centre were two men already active in other causes and associations. Alan Plaunt and Graham Spry were both Oxford-educated nationalists with the enthusiasm and the funds (Plaunt's) to take up the challenge of Spry's own editorial in the Nation 18 months earlier. Before long they had put together a well-organized lobby that, as Spry later put it, had 'affinities with Machiavelli as well as with Sir Galahad.'[41]

The mood of nationalism and the web of connections within the intellectual community were already well enough established that the League found widespread support almost from the beginning. Especially important were two sets of connections. The first was with key figures in the newspaper world. Throughout these years there were always a few journalists who, through inclination and ability, became involved with the intellectual community in its pursuit of reform causes. In the First War, Joseph Atkinson of the Toronto Star was, as already indicated, a participant in King's plans for social reform. Future years would see close ties between the parliamentary reporter of the Winnipeg Free Press, Grant Dexter, and the civil service mandarins. In the case of the Radio League, Plaunt got editorial and financial support from powerful editors like Atkinson and J.W. Dafoe of the Free Press.

The second set of connections was that with men of influence within the Conservative party. In particular, Spry and Plaunt recruited R.K. Finlayson, Winnipeg lawyer, Canadian Club supporter, and later Bennett's secretary. Also in regular contact with the League was W.D. Herridge, a speech writer for Bennett, who received his reward with the ambassadorship of Washington.[42]

The importance of previous contact was shown in the way that Spry and Plaunt could call upon individuals who, at least initially, did not find the cause all that compelling. Friendships as much as the cause of Canadian radio broadcasting helped make the League as successful as it was. Thus when Spry was forming the League, he naturally looked to colleagues within the Canadian Club for a nucleus of advisers and supporters. The previous summer, for example, Claxton and Spry had served together on the publications committee of the National Association of Canadian Clubs. The committee had also included figures like Lester Pearson, while Jim Macdonnell was president of the association and involved in the meetings.[43] It was not surprising, therefore, that Spry wrote Claxton to ask his support.

The reply was less than encouraging. 'I received your manifesto about radio,' Claxton wrote. 'As you know I have no radio and have never listened to radio if I could possibly avoid it. I am really keen to have the programmes given to the Canadian people made as bad as possible in order that the radio may pass out.' Only in a jocular concluding remark was there any indication of sympathy for Spry's new endeavour. 'For this reason alone I am in favour of government control.' It was good enough for Spry and the Canadian Radio League. Claxton was immediately put on the executive committee! It was not until several weeks later, with reports of an executive committee meeting circulating, that Claxton found this out. At that point, however, Spry won. Having apparently been present at the meeting and having voted for resolutions he had never seen, Claxton decided he might as well join in fact as in name. From that point he undertook the task with the same energy he had shown in Canadian Club work, writing copious letters in favour of the League's position and acting as its legal counsel in the jurisdictional fight that developed between the Dominion and the provinces over radio broadcasting.[44]

The formation of the Canadian Radio League and the recruitment of members and supporters serve as an early example of the way in which the loose network of intellectuals that had developed in the years since the First World War could come together to push for a cause. It was, in fact, an initial example of the sort of activity that would become common during the Depression. By the end of the 1920s Canada had a number of individuals who were members of the well-educated minority, strongly nationalist for the most part, willing to use government intervention in social or economic matters to achieve needed changes, and personally connected by a complex web of friend-ships, professional ties, similar backgrounds, and mutual causes. All were vitally interested in public issues. Some, as with Massey and Macdonnell, were well off. Most were well enough established as ac-ademics or lawyers to have at least the necessary contacts with the powerful and wealthy. Most, if not all, had strong ties to the university community in Canada and because of their own academic background, the age in which they lived, and their own approach to issues tended to employ social scientific methods as a tool for problem-solving. This was Brooke Claxton's 'group,' or the 40 to 100 men and women men-tioned by Graham Spry.

It would be a mistake, however, to see this group as a homogeneous club of crusaders seeking a fixed goal with unanimity. They did not always agree on all things – far from it – nor was the membership of this elite completely stable. It was really a pool of available talent operating under certain assumptions and values derived from a com-mon generational and similar educational experience. Within the gen-eral elite, however, there were continual formings and reformings of elements into structured bodies to promote various causes. In some cases, as with the Radio League, the cause might be specific, and the body formed would disappear once its purpose was accomplished. In other cases, as with the Canadian Political Science Association, the purpose might be professional and the institution ongoing. Finally, in the case of the emerging mandarinate of the civil service, the structure might be given by the occupational pursuit of individuals. Their sep-aration from others in that occupation and their inclusion in the elite would depend on the characteristics and outlook of the individuals. In all cases, however, they remain tied by a network of connections and attitudes to other elements of the activist intellectual community in Canada. As such they remain distinguishable from other Canadians both to themselves and, as their activities assumed greater significance, to the public as well.

In the end, ideas as much as connections and institutions bound the elite. Though there were often lively disagreements between members of the elite, there was a general commitment to two underlying principles. The first was to the ultimate rationality of decision-making. Members believed in intellectual discussion, investigation, and debate and held themselves superior to those who employed emotions and demagoguery to appeal to the public. Underlying this approach was an assumption that also ran through the formation of the social sciences in Canada. Proper investigation and intelligent analysis, many still presumed, led inevitably to agreement. It was a view that created certain contradictions. On the one hand, it encouraged widespread investigation and debate as members of the intellectual community sought to understand modern problems. The years of the Depression saw lively and often heated exchanges on the economy and society. On the other hand, if and when the elite began to assume a common position on an issue, it could be intolerant of those who dissented. Such dissent, they tended to presume, could come only from ulterior motivation, intellectual laziness, or sheer stupidity. Once this was concluded to be the case, the intellectual debate could quickly turn to scorn and belittlement.

Also tying the elite together was the growing orientation towards the governmental process. As the 1930s went on, this generation of intellectuals and reformers extended the tendency begun by their forbears. They were less interested than their predecessors of the First War in voluntarist organizations and more in lobbies to pressure government, less in philanthropy and more in politics, hardly at all in a career in the church but very much in one in the civil service. Indeed, their greatest effort in the first part of the decade was directed at finding some vehicle within government, either in the bureaucracy or in some political party, to allow them to develop their views on the social crisis of the age into concrete policies for, as they saw it, the improvement of Canada.

7

Moving into the inner councils
1930-5

From the First World War on, various groupings of middle-class urban reformers, increasingly anchored in the universities, had sought influence over government policy in order to promote reform. Yet when Brooke Claxton commented in 1935 on the existence of an elite group within the 'inner councils' of the national political parties, it marked a significant and recent shift in the relation between the intellectual and the state. Of course there had been connections in other generations between reform intellectuals and politicians. It was in the early 1930s, however, that direct involvement in the political process by the intellectual community began to take place. Men like Norman Rogers, Brooke Claxton, and Graham Spry would run for political office, while Frank Underhill, Frank Scott, and R.K. Finlayson would become involved in the drafting of party policy. Many others would see themselves consulted by politicians as never before.

Forcing the changes were the circumstances of the early 1930s. Nationalist issues were joined and eventually dominated by the problems of the Depression. The elite saw the reform of economic and social policies as imperative if order were to be brought into a chaotic world. Outmoded means of policy formation had to be abandoned and a systematic approach to planning accepted. If this were to take place, men awake to the necessary changes had to become involved in the political process. The intellectual reformers thus renewed the efforts of their predecessors to gain increased influence over the governmental system. They were remarkably successful, and by 1935 Claxton's comment about their presence within the 'inner circles' was no exaggeration. The intellectual and governmental spheres of activity had become connected as never before. This is not to say that these years brought about the rise of systematic planning of government policy. That would come later. Rather, the first half of the 1930s was marked by an expansion of the political activities of the elite in an effort to gain acceptance for such systems. As O.D. Skelton put it at the end of the decade, it was a heyday not of plans but 'of plans for planning.'[1]

The growing influence of the intellectual reform movement is more readily understood if the slide into the worst depression in Canadian history, which began in 1929, is viewed not only as an economic crisis of the first magnitude but also as a psychological one. The Canadian government under the leadership of Mackenzie King seemed unable or unwilling to comprehend what was happening to the nation. R.B. Bennett rode Liberal obliviousness to power, but the rhetoric of action that marked his campaign proved impotent against the downward spiral that gripped the Western world. The traditional political parties had failed, and, not surprisingly, new parties would spring forth in the next few troubled years. Perhaps even more devastating psychologically – at least for the middle class – was the patent failure of the 'capitalist entrepreneur' to find adequate responses to the crisis. The businessman's reputation thus suffered as it became apparent that the clichés of individual initiative and entrepreneurial talent could not provide the answer to depression. As W.L. Grant wrote in 1931, 'the pre-war combination of individualistic capitalism and Protestant Christianity has been largely debunked ... Now, the theory of life which satisfied the ordinary middle class man in Canada up to 1914, has largely lost its halo, and this will be very difficult to restore.' Through the years from 1929 to the bottom of the Depression in 1932 or 1933, too many false starts and a great deal of unfounded optimism caused public disenchantment with the traditional guardians of Canadian material well-being.[2]

Such disenchantment provided an obvious opportunity for various reform groups to assert their influence over the process of government. The emerging intellectual elite of these years rested its claims on traditions of urban progressivism that stretched back to the turn of the century. Indeed, at the end of the First World War it had appeared as if that group of reformers, in partnership with agrarian reform, were about to assert its power in the political arena. As many have since noted, however, the great hopes for reform that existed in 1919 had died. As Frank Underhill remarked in 1930, there was a belief in the 'new Era' back then. 'How strangely remote this enthusiasm seems today.' The intellectual had neither formed the close alliance with the progressive farmer that was necessary nor penetrated the traditional political parties. The short-lived Canada First movement of the 1870s, Underhill concluded, remained the only instance in Canadian history when those who considered themselves intellectuals proved a force in Canadian politics. As the 1920s went on, Mackenzie King's deficit-pruning made it apparent that his government did not want traditional patterns shattered by the presence of new theories or ideals. As Graham Spry remarked sarcastically in 1927, the Liberals were 'no more Liberal than the Czar of Russia.' With the Depression, however, new ideas were patently necessary, and the intellectual community had in place a series of connections that enabled it both to tender advice and to challenge the traditional methods of policy formation. The fact that these individuals had little influence in national politics freed them from at least some of the criticism and loss of reputation suffered by businessmen and politicians after 1930.[3]

For years a segment of the intellectual community had preached jeremiads against the flaws in modern civilization. Now, as with flood or famine in earlier times, the prophets of doom gained prominence. Here was the proof that the system built by the businessman and the old party politician was defective. The men who had presided over the construction of a complex modern civilization apparently did not know how to keep it running smoothly. 'We have urbanized our population without planning for the continuance of such urbanization. We have universalized, and even glorified the profit, motive without planning to ensure the continuance of markets. And we have failed egregiously to control the machine.'[4]

The situation was made more critical because the stability of Western democracy seemed tied to the success of industrialism. With the collapse of the economy the foundations of the political system appeared increasingly fragile. In Europe increasingly polarized political communities raised fears that the fascism of Italy and the rising Nazism of Germany would continue to spread. As sociology student S.D. Clark reported, even the home of the mother of parliaments, the United Kingdom, seemed under increasing pressure as socialism moved left-ward and conservatism to the right. Nor could one presume that this contagion was simply another manifestation of the European vortex. Hearing of the attempted assassination of President Roosevelt in 1933, Frank Scott predicted that such violence would become more common as desperate men pursued desperate solutions. Even Mackenzie King, his sense of the crisis sharpened by electoral defeat, worried that 'the old capitalistic system is certain to give way to something more along communist lines.'[5]

For most of the intellectual community, however, the danger was not from the left but from the right and due not to pressure from below but demagoguery from above. Various politicians and political groups, including William Aberhart, Mitchell Hepburn, and Maurice Duplessis, were singled out as leaders of near-fascist movements in Canada. Whatever the specific malaise pointed to, however, there was a widespread belief that, as O.D. Skelton argued, the coming years 'will be the testing time for parliamentary institutions in this country and elsewhere.' The ability to end the Depression, or at least to make it endurable, thus involved much more than the happiness of the unemployed and their families. The question was whether democracy could adapt itself to modern circumstances sufficiently to control the industrial machine. 'The political task of our generation,' wrote social democrat J. King Gordon, 'is that of preventing the rise of the totalitarian state in the remaining democratic countries of the world.'[6]

In the search for a solution there were several traditional themes that appeared in the analysis of the situation. The complexity of the modern era, the high degree of urbanization and industrialization, and the decline of local economies in favour of national and international interdependence were all pointed to in the early 1930s, as they had been over the previous decades, to argue that greater government planning and state intervention were necessary. Private philanthropy and untrammelled free enterprise were no longer sufficient.[7] The state, as one writer argued, could 'no longer simply remain an arbitrator between man and man, against anarchy, and allowing the individual members of that society to work out their economic destiny unhindered within these limits.' For as the society and the economy became more complex, the politician became increasingly unable to deal with the problem.[8] To move from these long-standing generalizations to the specific role the intellectual should assume in politics was a more difficult matter. Within the community a heated debate soon developed as to the proper function of the academic. For the social scientists involved, with their discipline's conscious assertion of kinship with the sciences, such values as detachment and objectivity were deeply ingrained. Challenging this notion, however, was the personal commitment of many to the use of their knowledge and position to assert influence over public policy. The paradox that developed was thus

argued in terms of commitment versus detachment. On the one hand
the scientific tradition stressed objectivity and impartiality in the pursuit of truth, while on the other hand the progressive intellectual tradition and the problems of the modern world both seemed to call for
a commitment to social goals and policy choices.

The principles involved were often muddied by overlapping positions, contradictions, and shifting arguments. In spite of this, there did
develop a fairly well defined spectrum of opinion by the middle of
theend were those advocates of both public and partisan involvement
in the issues of the day. These committed advocates of reform were
the ones D.A. MacGibbon termed the 'hot gospellers,' those who felt
that detachment was ultimately an illusion behind which a reactionary
status quo could disarm the intellectual community. The best known
of this group was historian Frank Underhill. A man with an acerbic
pen and an iconoclastic temperament, Underhill had long chided both
his fellow intellectuals and the Canadian public for their complacency.
By 1931 his criticism had begun to shift towards a call for action.
Looking to the success of British intellectuals in developing a committed forum for discussions on social democracy, he called for a 'Canadian Fabian society' to bring social issues before the public in an
intelligent and rational manner.[9]

Underhill's summons bore fruit the next year when he and Frank
Scott of McGill joined with Eugene Forsey, Harry Cassidy, Graham
Spry, and Toronto economist Irene Biss in the League for Social Reconstruction (LSR). Designed to provide an analysis of current problems
from a social democratic viewpoint, the League reflected Underhill's
belief in political commitment as a necessary part of the academic's
role. It was a view that attracted many of the most active members of
the intellectual network of the 1920s. The nature of intellectual reformism in the Depression can only be fully understood, however, if it is
recognized that the LSR was but the best-known focus for those who
believed in commitment. Its founders had hoped that the body might
become an umbrella organization for Canadian intellectuals interested
in reform. In this sense it was fulfilling the call made by McGill historian (and brother-in-law of Brooke Claxton) Terry MacDermott, who
had called for 'radical thinking in Canada,' whether of the socialist,
liberal, or conservative variety, for 'lest we be misunderstood, it may
be said that even Conservatism has its radicalism.' His involvement in
the early stages of the League's activities testified to his own commitment to such an ideal. Given this view of its purpose, the founders of

the League approached not only MacDermott but men like Brooke Claxton, Harold Innis, and even a man as visibly tied to the Liberal party as Norman Rogers. 'Perhaps you see more hope in the Liberal party than I do,' Underhill wrote Rogers in early 1932, 'but there is no reason why we shouldn't work to supply them with ideas.'[10]

Yet there was a contradiction in the purposes of the League. At the same time that it sought to be all inclusive, men like Underhill were moving it towards affiliation with the emerging social-democratic CCF. By January 1933, the enthusiasm for the new party and the access to policy formation that alliance seemed to provide overcame the reservations of men like Scott. By a narrow majority the League voted for formal alliance with the new party. As the once-reluctant Scott commented of the decision to adopt a specific partisan stance, 'If you want to scrap either the left or right wing elements, there can surely be no doubt as to which must go.' For many, however, it was a question not merely of left or right but of the particular party chosen as a vehicle for reform. 'With the general aim of social reconstruction and with most of the objectives in the manifesto I am in agreement,' wrote Rogers. He was not willing, however, to become involved in a body that might prove hostile to the Liberals: 'To my mind the new social order will come to pass in two ways: – lst. By the education of public opinion beyond the present social objectives of the mass of the people ... 2nd. By instalments of legislation enacted by a Government which is in sympathy with some of the objectives we have in mind and open to conversion with respect to some of the others. I have not yet despaired of definite progress in that direction.' For Rogers, 'the human mind is not taken by assault but by persuasion, and I am inclined to think that the existing order may be challenged more effectively from the vantage point of independent criticism than by adopting a position and a creed which will certainly be exposed to misrepresentation and may readily impair the success of the educational function.'[11]

Thus, while the LSR has attracted considerable attention historically and was a significant intellectual force in Canada through the 1930s, it ultimately became a vehicle for a particular partisan reformism and thus could not become a clearing house for intellectual reform. Nor could its membership include even those intellectuals who were willing to become committed politically. Norman Rogers, who continued to work for the Liberal party, serves as one obvious exception, as does Stephen Leacock, whose 1935 call to social scientists to 'make things happen' coincided with his own support for Bennett's New Deal.[12]

At the other end of the spectrum was a smaller group of intellectuals who denied the desirability of committed partisanship. Though small, it was powerful and influential both because it represented a tradition deeply embedded within the university system and because it included two successive heads of the Political Economy department at the University of Toronto, E.J. Urwick and Harold Innis. The arguments varied, but two concerns dominated. The first was that scholarly analysis, essential to the understanding of the problem at hand, was inimical to the pre-judgment involved in partisan activities. The second was that the social sciences were not sufficiently developed to provide the solutions to specific modern issues. Those social scientists who sat around writing policies for the future, and the eager public that seemed increasingly to await their pronouncements, had elevated a new priesthood. They were the 'new millennialists' who, like their predecessors, would ultimately fail the people. Yet the recently acquired mantle of professional expertise gave their utterances a meaning beyond their true significance. The public might thus be falsely led to sit patiently, listening to the outpourings of the new religion, rather than seeking the needed political solutions themselves. 'The social sciences,' Innis warned, 'tend to become the opiate of the people.'[13]

There was also a third concern that was just beginning to surface in the early 1930s. Would influence of the expert, which Canadian intellectuals had been advocating since the time of Adam Shortt, be compatible with democracy? The institutionalization of expert advice in an increasingly interventionist state implied greater use of bureaucracy and regulation. In the early 1930s the Canadian bureaucracy was hardly a juggernaut, but individuals like law professor J.A. Corry of the University of Saskatchewan were influenced sufficiently by Lord Hewart's *New Despotism* to raise questions about the relation between bureaucracy, the modern regulatory state, and democracy.[14] As the drive of the intellectual community towards greater influence continued, such concerns were bound to grow apace.

Deeply held principles, including the very definition of the intellectual, were at stake in the differences between men like Innis and Underhill. In an age that was redefining both the role of the intellectual in society and the relation between society and the state, debate on these principles became acrimonious. Thus, for example, by 1935, Innis became increasingly critical of Underhill, whose political activities he believed to be at odds with his academic position. So harsh were Innis's views, in fact, that as D.A. MacGibbon later wrote to him, it seemed 'you think such persons as he and Bell Alexander at Edmonton should be rubbed out.' Irene Biss, who was a colleague of Innis at the University of Toronto, sprang to Underhill's defence. This only heated matters up. In the exchange that followed, however, a clear statement developed of the two poles that existed within the academic community.[15]

'Must you lose a friend because he [Underhill] goes off on a line you don't agree with?' asked Biss. To her there was nothing in Underhill's activities that diminished his status as a scholar. Indeed, those political activities were the logical conclusion of scientific reseach, for at some point that accumulation of facts inevitably led to some sort of conclusion that demanded action. 'For a social scientist the way of handling material involves influencing people – I suppose preaching,' wrote Biss. The question was, therefore, 'not the fact of the preaching, but the adequacy or relevance or quality that counts.' Innis was not mollified. To become a preacher implied that the intellectual was prepared 'to sell out to any bidder,' and he simply did not believe that, as Biss argued, she would abandon her political position 'if my researches convince me of the reverse.' At one point the argument became so heated and Innis so frustrated with the obstinacy of a junior colleague that he suggested they cease to teach a joint course while Biss retorted that some of Innis's comments were 'gratuitously insulting.' Even, or perhaps especially, among colleagues and scholars, rational debate could quickly turn emotional as personality and partisanship intervened.[16]

Biss and Innis represented opposite ends of the spectrum as to the possible role of the intellectual in Canada. Most were neither as sanguine about the possibilities of political commitment as were some members of the LSR nor as worried about the preservation of the sanctity of scholarly analysis as Innis. Indeed, for many of those interested in public policy there seemed to exist a reasonable compromise position that would preserve detachment while allowing active involvement in policy formation.

For this group the ideal was that represented by the senior civil service. Its model was found in the careers of men like Adam Shortt, and even more, O.D. Skelton. By bringing expert advice to the government the intellectual could assist in comprehending the complexities of modern civilization while remaining detached from the partisanship and popularization inherent in political commitment. It was not always that clear-cut, of course. As Skelton himself commented in 1932, 'Occasionally a question of professional ethics has been raised – how far is the economist working for a government or a business corporation to find his model in the lawyer, accepting and arguing a brief, or in the priest, dedicated to the advancement of an accepted belief?' For Skelton, neither was a proper analogy. 'Objective analysis and fact-finding' and the application of relevant theory 'to light the way through the changing maze of facts' defined the proper role of the social scientist, whether in government or university. The employer could be changed without altering the tenets of professionalism.[17] It was an image of detached involvement that mirrored MacIver's image of the managerial state. It would also have been viewed cynically by both Underhill and Innis, but it was probably more typical of the attitude of the forming intellectual elite than was either of the extremes.

Perhaps surprisingly, the intellectual community was less heated in its discussions about the specific political parties than it was in its discussions about its own role. In fact, in the early stages of the Depression the intellectual network that had formed in the 1920s had a relatively inchoate set of political views. The reason for this was straightforward. Neither of the traditional political parties showed much commitment to economic or social reform or, for that matter, to any systematic planning whatsoever. The Conservatives under R.B. Bennett retained an emphasis on protectionism and the rhetoric of traditional imperial sentiment. The Liberals under Mackenzie King replied with lower tariff proposals and rhetoric about being a reform party. For the intellectual community, however, the rhetoric meant little in the wake of a decade of unimaginative budget-pruning. Frank Underhill's sarcastic comments about the Liberals in 1931 summed up the mood of many intellectuals towards the parties. What the country needs, he said, is less of King's 'gush about the necessity of the forward-looking elements in the community getting together' and more definition 'of the goal to which the forward looking elements are looking forward.'[18] Though individuals had commitments to parties, nothing in 1930 gave any indication that the emerging network of intellectuals saw one party as a natural vehicle for social reform. Disdain for Tory imperialism was neatly balanced by hostility to the inaction and record of that apparent ex-intellectual, Mackenzie King.

As the Depression went on, choices tended to be made and the partisan affiliations became somewhat deeper. When the CCF was formed in 1932-3 it attracted many intellectuals because it seemed the party most willing to use the state in a interventionist fashion. Others, whether for personal, ideological, or other reasons, became tied to different parties. Even as these partisan loyalties strengthened, however, there remained a sense of community within this intellectual group. Thus, for example, that socialist scourge Frank Underhill, who caused so much commotion at Queen's Park and in the president's office of the University of Toronto, remained in close contact with businessmen like Liberal J.S. McLean of Canada Packers and Conservative J.M. Macdonnell of National Trust. On the publication of the LSR's *Social Planning for Canada* in 1935 he ensured that both were sent copies, having as he did 'a certain amount of anxiety about the state of your soul.' McLean wrote back to thank him for the privilege of being on the mailing list of a bunch of socialists. 'I try to keep in touch with what you reds are doing, as I would like to know at least six months in advance when I have to hand over my job. Besides, if I must confess it, I enjoy the company of reds rather better than all the captains of industry.'[19]

For his part Macdonnell, though a Conservative in a group that was increasingly radical in outlook, seems to have received almost universal respect within the intellectual community. Thus, for example, when LSR member Eugene Forsey sent an article to the *Canadian Forum* that implicated National Trust in some shady dealings, both Forsey and Underhill were unhappy that Macdonnell was displeased by it. 'I am distressed about this whole thing since Macdonnell is a friend of mine,' wrote Underhill, 'and I don't want to do anything that is unfair.'[20] It was with a visible sigh of relief that both dropped the issue after Macdonnell pointed to some flaws in the original article. Even muckraking was kept genteel within the confines of this group of peers.

Personal connections and friendships across partisan boundaries were common. In some cases the ties were personal, as with Forsey, who, in spite of quite radical writings in favour of the Soviet experiment could look to the support of Conservatives like C.H. Cahan. Through the 1940s Forsey and Arthur Meighen were regular correspondents, trading advice and ideas, and defending each other in the face of criticism in spite of their considerable difference in ideology. Meighen also acted as a reference for a Guggenheim fellowship for Forsey. On other occasions, personal acquaintance was reinforced by the belief that partisan differences masked common views. This would seem to have been the case in the continued contacts of men like Macdonnell and McLean with even the more radical members of the intellectual community. It may also have explained the loan of an automobile by the future Liberal cabinet minister Walter Gordon to Graham Spry during the latter's bid for office in a 1934 by-election. Its spirit was best summed up, however, in the 'heartiest congratulations' with which Frank Scott acknowledged Norman Rogers's victory as a Liberal in the 1935 general election. For, as he said, 'If I cannot have actual or potential socialists like yourself sitting with the elected members of my own party, then I prefer to have them elected members of some other party.'[21]

Scott's comment to Rogers raises an important point. Though the 1930s were a time of political polarization and though the intellectual community often seemed to mirror this sense of division in its debates, there was a sense of common purpose that bound the elite together. Though personal ties abounded, they would not have survived nearly as well had their not been something more: the sense of educational superiority and common ideological threads that survived all the anguish and partisanship of the decade. This thread linked the elite all the way from members of the LSR through Liberals like Rogers to Finlayson and Macdonnell and finally to Innis.

The most basic link was the perception of the intellectual elite as to its place in the political process. This, in turn, derived from the progressivism that had developed in Canada over the previous thirty years. This tradition had asserted the importance of extra-parliamentary input into policy formation by those with superior knowledge and ability. Parties were necessary, but they were insufficient to shape policy in the modern world. The nature of politics tended to put the focus on tactics and power rather than ideas. Left alone, the politician would invariably dilute or abandon reform in favour of expedient popularity contests. Even Harold Innis accepted this argument. Further, Innis was active himself in public policy areas, serving as an adviser to a Nova Scotia Royal Commission of Economic Inquiry in 1934. At one point he wrote R.B. Bennett with advice on railway policy.[22]

Also stemming from the progressive tradition and inherent in the academic orientation of the intellectual community was a rejection of the 'babbitry' that marked modern industrial society. The vulgarity of capitalism was distasteful to the values and social practices of the intellectual community. This instinctive distrust of capitalist activity was easily translated in the progressive tradition into an argument against the high accord granted the businessman in the modern world. The Depression merely reinforced a long-standing insistence that 'unregulated capitalism' would not provide for the security of the populace or the maximization of its welfare. 'It is significant to note,' one writer commented in the Canadian Banker in 1932, 'where the needy are turning in their distress. It is not to their erstwhile employers who could use their services while prosperity lasted – but rather to the public treasury.' Queen's historian Duncan MacArthur concluded in 1934: 'In all circles except the most reactionary it is now admitted that the principles of *laissez-faire* with their corollary of unrestrained individualism have failed to promote the best interests of the community. Some form of control of economic relationships is deemed essential and the state as the most effective agency of the larger community is being considered as the proper instrument for the exercise of this control.'[23]

The basic distrust of raw capitalism was complemented by a continuing belief, to restate MacIver's phrase from the 1920s that change must not tear down all the old systems. The adherence, without exception, to what Norman Rogers termed an 'evolutionary method of social reconstruction' transcended all political partisanship. Indeed, within this intellectual community ideology was somewhat truncated by the 1930s. Not only was violent upheaval ruled out but views that would have been quite respectable a generation earlier were equally unacceptable. The dismissal of classic nineteenth-century liberalism was matched by the fading away of any explicit defence of the state as an organic entity. The rhetoric of organicism did appear from time to time in the 1930s, especially in the writings and speeches of those of the pre-war reform generation who were still active, including Mackenzie King. It remained, however, only as a residual influence rather than a primary belief of the intellectual community in Canada.[24] For the great bulk of these interconnected intellectuals of the 1930s, the depiction of the state as an organic expression of society was as alien and as dangerous as the image of it as night watchman. In its place had developed a dominant viewpoint based on the concept expressed by MacIver of the state as a mechanism to be used as necessary for the promotion of social well-being. That social well-being, moreover, was increasingly defined not in the spiritual or moral terms of an earlier generation but in terms of material standards of living.

The problem of class structure is more complex. Certainly members of the LSR would have argued in the 1930s, and still might, that their acceptance of the realities of class in Canadian society separated them both from the progressive tradition of earlier years and from contemporary liberal intellectuals. The concept of 'class,' after all, had been a basic factor in Underhill's call for a new party and in the CCF Regina Manifesto, drafted with the assistance of LSR members.[25] Such a viewpoint would seem to challenge the argument that there was ideological similarity that transcended partisan differences.

Yet there are limitations in the importance that can be assigned to class even in the writings of the LSR. As the surviving members commented in a 1975 reprint of their *Social Planning for Canada*, 'The general approach was more pragmatic – not to say reformist – and less socialist, than we might have admitted at the time. On economic questions, for example, the conclusions were not always doctrinaire. They can be better described as a mixture of Fabian socialism, Keynesianism (a new thing in 1933-5), and the Welfare State (still unchristened as such).' The words 'pragmatism' and 'reformism' hold the key. For though the writings of the LSR drew on Fabian and Marxist sources on the importance of class relations they also retained a strong attachment to the vision of the classless liberal society. An obituary to Richard de Brisay, the editor of the *Forum*, who died shortly before the formation of the League, sums up this attachment. 'The democracy of the future of which he dreamed was one in which all men could have been aristocrats.' The potential of the individual rather than of a class remained paramount.[26]

This view was also revealed in an article written in 1932 by Frank Underhill. Entitled 'Bentham and Benthamism,' it sought to establish the intellectual roots both of the LSR and of Canadian social democracy in mid-Victorian liberalism. Bentham, Underhill argued, was not quite the straightforward advocate of individualism and laissez-faire that many assumed him to be. Instead, his thought contained two 'mutually incompatible' strains. One viewed man as actuated by self-interest, and the other, drawing on the Enlightenment, took a more optimistic view, looking to man's perfectibility. It was this combination that produced the doctrine of laissez-faire with its assumption that when a man was left to pursue his own self-interest the result could be social progress for all. According to Underhill, Bentham 'never quite plumbed the depths of human selfishness.'

As he matured in his thinking, Bentham altered his views and adopted a more interventionist view, becoming, concluded Underhill, a democrat, technocrat, and mild collectivist. 'It is interesting to note that the ideal which Bentham elaborated of a mathematically complete political democracy at the bottom with a bureaucracy of administrative experts at the top is exactly the ideal of such socialists as Mr. and Mrs. Sidney Webb in our own day.' It is also interesting that it encompassed the views of much of the Canadian intellectual elite with which Underhill was connected. To Underhill, however, the key point was that modern democratic socialism was an extension rather than a contradiction of modern liberalism. The individual, not the class, remained the paramount concern. 'Extension of the state's functions was necessary,' Underhill concluded, 'because experience had shown that in no other way could individuals be given that opportunity for happiness which it is the function of the legislator to guarantee. English socialism has always emphasized that it is only another method of seeking the same ends which the individualistic generation which preceded it had in view. Its end is the emancipation of the individuality, the free development of personality.'[27] Circumstances, according to Underhill, had forced the true liberal to collectivism. The continuity was there, however, and should circumstances change once more the true liberal might find his way back again.

Thus while the differences in partisan affiliation and specific programs within the intellectual community could be quite deep, there were countervailing factors, not merely personal but ideological, that held it together and gave it a sense of common purpose. As later switches in political allegiance among members of the community indicated, the specific party platform was less important than a general commitment to reform and a particular vision of Canada. Political affiliations were but a means to an end and could be discarded if no longer useful. Thus Frank Scott could conclude his letter of congratulations on Rogers's electoral victory with the prediction that 'if the issue is as clear as I think it will be, you will scrap your party before you scrap your social objectives; but if you and others can liberalize the party sufficiently then I shall be equally content.'[28] The party that could convince these intellectuals that it was sincere in the desire to reform and had a realistic chance of carrying it out would capture their support.

The relation of ideology and politics can be observed in the search for a suitable home for his views by Brooke Claxton in the period between the beginning of the Depression and the 'New Deal' election of 1935. Claxton, who had been a soldier in the First World War, had strongly supported Borden's Union government in 1917 – seeing conscription as necessary for national survival. With the end of the war and the return to Conservative government by 1921 he had supported Arthur Meighen. Even late in the 1920s he remained a Conservative, though, as he later admitted, he did so more or less instinctively. Certainly his widespread connections through the Canadian Club of Montreal and his support for national autonomy indicate that his Conservatism was matched by a growing attraction to various reform ideals.[29]

During the 1930 election Claxton became somewhat more enthusiastic in his Conservatism, largely because, though he was wary of

R.B. Bennett, the new prime minister at least seemed willing to face the issue of the Depression and to promote Canadian nationalism through the use of the tariff. Mackenzie King also had a role in renewing the Montreal lawyer's Conservatism. Claxton had few kind words to say of the Liberal leader at any time in the early 1930s, describing him variously as 'a complete washout' and a 'laissez-faire Liberal of the 1850 vintage.'[30]

Yet at heart Claxton was a modern interventionist liberal, if not a Liberal, and what he wanted from Bennett was both social reform and a sign that he was willing to listen to the right sort of advice. The presence of Herridge in Bennett's inner circle was a small comfort, and the recruitment of Finlayson even more of one, but for Claxton the record of the government was disappointing. As early as the spring of 1931 he wrote Finlayson: 'I can no longer be treated as a Conservative.' Instead, he began to argue for a more radical response to the mounting social and economic crisis in Canada. What was needed, he concluded, was 'a Party very much further to the left than the Liberal Party, or in King's moving to the left. Probably what will happen will be a Western party ... with close affiliations with independents representing industrial communities in the East.' By the autumn of that year Claxton was involved with Terry MacDermott, Frank Scott, and others in trying to draft reform proposals that would represent the views of the intellectual community.[31]

Considering Claxton's increasing disillusionment with the government and his close ties with people like Scott, it is somewhat surprising that he did not become a member of the LSR when it was formed in 1932. He, like it, had called for a new reform program, and he, like it, was committed to the importance of the intellectual in Canadian politics. Even before the Depression he had been exploring the potential for the formation of 'study groups' that could advise the Conservative party. The LSR seemed exactly such an organization. Yet Claxton's early involvement with the founders of the League never led to any meaningful connection with it. The reason for this seems, once again, to have been the League's association with the CCF. Claxton, like many other intellectuals of his generation, appreciated the importance of power. Men of progressive sympathy were only going to be able to reshape the nation if they were in positions where policy was determined. For Claxton, as for others, the problem of the modern nation was at least partly managerial. An efficient and well-educated bureaucracy, with the political levels dotted with men of training and intelligence, would solve many of the problems inherent in the modern world. There was no reason to suppose that democratic socialism was necessary or that the idealism of the CCF was sufficient. 'While the CCF shows every sign of sincerity and high principles,' he commented in 1933, 'it lacks political experience and judgement and certainly would give no reason to suppose that it had any administrative or executive ability.' To a man as pragmatic and technocratic in orientation as Claxton, idealism was not enough.[32]

Thus by the low point of the Depression Claxton was adrift. His traditional Conservatism was gone, though he remained close to Finlayson and retained a certain admiration for Bennett's forcefulness. His contempt for King was as great as ever, but he continued to hope for leftward movement in the Liberal party. The CCF had his admiration but not his support. It was not, as Claxton admitted, a satisfactory situation. The Canadian political system had yet to show the leadership that was required. He was, he wrote, one of a large number of Canadians who felt that 'Bennett has made too many mistakes and the CCF is too uncertain to justify their being either Conservative or CCF and yet feel that Mr. King does not show any sign of the qualities of leadership needed at the present time.' Personally, concluded Claxton, 'I play with them all.'[33]

This scepticism towards all the major political parties might, under other circumstances, have led to the alienation of the intellectual community from the political process altogether. This was not the case with Claxton and others of this group. The times were too political, and the group thrived on politics. Discussions of the political world filled their correspondence and shaped their conversations. To have withdrawn into the ivory tower or philosophical cynicism would have been unthinkable. Rather than indicating alienation, Claxton's position reflected a pragmatism in which the best of imperfect alternatives were weighed. Ideals had to be coupled with power and personal ability. For the intellectuals of the 1930s, reform was as much a technocratic concept as an ideological one.

Ultimately, of course, Claxton drifted into the Liberal camp. Though he sympathized with many of the goals of Bennett's New Deal he felt the proposals were not well worked out; further, in his pragmatic fashion, he reasoned that King would win in 1935. The danger was that he would be 'returned with an overwhelming majority and will do as little as possible.' It was up to Claxton and his 'sort of group' to try to ensure that the incoming government did not drift back into the cautious laissez-faire attitudes of the 1920s. As for Bennett, he had ultimately been written off, not because of economic or social policy, but because 'I felt that the country simply could not stand any more of his bullying.'[34] Even as Claxton found a new political home, which would lead him into Parliament within a few years he remained sceptical of the traditional political leadership of the country. His real hope was that the network of intellectuals with which he had been associated for years was beginning to make its influence felt. For Claxton, there was at least the hope that the Liberal party was beginning to listen to the right people and that, for that reason, it could become the reform vehicle that he felt the country so desperately needed.

Claxton's hope that new intellectual forces might gain influence within the political parties was, as has been argued, nothing new. The 1930s, however, brought about not only an increase in the number of connections between the intellectual elite and government but a qualitative change in the nature of those links. For one thing, the emphasis shifted between levels of government. Before 1930, in spite of well-publicized figures like Skelton, the real advances in the influence of the network of intellectuals had been at the municipal and provincial levels of government. It was in those jurisdictions that government needs most closely approximated the professional drive of the intellectual community. Social work, urban reform, sanitation, and similar areas provided the route to greater involvement for a new professional middle class of experts. It was only with the Depression that the focus shifted away from such social engineering and toward the larger-scale problem of controlling the economy. Such dilemmas were, those at the time felt, manageable only at the federal level. The intellectual generation of the 1930s thus became less inclined to focus on municipal or even provincial issues and turned instead to the national political parties and the Ottawa bureaucracy.

Moreover, the tendency to 'extra-parliamentary organization' that has been traced in areas like party fund-raising[35] was present also in areas related to the formation of party policy. Of course such activity was hardly new to Canadian history. The Canadian Manufacturers' Association, the Grain Growers' Grain Company, the CPR, and numerous other interest groups had through the years sought to influence government policy. What was happening in the 1930s, however, was somewhat different. The intellectuals seeking influence in party policy had little or no vested interest in the outcome of that policy. They were not lobbyists seeking profit through adoption of specific policies.

Though prestige and research contracts often flowed from such influence, there is an obvious difference between the interest of an Underhill, Scott, Claxton, or Macdonnell in reform, and that of low-tariff farm organizations, high-tariff manufacturers, and other such groups. The intellectual network of the 1930s was interested not so much in the adoption of a specific policy, for on specifics they were often divided, as in the adoption of a particular approach to government. The intelligent use of the expert to plan the pragmatic intervention of the state to meet social and economic needs was the key concept linking this new type of extra-parliamentary force.

The specific nature of the influence varied from party to party. The LSR's relation to both the CCF and the intellectual community was so close that, as has been indicated, there were hopes of making it an umbrella organization for reform thought in the 1930s. Though that plan failed, the key role that Underhill played in drafting the CCF's Regina Manifesto and the direct contacts between the leaders of the LSR and parliamentary leaders like Woodsworth all provide clear instances of direct influence by the League on party policy. Indeed, through its early years the LSR was so dedicated to the party and so successful in gaining recognition by other elements of the party that one can talk almost of an 'intellectual class,' joining farmers and labourers, in comprising party support.[36] The political advisers from the intellectual community were in place when the party was formed. This meant that they were seen as an integral part of the organization and were readily accepted by the political level.

In the traditional parties, the relations were more complex. Those between R.B. Bennett's Conservative government and the intellectual reform community were a mass of contradictions. In some ways Bennett and his party were almost as advanced as the CCF in forming contacts with various interested intellectuals. Thus, for example, the party developed the political 'summer school.' This rather strangely named practice involved bringing together various experts on social and economic problems in a scholarly conference with politicians. Formal papers, discussions, and informal contacts were supposed to give the intellectual access to the politician while allowing the politician to gain information on current social problems and possible remedies. The Conservatives held such a conference at Newmarket, Ontario, in 1932. Taking over the classrooms and boarding facilities of Pickering College, Bennett and Ontario premier George Henry presided over an unusual mixture of academics and politicians. The topics ranged from government ownership through public administration to social services. Those attending included intellectuals from Harold Innis to LSR member and social work expert Harry Cassidy.[37]

That same year Bennett had to deal with the central economic issue of his administration – trade relations with the United Kingdom. Recognizing the complexity of the problem he followed King's precedent and called in outside advisers to assist him. Several professional economists, including Burton Hurd of McMaster, Hubert Kemp of Toronto, and Clifford Clark of Queen's, worked with the prime minister as researchers and consultants in the months leading up to the conference. Bennett obtained further expert advice from men like Dominion Statistician R.H. Coats and D.A. MacGibbon within the civil service. To a greater degree than even before, the prime minister looked in 1932 to a group of non-political experts to guide him in a major conference. It marked an important step in increasing the profile of the specialist. The consultations that Bennett undertook for the Imperial Economic Conference of 1932 were especially significant because they brought him into contact with the considerable talents of Clifford Clark. Clark, though a protégé of Skelton's, had not been involved with the various intellectual circles that developed in the 1920s; he had left Canada for the United States to work as an economic adviser for Strauss and Company. The Depression, however, had ended his career in private business, and he had returned to Queen's as a professor of economics.[38] Before long he was serving as an adviser to Bennett for the conference.

At this point three circumstances came together to shape both Clark's career and the direction of Canadian bureaucratic development. First, there was a vacancy in the deputy ministership of the Department of Finance. Second, O.D. Skelton had by this time won Bennett's trust in spite of his Liberal ties, and Skelton pleaded Clark's abilities to the prime minister. Third, the prime minister was reinforced in his impression of Clark by the good work he did at the conference and because he engaged Bennett's minister of trade and commerce, H.H. Stevens, in debate. According to Ottawa tradition, Clark took apart Stevens's bi-metallist arguments so effectively that Bennett decided this was the perfect deputy minister of finance.[39] By October Clark was deputy minister, and over the next two decades he would preside over the expansion of the Department of Finance into the sort of economic planning agency that the intellectual elite saw as essential. For the first time a professional economist was in charge of planning the government's finances and, increasingly, the nation's economy.

Bennett's ties to the intellectual community within the civil service were reinforced by some of his political appointments. In particular, R.K. Finlayson's appointment as Bennett's private secretary gave direct access to the prime minister to a man intimately involved in the Canadian Club circuit. W.D. Herridge, though less connected personally to these intellectual circles, was important in that his advocacy of Roosevelt's New Deal policies reflected many of the enthusiasms of the intellectual community. It was Herridge and Finlayson who, with 'the always available bottle of Haig and Haig,' wrote many of the New Deal speeches at Herridge's Harrington Lake cottage. As Claxton wrote to Herridge in 1934, the reforms would be too late to save the government this time around, but if the party showed a willingness to embrace such ideas it would at last be accepting the needs of modern society. The defeat would be the beginning of the rebuilding process, for the party would lose its reactionary wing and emerge as 'a young and vigorous fighting force stripped of deadwood.'[40]

A close examination of these various connections also reveals some of the weaknesses in the Bennett administration's ties to the intellectual community. Neither Bennett nor his top advisers ever developed any close personal ties with any of the university-based intellectual community. In part this was a matter of personality. Bennett seems to have felt uncomfortable in the company of intellectuals and was, as Finlayson complained, 'contemptuous of anyone who claimed to have a brain in his head.' His response was often to react by blustering.[41] It is not that he was more anti-intellectual than other politicians of his day. His hiring of Clark and support for Skelton reveal that. It is simply that unless his relation with intellectuals were precisely defined, as with Finlayson, Clark, or Skelton, he avoided contact.

What was true of Bennett was seemingly even more the case with his front benches. Though Finance Minister E.N. Rhodes worked reasonably well with Clark, he established no other contacts within the Canadian community of economists. H.H. Stevens seemingly had even less contact with the universities, and his near-libellous accusations during the Royal Commission on Price Spreads earned him criticism from numerous intellectuals, not because he was attacking business but because of the demagogic way he was doing it. Indeed, aside from Bennett himself, the only leading Conservative with strong affiliations to the network of clubs, societies, and causes that defined the elite was former prime minister Sir Robert Borden, who, with Liberal Newton Rowell, acted as the elder statesman on numerous committees and was in continual correspondence with various political writers and thinkers.[42]

The relatively weak ties between Bennett's Conservatives and the intellectual community were partly due to the antipathy of this generation of intellectuals to the imperialist rhetoric of the Conservative party. There were also various government policies on the domestic front that offended it to one degree or another. Thus, for example, Bennett handled the removal of Vincent Massey as minister to Washington in a fashion calculated to ruffle feathers. Massey was a political appointee, and his dismissal was not improper, but rather than talk to him personally Bennett passed the duty on to Herridge. Herridge phoned Macdonnell at National Trust. Macdonnell, in turn, called the president of the company (and a Liberal), Jim Rundle. Finally, in this long and convoluted process, Rundle called Massey and suggested his resignation. Even Macdonnell found both the dismissal and the means used to obtain it unfortunate and distasteful. For others it was proof of the arrogance and high-handedness of the new prime minister. As W.L. Grant commented of the incident, 'he seemed to me to talk more like a ward-heeler and a thug than the Prime Minister of a great dominion.'[43]

The Massey firing was a relatively minor incident and would have done Bennett no real harm within the intellectual community had it been an isolated event. Over the next years, however, his personal style of blunt aggressiveness continued to give offence. When he reinforced it by an increasing penchant for 'law and order,' many within the community began to fear, as did Claxton, his authoritarianism. Even Macdonnell at one point raised the unthinkable possibility that he might have to support the detested Mackenzie King.[44] He resisted the temptation, but others did not.

The generally poor relation between Bennett and much of the intellectual community in the 1930s is somewhat ironic. In the creation of the Canadian Broadcasting Corporation (CBC), and the Bank of Canada, the transformation of Finance under Clifford Clark, and the New Deal election of 1935, the Bennett government undertook the sort of expansion of state activities and systematic planning that so many of these individuals advocated. Even the best efforts of men like Finlayson, however, could not bridge the gap between the prime minister's blustery demeanour and the intellectual community, nor could he overcome the historical memories of 'Ready, Aye Ready' within a network that had been founded on nationalist issues.

So long as the Conservative party was in office these difficulties were masked to a degree. The fact that the intellectual community had to look to Bennett for policies and the presence of able civil servants like

Clark and Skelton provided essential connections. After 1935, however, the party found itself increasingly estranged from the new elite that was developing. Those, like Macdonnell, who were committed to the newer concepts of social security and state intervention and who remained within the party would find themselves in a difficult position, surrounded by MPs and supporters who regarded intellectuals with distrust and who increasingly looked to nineteenth-century liberalism for their political inspiration. It was an epitaph on the Bennett government when one of the brightest young men to drift from the party during these years, Brooke Claxton, commented of Bennett's impending defeat that he 'does not deserve any such fate for his has been from every normal point of view, one of the best administrations in Canada.'[45] The times, however, were not normal, and, for better or worse, Mackenzie King's Liberals returned to power with a large majority in 1935.

If the Conservatives failed to develop strong links with the intellectual community because of their leader and despite their policies, then the Liberals succeeded despite both their leader and their policies. The Liberals of 1930, it was true, did have aspects that appealed to the intellectual community. Mackenzie King's record on national autonomy was acceptable, and the party as a whole was free of the taint of authoritarianism. On the economic side the low and moderate tariff positions that King had adopted through the 1920s in response to Progressive pressure were generally supported by the Canadian economic community.[46] King's tariff policy took on an especially progressive light when Bennett revised the tariff schedule upward after his election. The tariff played a symbolic role in the political life of Canada. High tariffs equalled big business and the Canadian Manufacturers' Association, while low tariffs represented the farmer and consumer. Mackenzie King was here on the side of the angels, even if, on occasion in the past, he had been tempted by protectionist devils.

The Liberals had their flaws, however. Though the tariff policy was moderate there were many, including men like J.W. Dafoe of the powerful *Winnipeg Free Press*, who felt that there was too much attention being paid to protectionist voices in Ontario and Quebec. Moreover, and especially distressing to the social scientific community, the party seemed fixated on the tariff as the only meaningful agent of economic adjustment. Fiscal caution demanded balanced budgets and thus ruled out economic adjustment through deficit financing, while King remained cautious, if not hostile, to the manipulation of interest rates

or money supply as a means to achieve economic control. Though King
was a trained economist, he was far from comfortable with the newer
versions of economic thought and preferred to retain his own 1918
Industry and Humanity as a guide for both social and economic policy.[47]
For the emerging technocratic elite, this sort of religious moralism and
lofty rhetoric appeared impossibly outdated in anage that increasingly
looked to the touchstones of planning and efficiency rather than 'harmony' and 'uplift.'

Unlike Bennett, King did have strong contacts within the intellectual community. As prime minister he was especially reliant on O.D.
Skelton, who functioned not just as deputy minister of external affairs
but as a senior adviser on most everything. He had also brought in
Norman Rogers as private secretary. Even after Rogers went to Queen's,
King continued to look to him for advice, and both he and Skelton
were actively involved during the 1930 election campaign. The bond
was mutual, and when King lost, Skelton confessed that he wished he
had left the civil service to assume the principalship of Queen's. Instead
he was effectively cut off from King for the next five years. As the
defeated prime minister commented in his diary, 'to be separated from
him will be a terrible loss.' Henceforth Rogers became even more important to King. Over the next few years pilgrimages were regularly
made between Ottawa and Kingston, with the Queen's political scientist acting in a multitude of capacities – speech writer, policy adviser,
link with the academic community, and reassurer of the tempera-
mental King. Rogers was seemingly more trusted by the leader of the
opposition than most other academics with whom King had contact,
in part perhaps because they shared the same spiritualist inclinations,
or at least so King thought. In those massive diaries in which King so
often criticized those closest to him, there are few if any negative
comments on Rogers. The 1932 comment that 'he is an exceptionally
fine fellow' is both consistent with others and an amazing comment
from a man who rarely gave unstinted praise.[48]

Ironically, however, the man who was probably the most crucial in
shaping the relation between the Liberal party and the intellectual
community was neither so close to King nor regarded by many as an
intellectual. This was Vincent Massey, whose services became suddenly
available to the Liberal party after Bennett removed him from his
Washington post. Massey's independent wealth and his desire to retain
a public role suited King's purposes well. The ex-prime minister, as
politicians are wont to do, believed that his party lost in 1930 not
because of bad policies but because of bad organization. For King, the

key to victory in the next election was an improvement in the admittedly deplorable state of party organization at the national level. Vincent Massey was cajoled in the name of Liberalism, and with hints of future ambassadorial postings, into the office of party president. With Norman Lambert, he was to create an effective party network, backed by sufficient funds, to ensure that the party got its message across.[49]

Mackenzie King got more than he bargained for. What he wanted was a man on whom he could unload the grubby and time-consuming chores of fund-raising and organization while leaving the leader of the party alone to deal with parliamentary and policy matters. What he got was a man committed to reform, who was determined to drag the party loose from its laissez-faire traditions. Massey saw himself as an intellectual adviser as well as an organizer, and from the time he left Washington he continually pushed his liberal-progressive brand of reformism on the party. As he wrote Dafoe, if Liberalism was to become a viable alternative to the Bennett, government then it must, unlike 1930, show that it was aware of the problems and requirements of governing a modern industrial society. 'I can see great possibilities for the party,' he commented, but 'only if it is bold and progressive in its policies.'[50] By the summer of 1931 Massey was regularly popping up at Liberal functions, at King's Ottawa home, and even at the hallowed Kingsmere, cajoling the party into what he conceived of as the dual challenge of organizational and intellectual refurbishment. By the time he was officially appointed president of the National Liberal Federation in March 1932, Massey had become much more than the compliant functionary.

Massey had not set himself an easy task. The party membership was in many instances as old-fashioned as critics like Claxton and Underhill had charged. Moreover, Massey found himself working with a party leader who, though sympathetic to reform in the abstract, was both extremely cautious when it came to specifics and inordinately sensitive to any implied criticism. The combination of personalities and the clash of ideas proved volatile. Practically from the time Massey began to assist the party, King complained about the nature of that assistance, about Massey's pretentiousness, and about numerous other faults. At one point in 1931 he even had his Kingsmere telephone number changed 'to avoid Massey.'[51] Amid the stormy and contradictory relationship made up of flattery and insults, recriminations and congratulations, however, Massey persisted in asserting a new intellectual presence in the party even as he undertook reorganization and refinancing.

Important in Massey's persistence was the role undertaken by his wife, Alice. In an age when the wives of public figures rarely appeared, Alice Massey gains repeated mention as an active figure in Massey's activities and especially in his reformism. She was often present at discussions between party officials and Massey at Batterwood, the Massey estate near Port Hope, and she was often the one whom contemporaries remember as the person most interested in the philosophic aspects of reform. Diplomat Hugh Keenlyside, after dining with her in Japan, noted his 'surprise' at her well-informed views on the necessity of the Liberal party adopting a more radical program. 'She admires Woodsworth, Dafoe and [Charles] Bowman and in general talked like an editorial in the "Canadian Forum." ' A daughter of Tory idealist George Parkin, sister-in-law of W.L. Grant, and a woman with a penetrating intellect, Alice Massey came from a tradition of the intellectual as public figure. Every indication is that she, as much as Vincent, was a force in pushing the Liberal party toward closer ties with the intellectual community and with the new reformism. She also had one great advantage that was singularly lacking in her husband – tact. On a good many occasions King's wrath against Vincent was allayed by a timely intervention on the part of Alice.[52]

For the Masseys, the key to reforming Liberalism was the injection of new ideas into the party from within the intellectual community. As Claxton had proposed for the Conservatives in 1929 and as Underhill was suggesting for the left in 1931, the Masseys in the summer of 1931 urged the formation of a series of study groups formed of intellectuals to look at various aspects of Liberal party policy and, in concert with politicians, to develop party policy. As in the case of the other parties, the inspiration was once again British and owed much to Massey's reading of the biography of former British Liberal party president Robert Hudson – a man whose fund-raising work did not detract from his influence on policy. For King, who sent Massey the biography, such activities were at best a tolerable nuisance to keep the party president from finding the more grubby aspects of the work intolerable. He did little to hurry the development of intellectual study groups along.[53]

By 1932 changes were occurring. First, King himself was in contact to a greater degree with a number of intellectual advisers, while Massey had had enough sense to develop ties with men like Dafoe and Rogers, whom he knew had King's trust. The renewal of ties with Dafoe was especially important. Throughout the reform movements of the early twentieth century, journalists played an important part both as advisers and, especially, as transmitters of new ideas. In the 1930s a group of journalists centred on the *Winnipeg Free Press* became an integral part of the intellectual community working to make the Liberal party a vehicle the public could trust in a new era. In Winnipeg there was Dafoe himself who, with his associate George Ferguson, actively supported Massey's efforts. There were also connections between *Free Press* newspapermen and the intellectual community through Winnipegers like Finlayson and E.J. Tarr. Indeed, as the decade went on, it became customary for Dafoe, Ferguson, Tarr, and various others to meet regularly at the Manitoba Club to discuss the issues of the day. Known as the Sanhedrin club, this informal group provided a link between the intellectual community, the politicians, and some of the most powerful newspapermen in the country.[54]

Nor were the journalistic connections confined to Winnipeg. In Ottawa, Massey and the Liberal reformers had a most capable supporter in Dafoe's Ottawa correspondent, Grant Dexter. Dexter was of the same generation as much of the intellectual elite, and, like them, he had served in the First War. After the war he was posted to Ottawa by Dafoe and over the years became the journalist who, more than any other, was able to pry information loose from politicians and from civil servants with whom he shared a common sense of purpose. As the intellectual community moved to gain influence in political circles, it found in Dafoe and Dexter allies who could use publicity and propaganda to encourage movement in new directions. Many of the editorials in the *Free Press* through the 1930s and 1940s were products of the interchange between activists like Massey, reformers like Rogers, civil servants like Clark, and journalists like Dafoe, Ferguson, and Dexter.[55] So close had the connections become by the end of the Depression that the intellectual elite that formed in the 1920s has to be enlarged to include these and other key journalists.

By 1932 the involvement of Dafoe in political consultations with Massey forewarned of the emerging alliance between the *Free Press* journalists and the extra-parliamentary reformers. As early as February of that year Dafoe was, with Massey and Rogers, writing speeches for King, and all three were urging him to accept the idea that party policy should be directly influenced by semi-formalized groups of non-politicians coming together to discuss issues. Their efforts bore fruit the next fall. First, in a weekend meeting at Batterwood, King, Ernest Lapointe, and J.L. Ralston met with the Masseys, Norman Lambert, and J.W. Dafoe to discuss policy matters. Working from a memo drawn up by Dafoe, Tarr, Crerar, and Fowler, Massey and Dafoe led the discussion, with Lambert and Ralston joining in. Mackenzie King watched, as did Lapointe, commenting much less frequently than the others. Massey's approach was straightforward and consistent with his earlier positions. 'Massey was quite precise,' Dafoe later reported, in saying that 'it was essential if the effective organization of the party were to be made possible, that it should stand for a program which would sharply differentiate itself from the Government program by being radical, and both Mr. Lambert and I reinforced this presentation of the case as strongly as we could.'[56]

Not too much should be made of the detailed decisions that resulted from this meeting. Though there was a far-ranging discussion on social security and economic planning, the only specific matter on which there was a firm decision – that is, accepted by King – was in favour of a central bank. Even here the details were vague.[57] What was important was that Massey had succeeded in bringing the political leadership of the party into policy discussions with figures outside the parliamentary process. It was the beginning of what Massey hoped would be a new era of regular discussions between intellectuals and experts on the one hand and the politicians on the other.

With this meeting over, Massey began the organization of study groups that would develop policies and undertake analysis of contemporary problems. As with others interested in forming such groups, Massey called on the members of the intellectual elite who might be disposed toward using the Liberal party as a vehicle for reform. In Montreal this meant those members of the McGill-Canadian Club circuit who had remained outside of the LSR. Correspondence was struck up with both Claxton and MacDermott to ascertain their views on the political future of Liberalism. At Queen's, of course, the initial contact was Norman Rogers, who brought in economist C.A. Curtis, a dedicated Liberal and expert on banking. A.F. Plumptre of the Political Economy department at Toronto also made the pilgrimage to Batterwood on various occasions, as did other academics within striking range. These meetings were usually more technical and specific versions of the one in September, 1932, and their results were transmitted by Massey back to King and to other sympathetic members of Parliament. Though the reaction of the politicians varied depending on the issue, the study groups that began to take shape over the winter of 1932-3 provided an ongoing series of links between the intellectual community in Canada and the Liberal party at the national level.[58]

In this transmission of information Massey was both the bearer and the buffer, often acting as a lightning rod for new ideas, testing the reaction of party regulars. It was not always an easy task, and the president of the party took a great deal of criticism of his support of the ideas of intellectual liberalism. Thus, for example, King repeatedly criticized Massey for his failure to understand the complex personalities in the parliamentary caucus and for not realizing that he could not 'ride roughshod over the heads of the party caucus.'[59] This criticism was not completely unfair. Massey, like many members of the intellectual elite, had a certain disdain for political professionals and especially for the seeming pettiness of the backbenchers, with all their unintellectual concerns with local constituency issues. The emerging 'brain-trust,' as it was increasingly termed, believed in its own abilities and in the necessity of expertise being employed in the shaping of policy.

Tension with the caucus became most explicit on the question of the party's stance vis-à-vis the CCF. Both Massey and Rogers believed that the Liberals must move left of centre and that it must compete with the CCF for the 'progressive' vote in the country. The idea that there were natural links between the Liberals and the CCF is understandable from the perspective of the intellectual community. The line between LSR members like Scott and those moving into the Liberal camp like Claxton and MacDermott was fine indeed. Many of those involved with the CCF were men that both Massey and Rogers admired and knew well on a personal level. To others, however, the combination of farm populism and labour radicalism that underlay the CCF was too explicitly socialist to have anything in common with Liberalism. As J.W. Dafoe warned, the situation was not analogous to the 1920s. when Progressivism and Liberalism discovered much common ground. 'The CCF has become the plaything and experiment ground of pseudo-intellectuals, monetary cranks, advocates of "Socialism in our time" and faddists who want to reconstruct the world and make over human nature.'[60]

The tension between the intellectuals' and politicians' views of the place of Liberalism on the political spectrum led to a revolt against Massey's growing influence in the spring of 1933. Though the discontent had been developing for some months, the incident that brought it into the open was a speech given by Massey in Windsor, Ontario. Proclaiming the 'new Liberalism,' Massey warned that there were elements of the party that found the new approach difficult to accept. He went on to imply that he and those other 'progressive' Liberals had as much or more in common with the CCF than with the right wing of his own party: 'The second thing that I wish to say about the third party movement in Canada today is this. I believe that the rise of an organized protest against abuses and evils in modern society is to be welcomed. It has provided a valuable stimulus to political thinking. The protest has abundant reality. The vast majority of persons behind it are people who are themselves suffering present wrongs and wish to make an honest examination of the causes of those wrongs and desire to bring about changes sufficient to redress them.' The only possible response to this political protest, he continued, was 'a national plan for our political and social and economic regeneration and it will be the privilege and the responsibility of the new Liberalism to provide it.'[61]

Several members of the parliamentary wing of the party were not amused to see the party president defining the future direction of party policy and its relation to an upstart third party. When reports of the speech reached Ottawa, King received several complaints from MPs. The prime minister did little to defend his party president. 'He thinks he knows more about politics than anyone else, and is always driving ahead,' he commented after a stormy caucus meeting. Later, after actually seeing a transcript of the Massey speech, King was horrified. 'His references to the CCF were mistaken politically, his references to myself were little short of contemptuous ... Massey has made no end of trouble for me trying to force the pace.'[62]

Massey's most ambitious effort to 'force the pace' came in September 1933 when he brought politicians and experts together in a 'summer school' along the line, of the Conservative one at Newmarket and modelled on the concept of the Chatauqua meetings that had been so much a feature of Canadian life in recent years. Held at Trinity College School in Port Hope, the 'first Liberal summer school,' and the only one for a generation, has been viewed as being at best a mixed success. Mackenzie King was obviously uncomfortable with the notion of exposing party thinking, even unofficially, to public scrutiny. He was also far from a convert to the miracles of planning and saw in many of the papers a danger to basic liberal freedoms. The best thing about the conference to the leader of the opposition was undoubtedly its end, and as one writer has commented: 'It is a bizarre commentary on the relationship of the party leader to policy-making in this era that one of the major effects of a policy conference was to make the party leader constipated for the duration, as duly noted on a daily basis in his diary.' Nor can it be argued that the papers by people like Curtis, H.M. Cassidy, MacDermott, and MacIver had much immediate effect on party policy.[63]

Yet at the time Massey termed the summer school a success beyond 'my wildest expectations' and even thirty years later commented in his memoirs: 'It seems extraordinary that a gathering that did much to vitalize Liberalism in Canada should have met with such strong opposition.' From his perspective the enthusiasm was justified. Ever since the defeat of 1930 he, Rogers, and others had been attempting to wean the Liberals from the laissez-faire traditions of the party to a new, more technocratic and interventionist view of government. Though it was to be a long while before the ideas presented at Port Hope were to become legislation, the public association of the party with those ideas seemed an important step in committing the party to both a 'new Liberalism' and reliance on the use of outside expert advisers in achieving that goal. The goal to which the forward-looking elements were looking forward, as Underhill had put it two years before, was emerging. As Massey said in his introduction to the published papers of the conference, 'It may be said – and this would seem to be one of the things on which the contributors to this volume are in substantial agreement – that while freedom at one time meant freedom from government regulation, it now must mean freedom by government regulation. Individualism, however "rugged" it may be, can no longer be left to itself. It can, in fact, be safeguarded only by means of the control which the State provides.'[64]

So few of the policies necessary to bring Canada into the age of the positive state were actually implemented in the early part of the Depression that the significance of what was happening to Canada's national parties has been understated by historians. Though the concrete developments would largely come later, the movement of the intellectual elite into the 'inner circles' of the parties was a matter of major historical portent. All three national parties found their perceptions of their own role altered by intellectual input in these years. The 'new Liberalism,' as with emerging currents of Conservative and CCF reformism, possessed two major characteristics. First, all parties had looked increasingly to the ideas of an extra-parliamentary elite of intellectuals. These intellectuals, whether based inside or outside the university, were familiar to each other and espoused a reform agenda based on the methods of the emerging social sciences and oriented towards the urban middle class. Second, though there were differences in the degree of reform thought necessary, this technocratic thrust had at its base a marriage of the utilitarian and liberal ideals of individual happiness with a perception of the state as a mechanistic agency that should be freely used to provide the services the community found desirable. It also implied that policy must be formed with an eye to efficiency. As Massey argued, 'Efficiency must serve the common weal, and on the other hand, if the humanitarian task is honestly performed, we will have the basis of an enduring efficiency.'[65] Efficiency, happiness, and justice were all thought compatible within a process of systematic planning that looked to the social sciences as the inspiration and the state as the agent.

At this basic level there was little difference in the expression of the new reformism within the three parties. Given the common background and connections of the individuals expressing these views, this is hardly surprising. Herridge's new deal outlook, Underhill's extension of utilitarianism to collectivism, and Massey's call for state intervention all rested on the same basic premises. There is a difference, however, in the degree to which the parties took to these new ideas. In the case of both the Liberals and the CCF the intellectual elite had considerable success in achieving influence within party councils. CCF ties with the community were the strongest due both to the left-of-centre orientation of the party and to the existence of the LSR, but by the end of 1933 the Liberals too were influenced by these currents of reform, even if the older Christian reformism and innate caution of their leader worked to slow things down. By 1933, whether King was completely comfortable with the idea or not, the Liberal party was fast shedding its traditional position that government intervention was dangerous to civil liberty and moving towards a vision of the party more in accord with what Rogers termed 'the left wing of Liberalism.' Moreover, its growing allegiance to the new principles was revealed in speeches by Massey, by enthusiastic younger MPs like Ian Mackenzie of British Columbia or Paul Martin of Ontario, and by the publicity attached to the summer school. Given this, the drift of Claxton and others towards the party was somewhat more definite than appeared to be the case on the surface.

The connections between the Conservative party and the intellectual elite were more tenuous. Though, as has been indicated, there were various ties built up during the Conservative years in office, there is no doubt that by 1935 the Conservatives had neither the strong links to the intellectual elite possessed by the other parties nor the commitment to the new reformism that the elite represented. Indeed, by the time of its defeat and the collapse of Bennett's New Deal experiment, the Conservatives were left in somewhat of an ideological limbo, between a pragmatic interventionism that stretched back through Canadian history and a growing identification with what Massey would have termed the old liberalism – a view emphasizing the limitations of the role of the state and the importance of the market-place in shaping Canadian society. The party's intellectual reformers, men like Macdonnell, would continue to work after 1935 to bring the organization into line with trends in other organizations. The presence of such individuals, and their eventual success in nudging the Conservatives toward a more interventionist philosophy of the state, indicates, however, that by the middle of the Depression the intellectual elite that had formed in the late 1920s had at least some involvement in all three national parties. Add to this the growing presence of members of that same community within the federal bureaucracy and the result is a degree of influence that would have been impossible even five years earlier. Moreover, that influence was just reaching the point where it could begin to shape major policy decisions. It is thus of some relevance to see how the principles of technocratic reform translated into specific courses of action. This will be the focus of the next two chapters.

8

The 'new millennialists': economics in the 1930s

Economics in Canada came of age in the 1930s.[1] A discipline that had only recently become an established part of the university curriculum in Canada began, under the stimulus of the Depression, to challenge traditional descriptions of the way in which the economy worked. As it did so, it increasingly undermined the theories on which those descriptions were based and began in a serious fashion to search for a new approach to economics. By the time that English economist John Maynard Keynes published his famous *General Theory of Employment, Interest and Money* in 1936, Canadian economists were more than ready to abandon an obsolete view of the economic universe in favour of a structure that offered greater hope for comprehension of the world around them.

The change in theory was accompanied and its impact accentuated by a dramatic rise in the authority of professional economists. To an unprecedented degree the Depression caused the public to look to economists for advice on public policy. This change was the result of a conjuncture of circumstances, including the relatively improved state of economics departments in Canadian universities in the years after the First World War, theoretical developments at the national and international levels, and the quest for a solution to the worst economic crisis in Canadian history. Together these factors catapulted the 'dismal science' into a prominent role in Canadian governmental planning and reform. Thus, for example, in 1930 the Canadian civil service had only one civil servant with graduate training in economics, O.D. Skelton, and he was in External Affairs rather than in an economic position. A decade later, when Skelton died, he had been followed by experts like W.C. Clark, R.B. Bryce, W.A. Mackintosh, and his own son, Alex

Skelton.[2] The Second World War would see the proliferation continue unabated as economists flowed from academic positions or graduate schools into increasingly central positions in the public service.

The influence of economics was not merely a matter of the number of economists in powerful positions. This rise of the economist to new prominence was intimately bound up with the direction of the intellectual community of public activists in Canada. That community had, since the First World War, increasingly looked to the empirical methods of the social sciences as a means whereby solutions to modern problems might be found. As depression faded into war, it became increasingly apparent that the language that would be employed to translate the hopes and ideals of the intellectual community into the policies and plans of governments was the language of economics. During the Depression the intellectual network found its focus in economic issues and in an economic approach to social and governmental reform. It was a change of some significance. Economics was fast becoming what religion had been until the early twentieth century – the keystone by which the intellectual community communicated with politicians and public alike.

Such a dramatic assertion of authority on the part of a single discipline was bound to meet with opposition. There were many individuals who both resented the claims of economists and doubted their abilities. Not surprisingly, claims of importance were often met with cynical responses. Thus, in spite of his own professional background, Mackenzie King got enjoyment out of Lord Hailsham's remark to him in 1932 that if one put six economists in the same room there would be seven opinions, 'Keynes giving two.' Stephen Leacock was more sarcastic about his own profession, terming it an 'obstinate and crabbed science, living on facts and figures, untouched by imagination. Worse than that, it is now crippled and discredited with controversy.' Both for those who doubted the pretensions of the profession and for those who felt that professional guidance of the Canadian economy was long overdue, the Depression marked a turning-point in the way in which Canadians approached the solutions of contemporary problems.[3]

Commenting on the state of the economic profession in 1929, Harold Innis complained that it 'must be brought level with history and political science' in Canada. Further, he argued that 'Canadian economic history is in a sense at the root of the problem. Its elaboration will strengthen the anchorage of economics which is so essential to a rapidly growing young country such as Canada.'⁴ Given the relatively established state of economics within the social sciences, these comments appear somewhat overly critical. They are nevertheless revealing, for in his emphasis on the relation to political science and history and in his own emphasis on the importance of economic history, Innis correctly noted the prevailing tendency of Canadian economics on the eve of the Depression.

The most obvious fact about that tendency is that the importance that Innis assigned to economic history was widespread within the profession. The orientation towards history within Canadian economic writing was deeply rooted. Adam Shortt had seen history as the key to economics, while W.J. Ashley, the first political economist at the University of Toronto, had also been appointed a professor of constitutional history. As the discipline developed the tradition remained intact. In the years after the First World War, many of the best-known publications of Canadian economists were in economic history. Innis followed his 1920 publication on the Canadian Pacific Railway a decade later with the monumental *The Fur Trade in Canada*. O.D. Skelton had written more historical monographs than economic ones by the time he joined External Affairs. His biographies of Laurier and Galt, his historical studies of railway construction in Canada, and his 1914 *General Economic History of Canada* testified to his orientation. Indeed, when Queen's University set out to find a replacement for Skelton as head of the department, it passed over one able economic historian, W.A. Mackintosh, in favour of another, Herbert Heaton. So powerful was the trend to economic history in these years that a whole generation of economists gained reputations as being among Canada's top historians. For a younger generation of historians proper like Donald Creighton and A.R.M. Lower, inspiration came not from the constitutional orientation of their own profession but from the economic studies of men like Innis and Shortt.⁵

There was also a second major concern of Canadian economic writing in the post-war years. This was with the agrarian sector, particularly, with western Canadian agriculture. The importance of the wheat boom in the years before 1914, the long-standing belief in the necessity of western development, and the great political upheavals originating in western Canada after the First World War all provide explanations for this focus. The belief was that, in the frontier experience of the west, there existed problems that mirrored the difficulties of new societies while in the experiments with co-operative ownership, government regulation, and populist politics lay the possible future of democracy. Economic writings on the frontier regions of Canada were as popular as writings on its history. The tradition was especially strong at Queen's, where Clifford Clark wrote on the country elevator, Humfrey Michell on agricultural credit, and W.A. Mackintosh on the problems of the prairie provinces. By the Depression, the interest in the west led to major publications from other institutions. Thus D.A. MacGibbon of the University of Alberta and later of the Board of Grain Commissioners was publishing work on prairie settlement and, in 1932, *The Canadian Grain Trade*, while P.C. Armstrong undertook a major work entitled simply *Wheat*. The Depression also brought about the most ambitious scholarly studies of the west to that time in the Canadian Frontier of Settlement series under the general editorship of Mackintosh. In an increasingly urban society Canadian economists still saw the agricultural sector as central to understanding economic development.[6]

Of course other sectors received attention. Transportation was a much-studied topic, and primary resources other than agriculture interested several economists. These studies, however, simply reinforce the conclusion that Canadian economic writing had distinct biases in these years. That writing was infused with historicism and focused on specific events and institutions rather than working with abstraction or theory. It revealed, in other words, strong ties to the historical school of nineteenth-century German economic thought or, perhaps more directly, to its North American offshoot, the 'institutional school' of the turn-of-the-century United States.[7]

This historicism was reinforced by the state of economic theory at the beginning of the Depression. As early as the decade before the First World War economic theory had become relatively fixed. This does not mean that there were not economists looking for new approaches to problems. The work of Veblen in the United States or Schumpeter in Austria and the United States provided interesting theoretical challenges. Nevertheless, classical economic theory, modified by the marginal utility theorists of the late nineteenth century, had become so strongly entrenched in economic thought that the most promising direction for the economist who wished to contribute something to his discipline did not seem to be a restatement or modification of hypothetical arguments on the way in which the economy worked. Only through high-quality studies of specific problems in real-world circumstances would a means be found to test theory. Theory became less relevant in the short term than empirical testing. Macro-economic theory was pushed into the background as micro-economic analysis predominated. The argument of Dominion Statistician R.H. Coats in 1931, that 'the need for economic and social research lies wholly on the inductive side,' would not have been disputed by many of his economic colleagues.[8]

This outlook affected not only the specialized monographs but the whole approach to the discipline. Robert Lekachman's 1966 study of John Maynard Keynes underlined the contributions of his subject to economics by comparing two general textbooks written in the United States: Garver and Hansen's 1937 edition of *Principles of Economics* and Paul Samuelson's 1964 edition of *Economics*. Not only the details and conclusions had changed, he noted, but the whole organization of the subject. The same test applied to Canada leads, not surprisingly, to the same result. Thus, for example, D.A. MacGibbon's popular *Introduction to Economics*, first published in 1924 and republished in 1931 and 1935, taught economics by setting the principles of the discipline firmly within historical and institutional frameworks. Such subjects as production, credit, and consumption were described not as a set of economic laws but in terms of specific Canadian events. Whole chapters were devoted to descriptions of Canadian labour unions, primary industries, manufacturing, transportation, and other similar matters. In the 1924 edition, the business cycle was not even mentioned, nor were the concepts of elasticity of demand, national income, recession, or depression. However, there was discussion of the Canadian merchant marine, trade with New Zealand, and the Hudson Bay route. As one reviewer commented, 'It seems clear that one criterion of a good general textbook will be that it contains the least possible economic theory as such.' Ironically, MacGibbon was criticized as being too theoretical. The gap between this work and that of Samuelson or of any other standard post-war textbook on economics is as marked in Canada as in the United States. As Lekachman commented, 'In a generation economists have learned to concentrate on different problems, redefine the scope of their principles, reinterpret public policy, and transform their nomenclature.'[9]

There were many advantages to the historical and inductive approaches taken by MacGibbon's generation. In an educational milieu in which most Canadian economists received their graduate training abroad, they helped ensure that Canadian aspects of issues would not be ignored and Canadian economists not remain American or British in their outlook and approach. Thus, for example, the historical approach spawned in the work of men like Mackintosh and Innis a better understanding of Canadian development and a particular Canadian contribution to economic thought. In the development of the staple theory these two individuals and others combined historical, economic, and geographical methods in order to come to an understanding of a major aspect of Canadian economic development.[10]

Another important if more mundane advantage of this approach was, to put it simply, communicability. The free borrowing of concepts from other disciplines as well as the general descriptive framework in which most economic studies were written meant that, with a few exceptions, economic writing in Canada before the 1930s was easily understood by the educated layman. The orientation of the Canadian Political Science Association towards both the professional and amateur 'political economist' testifies to this, as do the formation and the early articles of the interdisciplinary *Canadian Journal of Economics and Political Science*. The absence of highly technical language and thus the ability of economists to communicate with other members of the intellectual community were essential to the continued existence of a distinct intellectual elite that remained oriented toward public reform and, increasingly, as the decade went on, looked to economics to point out the means by which those reforms might be achieved.

By the 1930s, however, the historical foundations of Canadian economics were under challenge. In the years after the First War and culminating in the Depression, a series of challenges confronted the intellectual traditions of the discipline. First, and perhaps most important, the rising importance of the social sciences and the secularization and professionalization of social work in the 1920s altered conceptions of the causes of social ills. Before 1914 a jumble of 'causes' had been assigned in searching for the root of social problems. These could vary from personal failure, such as laziness, self-indulgence, or immorality, to environmental factors, such as poor living conditions, lack of education, 'demon rum,' or other forces, but in most cases the sources of the problem tended to be immediate. Moreover, the basic economic problem of poverty or unemployment tended to be viewed as an effect rather than as a cause or, at most, as an intermediate cause stemming from a previous one.[11]

Tendencies within the progressive movement and the growing influence of social scientific thought, however, altered these assumptions. The declining influence of religion had decreased expectations about the possibilities of ethical reform, while the growing sense of the complex interdependence of modern society led observers to assign increasingly remote causes in the assessment of problems. From the individual, social workers and social gospellers moved the perspective outward to physical environment and family living conditions. Urban reformers looked to neighbourhood and city. By 1914 causation had shifted to the basic industrial trends that had determined the flight from the farm, the rise of the city, and, therefore, the urban environment in which so many social problems arose. Finally, by the 1920s, the key to that environment, to the demographic shifts that had taken place, and to many of the other social forces present was seen increasingly as man's search for economic security. As social worker Charlotte Whitton argued, social workers had to accept the fact that the problems they face 'are economic rather than moral in their origins.' 'Poverty,' as another social worker commented, 'must be viewed as an economic ill.' Economist Bryce Stewart took this new attitude to its logical conclusion when he warned that the 'opportunity to earn a living and to strive after accomplishments day by day is the foundation of public order.'[12]

The Depression reinforced this trend. Here was demonstrable evidence that remote economic events could shape the lives of thousands of men and women whose past environment, habits, and outlook had none of the classical symptoms of social problem groups. By the 1930s few within the intellectual community and fewer still within the social sciences would have argued with the notion that the 'sources of unemployment may generally be found in causes wholly independent of the workmen involved and over which they have no control.'[13] The belief developed that economics determined other environmental and personal conditions and that those economic factors were largely beyond the control of the individual. As this perception of social conditions grew, those who could claim some expertise in the mysteries of economic causation rose in prestige accordingly.

Moreover, as James Struthers has noted, the Depression tended to lay to rest one other important myth concering social problems. For years, as has been argued, there had been a widespread belief that one of the basic problems of Canadian society resulted from an excessive drain of population from the farms to the city. Urbanization created social ills and economic dislocation in the face of periodic changes in the business cycle. The farmer, however, was seen as at least partly immune from the vulnerabilities of the modern economy and the demand for farm help seen as infinite. As Finance Minister James Robb put it in 1924, 'There is work for them on the farm if they want it.' So long as this view persisted there was a moral judgment implicit in the choice of the unemployed individual to remain in the city rather than go to work on a farm. The individual who failed to assume the burdens of agricultural work, when it was available, thus had to bear at least part of the responsibility for his or her predicament. The years 1929-32, however, did much to destroy forever the long-standing Canadian belief in the limitless opportunities of the countryside. The devastation of the western agricultural sector was a source of genuine shock, even in an age when economic hardship was so common. It was hard for reformer or politician to call for a return to the land as thousands of farmers abandoned hope and left behind a lifetime's work. As economist Burton Hurd wrote in 1936, 'Any substantial attempt to relieve the urban unemployment situation by putting more people on the land promises to prove costly and relatively ineffective.' After 1930 Canadian economists increasingly looked to the agricultural sector as basic to the problems of Canada rather than as central to their solution. The long-standing safety valve that had conjured dozens of resettlement schemes and colonization companies into existence over the years had proved chimerical. Any solutions to the difficulties of modern Canada would have to deal with the improvement of the economy as a whole.[14]

Together these factors thrust the economist to the forefront for the first time in Canadian history. With the Depression came the opportunity for these academics to assume a new role in Canadian life and acquire new personal and professional prestige. As Harold Innis commented, 'Periods of prosperity may be characterized by the most intensive work in economics but periods of depression have been characterized by attempts at application.'[15]

Sudden prominence brought not only opportunity but also problems. No longer could the academic economist toil away quietly at his historically oriented work with little or no thought to the more immediate problems facing the country. As economics acquired new importance, those who practised it suddenly found their pronouncements being widely discussed in the papers and among the wider public. Economists were newly sought after, in the cynical words of one of them, to play the role of 'Medicine Man' and 'to cause the buffalo of peace and plenty to appear.' Public and political expectations for the profession were all too often unrealistic, given the state of the profession and the complexity of the problems it faced. As Saskatchewan economist George

Britnell wrote to Innis, 'There are times when I get really frightened at the things which lawyers and politicians think economists should be able to do by turning a handle and mixing a few statistics in a hat.' Whatever the anxiety, there was general agreement among economists that they could help solve the crucial problems facing the nation. Even Innis argued that 'political parties must draw to an increasing extent on the economic intelligence at hand.' The central question was whether the theoretical base of Canadian economics was adequate for the task ahead.[16]

It is impossible to deal with the evolution of economic theory in the Depression without first considering the place of Cambridge economist John Maynard Keynes. His importance to this and succeeding generations of economists cannot be disputed, for *The General Theory of Employment, Interest and Money* (1936) was a major force in reshaping economic thinking in Canada, as it was elsewhere. There is, however, somewhat of a myth surrounding the impact of Keynesian theory, and it leads to two dangerous simplifications.

First, some later Keynesians have seen *The General Theory* as not merely good economic theory but as permanent economic law. All too may have seen Keynes as having cut the Gordian knot of business cycle theory and ushered in a new era in which severe economic dislocations were unthinkable.[17] Such interpretations, more common twenty years ago than they are today, overstate the case. Economists have not resolved their debates on basic principles and are unlikely to do so within the foreseeable future. In the general context of economic theory, therefore, Keynes must be accorded a prominent place without being deified.

There is also a danger in portraying Keynesian theory as bursting upon the mid-Depression as a revelation out of nowhere. The emphasis accorded the 'Keynesian revolution' in economic literature tends to leave the casual reader with an image of two distinctly defined eras in economic thought. The first begins with Adam Smith's *Wealth of Nations*, published in 1776, and stretches barely perturbed by the work of Malthus, Ricardo, Jevons, Marshall, and others throughout the nineteenth century and into the twentieth. The second comes into being when economists read *The General Theory*, see the light, and convince politicians of the error of their ways. This is a deliberate overstatement, of course, but it emphasizes the problems contained in the concept of a 'Keynesian revolution,' occurring sometime in the few years after

1936. Instead, the influence of Keynesian writing on Canadian economic thought must be assessed with two facts in mind. First, Keynes was important before 1936. From at least 1919, with the publication of *The Economic Consequences of the Peace*, he was an economist of international repute. Later publications such as *Essays in Persuasion* (1931) and the two-volume *A Treatise on Money* (1930) enhanced an already significant stature within the profession. Not only professional economists in Canada but also 'amateurs' with an interest in economics, like J.W. Dafoe, felt it important to try and wade through Keynes's works.[18] Thus the economic profession in Canada was aware of the line of Keynes's thought and of the modifications he was making to traditional economic theory.

Second, long before 1936 there were doubts about the relevance of classical economic theory to modern conditions. The problem, as D.A. MacGibbon pointed out, was that the world of the classical economist rested on philosophical and sociological assumptions that seemed increasingly dubious as the twentieth century wore on. Bit by bit Canadian economists began to discover rot within the edifice of classical economic theory. By the time of the Depression, much of the basis of nineteenth-century economic thought was, if not discredited, under serious challenge. Only some reasonably acceptable alternate theory was necessary to convince the bulk of Canadian economists that the structure wasn't worth saving.[19]

The essential problem with classical economics was its assumption of the inherent stability of the economic world. The great Cambridge economist Alfred Marshall opened his 1890 work, *Principles of Economics*, with the comment that the 'general theory of the equilibrium of demand and supply is a Fundamental Idea running through the frames of all the various parts of the central problem of Distribution and Exchange.' He made economic principle inseparable from assumptions about social organization and from personal observations as to how society in fact operated. Late Victorian society, as viewed from Cambridge, gave the impression that stability was indeed the natural order of things.[20] For Marshall and for those many who followed his writings, equilibrium was not only one aspect of economics but a central notion that carried with it subordinate notions of social stability and a self-correcting price system.

Though the variables could be bewildering, the process by which the price system achieved equilibrium was relatively straightforward. As economists like the young W.C. Clark argued, in a recession manufacturers would cut production and wages to rid themselves of excess inventories and reduce production costs. At the same time investment in manufacturing would decrease and money would, like labour, become a cheaper commodity. At some point, however, inventories would be run down and the costs of production lowered sufficiently to encourage an increase in production. Demand would also increase because of the lower costs for the goods. The need for workmen would thus increase until unemployment eased and wages rose. The increase in demand would also make new investment worthwhile and cause interest rates to recover. Equilibrium would have been achieved, under conditions of full production and employment. Eventually, of course, excessive demand could push up the cost of wages and money to the point where prices of the product would increase, excessive new capacity come onstream, and the downturn begin. Through it all, however, was the assumption that the business cycle was self-correcting in its effects and that its natural tendency was to move toward full production and employment – that magic point where demand met supply.[21]

Closely related was a theory of money that also reflected the stability of the nineteenth century and emphasized the self-correcting systems within the market-place. The 'quantity theory of money,' as it had evolved under the guidance of the Cambridge theorists, assumed two basic points. First, any change in the quantity of money in circulation had a direct effect, all things being equal, on the price level. The expansion of the money supply was thus, in most cases, inflationary, and a more or less constant money supply was seen as characteristic of a sound economy. Second, money affected the achievement of equilibrium in that the demand for investment would increase demand for this relatively fixed good, thus forcing an increase in interest rates. In accordance with the normal laws of supply and demand, the demand for money would thus decrease and the pressure for investment ease. Conversely, in recessionary times the demand for money would be low and interest rates would adjust downwards, making investment more attractive.[22]

Demand and supply functions thus worked in both the financial and commercial worlds to adjust the economy towards full employment and production. Disruptions could occur, but the emphasis in much of the writing of the Marshall school was that politicians must resist the temptation to interfere in the economy when such disruptions did happen. They would only make matters worse. This does not mean that Marshall, or those Canadians who accepted his principles, opposed all government activism. What they did fear was a return to medieval principles of guilds, legal monopolies, and excessive regulation designed to destroy the price system's natural workings. 'Nearly all the founders of modern economics were men of gentle and sympathetic temper,' Marshall reminded his readers. They insisted that the government allow the economic system to work unhindered because excessive interference would have hurt rather than have helped the people most vulnerable to economic downturn.[23]

In placing Canadian economic writing to the 1920s within this classical-marginalist tradition qualification is necessary. There was always a distinction in Canadian economic writing between the workings of the market-place and the necessities of ameliorative action. Few, if any, Canadian economists took their defence of classical economic theory to the point where they translated it into a social philosophy. The idealist tradition in Canada was simply too strong, as indicated by the involvement of men like Shortt and Mavor in reform movements that accepted increased government participation in social matters. Mackenzie King, another economist and idealist, had been active in drawing the Laurier government into some involvement, however modest, in the protection of many groups affected by rising industrialism. The Canadian academic community thus never saw the extreme defences of laissez-faire typified by such American economists as Amasa Walker and Laurence Laughlin. Instead, Canadian economic thought sought to preserve the integrity of the price system while recognizing the role of government in ameliorating the negative side-effects of modern industrial capitalism.[24]

In the years around the First World War, as the Christian idealist impulse weakened, this ameliorative tendency began to become integrated into basic economic theory. The emphasis on equilibrium was joined by a concern for the fluctuations between the points of equilibrium, for the basic reason that points of disequilibrium began to seem as prevalent as those of relative equilibrium. The first Canadian 'industrial' recessions, in 1907, 1912-13, and 1919-20, revealed the vulnerability of the Canadian economy to economic downturns. Economists became less sanguine about allowing the automatic forces within the market-place to make the necessary corrections. As early as 1909, O.D. Skelton urged the government to plan its spending in such a way as to act as a 'flywheel' in the business cycle. By planning public works ahead of time but postponing them in good times while accelerating them in bad, it could ease inflationary pressures at the top end of the cycle and increase employment at the bottom. The idea was restated by the Ontario Commission on Unemployment in 1913 and became increasingly common thereafter.[25]

The market-place was thus inadequate for regulating economic activity. First, Canadian economists had from the beginning thought it necessary and desirable for the governments to ease individual hardship. Second, by the 1920s there was at least discussion of the possibilities of reacting to the cycle through the use of public works that could both assist workers by providing additional employment and 'prime the pump' by moving public funds into the market-place. These limited concepts of involvement in the market-place were a long way from the later self-confident assertions that the business cycle was controllable, but they were not pure classical economics.

The results of these changes were somewhat paradoxical. Canadian economic writing remained classical in outlook yet in several specific instances ignored classical theory in the face of modern problems. Economists explained that the classical theories propounded by people like Marshall were correct and made complete sense, but only for Marshall's world. That world, unfortunately, had ended with the First World War. Marshall's theories of equilibrium depended on a world in which international trading relationships were stable and unhindered by artificial barriers. Specifically, they required stable prices domestically and stable exchange rates internationally. For the actual situation of late-nineteenth-century Europe, such assumptions were not unreasonable, especially from the vantage point of the British Empire. The gold standard was intact, buttressed by the strength of the British pound and the belief in free trade. Such stability in key areas allowed market forces to work their way through the system in a relatively smooth fashion, thus balancing supply and demand at the point of equilibrium. Between 1914 and 1919, however, the economic order had been seriously disrupted. Monetary relations were destabilized by the costs of fighting the war, the abandonment of the gold standard by many nations, and the rising creditor status of the United States. Attempts to restore that standard in the post-war years had only made matters worse, because key currencies like the pound sterling were valued incorrectly. Also, drawing from Keynes, Canadian economists criticized the peace conference of 1919 and the hefty reparations forced on Germany, which they saw as unrealistic and exacerbating the imbalances that were already so chronic in the modern world.[26]

Most of this analysis is unexceptionable today both as history and as economic theory. Such writings, however, implied that theories that applied to the stable pre-1914 period were of doubtful applicability in an era that experienced depression, hyper-inflation, speculative boom, and crash, all within the space of ten years. This was not a world that mirrored Marshall's state of equilibrium or exhibited the smooth workings of Adam Smith's invisible hand. Faced with new and volatile circumstances, Canadian economic writing shifted from an emphasis on stability to a concern with the problems of change and dislocation. The authority of Marshall was increasingly challenged by the ideas of Veblen, Schumpeter, and Keynes. In formal terms, classical economic theory still held that the natural point of equilibrium was at full employment and production. So many destabilizing forces had come into play, however, that the point of equilibrium seemed more a utopian ideal than the normal state of things.

It was thus with, at best, a qualified adherence to the traditional tenets of classical theory that Canadian economists turned their attention to the Depression when it hit in 1929-30. Various specific factors were assigned blame for the downturn. Imbalances in Canadian trade, excessive reliance on foreign markets, lack of protection for domestic production, the collapse of the wheat market, the end of an era of expansion and other themes appeared and reappeared in popular journals, scholarly articles, and learned monographs as central to the coming of the Depression. It would be overstating the case to imply that all Canadian economists were moving clearly in one direction. The Depression was a massive shock, and it took time to adapt views to new circumstances. Traditional ideas die hard, and there was a great deal of moralizing by economists to the effect that Canadians and others in the Western world had simply become too greedy. The search for material success in the post-war world had allowed the promoter to undertake an 'orgy of speculative development.' Banking expert and University of Toronto professor Gilbert Jackson charged in 1933 that the 'root cause of the depression lies in no fault of this economic mechanism by which we live, but in ourselves.' The Depression merely proved to him that economics was 'an exemplification of the moral law.' Man had become too greedy and now was paying the price.[27]

While all these factors were, to one degree or another, relevant in assessing the coming of the Depression, none went beyond malfunctions in the economy to what Innis termed 'the Canadian problem.'[28] It was one thing to point to specific, and usually obvious, vulnerabilities in the economy. It was quite another to understand the business cycle well enough to explain why, in this instance, that cycle was so severe. Even seeking such an understanding was part of the process, for government and public looked to economists not merely to discover what had gone wrong but also to find remedies. Identifying the problem accurately, therefore, was the important first step in finding a solution.

A 1932 editorial in the *Canadian Banker*, probably written by W.A. Mackintosh, thought it had discovered certain patterns in the various assessments of the Depression. There was, it concluded, a 'monetary school' and a 'disequilibrium school' on the causes of the collapse. The monetary school looked back to the First World War and emphasized the shortage of gold and its misallocation. The disequilibrium school also looked back to the war but argued that massive upheavals in production and technology had left 'the world with greatly expanded productive equipment in food and raw materials producing countries especially.' Normally, adjustment would have occurred in the post-war period. In democracies, however, public pressure had led government to seek popularity by means of price regulation and other schemes designed to thwart the necessary market changes. The readjustment was thus not allowed to run its course, and pressures continued to build within the system. Thus 'the severity of the present depression is not to be regarded as primarily cyclical but rather as the result of the necessity of working through these accumulated maladjustments suddenly.'[29]

Though it is impossible to separate completely the monetary and disequilibrium factors brought about by the war, the *Canadian Banker* was correct about the existence of the two schools. The monetary school began with two beliefs strongly held within the Canadian economic community. The first was that the gold standard was the best means of ensuring stable international price relations. In spite of the occasional bi-metallist like Humfrey Michell of McMaster University, most Canadian economists remained convinced of the wisdom of this traditional economic system. The second was the that gold standard was in a shambles. When the United Kingdom abandoned gold in 1931 it aggravated an already chaotic situation and marked the end of the attempts to patch up the monetary system on the basis of pre-1914 standards. If the gold standard were no longer possible, then what was needed, economists agreed, was an orderly readjustment of international monetary relations. What was actually occurring had, as Clifford

Clark noted, an 'every-country-for-itself, devil take the hindmost character.'[30]

A variation of this monetary theory argued that the world faced a 'price crisis, the result of a prolonged and apparently not yet completed rise in the scarcity and value of the monetary unit.' Drawing on the quantity theory of money, this hypothesis argued that the First World War and other events had forced an increase in nominal prices, thus leaving the quantity of money available for the carrying on of normal transactions insufficient. Inevitably money supplies had to increase or prices fall. Since the world had clung to gold without allowing for sufficient revaluation of its price, the 1920s had seen a serious disequilibrium develop, as too little money chased too many purchases at an ever-increasing rate. With the speculative frenzy on the stock exchanges in New York and elsewhere, the shortage of funds became even more acute, and before long there 'was not enough money left in the ordinary channels of business to conduct the trade of the world and the trade of the world broke down.'[31]

As this and other theories held by the monetary school recognized, the self-righting mechanisms of classical theory were, at best, going to take effect only in the long run. The continued instability of the international monetary structure, the increase in currency restrictions, and barriers to international trade all meant that the situation was being subjected to new shocks on an almost weekly basis. The forces of stabilization thus had no opportunity to make themselves felt. A combination of co-operation on foreign exchange rates, the place of gold in future monetary arrangements, and domestic efforts to achieve a stable price level would resolve the basic problems underlying the collapse of 1929-30. There was, however, no indication that the necessary co-operation was developing or even that economists, bankers, business, and government could agree as to what direction prices should be heading.

The other, disequilibrium school of thought had at its basis the traditional arguments of classical theory. Various forces had thrown the economy out of equilibrium. The Depression was but another trough in the ongoing business cycle similar to those of 1873, 1893, 1907, and 1912-13. Each economist had his own theories as to why this trough should be more severe than earlier ones, though the most popular centred on the dislocations of the First World War. Harold Innis, for example, saw the war as marking a fundamental watershed in the nature of industrial production. The first stage of the industrial revolution had been developed on the basis of coal and iron. Areas with abundant supplies of these materials became economically powerful. The war had brought a shift away from these materials, however, and the old 'palaeotechnic' capitalist economy began to yield to the 'neotechnic' world of internal combustion engines, hydro-electricity, and other sources of power. Paleotechnic areas sank into an increasingly depressed state while investment flowed to new areas. The result was severe structural dislocation. 'Neotechnic industrialism superimposed on paleotechnic industrialism involved changes of great implication to modern society and brought strains of great severity.'[32] Until the transition was made, the economic disequilibrium would remain.

It was but a short step from the idea that modern society was undergoing basic technological shifts to the conclusion that the Depression marked not the evolution of capitalism but its most severe crisis to date. In many writings, and not just those of Marxists, there was the suspicion that capitalism itself was one gigantic business cycle, containing within it many smaller ones. That cycle had begun its rise in the eighteenth-century, peaked in the nineteenth, and exihibited increasing signs of instability in the twentieth. Finally, in 1929 it began the collapse. When the cycle began again it would be under a different socio-economic system.

There were, many economists felt, elements within the capitalist system that foreshadowed impending collapse. Most importantly, the efficiency of production appeared to have had run ahead of that of consumption. There were too many goods and too few markets for those goods. In 1932, for example, W.B. Hurd of Brandon College argued that the 'greatly enhanced efficiency of large scale production is perhaps the strongest argument for the prevailing competitive system; yet the widespread adoption of capitalistic technique has created a series of business problems of unprecedented magnitude.' Writing three years later, Stephen Leacock made essentially the same argument. Adam Smith's classical economic theories were a failure, Leacock concluded, because they did not comprehend the problems of long-term over-production. Even R.B. Bennett picked up on the theme in his opening New Deal speech in 1935. Only a redistribution of wealth would allow the preservation of the capitalist system: 'It has become increasingly clear to thoughtful minds in all industrial countries that what is needed for the restoration of industrial equilibrium is practically a change in our social system.' The 'invisible hand' seemed no longer to function, and only a basic restructuring of the economy could remove the basic flaws of modern capitalism.[33]

Such views raise the issue of what had happened to those classical self-correcting forces that were supposed to lift economies out of recession. Specifically, classical theory argued that if over-production were a problem, falling sales and rising inventories would lead businessmen to close down production and workers, faced with rising unemployment, to accept lower wages. The combination of fewer goods being put on the market and being produced at less cost would eventually remove the glut. According to Hurd, however, this pattern was no longer quite so automatic. Large-scale industrial enterprises had high fixed costs in plant and machinery. These fixed costs encouraged the continuation of production even after a glut had developed for a particular product. Industries were under continual pressure to keep plant and machinery functioning. If things continued to worsen, of course, the company would reduce production, but as soon as the upturn began the pressure to use idle machinery would increase and production would resume long before the economy had fully disposed of the glut. Pressure would then be brought to bear upon governments to preserve domestic markets for domestic industry, thus encouraging a series of barriers to trade such as quotas and prohibitive tariffs. The results could be seen simply by looking around. 'The effect of increased competition, coupled with the practical closing of foreign markets, on industrial centres with economies and population structures geared up to productive capacity much beyond requirements has verged on the catastrophic.'[34]

Though the theories of Hurd and others were open to criticism on points, the Depression led many economists to chip away yet more away from the already crumbling edifice of classical economics. Most importantly, the belief that equilibrium existed at the point of full employment and production had been thrown into serious doubt before the publication of *The General Theory*. For both monetary and disequilibrium theorists, the frictional problems in the way of reaching equilibrium were so great that stability at full employment and production was at best an illusory goal. For the more pessimistic, who saw in the Depression a crisis of capitalism, the problems with classical theory were even more fundamental. Classical economics had developed to explain capitalism, and capitalism was on the verge of collapse. The theory could become as obsolete as the system under which it developed. Given these criticisms and doubts, it is no wonder that

Keynes was well received when he published his *General Theory* in 1936 and provided the theoretical justification for laying to rest the concept of equilibrium at full employment.

From an analysis of the problem it was necessary to move toward solutions. Proposals of varying sophistication and relevance were suggested, but it is probably best to categorize the major writings of academic economic thought in the decade in terms of the monetary and disequilibrium schools already mentioned.

On the monetary side, economists were able to come up with a clear proposal for change. Moreover, they set out to have it implemented by the federal government. What they wanted and eventually got was a central bank for Canada. Yet the campaign for the bank, though successful, must be viewed as a modest first step in the minds of economists. They campaigned hard for it not because they saw it as a panacea for depression but because it was the one feasible step that could be taken domestically on monetary matters.

The rapid development of support for the central bank has to be set against its historical backdrop. First, a decline in prices occurred during the period 1929-33. Though it helped those with savings, it severely aggravated the problems of groups like farmers who were faced with large fixed debts and declining income. Second, there was a strong tradition in North America, especially within the agrarian sector, of responding to this predicament, with demands for deliberate inflation of prices. Some of the most powerful waves of rural protest had gained their momentum from the cry for currency reform. Stretching from the Greenback and free silver movements of the nineteenth-century United States through the Non-Partisan and Progressive movements of Canada, 'easy money' had been a regularly raised cry on the frontier. In the 1930s the theme was revived most persistently in the writings of Major C.H. Douglas, the social crediter whose teachings were appearing with ever-increasing regularity among the splintered ranks of farm parties in the Canadian West. The continuing force of these ideas would be dramatically revealed in 1935, when William Aberhart swept to power in Alberta on the basis of social credit theory.

Though a recurring theme in Canadian and American history, the idea of easy money had never been acceptable in traditional business and academic circles. For the economists the ideal was price stability because, as has been pointed out, it removed one more source of disequilibrium. For the banker and businessman not only was sound money thought good for the economy, but there was also a strong belief that a contract between the debtor and creditor was violated, at least morally, when the value of money changed dramatically. The gold standard, because it restrained expansion in the money supply, provided the desired stability.

Yet, as has been indicated, by the early 1930s there was no clear choice between a stable gold system and some other less favoured approach to the monetary structure of the nation. Economists had to find some means of achieving the monetary stability that had been so routine before the war.[35] The international situation was so chaotic that few held out much hope that it would be resolved in the near future. Domestically, however, improvement seemed possible with the formation of a Canadian central bank to oversee matters of currency, credit, and foreign exchange rates. It was thus not economic theory, but circumstance, that had altered. A stable price level and a monetary structure remained the goal of the economic profession. What had altered was the belief that such stability could be achieved only if the government became directly involved in monetary matters.

As with so many other changes in Canada, this one must be traced not from the Depression but from the First World War. Until 1914 the Canadian government had, as one writer has observed, seen 'the preservation of the established external value of the dollar' as 'the sole monetary objective of the government.' Banks, though restricted in terms of procedures for note issue, necessary reserves, and other matters, were generally expected to handle most other monetary and exchange functions. Generally the system did not work badly, and early suggestions for change were scorned. 'In this pre-1914 period,' as one historian has noted, 'bankers and government officials enjoyed an easy and confident support.' Moreover, with the economic profession in Canada just beginning to develop, it was the banking profession that had the reputation among government officials as the real experts on the economy, and they were widely respected within the intellectual community. Typical was Sir Edmund Walker, president of the Bank of Commerce from 1902 to 1924. Author of a history of banking, chairman of the board of governors of the University of Toronto, and a confidant of both academics and politicians, he represented the wide range of activities that might be expected from a senior banker. He was also the sort of person to whom the government looked when it needed economic advice. Also typical of this earlier period was Thomas White. When the government of Sir Robert Borden appointed this 'near banker' minister of finance it received high praise from those interested in planning and reform. Thus the banking community played a central role as the arbiter of economic wisdom and financial planning before 1914, just as the economic community would after 1930.[36]

Ironically, it was under the administration of White that changes began to occur. The necessities of war forced the government to alter previously acceptable arrangements and to pass the 1914 Finance Act. This act, which tied bank deposits either to gold or Dominion notes, eased pressure on the gold standard by effectively suspending it. It was touted as a war measure but remained in place when peace returned. The result was a contradiction in Dominion monetary structures. The system no longer operated automatically, because it was not based purely on gold, yet the government had neither the power nor the expertise properly to manage the monetary system. Over the next few years various amendments only patched up a rather cumbersome and inefficient structure of monetary management.[37]

By the 1930s positions had hardened. On the one side were the great majority of commercial bankers who felt that, whatever the shortcomings of the Finance Act, it left the making of basic decisions on monetary and credit matters to those best qualified – themselves. Moreover, any central bank was all too likely to be structured in such a way as to compete with them or remove their long-standing privilege of note issue. Most important, they feared that a government-controlled central bank would, whatever the intentions of the government of the day, eventually become a pawn in political moves to inflate the currency and thereby undermine its soundness. They constituted a formidable lobby, especially given the high opinion that government circles had of Canadian banks, which was enhanced by their success in surviving the economic collapse.

Opposing the bankers were the majority of Canadian economists. Their basic criticism of monetary policy in the Dominion was, in the words of Toronto professor A.F.W. Plumptre, that 'it did not exist.' A group of Queen's economists termed the Finance Act, which was supposed to provide a framework for that monetary policy, a 'dangerous piece of legislation' on two grounds. First, it required no reserve for notes issued under its provisions, and, second, it was under the control of the Department of Finance, a politically controlled body that could manipulate the bank for partisan purposes. For economists the management of credit was too important to be left in the hands of commercial banks, even if, as most economists accepted, they were generally competent in their operations. 'The world in which we live,' wrote the Queen's professors, 'is a very different one from that of pre-war days and it is doubtful if we could recover the environment in which our pre-war monetary legislation operated.'[38]

In theoretical terms, Canadian economists saw a central bank as a potentially important agent of government economic policy. 'The function of a central bank is to determine the quantity of credit that will be made available by the commercial banks to the business public,' noted the Queen's Department of Economics, but that function could operate in numerous ways. The issue of notes, reserve requirments, open market operations, and other activities could make the bank a major force in the determination of price levels and interest rates. Moreover, the bank could operate so as to stabilize foreign exchange rates and thus affect Canada's international trading relations. It would be, all in all, a powerful tool to aid in the control of business cycles. As C.W. Hewetson of the University of Alberta commented, 'In the light of our present knowledge of economic matters it would appear that the greatest hope of bringing trade fluctuations under some measure of control lies in the artificial regulation of bank credit with a view to greater stability of the general price level.'[39] The drive for the bank among Canadian economists thus indicated a growing belief that, given the right tools, society could indeed manipulate business cycles. Macro-economic management, so long submerged by the rhetoric of self-correction and inevitability, was beginning to surface in Canadian economic writing.[40]

Canadian economists thus stood pitted against the bankers in the debate over a central bank. At this point the changing nature of the relation between the government and the intellectual community becomes apparent. The economists found themselves with as much access to key figures in the political world as did the leaders of the banking community. Thus, for example, the Queen's economists, proponents of a strong bank, found various ways in which to steer discussion in the right direction. Initially, of course, they had access to O.D. Skelton, who was himself sympathetic to a central bank and who had the ear of Prime Minister Bennett and other leading politicians. Further, Queen's political scientist and Liberal adviser Norman Rogers introduced his colleague C.A. Curtis to Mackenzie King as an expert on banking. Before long Curtis delivered a memorandum on central banking to the leader of the opposition that King used to good effect in the House of Commons. It was, he said, 'an excellent memo, most helpful.' Most important, however, was the presence of Clifford Clark as deputy minister of finance. As with so many of his Queen's colleagues, he was committed to the formation of a central bank, and as the man charged under the Finance Act of 1923 with responsibility for its regulations, he was in the perfect position to argue that the act was deficient. Over the next two years he did everything he could to ensure that the government adopted the view of the Queen's economists.[41]

By 1933 the economists had gained the upper hand over the bankers. The Liberal party had come out in favour of the principle of a central bank, while R.B. Bennett's Conservatives, noting the drift of public opinion in the country, appointed a royal commission to investigate the matter. At the annual meeting of the Canadian Political Science Association that year, Clark found a great deal of sympathy for a bank, and as it was up to him to find a secretary for the royal commission he naturally looked among his supportive colleagues. The man he chose was A.F.W. Plumptre of Toronto. As Plumptre had been involved with Curtis and others in Massey's study groups on central banking, his pro-bank views were well known. The commission was thus given a gentle prod in the right direction by the placement of a pro-bank economist in a key position.[42]

The Royal Commission on Banking, or Macmillan Commission, saw the next stage in the debate between the old and new elites of economic experts played out. The great majority of bankers remained opposed to a central bank and argued that the existing system, while far from perfect, had proved its worth over the years. The tone was set on the first day of hearings when the president of the Canadian Bankers' Association concluded that the system 'has provided Canada with a financial structure which is at the same time extremely strong, and singularly flexible; with a structure well adapted to the needs of the country.'[43] As the hearings moved across the country, banker after banker pointed with pride to the accomplishments of his company and, explicitly or implicitly, challenged the need for a central bank.

On the other side the great majority of economists called the formation of a central bank a necessity. Most enthusiastic were the Queen's economists Mackintosh, Curtis, and F.A. Knox, who urged wide latitude for the central bank in its activities and significant powers over commercial banks. Others were slightly more cautious, but there was widespread support for the principle from men like W.B. Hurd of Brandon College, Elliot and Hewetson of Alberta, and Carrothers, Topping, and Drummond of British Columbia. There were opponents, of course, but the reasons for opposition help prove that most economists favoured a central bank. First, of seventeen economists who appeared before the commission, only four opposed the bank. Second, two opponents, Edouard Montpetit and M. Grégoire of Laval, seemed to be as concerned with centralized government control and its effect on Quebec as with the economic functions of the bank. Their monetary views were thus affected by their desire to preserve provincial autonomy. The other two opponents were men with somewhat unorthodox views. H. Michell of McMaster was, as has been mentioned, about the only bi-metallist among academic economists in Canada, and it was his view that bi-metallism rather than a central bank would resolve any monetary problems. W. Swanson of Saskatchewan was extremely conservative and looked to aesthetic solutions to the Depression, but even he admitted that changes were needed.[44]

In the end, the economists won out over the bankers. The Macmillan Commission's analysis of the problem and limitations of the Finance Act and its operations in Canada paralleled in all essentials the viewpoint of the majority of economists testifying before it. The act, the commission concluded, 'did not provide Canada with the organization needed to undertake the task which the maintenance of the restored gold standard implied.' Only a central bank could provide the necessary objectivity, expertise, and facilities for the sort of credit management that was needed in modern circumstances. The decision was close, however. Two of the five commissioners, Sir Thomas White and Beaudry Leman, dissented, believing that a central bank would hinder rather than facilitate monetary objectives in Canada. Given such a narrow victory for the principle of a central bank, the role of the professional economic community, both inside and outside the commission, may well have been decisive.[45]

In 1934 the Conservative government established the Bank of Canada, and, though there was considerable controversy to come over the relation of the bank to the government and over other matters, the important battle had been won. The economic profession had demonstrated the degree of influence it had in Ottawa. Clifford Clark then sought to consolidate that influence by ensuring that the Bank become an agency of economic planning run by economists. What was needed in the way of a governor, he told Bennett, was not a banker but an economist. 'The major problem of central banking is not one of routine administration but rather of economic interpretation and monetary principles.'[46]

An economist was not appointed. Instead the government brought in Graham Towers, assistant general manager of the Royal Bank and one of the few commercial bankers who had not been opposed to a central bank. Though not an academic economist, Towers was regarded with some respect within political and economic circles as an innovative banker. He also had credentials in economics, having studied under Leacock at McGill and being one of the few bankers in Canada to belong to the Canadian Political Science Association. Finally, in both his background and age (he was 37 at the time of his appointment), he possessed characteristics similar to the group of interconnected intellectuals that had formed in recent years. Though not a member of this network at the time of his appointment, he was able to feel comfortable with it and to work with those linked to it.[47]

Nor did Towers's appointment mean that the economic profession was without direct influence on the Bank of Canada. On the contrary, the Bank provided a whole new area of recruitment for bright, well-trained intellectuals. Here, as in so many cases, personnel were drawn from a specific social-intellectual class with common acquaintances and similar university backgrounds. At the centre of this group in the Bank was Alex Skelton, Rhodes scholar and son of O.D. Skelton, who was hired to head up the bank's research department. The brilliant and somewhat erratic Skelton would attempt over the next few years to ensure that the Bank was imbued with reformist zeal. In future years many of the brightest and best students of the Canadian economic profession found their way into the bank. Men like John Deutsch and Louis Rasminsky ensured that the influence gained in the 1930s would remain intact in the Second World War and afterwards.

For all the potential of the Bank, however, the economic community recognized that this institution would not, in itself, provide sufficient control over the economy to make a real difference in the Depression. The Bank, it was sensed, was likely to be cautious in its approach to monetary problems. 'In the present state of the science of economics and the art of central banking there has been achieved no great exactness in the control of price levels through central bank operations. The direction in which the control operates is well understood, but the degrees to which it operates are not to be predicted accurately.' Thus even those who most strongly advocated the creation of the Bank did not expect too much from the institution. It was just as well. Graham Towers and his senior staff were carefully orthodox in their monetary policy and cautious enough not to push the bank into new ventures too quickly. Even with the arrival of the *General Theory*, the governor of the Bank remained concerned lest enthusiasm for monetary reform lead to debasement of the currency. As Towers warned, 'Inflation was a form of taxation' and one that hit fixed incomes the most. It was thus to be some time before the bank moved into the full range of monetary operations. Other measures were patently necessary if the nation were to take full advantage of the possibilities of economic control of the economy.[48]

One obvious possibility was to tackle the Depression on the assumption that disequilibrium was the basic factor in determining its nature. Perhaps steps could be taken to remove some of the forces creating or continuing that disequilibrium and thus allow the business cycle to move toward full employment and production. The most obvious tool for dealing with disequilibrium in current circumstances was the long-standing concept of pump-priming, that is the injection of funds into a slack economy in order to create jobs for workers and business for employers. Earlier Canadian proposals had been given added legitimacy when, in 1930, Keynes, testifying before the British Macmillan Commission, had advocated massive government works as a response to the downturn.[49] Moreover, the use of public works to combat the Depression was an issue of immediate importance. The Conservative government passed a series of public works measures, first becoming involved directly and then providing a series of grants to the provinces. Thus Canadian economists were well aware of the use of government funds to encourage recovery, both as a practical policy and as a theoretical tool of contra-cyclical economic management.

Yet the reaction of Canadian economists towards such schemes reveals the conservative side of the profession. If anything, most economists were cooler towards such-large scale expenditures in the name of recovery than were politicians. On the one hand, they recognized that if the public works expenditures were to be meaningful they would have to be on a large scale. Thus, for example, the $50 million proposed by Bennett in 1934 was criticized by Gilbert Jackson and others as insufficient to prime the pump. 'We must spend on a large enough scale.' On the other hand, economists were as convinced as the most cautious back-bencher that government spending was dangerously out of control. The First World War, they argued, had pushed the total Canadian debt load dangerously high. In addition, the creation of the Canadian National Railway system and other modern acquisitions had aggravated the situation. Then, with the Depression and the decline in government revenues, the debts, which remained fixed, became a millstone around the Canadian economy. Thus, although deficit financing was an accepted economic principle, as was the use of public works for recovery, Canadian economists doubted whether they were desirable in Canada at present. 'The increasing proportion of national incomes which is now being diverted by governments, together with the increasing burden of debt charges,' warned D.C. MacGregor in 1934, 'raises the question of whether or not public finance is approaching the limits of its effectiveness and soundness within a capitalistic economy.' Jackson, after criticizing Bennett's public works expenditures as too small to have an effect, argued not for greater expenditure but for the 'ruthless balancing of all budgets, governmental and municipal.' R.H. Coats asked with concern about the various unemployment insurance schemes being promoted how they 'could possibly avoid bankruptcy.'[50]

The orthodox economic viewpoint was best revealed in the actions of Clifford Clark in his first years as deputy minister of finance. Clark was well aware of the possibilities of deficit financing, having trained under Skelton. As with the majority of economists, however, he was cautious about its use in Canada. For him, wartime debts and problems brought on by German reparations and currency instability lay at the bottom of the Depression. Frivolous or excessive government expenditure would only aggravate an already serious problem. Fiscal conservatism thus continued to be the style of the Department of Finance even after it came under the control of its first professional economist.[51]

If it was not possible to spend one's way out of the Depression, perhaps some structural or institutional reform might improve the situation. Not surprisingly, for example, the LSR, which included economists like Biss and Forsey, argued that the Depression was linked to the evolution of capitalism. Years of growth and innovation as new technologies developed and new lands opened had now been replaced by depression in the era of 'monopoly capitalism.' Serious maldistribution of wealth and problems of over-production would continue to plague the system. Only a basic reform of institutions and the development of 'socialized monopoly' would remedy the basic problems of the Canadian economy. 'Planlessness, rigidities and above all the restriction of markets enforced by pursuit of profit produces a situation in which consumption chronically lags behind capacity to produce.'[52]

Even those who rejected socialism often accepted the critique of capitalism and the argument that basic structural changes were necessary. Terry MacDermott and Francis Hankin, both members of the Montreal 'group' that included Claxton and Scott, wrote *Recovery by Control* in 1933. Drawing its inspiration from Franklin Roosevelt's New Deal, its basic premiss was that the only way to overcome the blind forces of 'economic anarchy' was to curb capitalist excesses in the name of social security and stability. Uncontrolled private ownership would have to yield to public interests. Pointing to the Post Office, the CBC, Ontario Hydro, and other publicly controlled operations, they argued that the basic principles in operation in these bodies should be widely extended. The reasoning was economic. In spite of Adam Smith, they concluded, the reconciliation of self-interest among millions of individuals was impossible. The invisible hand was an illusion. The world was forced to operate in ruthless competition which created maldistribution of wealth and 'gives rise to the violent fluctuations in the purchasing power of consumers. That it is which bedevils economic security.' Brooke Claxton found their arguments impressive and even sent a copy of the book to Bennett's private secretary, R.K. Finlayson, with an urgent appeal that the prime minister consider it as a possible means of dealing with the Depression. The tone of Bennett's New Deal program, though drawn from American rather than Canadian sources, indicates that the belief in the need for structural changes was deeply ingrained in Canadian thought by the mid-1930s.[53]

The reform orientation of the intellectual elite, the failure of business to prevent the Depression or to respond adequately to it, and the seeming failure of the self-righting mechanisms of classical economics all prompted this argument that structural change was necessary. It also reflected the degree to which economic method was becoming the standard approach to social issues even among non-economists. The writings of people like MacDermott and members of the LSR mirrored those of professional economists. Thus in 1934, when the Canadian Institute of International Affairs held a study group on the Canadian economy in Montreal, problems of structural reform consumed much of the conference. Present were a cross-section of Canadian economists, with such well-known individuals as Harold Innis, Vincent Bladen, A.F.W. Plumptre, Robert McQueen, G.E. Britnell, and H.R. Kemp. Also present were non-economist intellectuals like Norman Rogers, Frank Underhill, and a young Manitoba historian, J.W. Pickersgill. Various solutions were debated, with lively disagreement as to whether Underhill's defence of 'radical political and economic reconstruction' made sense. In the end, though the group refused to accept Underhill's more radical proposals, there was a strong feeling that social and structural reforms were necessary if recovery were to take place. The market-place could not be left to work the disequilibrium out of the economy. Instead a new view was developing: disequilibrium must be managed through direct and ongoing intervention. The conference decided in favour of a national planning council 'with the implication of a considerable degree of social and economic planning.'[54]

Thus professional economic opinion was, by the mid-1930s, increasingly despairing of classical theories of recovery from depression. As with so many other intellectuals of the age, economists began to argue that economic recovery involved reforms that would remove structural problems within the economy and facilitate government intervention to assist in the recovery. The Bank of Canada had been but a first small step. The acceptance of the need for widespread reforms produced a dilemma in the late 1930s. Serious fiscal imbalances and constitutional obstacles, largely resulting from Canada's federal character, seemed to interpose themselves between the planners and their reforms. The very constitution of Canada appeared to be a 'structural problem.' Reform of federal-provincial relations became, for many, the key to all the other necessary changes. Economics, which was already blending with social reform, now blended with politics as the intellectual elite sought to strengthen the power of the federal government in the name of economic recovery and social reform.

9

The problem of national unity
and the Rowell-Sirois Report
1935-40

Emotional nationalism had always been an inherent part of progressivism between the two world wars. As has been argued, national causes had, more than anything else, helped form the intellectual network in the post-First World War period. Until the mid-1930s, however, the cause of nationalism had been only loosely connected to ideas of social and economic reform in the writings of the intellectual community. Reform and proper planning would, it was true, contribute to Canadian nationalism by making the country a better place to live. Indeed, in cases like the Canadian Radio League, nationalism had been the primary justificastion for state intervention. For the most part, however, the ties between the two causes were less direct. One was viewed as a defensive resistance to British machinations for greater Imperial commitments by Canada while the other was seen as a positive assault on the traditions of laissez-faire and political amateurism within Canada. In the latter part of the Depression decade, however, it became impossible to consider the issues of social and economic planning without dealing with the nature of Canadian nationalism.

There were several reasons for this. First, it became apparent that questions of constitutional jurisdiction could not be treated lightly by those who would launch government on major new programs. This was shown in 1935 when R.B. Bennett's New Deal legislation ran into criticism from the Liberal opposition and from observers outside Parliament for its dubious constitutionality.[1] When the Liberal victory of 1935 halted Bennett's initiative, few reformers outside the Conservative party mourned its collapse, but all were left with the same problem. Any large-scale program of social and economic reform would have to face the realities of constitutional limitations on the Dominion government.

Also bringing national questions to the fore in these years was the rise of several powerful and unorthodox provincial political administrations. In rhetoric and policy they challenged Dominion supremacy and the vision of technocratic reform that was so important to the intellectual community. William Aberhart's populist Social Credit government, elected in the same year that King returned to power, provided an obvious target for critics of provincial governments. Based on the heretical monetary policies of Major C.H. Douglas and on evangelical oratory, this party with no national context represented, to many intellectuals, a vigorous and reactionary regionalism that offended many of their basic values.

Things were no better in Quebec. Premier Taschereau's Liberal government had always been seen by observers within academic circles as a particularly reactionary brand of Canadian Liberalism. As Eugene Forsey complained in 1933, 'We shall soon have all our rights filched away from us.' The government that succeeded Taschereau's, however, was even worse. The Union nationale under Maurice Duplessis espoused a right-wing populism that many intellectuals felt verged on outright fascism. To cite Forsey, this time from 1937, 'Quebec has been for some time the scene of a formidable, carefully organized campaign to transform the province into a clerical-fascist state.' Brooke Claxton accused Duplessis of working with another favourite target of the intellectual community, Mitchell Hepburn of Ontario. The two of them, he warned British historian Arnold Toynbee, had formed an axis backed by big business to take control of the Dominion government. 'If this axis does come into power in the next two or three years, it would mean the suppression of all liberty except the liberty of Quebec and the mining magnates to do what they liked. It would be fascist in tendency and in practice.' By 1937 even the relatively staid O.D. Skelton was complaining to Mackenzie King of the 'semi-Fascist attitude' of several provincial governments, while in a somewhat lighter vein Frank Underhill summed up a prevailing concern of the intellectual community. Provincial administration, he argued, was characterized by a tendency toward long periods of bad government alternating with relatively brief periods of competence. The exception was Quebec, which was privileged to have bad government all the time.[2]

Though the harsh criticism of many provincial governments was justified, the strength of anti-provincial sentiment was accentuated by the fact that the ties of the intellectual community were increasingly with the Dominion government. This had not always been the case:

an earlier generation of reformers had concentrated on issues like housing, city beautification, health, and child welfare. All these activities
had led to involvement in municipal and provincial political issues.
Men like Morley Wickett, Newton Rowell, and the economists who
worked for the 1913 Ontario Commission on Unemployment had thus
seen the province as a natural vehicle for their social and economic
goals. Even in the post-war years, the rise of professional social work
had made the province central to the development of new ideas on
planning. The Dominion government of Mackenzie King, moreover,
had in the 1920s seemed especially barren ground upon which to spread
the seeds of reform.

The shift to the Dominion occurred in part because the Depression
was manifestly not manageable at a local level. It was a national and
international phenomenon that demanded a broad range of action over
the widest possible area. The collapse of municipal finance and the
disparities in the treatment of the unemployed across the nation testified to that fact. Neither the provinces nor the cities had the resources
or the power to deal with the vast problems of the 1930s.[3] Related to
this was the changing nature of social analysis by the 1930s. As city
beautification and urban renewal became subordinate to the evolving
concept of economic analysis, the solution to the myriad of social and
industrial ills began to be sought in the realm of fiscal and monetary
measures that were best handled at the national level.

The perspective of the intellectual community accordingly became
ever more national in orientation. Outside social work, where the
provinces remained dominant, most reform activity was developing at
the national level. It was the Dominion civil service that was absorbing
men like Clark and Skelton, and it was to Dominion politics that
individuals like Norman Rogers, Vincent Massey, Frank Underhill, and
F.R. Scott looked. Even where there were exceptions, as in the work
of Rogers and Innis for the 1934 Nova Scotia Royal Commission on the
Economy or in the work of H.M. Cassidy, E.J. Urwick, and W.A. Mackintosh for the Unemployment Research Committee of Ontario, it was
clear that both the problems and the solutions extended far beyond
provincial boundaries.[4] A distrust of the political tendencies of many
provincial administrations, an emotionally based nationalism, and the
belief that the problems to be solved were best dealt with at the Dominion level all worked to make the intellectual community supporters
of strong central government.

What concerned many individuals was that the trend in Canada

seemed to be going in the opposite direction. Sectionalism and regionalism seemed dominant. Brooke Claxton warned as early as 1929 that
for the true nationalist the real concern was no longer imperial relations but federal-provincial ones.[5] The British North America Act had
evolved into a rigid document that seemed destructive of national
unity. Norman Rogers at Queen's wrote Claxton to say that he was
'entirely in accord' with this interpretation.[6] Over the next years both
Rogers and Claxton would become tireless crusaders for constitutional
reform. In published writings, speeches, and personal intervention with
politicians they sought to convince people that provincial power had
become excessive. Rogers and Claxton were joined by an increasing
number of individuals who sensed as the 1930s went on that social
reform and constitutional change were connected. This was perhaps
most obvious on the left, where members of the LSR argued in favour
of a strong central government as a prerequisite to socialism. As Frank
Underhill wrote in the Forum, 'The real question at issue now is whether
we are sufficiently nationally-minded to insist upon a national authority which shall be strong enough to supervise and direct our social
and economic life or whether we mean to parcel up so much of the
authority among nine provincial governments that our national government will remain impotent to meet national responsibilities.' Such
views were not confined to the left. Among Conservatives, individuals
like Herridge and Leacock voiced concern about growing regionalism.
Canada, the latter warned in 1934, 'is almost visibly turning – from
what was meant to be a united nation into a confederate group of
autonomous units.'[7]

So strong was the nationalist orientation of the intellectual community in these years that those who took a different perspective found
themselves standing almost alone among academics. Thus when Harold
Innis, in his work for the Nova Scotia Royal Commission on the Economy, defended provincial rights he was widely criticized by fellow
social scientists. Typical was A.F.W. Plumptre's comment: 'I am not
persuaded that any general movement of powers and authorities back
to the provinces is as yet – if ever – desirable.'[8] Plumptre was mild in
comparison to historian Arthur Lower, who, on hearing of the proposal
that provinces be consulted concerning the tariff, wrote that the whole
concept was 'impracticable and anti-national.' For him Nova Scotia's
relative impoverishment was less important than the development of
a national community. 'I for one would be prepared to say, in last
resort, that whatever N.S.'s hard fate, she must look forward to con-

tinued submission of her well being and interests to those of the Dominion at large.' Given such sentiments, his comment that he was 'not a "states rights" man' seemed somewhat superfluous.[9]

In spite of the growing chorus of concern reflected in the comments to Innis, things seemed only to be going from bad to worse under the Bennett government. A series of ad hoc policies toward the provinces and the failure to recognize the underlying relation between the constitution and other issues had led to further deterioration in the prestige and power of the Dominion government. As Claxton warned Herridge in 1934, policies of social reform were not enough. The national unity of Canada had been so weakened that the first task was to reunite the various constituent parts of the nation. 'The manner in which unemployment and financial relief has been handled and the delay of the government in taking a strong lead in most issues has allowed provincial feeling to develop and provincial governments to take the lead in nine different and very pale conceptions of the NRA [American National Recovery Administration]. The story of Dominion relations with the Provinces during the depression is pathetic.' The constitution had become a roadblock to progressive reform, and unless it could be altered all attempts at change were likely to bear little fruit. By 1935 much of the intellectual community had come to see development of social and economic planning as inseparable from alterations to the constitution. That was why Bennett's blindness to the constitutional problems confronting his New Deal legislation was viewed both as tragic and as evidence of his political cynicism. It was also why the political candidate of the intellectuals, Norman Rogers, stated during his 1935 campaign that 'one of the first important tasks that will confront a new administration at Ottawa will be a redistribution of powers under the British North America Act.'[10]

Concerns over the constitution meant that the intellectual elite was, by the mid-1930s, shaped not only by background and training but also by the general acceptance of three common goals. The first was to gain acceptance from politicians and public of a pragmatic, interventionist role for the state. The second was to translate this principle into a series of concrete policies and techniques to ensure that economic security and social justice, as they envisioned it, were increased. A lively debate existed on the details of this second goal, but there was also a general set of parameters defined by the principles of positive liberalism and parliamentary process under the guidance of an expert bureaucracy. The third goal of this predominantly English-Canadian group was to reform the constitution for the sake of preserving the nation and to futher the other causes that it propounded. As the decade went on, constitutional issue began to take precedence because it was thought a necessary preliminary to other changes. As Frank Scott warned the Association of Canadian Clubs, 'No issue which faces the Canadian people is of greater importance than the problem of bringing the constitution up to date. Other matters loom more large upon the immediate horizon – unemployment, wheat marketing, the revival of trade generally must be seen to. But it is to be hoped that these difficulties are of a temporary nature, and in any case their solution involves us in constitutional questions which force us to examine with critical eye the present working of our governmental machinery. Even if they were solved tomorrow, however, the constitutional problem would still remain.'[11] Those intellectuals who in the early 1930s had worked to gain influence in the civil service and within political parties thus turned their attention increasingly to the cause of constitutional reform after 1935.

By the time Mackenzie King took office in October 1935, the general concerns of the intellectual community were reflected in two related crises in federal-provincial relations. The first involved what Claxton termed the 'pathetic' handling of the relief problem in Canada. The second concerned the rapidly increasing strain on the fiscal resources of the provinces. By 1935 the possibility of provincial default loomed, and neither the provinces nor the officials of the Dominion had any clear means of resolving the problem. Of course the first crisis triggered the second, as many observers realized, but, as James Struthers has noted, King treated the 'issues of constitutional reform, financial relations and unemployment relief as if they were in separate compartments.' Moreover, though Bennett had made many errors in his handling of the situation while in office, King also bore some of the blame for the emerging crises. Through the 1920s, while prime minister, he had consistently sought to distance the Dominion government from any responsibility for unemployment. It was a convenient policy for a government primarily concerned with reducing the war debt, but it left the nation in a precarious position when unemployment went to unheard-of levels in the 1930s. It was thus far from certain that King fully appreciated the interrelated nature of the federal-provincial problems his government faced or that he would shoulder responsibility for handling the crises.[12]

The two crises were related because the municipally based relief system had proved totally unable to handle the levels of relief common to many parts of the country. Especially in the west, where the economy was the hardest hit and where some governments entered the Depression with a large debt burden encountered in coping with earlier growth, it had become apparent that the supposedly clear jurisdictional distinctions between Dominion and provincial responsibilities were impossible to maintain.[13] Understandable pressure mounted on the federal government from the provinces, municipalities, and public to take action in the face of a worsening crisis. Indeed, Mackenzie King had been defeated in 1930 in part because he refused to consider such Dominion intervention, thereby appearing indifferent to the plight of the unemployed. Bennett, in contrast, had promised quick action, and upon his election had undertaken a series of relief and public works measures that brought the Dominion into the area of relief in a major way, though the matter remained formally within provincial jurisdiction.

The next five years saw the Dominion become ever more entangled in 'provincial issues' like relief. The vote of $20 million in 1930 for the relief of unemployment was only the beginning of a flow of federal money into a seemingly bottomless pit. By 1935 Dominion loans to the provinces had reached a level of $33 million, while total relief expenditures by all levels of government had risen to a massive $172 million. In addition, a complex series of federal programs, grants, debt guarantees, and other measures created an expensive and inefficient patchwork of policies that varied from session to session as the administration fought to keep abreast of the rapidly evolving situation.[14]

From the perspective of the Dominion government, this situation led to three undesirable results. First, the federal government faced the prospect of continuing to pour money into programs and projects over which it had no control. The constitutional barriers that existed had, in effect, led to a series of unconditional grants to the provinces that made accountability difficult if not impossible to achieve. Second, the measures were ineffective. The quality of relief remained grossly inequitable between various parts of the nation, with the unemployed in poorer regions facing greater hardship than those in the relatively affluent ones. Transients who moved from community to community in search of work found themselves excluded from relief rolls because they did not meet local residency requirements. As a greater percentage of relief funds came from federal coffers such discrimination became increasingly unacceptable. Third, the continued flow of federal funds seemed to be failing to stop the fiscal collapse of the provinces. Whether because of costly overlaps, profligate provincial administrations, or the impossibility of planning on the basis of short-term ad hoc grants, the financial situation was continuing to deteriorate. The federal government thus seemed faced with an impossible choice. It could pour even more money into relief and thus see control of its own revenues continue to erode, or it could cut the provinces off and allow them to default.

It was at this point that the first issue merged with the second. Relief expenditures were destroying the fiscal soundness of the provinces, and by the autumn of 1935 there was imminent danger that one or more might default on outstanding loans. British Columbia had already come close to doing so under the Bennett administration, and by the time King assumed office the situation was becoming increasingly grave in the other western provinces. Even before King was sworn in as prime minister, Bennett warned him that several provinces were effectively bankrupt. A few months later King recorded fatalistically in his diary: 'It seems to me we have to face in Canada the possible default of the provinces and municipalities and might as well do so sooner rather than later.'[15]

Against this gloomy background the Dominion-provincial conference of December 1935 convened. The conference was held due to an earlier promise by King to meet with the premiers should he be elected. It also reflected the belief that Bennett's bad relations with his provincial colleagues could be worked out by face-to-face compromise, especially given the predominance of the Liberals at the provincial level. Yet King's actual goals for the meeting were fairly limited. Aside from the political value involved, his main purpose seems to have been to find a way to stop the drain on the federal treasury. The exact means by which this would be done were left vague, and the new prime minister, preoccupied with closing a trade agreement with the United States, spent little time in the weeks preceding the conference in thinking about it.[16]

The main preparatory work for the conference thus fell to King's new minister of labour, Norman Rogers, though Clifford Clark and Alex Skelton were also very much involved. It was natural that the new cabinet minister, Rogers, should assume such a role. He was well known within intellectual circles both as a leading expert on constitutional matters and as an exponent of reform. In coming into government he had expressed the opinion that he should be given a task involving federal-provincial relations. King, for his part, continued to think highly of his long-time adviser and considered Rogers, like himself, representative of the sort of intellectual whose presence around a cabinet table raised the level of debate: 'I had some sort of vision of myself and Norman Rogers at the outer edge as it were of a complete sweep. Most else seemed to be washed away. This seemed to have significance of our part in the campaign on a high plane, and possibility of our association together in a closer relationship for years to come.' It was thus highly symbolic, as King pointed out, that Rogers was assigned the Labour portfolio, the same one held by King when he first joined the cabinet. Also, in assigning Rogers the complex and delicate task of convening a Dominion-provincial conference, King was both expressing confidence in his new minister and testing his abilities.[17]

By the time the conference convened it was apparent that Rogers had done his work well. The provinces were generally agreeable to Dominion proposals, and Rogers was able to achieve several of his goals. A program was agreed to for the registration of the unemployed, and the principle was accepted of a larger relief grant to the provinces in exchange for the formation of a federal Employment Commission to supervise the handling of relief and investigate the whole problem of unemployment in Canada. Behind this was the growing recognition that part of the ongoing problem arose from disparities between taxation powers and jurisdiction at the various levels of government. Finally, there was discussion on the possibility of constitutional amendments to remedy some of the problems of federal-provincial relations and an acceptance in principle of the need for an amending formula. As it turned out, the provinces were more amenable at the conference than they would be when it came time to implement these proposals. Later meetings at the ministerial and official levels would see much of the promise of 1935 come to nought. H.B. Neatby has noted that as the Dominion proposals became more explicit, relations with the provinces became 'more strained.' Nonetheless, the three major areas of discussion – an unemployment commission, transfer of taxation powers, and the possibility of constitutional amendments – shaped the main lines of policy debate of the next four years.[18]

The first of these proposals – for an employment commission – was the particular enthusiasm of Rogers, and he immediately began to push the cabinet to follow up on the conference with the formation of such a commission. Here was the opportunity to show the way in which federal-provincial fiscal relations and social and economic reform were but two aspects of one problem. Rogers's hope for the commission rested on his strong belief that careful study would produce clear answers. Such a body, if well run, could both demonstrate the needs of the unemployed and ensure that federal funds were being used as effectively as possible. Rogers was determined to show King and the government how rational investigation could produce systematic reform.[19]

Yet, notwithstanding King's personal regard for him, there were limits to Rogers's influence within government. In an administration obsessed with the deficit and led by a prime minister who continued to regard planning 'as a form of dictatorship,' Rogers often found himself alone in the cabinet. Thus, for example, in his hurry to get the bill approved that would create the employment commission, Rogers pushed so hard that King recorded a rare criticism of him for his 'blank cheque frame of mind.'[20] As well, when the government decided in March 1936 to reverse itself and cut relief grants to the provinces, only Norman Rogers stood opposed of all the federal cabinet. The first attempts to influence government at the political rather than at the bureaucratic level were thus often mixed in their results. Mackenzie King, in spite of his vision to the contrary, did not move on the same plane as the intellectual community of Norman Rogers's generation.

The tension between King and Rogers that developed in the spring of 1936 grew in part from their differing perceptions of Roger's National Employment Commission (NEC). Mackenzie King and others in his cabinet saw it as a body designed to supervise federal relief grants to the provinces and to ensure that their money was not being wasted. It was, in brief, a means to reduce relief costs. Rogers, the minister under whom the commission was placed, envisioned a much larger role for the body. Ultimately it might save money through the efficient allocation of the resources of the nation, but more immediately he hoped that studies by the commission would be the first step in a series of far-reaching reforms, including possibly national unemployment insurance. The National Employment Commission thus was seen as following in the tradition of bodies like the Aird Commission on radio broadcasting and the Macmillan Commission on banking. Once a systematic study was undertaken, the results would be obvious and the necessary reforms undertaken.[21]

The membership of the commission should have given warning to Rogers of King's attitude. Rather than having principally social workers, economists, and other 'experts' in the field, the commission was dominated by what the *Canadian Forum* sarcastically referred to as 'business tycoons.' Aside from its chairman, Arthur Purvis, Montreal president of Canadian Industries Limited, there was shoe manufacturer Alfred Marois, businessman Neil Maclean of New Brunswick, and E.J. Young and Mary Sutherland, who were from rural areas and known to be 'responsible' individuals. Only in the appointment of labour representative Tom Moore and above all Rogers's colleague from Queen's, W.A. Mackintosh, were there representatives who began their studies with strong sympathies for substantial reform.[22]

Nevertheless, the argument in favour of reforms involving unemployment was clearly placed before the commission. Mackintosh was tireless in his efforts, and social workers like Charlotte Whitton brought their experience with the problem to the body with a series of studies for the NEC. Thus the traditional notion that the individual was primarily responsible for his unemployed condition, rejected by economic and social work professionals a decade or more before, was challenged before this conglomeration of businessmen and others. 'The modern concept of the humanitarian state,' went one report, 'precludes such an attitude in a day when national and international factors contributing to distress and the interdependence of all community life are so generally recognized. It places upon the whole state an obligation for the maintenance of at least minimum standards of survival for its people.'[23]

Initially the commission made cautious, if not innocuous suggestions. The interim report, released in 1937, stayed away from major reform issues, pleading the need for more information and study. Even the traditional nostrum of public works activity was rejected on the grounds that it might interfere with the recovery of private investment. Instead a Home Improvement Act and a Farm Improvement and Employment Plan, both of which would use government guaranteed loans, were recommended. As the commission continued its studies, however, more far-reaching plans began to emerge. In particular, it looked as if the viewpoint of the academic reformers had carried the day, at least to the extent that the commission began to inquire seriously as to the possibilities of a National Unemployment Insurance Act. Mary Sutherland objected strenuously to this idea, however, and carried her objections to the prime minister. King was horrified at the implications of such a recommendation at a time when federal-provincial relations were in such a delicate state and at a time when the prime minister remained concerned with reducing the cost of government. King accordingly told an unhappy Rogers that the report would have to be revised. While Rogers protested to King and Mackintosh to Purvis, the die was cast. The final report was a compromise in which the principle of a National Unemployment Insurance scheme was defended but the question of implementation and details referred to the sitting Royal Commission on Dominion-Provincial Relations.[24]

The battles over the final report of the NEC were symbolic. Two views of the political process in general and of the relation between the problems of relief, the role of the state, and federal-provincial relations had clashed. On one side were Mackenzie King and the majority of his cabinet who still saw massive relief problems as essentially financial in nature. On the other side were men like Rogers and Mackintosh, the academics, of whom King complained that there was too much concern for theories and goals but not enough for the 'human factor,' by which he meant the political. The interesting thing in all this is not only that the practical politician found it necessary to trim the sails of his newly elected resident intellectual, but that Mackintosh and Rogers had also had considerable success in swaying the business majority of the commission. It was the disturbing nature of the emerging consensus, after all, that had forced Sutherland to go to the prime minister. Nothing in the whole experience dictated any revision in the intellectual community's confidence in its own position. Henceforth it would simply have to take greater account of Mackenzie King's 'human factor.'[25]

The Dominion-provincial conference of 1935 had been concerned with more than the unemployed and their efficient handling. General problems of taxation power and fiscal soundness had also emerged from the various committees of the conference and from the follow-up meetings of the Continuing Committee on Financial Questions. These subjects were, not suprisingly, anxious matters for study in parts of the Ottawa bureaucracy. Perhaps the most concerned of these government bodies lay within the newly formed Bank of Canada. The Bank's outlook had already been revealed in an arrangement developed under the Bennett government. Concerns over the credit rating of the provinces had led to an informal understanding between the Bank and the Bank of England. No provincial attempt to raise money on the London markets was supported by the Bank of England without prior consultation with Bank of Canada officials.[26] The Bank of Canada was thus acting as an unofficial adviser to the international money markets on provincial financial matters without provincial consent. Such control was limited, however, and probably unconstitutional. It was certainly unacceptable to Mackenzie King, and he ordered the practice stopped. The fiscal crisis would have to be resolved by other means, and those in the Bank obviously felt these means would have to include greater Dominion control.

The Bank was thus deeply involved in the question of provincial finances, and by the end of 1935 it had assembled a research department made up of economists who were among the most able in government. Men like J.J. Deutsch and J.R. Beattie were on the permanent staff, while academic social scientists like A.E. Grauer of the University of Toronto were occasionally called in to undertake special projects. Presiding over them was the brilliant and mercurial D.A. 'Sandy' Skelton.[27] A committed reformer and ardent enthusiast for the causes he adopted, Skelton was to have a major influence on the direction not only of Bank policy but also of that of the government as a whole toward the sensitive problem of Dominion-provincial fiscal relations. Within the confines of the carefully orthodox organization of Graham Towers, there thus existed an active group of advocates for constitutional and economic reform.

. As with so much of the intellectual community in these years, Skelton was resolutely centralist in his view of Dominion-provincial relations. Memo after memo from the research department urged 'more centralized control of Provincial finances' and warned that 'in any plan' that might be developed 'greater centralization of control and coordination of policy are evidently necessary.' Any arrangements that might be made between the Dominion and the provinces had to include a greater degree of Dominion control than existed at present. 'For if the Dominion openly throws in its lot with the provinces and accepts the attendant obligations without adequate guarantees of future policy, it will prove an expensive undertaking.'[28]

Underlying this position was a mechanistic view of the nature of reform that derived from the pragmatic empiricism of the social sciences. The constitution was not some mystical document that should forever bind people, nor would its alteration significantly threaten either the Canadian social fabric or the Canadian spirit. 'The most important consideration,' wrote Skelton, 'must be the efficient and economical government of the country as a whole,' and the division between provincial and federal powers and duties should be determined by this: 'It is perhaps time to return to what should be, from the financial point of view at least, the guiding principle of federal finances.

National, provincial, and municipal governments are all fulfilling the same function for (and at the expense of) the same people. Presumably they should attempt to divide the functions of government in the most efficient manner possible, regardless of their respective legal, political and historical vested interests.'[29]

One possible solution to the concerns of Skelton and the plight of the provinces was raised by Clifford Clark in early 1935. The provinces' fiscal position was hampered by the relatively high interest rates they had to pay for loans because of growing uncertainty about their financial position. If the Dominion agreed to guarantee provincial bonds, then rates would be lowered along with the costs to the provinces. There was a catch, however. Clark warned that the Dominion should only agree to such a role if the provinces accepted some sort of role for the Bank of Canada in the process of budget formation. The intention was that all provincial budgets be submitted to the governor of the Bank for approval prior to submission to the provincial legislatures. It was an audacious proposal. As Clark himself commented, the provinces might well object and even the Bank might 'hesitate to assume the responsibility.' In spite of its audacity, a variant of Clark's proposal was discussed at the 1935 Dominion-provincial conference. At that conference there was considerable discussion of the possibilities of savings through debt conversion, the formation of a 'National Finance Council' to co-ordinate loans, and the guaranteeing of provincial securities issued henceforth by the Dominion. As for the Bank, it would seem that at least as far as Skelton was concerned, such a proposal would be accepted with alacrity. The only condition was that the Bank be given sufficient powers to make its new responsibilities meaningful.[30]

Indeed, Clark's proposal and the discussions at the conference gave Skelton the opening that he needed to pursue his own ideas on federal-provincial reform. These would have placed economic experts at the centre of fiscal management in Canada. For the problem, argued Skelton, was that complex proposals, such as those now before the government, could not be handled by casual discussions among politicians. It was up to the experts to unravel the complexities and come up with solutions. 'One of the most striking contrasts between Canadian and Australian conversion proposals,' he noted, 'is the thorough investigation by leading economists and politicians which preceded any move [in Australia].' The proposals that had been tossed around at the conference had not been well thought out and, if followed through, would damage the reputation of both the Bank and the Dominion. Discussions

on the issue were 'so limited and vague that it scarcely warrants detailed examination at the moment.'[31]

The only remedy to the problems was a decisive move not only to
have the Dominion government assert its influence in the whole matter, as Clark and others had urged, but to ensure that once in Dominion
hands the question of fiscal responsibility was kept one step removed
from the day-to-day world of politics. Skelton thus actively supported
the concept of a National Finance Council. What he envisioned, however, was not the casual advisory body such as he suspected the politicians wanted but a new super-agency that would transcend provincial
and Dominion areas of responsibility. It would be composed of officials
from both levels of government, and they would make the political
decisions. It would be up to a body of experts, however, to plot the
fiscal course of the nation. 'Everything hinges on the first requirement,'
he concluded, ' – a well-informed secretariat. Only if a secretariat can
build up a proper background, supply material of demonstrable usefulness which is not available elsewhere, and prepare a practical agenda,
will the Council meetings receive attention from the public and press
– not to mention the provinces.'[32]

A variant of this involved the concept of a Loan Council that would
have certain controls over provincial loans in return for Dominion
guarantees on those loans. Though the Bank was dubious about conversion, it did see the Loan Council as a possible means to the sort of
centralization urged in comments on the Finance Council. For ultimately it would be impossible to separate the problem of loans from
the more general questions of provincial budgeting. At least those provinces needy enough to require the loan guarantees would have to clear
fiscal policy with the Bank. Thus the concept of Dominion influence
over the provincial budgeting process, raised by Clark the year before,
reappeared in the memos of the research department of the Bank in
early 1936. In return for provincial access to Dominion credit worthi-
ness, the financial sovereignty of the provinces was to be limited.[33]

The myriad proposals and counter-proposals emerging from the Department of Labour, Department of Finance, and especially from the
Bank of Canada reveal the growing dissatisfaction within elements of
the civil service with the ad hoc responses toward federal-provincial
relations that had characterized the Bennett government and now
threatened to continue under the Liberals. There was a positive side
to the crisis, however. As those making the proposals well knew, the
desperate situation provided a rare opportunity to take action before

political indifference and public apathy reasserted itself. The attitudes of Clark and Skelton and the organizations they represented reflected the strong current of opinion within intellectual circles to the effect that current constitutional arrangements were outmoded and that the strong entrenchment of provincial powers was at best inefficient and at worst a deliberate and reactionary attempt to block needed reforms. For the Loan Council, National Finance Council, and other measures were never seen by these economists as more than half-measures. What they really wanted was for the third general area of discussion at the 1935 conference – the implementation of constitutional reform – to yield concrete results. Thus throughout all the discussions of financial remedies, officials in both the Bank and the Department of Finance, as well as intellectuals outside the civil service, worked to convince the government that what was needed was a full-fledged analysis of Canada's constitutional needs in the light of modern requirements.

Even before the convening of the 1935 conference, McGill economist H.C. Goldenberg wrote a memo to Clifford Clark warning that issues of public debt could not be dealt with unless the government was prepared to consider the basic constitutional questions that underlay them. The control of public debts, he argued, 'can be properly considered only in its relation to a redistribution of powers between the Dominion and the provinces.' Repeating a theme that was common in memoranda in these years, he concluded that 'provincial autonomy must not stand in the way of national solvency.' This was followed at the conference itself by the insertion of an item on the agenda to undertake 'preliminary' consideration of the question. As a result, a committee on constitutional problems was created, but, as in so many other instances in Canadian history, agreement was impossible, and nothing came of the proposal. In the weeks after the conference, Skelton continued to imply in his memos that a more comprehensive discussion of financial matters should include such a constitutional re-examination. The financial experts within the government bureaucracy thus worked to keep the issue alive at a time when most politicians were working hard to avoid such a contentious matter. The images of an activist core of experts that went as far back as Adam Shortt and the founding of the CPSA was a step closer to reality.[34]

The bureaucratic initiative surrounding the 1935 conference and subsequent discussions was matched by an ongoing campaign in scholarly journals and writings outside government in favour of a major study of Canada's federal-provincial relations at the constitutional level.

The LSR's *Social Planning for Canada*, published a few months before the Dominion-provincial conference, called for centralization of various social services in the name of justice and efficiency. Brooke Claxton wrote on the subject for the new *Canadian Journal of Economics and Political Science* in the same year, as did economist W.A. Carrothers. From Quebec the prize-winning essayist of the D.R. Wilkie writing contest argued that the nation would benefit by the abolition of the provinces altogether, though he admitted that some more moderate reforms were more likely to succeed. In Winnipeg E.J. Tarr continued to advocate a major study of the whole structure of federal-provincial relations in Canada. Most promising of all to the proponents of constitutional change was the continued support of a member of the cabinet. As recently as May 1935 Norman Rogers had publicly restated his support for the revision of federal-provincial constitutional arrangements.[35]

By the latter part of 1936 it became apparent that the federal-provincial initiatives emanating from the 1935 conference had failed. The provinces were not going to accept the supervision of either the National Employment Commission or a federal Loan Council. The Bank, therefore, turned from specific proposals for fiscal agencies to a call for a major study of the whole constitutional basis on which federalism rested. In August of that year, A.E. Grauer undertook a study of taxation in Canada for the research department and concluded, not surprisingly, that the progressive income tax was the best method of expanding revenues to meet social needs. More significantly, given the issue at hand, he concluded as well that 'the administration of the tax should be exclusively with the Dominion.' Then, in November, Alex Skelton wrote a memorandum urging the establishment of a royal commission to study the whole problem of federal-provincial fiscal and taxation needs and powers. 'No one can pretend,' said Skelton, 'that the present distribution of governmental functions and tax powers is giving Canada the most efficient and economical government possible.' An 'impartial' and independent commission, he argued, by careful scientific investigation, would be able to marshall the details of the problem with sufficient effect to force even the most recalcitrant and reactionary provinces to see the case that existed for centralization. It was time to map out a new constitution on 'rational and business-like lines.' In a ringing conclusion he warned: 'Ostrich-like tactics will no longer do; 1937 should become as memorable a date in Canadian history as 1867.'[36]

Reinforcing Skelton's call for a royal commission was the 1937 decision by the Judicial Committee of the Privy Council to the effect that the great bulk of Bennett's New Deal legislation was *ultra vires* of the Dominion government. The fears of the intellectual community had been confirmed by a decision from a British court that challenged the basic needs of modern Canadian nationalism. The vestiges of an imperial era now affected domestic reform. The *Canadian Forum* summed up the reaction of many when it commented in a gloomy editorial entitled 'Goodbye Dominion Status' that 'five old men in the Privy Council' had brought Canada back to something approaching colonial status and, in the process, had threatened the meaningfulness of nationhood. 'We are nine peoples,' it concluded, 'not one.'[37]

By 1937 there were thus three forces converging on the government to encourage a detailed examination of the whole field of federal-provincial social responsibilities and fiscal powers. First, the National Employment Commission had been unable to assert a meaningful supervisory role for itself, and people like Rogers and Mackintosh, if not the commission as a whole, realized that a rational attack on unemployment and relief would be impossible under the existing constitution. The reluctance of King and others to accept major new responsibilities did not alter the convictions of the reformers that the Dominion would soon have to enter into new areas of social and economic responsibility.

Second, it was obvious by 1937 that the Dominion-provincial initiatives of 1935-6 were a failure and that the King government had not been any better able than Bennett's to remedy the existing problems. Alberta had gone into partial default in 1936, and it was entirely possible that other provinces would follow suit. In the mean-time the attitude of the bulk of the cabinet and of the Bank of Canada toward the plight of the provinces was hardening. J.C. Osborne, deputy governor of the Bank, reached the point in the weeks before the Alberta default of advocating a policy of non-rescue as a means of forcing the provinces to accept prevailing Dominion arguments that 'certain constitutional changes are desirable.'[38] The Bank's position would change once default occurred, but it was an indication of the sense of desperation that the weakening of national prestige and provincial credit ratings could even be considered as more desirable than the status quo. This led directly to the third force. By the end of 1936 key officials in both the Bank of Canada and the Department of Finance strongly supported the appointment of a royal commission to investigate the whole situation. To the professional social scientists in both organizations such a comprehensive study made eminent sense, as it did to dozens of intellectuals outside government. Only by putting the situation into its overall context would it be possible to find a solution free of the sort of ad hoc responses that had characterized the response of the Dominion in the first seven years of the Depression.

The campaign for a review of the whole fiscal relationship between the Dominion and the provinces led to the appointment of one of Canada's best-known royal commissions. By the time of the appointment of the Commission on Dominion-Provincial Relations, the only question was why King had taken so long to act. From the time that Manitoba had requested such a study, in December 1936, it was widely expected that the government would move swiftly. Moreover, as early as February 1937 King had indicated in the House that he was prepared to appoint the commission. It was not until 1 August, however, that Newton Rowell, the new chairman of the commission, wrote to announce his appointment with the comment: 'This is the most important and difficult task I have been asked to undertake.'[39]

The Rowell-Sirois Commission, as it was to become, took some three years to investigate the complex problem it had been assigned. In the interval it travelled to each of the provincial capitals as well as Ottawa, listened to scores of briefs from provincial governments, municipalities, interest groups, and academics, accumulated thousands of pages of testimony, and cost the government more than half a million dollars. For the provinces and other bodies the Commission provided an occasion to list long-standing complaints about the state of Confederation. Alberta's Social Credit administration, still smarting from the refusal of the Dominion to aid it the year before, refused to recognize the legitimacy of the commission.[40]

Yet much of the public theatre that surrounded these hearings must be discounted. That is not to say that the reactions of the provinces and other bodies were unimportant. They were to be crucial in determining the fate of the report once it was released. This fate, however, must be kept distinct from the report itself, for the latter was not so much the product of the public hearings as it was the product of the intellectual network of the 1930s. The report of the Rowell-Sirois Commission was the full-blown statement of a generation as to what it saw as the proper future of Canadian federalism. Indeed, the results of the study had been conceived even before its appointment. Running through the earlier memos of Skelton, Clark, and others is the presumption that a centralized system of fiscal control and social service programs was best for the nation. The problem, therefore, resolved itself into the technical one of finding the best means of marshalling the data to make this conclusion obvious to others. A royal comission seemed to provide the means by which the public and perhaps even the recalcitrant provinces could be brought to the same position as the intellectual community.

The influence of the intellectual community can be demonstrated in various ways. Among the commissioners themselves, for example, two of the four, R.A. MacKay and H.F. Angus, were academic social scientists. The former was a political scientist at Dalhousie, and the latter taught at the University of British Columbia. The chairman, Newton Rowell, though of a different generation than the reformers of the 1930s, was, of course, a member of the founding generation of urban progressives in Canada. Also, as has been mentioned, in his involvement in the Canadian Radio League, Canadian Club Association, and Canadian Institute of International Affairs he remained tied to many of the younger generation. J.W. Dafoe, the final English-speaking commissioner, was also closely connected with many of those within the intellectual community most actively involved in discussion of public policy. He was also somewhat of a transitional figure between the older and newer versions of Canadian liberalism. He was both sympathetic to King's caution towards state planning and closely involved with reformers like Massey and Rogers. Only Justice Joseph Thibaudeau Rinfret and, after Rinfret's resignation due to illness, Joseph Sirois were unconnected to the new generation of reformers, a fact reflecting the increasing isolation that had developed between English- and French-Canadian intellectual communities.

If several commissioners had sympathies or connections with the reform network of the 1930s, the research staff that supported the commission embodied it. The research department of the Bank of Canada provided its core. On the recommendation of Clifford Clark, Alex Skelton was appointed secretary, and he brought J.J. Deutsch over with him as assistant secretary.[41] Lawyer, academic, and political scientist J.A. Corry also became closely involved in the research work of the commission as time went on. His name too had been recommended by Clark. This small core of permanent staff was complemented by a host of specially commissioned studies on various aspects of federal-provincial relations. It was a practice new to federal royal commissions and mirrored the growing importance of social scientific research in Canada. There were precedents for such studies, however, in the work of the National Employment Commission and in a 1934 Nova Scotia Royal Commission on the Economy. The introduction of this technique into the Rowell-Sirois Commission's deliberation ensured that the advocates of change would have their views reinforced by members of the social scientific community and others of Claxton's 'group.' Any careful observer of the individuals appointed to undertake the various studies by Skelton would have been able to discern the general tendency of the conclusions that these studies would reach before they were written. Thus, for example, both Brooke Claxton and H.C. Goldenberg of Montreal, well known for their views on federal-provincial relations, were commissioned to do studies that gave them another opportunity to state their arguments as members of a prestigious forum. The same was true of F.A. Knox and W.A. Mackintosh of Queen's, as well as D.C. MacGregor of Toronto. A.E. Grauer, who was to undertake a study of social assistance, was the person involved with Skelton the year before in an investigation of the federal-provincial taxation system for the research department at the Bank. Historian Donald Creighton had been less involved in public issues, but his arguments would reflect the nationalist orientation of the age.[42]

It was an impressive group. Some of the best academic minds in Canada were involved and, as the commission boasted, there was considerable diversity in terms of background and geographical location of commissioners, staff, and outside experts. At the same time it is revealing to note who was not included. First, nobody clearly identified with either of the opposition political parties received a commissioned study. This was probably not so much because of any narrow intolerance on the part of Skelton, who was himself reputed to have ideas to the left of the Liberals, but because the commission was sensitive to the need for credibility at the cabinet level. The NEC had been badly damaged because it had strayed from the governmental wisdom of the day, and the royal commission may have wanted to ensure that radically critical studies did not arouse the sensitivities of the prime minister. Also absent were those social scientists and other intellectuals who had been noted in the past for their opposition to changes dear to the heart of modern reform. Thus, for example, none of those who had opposed the formation of a central bank received any studies. Skelton and Clark would leave what they saw as the voices of an obsolete and reactionary view of the state to the public hearings. Their purpose was to employ not only the best minds of a generation but also to harness that generation's sense of mission. What they hoped for from the Rowell-Sirois Commission was a mature statement of the creed of modern social and economic planning.

The final report of the Royal Commission on Dominion-Provincial Relations was released in 1940, and, as might have been expected, the major thrust of the commission was centralist. Specifically, the commission recommended that the Dominion government assume responsibility for two key areas of social welfare: 'unemployed employables' and old age pensions. Costs of these two social programs had been the major factor in the spiralling rise of total welfare costs in recent years. In the first half of the 1930s alone, welfare costs had tripled, and it was this pressure that had created such an intolerable financial burden for provincial and municipal governments across the country. Thus, in order to ease administration, provide uniformity of benefits, prevent obstacles to labour mobility, and relieve local governments of a crushing burden, the commission recommended that the Dominion assume sole responsibility in this traditional provincial area. 'The matter,' it concluded succinctly, 'cannot be left to the provinces.'[43]

These recommendations also reflect a tendency that was to become increasingly important in the next years: a concern not just with social welfare but with the overall management of the economy. As the commissioners argued, assumption of responsibility for unemployment would presumably make the government more interested in the management of the economy. 'If the Dominion assumes full responsibility for relief of employables, it should have much stronger incentive than under the present system of divided financial responsibilities to adopt vigorous remedial policies and policies to prevent unemployment from arising.' With this in mind, the commission resurrected an idea that could be traced back to O.D. Skelton's pre-war writings and had been more recently advocated by the NEC, timed public works. Yet if the roots of the idea went to the senior Skelton, the specific proposal for its implementation reflected a particular enthusiasm of the younger. The commission recommended that the management of federal-provincial plans for such works be given to a new agency composed of experts and with officials from both levels of government.[44]

In return for this assumption of social and economic planning by the Dominion, the commission proposed a major revision in the tax structure of the nation. It recommended that the provinces yield all rights in the growing fields of income and corporate taxation as well as succession duties. The Dominion would then return to the provinces a 'National Adjustment Grant' that would replace all the 'illogical' subsidies that had developed over the years.[45] Especially tempting for the hard-pressed provinces was the statement that, as part of the arrangement, the Dominion would assume all provincial debt! The hope was that the offer was too tempting to refuse.

In concluding its report the commission remarked that it 'does not consider its proposals are either centralizing or decentralizing in their combined effect.' While it was true that the commission was moderate, even conciliatory, in its tone and that many of its arguments made eminent sense, this final remark was somewhat disingenuous. The recommendations had implications which, in two ways, would have altered power relations within the Dominion. In the first place, though the National Adjustment Grants were designed to provide the provinces with adequate funds to carry out necessary programs, they also helped ensure that individual provincial administrations would find it difficult to undertake a policy of deliberate aggrandizement. The National Adjustment Grant would be by far the most important source of revenue for provinces in most circumstances, and that grant could be increased only on the approval of a Dominion-appointed finance commission. The Dominion government would thus have, if not a veto, a degree of control over any attempts by provinces to embark on what in recent years has been known as 'province building.'[46]

The recommendations also would have increased the influence and power of the appointed expert. To all intents and purposes the finance commission was a variation on Alex Skelton's earlier proposals for a Loan Council, including the envisaged importance of the experts. 'These functions will require a small, but highly competent, permanent research staff and secretariat. Such a body would become a clearing house for economic, financial, and administrative information relevant to Dominion-Provincial relations and public finance policy.'[47] Given the complexities inherent in such cases, the members of the commission would have to rely on the experts around them as to whether a province's request for additional funds was needed or not. And while the political decision would, of course, remain with the commission itself, the role of the expert was seen as central to the proper management of the new system.

While these recommendations are both interesting and revealing, it is in the arguments used to develop them that the underlying philosophy of the commission is fully developed. It was a philosophy that represented the culmination of a stream of thought that had been developing over the past decade within the intellectual community. The official purpose of the commission was stated to have been to 'investigate the character and amount of taxes collected from the people' and to examine 'public expenditures and public debts in general, in order to determine whether the present division of the burden of government is equitable, and conducive to efficient administration.'[48] For most of those directly involved in the commission, however, the results that such an examination would bring were already known. Their vision of their purpose was to use that examination in a manner that would allow the restructuring of Confederation.

This sense of mission predated the commission, as Alex Skelton's deliberate comparison between 1867 and 1937 indicates. Once the commission was appointed, the parallel became commonplace. F.R. Scott praised the commission with the comment that it had a 'greater opportunity than has faced any constitutional body that has sat in Canada since the Quebec conference of 1864.' J.B. McGeachy of the *Winnipeg Free Press* portrayed it in medical terms as the 'Confederation Clinic,' in which the commissioners were attempting to diagnose and then heal the ills of the nation. Even the *Financial Post*, which had generally been resolute in its resistance to anything that smacked of government intervention in the economy, termed the commissioners the 'Fathers of Reconfederation' and admitted that 'centralization is inevitable.' The commissioners, it concluded, had a duty to adapt the work of the original Fathers of Confederation to meet modern requirements. One suspects that in the case of the *Post* the danger of provincial default was more of a factor in its respect for the commission than was any new-found enthusiasm for reform. The point remains, however, that across the political spectrum the Commission was touted as much more than just another sterile government investigation. The combined factors of industrialism, depression, new technologies, and new social demands had created the belief that an examination of their nation's most basic structures was necessary. The Rowell-Sirois Commission seemed to provide the means by which just such an examination could be carried out, and its results might shape the nature of the future of the nation in the same way that their spiritual forefathers had around the conference tables at Charlottetown, Quebec, and London.[49]

It was an awesome prospect. As Frank Underhill had warned on an earlier occasion, those who would change the British North America Act would face the 'objection of all those pundits who maintain that our federal union is a sacred legal contract upon which politicians must not lay impious hands.' For the commissioners, therefore, it made strategic sense to try and limit such criticism by showing that they, not their critics, were carrying forth the true spirit of Confederation. They thus set out both to show that their work was designed to preserve the work of the Fathers of Confederation by rectifying distortions that had crept in over the past seventy years. History, they argued, vindicated the quest of the constitutional reformers of the 1930s, for their aim was to restore the true meaning of Confederation.

Given this outlook, it is not surprising that the report of the commission began with a historical overview. For those who would assess that overview in terms of the biases of the times there are certain difficulties. The writings of the men who developed the historical interpretation – individuals like Mackintosh, Creighton, and Corry – have assumed a central role in the historiography of English Canada. The view put forward in these writings is so standard now that it is difficult to realize the degree to which the generation of the 1930s rewrote the history of the Confederation era and reinterpreted the meaning of Confederation itself. Before the Depression, Canadian Confederation had, for the most part, been viewed in the international context. It was part of the evolving relationship of the British Empire as a constitutional entity and as an effort on the part of British North America to ensure that its destiny remained distinct from that of the United States. In the 1930s, however, there had been a new interest in economic matters and a shift in emphasis from external to internal relations, from nation-building in the international context to nation-building in the internal context. Economic development, expansion, agricultural develoment, and, of course, federal-provincial relations assumed a new importance. This new emphasis was especially noticeable in the work of the Rowell-Sirois Commission, the general trend being reinforced in this case by its particular mandate. The intentions of the Fathers of Confederation were probed to discover what their vision of the nation had been. Not surprisingly, given the attitudes present within the intellectual community, the studies demonstrated that the Fathers of Confederation had wanted what the intellectual community of the 1930s now sought: a strong central government with sufficient powers to manage economic development.[50]

There was considerable evidence to support such a position, and in general terms its advocates used two sets of arguments. The first was based on an analysis of the British North America Act. The contents of that act, it was repeatedly argued, provided prima facie evidence of the intentions of those who had written it. As early as 1929, Brooke Claxton had argued that a perusal of sections 91 and 92 of the act led to inescapable conclusions concerning the division of powers intended in 1867. 'The layman often finds it difficult to understand a statute,' Claxton noted, 'but it is hard to see how anyone who can read English' could fail to understand that 'the effect of Sections 91 and 92 of the B.N.A. Act is to leave the residue of power with the Dominion and strengthen its hand, so that the Provinces could only deal with matters specifically given to them by Section 92 and not even these when they became of general interest and importance to the whole country.'[51]

To nationalists like Claxton, the interpretation of the act was so obvious that the continued pretensions of the provinces to additional powers were frustrating. In an effort to overcome provincial arguments, the Canadian Clubs had even commissioned Frank Scott to write an assessment of the act and its implications in the light of recent controversies. The result was an impressive attack on the doctrine of provincial rights that was circulated to all local clubs as part of the mandate of the association to promote nationalism. For Scott, as with Claxton before him and Rogers after him, analysis of the act made only one conclusion possible. 'Canada was conceived as a federation in which the people could co-operate through the central government for the management of all national matters, but would enjoy provincial autonomy in the administration of truly local questions.'[52] The division of powers, the residual clause, and the power of disallowance given to the federal government all proved that the Fathers of Confederation were economic nationalists.

It was not necessary to rely merely on the wording of the act. It was not a mysterious tablet from the distant past but a relatively recent document framed amid debate and public commentary. The historical record could thus be researched to discover the intentions that lay behind the words that became the Canadian constitution. When that record was analysed, the emphasis was on the drive toward unity that existed in the 1860s. The efforts of John A. Macdonald to establish a unitary state and, when that failed, to ensure a strong Dominion government commanded a great deal of attention both from individual writers and from the Rowell-Sirois Report. 'Yet nothing could be clearer,' wrote LSR member P.E. Corbett, 'than the determination of the most eminent protagonists of federation to set up a strong central government.' Frank Scott buttressed his analysis of the constitution with citations from Macdonald on the flaws in the states' rights orientation of the United States and closed his overall argument with a ringing quotation from Macdonald: 'If we do not take advantage of the time; if we show ourselves unequal to the occasion, it may never return, and we shall hereafter and bitterly regret having failed to embrace the happy opportunity now offered of founding a great nation.' The cumulative message was clear enough. Those who sought to reform the constitution and centralize revenue gathering and social services were, far from defiling the sacred constitution, upholding its basic tenets. Proposed reforms could thus be posed not as dangerous innovations but as basically conservative attempts to return Canada to its founding principles.[53]

The Report followed the logic presented in these arguments. Drawing freely on earlier writings and on the commissioned work of people like Corry, Creighton, and Mackintosh, it pulled together the various strands of argument into a cohesive depiction of the purposes of the Fathers of Confederation. The main reason for Confederation, the Report argued, was not external in nature, nor was it merely a question of political deadlock. Rather it was economic. Problems of colonial debt, aspirations for western expansion, railway construction, the improvement of borrowing potential, and the development 'of a broader base for government expenditures necessary to attain new and difficult economic objectives' were the ingredients involved in shaping Confederation.[54]

This conclusion was useful in emphasizing that the reason for Macdonald and the others developing a strong central government was their desire to deal with economic development and financial management. These were the primary areas of concern for the Rowell-Sirois Commission, and the parallel with 1867 was thus made more complete. Sound economic management, with its enormous significance for a people caught in depression, and reform of federal-provincial relations were shown to be but two aspects of a problem recognized and dealt with originally by the Fathers of Confederation. 'It seems generally accepted,' the report concluded, 'that it was the intention of the Fathers of Confederation, and indeed the only basis on which the Dominion could be built, that the central government should possess the revenues and carry the expenditures which were national in scope, while to the provinces and municipalities should fall the revenues and expenditures of a provincial or local nature.'[55]

What then had happened? Where had the Fathers of Confederation been betrayed? It was patently clear to any observer that the strong economic and fiscal powers given to the Dominion government in 1867 were largely dissipated by 1937. The problem was three-fold, according to the analysis undertaken for the Rowell-Sirois Commission. First, the constitution – so clear in its meaning to the intellectuals of the 1930s – had been the subject of numerous contentious court cases in the late nineteenth and early twentieth centuries. As Scott noted earlier, sections 91 and 92, the ones concerned with federal-provincial relations, had 'been the battlefield of judges and lawyers for over sixty years.' Beginning with Hodge vs the Queen (1883) and culminating in the Board of Commerce Case (1922), a series of successful challenges to Dominion authority had been mounted. Gradually the residual clause and other sweeping powers of the Dominion were reinterpreted by the courts until only the specific items listed as federal powers remained safely within Dominion jurisdiction. 'The examples,' lamented Scott, 'have swallowed up the rule.'[56]

The trend of the court decisions thus contradicted the argument of Claxton and others that the implications of the BNA Act were unmistakable. The unwillingness or inability to understand either Canada or the meaning of Confederation had led the Judicial Committee of the Privy Council into a series of traps in which narrow legal definitions, clever arguments, and other devices had vitiated the obvious spirit of Confederation. The result had been the 'interpretative attrition' of the BNA Act. There is no doubt, Claxton concluded, 'that the Privy Council has given us a constitution different from that intended for us by the Fathers of Confederation.' The Rowell-Sirois Report was more circumspect, but it made essentially the same point. The courts, it noted, were not allowed to look behind the words of the act to the historical event and were thus limited in their understanding of Confederation. And while it admitted that there were two sides to the debate over provincial powers, the fact that it devoted four times as much space to the narrow interpretation of provincial powers as to the broad one left little doubt that the commission essentially agreed with Scott, Claxton, and Rogers. As it concluded, 'the historical case presented by the critics of the Privy Council has not been accepted by all but it merits the attention and consideration of serious students of the problem.'[57]

While the judicial interpretations were important, however, men like Skelton, Scott, and the commissioners were strongly influenced by social scientific interpretations of events. The court decisions alone could not explain what had happened since 1867. Also crucial were forces embedded within the Canadian environment that had, over the years, altered the relative role of the Dominion and the provinces. The first of these forces was best described by W.A. Mackintosh in his study for the commission, *The Economic Background of Dominion Provincial Relations*. Mackintosh, in turn, was drawing both on earlier work of his own and on themes developed by O.D. Skelton in his 1914 study of the economic history of the Dominion. According to Mackintosh, and the Rowell-Sirois Report, Confederation had been part of an economic strategy for the rapid development of British North America, as witnessed in the expansion to the West and the National Policy of Macdonald. The Dominion Lands policy, development of the Canadian Pacific Railway, and other Dominion initiatives ensured that the expectations of the Fathers of Confederation were fulfilled, with a strong central government dominating the development of the Canadian economy. The existence of a federal system, however, created a series of political and economic relations that dictated that should the federal sense of initiative falter the provinces would immediately move to assert their own visions of development. The first signs of trouble occurred in the 1880s, when nagging recession and lack of immigration prevented the growth that the Canadian public felt necessary. The first provincial conference was, after all, held in 1887 in the midst of that depression. In contrast, after 1896, with the return of boom conditions, the dominance of the Dominion was reasserted. Major railway projects, the rapid settlement of the West, and the expansion of port facilities in both the east and the West once again meant that the federal government was central to Canadian economic development. Nationalism flourished. 'The wheat boom had finally brought the realization of the economic objectives of the Confederation scheme,' concluded the Rowell-Sirois Report. As a result, there developed 'a common material interest and a national spirit such as had never existed before.'[58]

The very success of the years after the turn of the century contained within it the seeds of current problems. The original economic purpose of Confederation had been so dependent on the development of the open lands to the west that it was inherently limited in scope. By the 1920s the great wave of agricultural expansion was finished. Though the First World War somewhat delayed matters, a shift in focus was inevitable. 'No obvious and pressing challenge' presented itself to the Dominion in the years after the war, and the burden of wartime debt turned policy-makers' attention from the shaping of new policies to fiscal caution. 'The Dominion yielded the initiative to the provinces.'[59]

The result was a new series of expensive burdens assumed by the provincial governments that were barely manageable in periods of prosperity. In depression, of course, they brought Canada to the brink of a major financial crisis. The end of the period of frontier expansion and development had thus left Canadian federalism in a state of disequilibrium, the fiscal position no longer in accord with the actual responsibilities of the respective levels of government. In this sense, the Judicial Committee of the Privy Council only aggravated a problem that was inherent in the nature of Canadian development.

Nevertheless, that aggravating factor was important because it prevented the political successors to the Fathers of Confederation from adjusting the orientation of the Dominion in response to changing conditions. Confederation, after all, had taken place during the height of Victorian laissez-faire theories concerning the role of the state. 'The prevailing idea was that the fewer functions surrendered by the individual to the government the better. John Stuart Mill was still the authority, and his ideas with regard to the limitation of government marked the general line of thought.' In other words, as J.W. Dafoe succinctly put it, Canada was formed and the initial division of powers undertaken before government had assumed the duties of 'almoner-in-chief.' This meant two things for the act. First, the lists of duties set out in sections 91 and 92 were as limited as the age's concept of government. Second, the evolution of new responsibilities, especially the major responsibilities of the provinces in education and social welfare, were not envisaged in the act or by its framers. As Corry wrote in his study for the commission, 'We did not have at Confederation any of the problems of a highly specialized and urban industrialized economy.'[60]

This was not to imply that the limited horizons of the Fathers of Confederation were responsible for the current federal-provincial problems. What had changed was not the wisdom of the politicians but the environment in which they framed policy. 'The self-sufficiency and the solidarity of the family carried a great deal of the burden of providing social security for the unfortunate. *Periodic unemployment generally meant no more than a temporary retreat to the family homestead.*'[61] This was in stark contrast to the circumstances of the twentieth century. Events rapidly broke down 'the former self-sufficiency of households and local communities.' Family autonomy declined as social and economic interdependence increased. Government was inevitably drawn into new roles. Social welfare was one of the more dramatic areas of increase. At Confederation total governmental expenditures at all levels in this area had amounted to little more than $1 million. By the time the commission was appointed, this figure had reached a quarter-billion dollars.[62] It was this evolution of governmental responsibility that created a dilemma for government and for federal-provincial relations. The new responsibilities were within the purview of the provinces. Yet the provinces did not have the funds to meet them.

This brought the argument back to the Judicial Committee of the Privy Council. The Fathers of Confederation may have been limited in their philosophic assumptions about government and in their ability to guess all that the future would bring, but, the nationalists of the 1930s argued, they had understood the dangers of an excessively rigid constitution. Their purpose had been to ensure that the principle of Dominion direction of economic development continue and that flexibility be left to allow future governments to make adjustments as required. This flexibility would have allowed the Dominion to shift from the settlement and development of an agricultural frontier to, as it turned out, the new economic frontiers of controlling cyclical swings in the economy and providing security. Unfortunately, the Judicial Committee of the Privy Council had not recognized the foresight of the residual and disallowance clauses of the BNA Act and had transformed a flexible tool into a rigid strait-jacket that threatened to suffocate Canadian nationality.[63]

The depiction of the transformation of Canada from the rural-agrarian world of the nineteenth century to the urban-industrial world of the twentieth had been basic to the progressive view of current Canadian problems. Thus the arguments presented in the 1930s were the culmination of decades of analysis by successive middle-class intellectuals into the problems of their era. Concerns about rural depopulation, growing interdependence, and the implications of the industrial economy had all surfaced before the First World War. Social, demographic, and economic changes, the argument went, demanded government response.

Yet there is another aspect to the writings for the commission. In the imagery of the nineteenth-century farm presented in the Rowell-Sirois Report and in Corry's study for the commission, there was a tendency to over-emphasize the self-sufficiency of the farm and the resilience of the family unit in times of depression. Discussions of a 'temporary retreat to the family homestead' had only a limited reality and failed to comprehend the hardship faced by individuals throughout pre-industrial Canada in times of economic collapse. Such over-emphasis in the midst of a carefully researched and documented report like the Rowell-Sirois reveals a touch of romanticism towards a lost world. As Corry commented, 'by moving eagerly into the full current of the Industrial Revolution, we have foresaken our pioneer self-sufficiency for economic interdependence.' Such romanticism is perhaps best explained by the fact that the generation that experienced the traumatic shift from country to city shaped the commission's view. Thus, for example, Corry himself, whose work largely shaped this part of the report, was writing in part as social scientist, assessing the trends of urbanization and industrialization, and partly reflecting his fondness for his rural childhood in southern Ontario in an era when the state was far away and largely unnecessary. 'Not being dependent for security and welfare on distant governments or fearful of their intrusion, these people believed that the best government was the one that governed the least and left them alone with their community initiatives.' Society had, for all its progress, experienced a loss in the transformation – a loss of independence – and it was this that necessitated the rewriting of the constitution.[64]

The Rowell-Sirois Commission was thus an expression not merely of a particular set of problems facing Canada but also a reflection of the mind-set of the intellectual community by the late 1930s. In both its brilliant aspects and its preconceptions it was the mirror of a particular group of intellectual social and economic reformers who, so its members argued, sought to preserve the original vision of Confederation by change. As Frank Scott wrote, 'It is not enough to found a great nation; its greatness must be maintained.'[65] The means by which this could be done was set out in both the Rowell-Sirois Report and in other writings of these years. With influence in the academic world and the bureaucracy, these reformers had set out to define the precise agenda for change. The Rowell-Sirois Commission was but the most elaborate example of that unfolding agenda.

By the time the commission reported, depression had given way to war. As a result, the careful marshalling of evidence and the ordered progression of influence and change had to give way to immediate and desperate activity. The role of the state was to be transformed not because the public and politicians had fully accepted the new reform views but because war forced government into new and expanded activities. The reformers were thus faced both with a tremendous opportunity and a real possibility of failure. With the outbreak of war, they found themselves riding the whirlwind of an expanding state and mushrooming bureaucracy. The reforms they had advocated henceforth unfolded not at a calm and orderly pace such as befitted a rational evolution of the state, but at the frenetic pace necessary to win the war. If these events could be shaped in a positive manner to turn temporary war activity into orderly social and economic planning, then success might finally be within reach. Out of the bureaucratic chaos of war might emerge the rational, efficiently planned, and humane state. If events took on a life of their own, however, or if the voices of change failed to convince the politicians and public, the opportunity might forever slip from their grasp. War was to provide the concrete test case of the modern state in fully developed form.

10

Bureaucracy, war, and reform
1939-42

When war came in September 1939 the reaction of the Canadian intellectual community contrasted markedly with that of its progressive predecessors of the First World War. Through the 1930s a good many members of that community had actively supported a foreign policy that would prevent Canada from being dragged into yet another British war in continental Europe. F.R. Scott's 1938 work, *Canada Today*, was perhaps the best-known statement of this position, but as late as 1938-9 Alan Plaunt and numerous others had sought to free Canada from the constitutional bond that tied Canada automatically to any British declaration of war. Even when war actually came, reluctance rather than enthusiasm typified the response within both civil service and academic circles. O.D. Skelton was in a position to show that reluctance clearly, and on a number of occasions Mackenzie King, no enthusiastic interventionist himself, had to prod his favourite civil servant to appropriate lines of advice. King's private secretary, Jack Pickersgill, complained in October of 'this meaningless war' into which Canada had fallen. Such comments came naturally from the generation that had fought or had friends and relatives in the First World War. The slaughter of that war and the disillusionment with its purpose were bound to shape the attitudes toward this new war. As C.R. Fay put it, any assessment of the war was impossible without taking into account the 'approaching slaughter of the young.' Poland was far away, and the image of another besieged nation in 1914 only drew the parallel with the First War all the more tightly.[1]

There was more to the reluctance than this, however. There was also concern that war might destroy the reform impetus that seemed to have been building in Canada. Memories of the way in which the

First World War had misdirected the energies of the state haunted these men who now faced another world war. The aftermath had brought the collapse of the reform wave and a backlash against the positive state. Now it was all too likely to occur again. A patriotic public, whipped up by war propaganda, might blindly support a state armed with the tremendous powers of the War Measures Act and other emergency instruments not for the purposes of reform but to preserve the status quo. As F.R. Scott warned, 'War is the handmaid of reactionaries; it seems to make reformers disloyal.' Arthur Lower commented cynically a few days after the declaration of war: 'When one is fighting for freedom in the abstract he must expect to lose it in the concrete.' The prospect of autocracy in war to be followed by reaction in peace was not one to encourage the domestic reformer.[2]

This general fear had a specific context. By the end of the Depression the interconnected groups of intellectual reformers had made substantial progress both in gaining access to power and in developing the broad outlines of the reforms that they felt essential in the modern state. Departments like Finance, under W.C. Clark, had moved toward Dominion assistance for housing and supported at least in principle most of the recommendations of the earlier National Employment Commission. The arrival of R.B. Bryce in the department in 1937 brought a committed Keynesian into a key policy area within the federal government. The 1939 federal budget gave indications that the long, if increasingly tenuous, hold of classical economics over Canadian fiscal policy was about to be broken. Most importantly, the Bank of Canada had, along with Finance, achieved the creation of the Royal Commission on Dominion-Provincial Relations. At the outbreak of war the commissioners and their staff were preparing the report that, it was hoped, would break the constitutional log-jam that made crucial reforms impossible. The fact that the report's long-awaited release was overshadowed by the beginning of the German assault on western Europe demonstrated the difficulties that reform causes faced in wartime. Moreover, reform was dealt another blow when Norman Rogers was moved to the Defence portfolio. It was a testament to Rogers's ability, but the tremendous burden of the post ensured that he would be less involved in pushing domestic causes. In his place in Labour was the relatively unknown Windsor MP Norman McLarty. He was not a man connected to the intellectual community and was not known as a reformer.[3]

At the same time the war offered some encouraging possibilities for those who advocated a more active 'planned' state. There were three reasons for this. First, as in the last war, the government assumed vast new powers to handle the crisis. Both politicians and public set aside any reluctance they might have had about the enlargement of the role of government, at least temporarily. In the process the government not only intervened to an unprecedented degree in the lives of Canadian citizens but also assumed a newly powerful position in its relation with the provinces. If, as the Rowell-Sirois Report argued, the Dominion had lost its primary role with the completion of frontier development, then it acquired a new one in directing the war effort. Armed with the War Measures Act and other emergency powers, the Dominion government moved quickly to assert paramountcy in national affairs. The defeat of Maurice Duplessis's Union nationale government in Quebec shortly after the commencement of the war removed a major obstacle to reform, and though other premiers would give King trouble on occasion the federal government was able to acquire the authority it had sought since the late 1930s. 'The war,' wrote economist B.S. Kierstead, 'has given us a temporary unity of purpose and a unique, if passing, national interest.'[4]

Second, the increased functions of the Dominion government demanded a proportionate increase in the size and complexity of the Canadian civil service. Sprawling temporary buildings and new departments and agencies abounded as the Dominion government hired the staff necessary to run a modern state during a total war. The federal civil service grew from 46,000 in 1939 to nearly 67,000 by 1941, 104,000 by 1943 and 115,000 by 1945 – an increase of some 69,000 over the war years. In contrast, the Depression decade had brought an increase of only 2,000.[5]

Third, the growth of the civil service brought a parallel increase in the use of 'expert personnel' within it. The advocates of the past generation had not gone unheeded, and there were enough former academics, social scientists, and well-educated professionals in place by 1939 to ensure that men of similar background, attainment, and outlook would be sought to fill the new positions as expansion occurred. In other words, the network of intellectuals that had developed within the university drawing rooms, club circuits, and advisory meetings was drawn to a greater degree than ever before toward the civil service. What began as a trickle in 1939 continually increased in volume over the next years, reaching a peak in 1943. By the end of the war, university professors could be found in most of the nooks and crannies of the sprawling temporary buildings around Ottawa. Thus, for example, Henry Angus of the University of British Columbia went into the Department of External Affairs, S.E. Bates left Dalhousie to enter the Department of Fisheries, Escott Reid of the Canadian Institute of International Affairs joined External, and C.B. Macpherson of the University of Toronto went to Leonard Brockington's Wartime Information Bureau. These were cases of individuals joining departments. In other instances, such as the Wartime Prices and Trade Board, whole university departments could have been created from a staff that included, at various times, J.F. Parkinson of Toronto, J. Macdonald of Manitoba, H.R. Kemp of McMaster, and G.E. Britnell of Saskatchewan. Presiding over them was K.W. Taylor of McMaster. The Department of Finance was not far behind in its recruitment of university social scientists and was probably more important in terms of actual power. The most significant appointment came when W.A. Mackintosh left Queen's for the duration of the war to act as special assistant to Clifford Clark. Over the years other important Canadian economists, including A.F.W. Plumptre and Vincent Bladen of Toronto and C.A. Curtis and F.A. Knox of Queen's, undertook duties of varying duration within the department.[6]

For the cynical, as with George Ferguson of the *Free Press*, Ottawa was a giant maw, pulling in all that came near and swallowing them up within a murky swamp of bureaucracy. Ottawa, he recalled after one visit, reminded him of Proverbs 1:12 and 17: 'Let us swallow them up alive as the grave and whole, as those that go down into the pit.'[7] For those swallowed up in the pit, however, all was not lost, and in reality the nature of wartime activity meant an intensifying of the connections that already existed. The early and relatively isolated figures of Skelton at External and Clark at Finance were now reinforced by newcomers of considerable ability and power. Key civil servants could now talk, visit, and relax with equally important colleagues of similar background and outlook. The informal network of ideas was becoming institutionalized within the more structured confines of the Ottawa mandarinate.

It was also becoming a tightly knit social network. In the large houses of Rockcliffe, at the Five Lakes Fishing Club, and in favourite dining spots around what was still essentially a small town, the contacts were continually reinforced. As was typical of this group, these social occasions were an electic mixture of serious scholarship and frivolous escapism. In the tradition of the 'clubs' of past decades, a group of economists soon got together to form an Economists' Dining Club to exchange ideas on mutual wartime problems. Of course, the Ottawa Canadian Club and other more established organizations continued throughout the war to attract the attention of these new civil servants. For less serious moments there were also dinner parties, informal social gatherings, and, on the part of some, considerable use of liquor as a means of escape from the ever-growing pressures of work. Whatever the activity, however, there was little doubt that the centre of intellectual reform in Canada was now passing into the hands of this group of Ottawa officials and allied politicians.[8]

Part of the reason the intellectual network was so visible and so close was that it was concentrated in just a few relatively small, though important, areas of government. A complete description of the often byzantine structure behind these numbers would demand a full study in itself. It is important to understand the basic orientation and structures of the wartime bureaucracy, however, in order to comprehend the way in which the intellectual community in Canada played a part in wartime activity. In general terms, the easiest way to picture Ottawa in wartime is to begin with J.B. Brebner's 1942 comment to Innis that the government had 'broken up into a few very vigorous government departments and agencies' with King and the powerful war cabinet trying to ride herd on them all.[9] In particular, three groupings involved with the war effort can be discerned.

The first group was, perhaps obviously, the military itself. From a chronically underfunded skeleton force in the 1930s the various branches of the military would expand tremendously, both after the initial declaration of war and again after the fall of France. With their own customs, chains of command, and specific function the military services operated somewhat apart from the normal Ottawa bureaucracy. Their purpose, to defeat the enemy, also meant that they were not directly involved in discussions of domestic reform except where those reforms might affect the war effort. The second crucial group was that which supplied the military. Beginning as a rudimentary War Supply Board in 1939, this area evolved under the energetic and capable leadership of C.D. Howe into the vast Department of Munitions and Supply. Employing thousands of civil servants and spending amounts greater than entire pre-war budgets, it became one of the most powerful bodies in wartime Ottawa. In July 1940, after passage of the National Resources Mobilization Act, a new Department of War Services took on responsibility for manpower aspects of supply.[10]

The third and final group was an interconnected series of departments and agencies concerned with the finances of government and the economy of the nation. At the centre, of course, were those bodies that had asserted their prestige and power through the Depression – the Bank of Canada and the Department of Finance. Ancillary bodies soon sprang up to meet the special problems of the war. The War Industries Board, the Foreign Exchange Control Board, and the Joint Committee on Economic Relations between Canada and the United States all spun off from government departments. Most important of all these adjuncts, however, was the Wartime Prices and Trade Board, which had become home to so many academic economists. Initially established in September 1939 under the Department of Labour, the body became influential when, in 1941, it was transferred to the Department of Finance, put under the energetic leadership of Donald Gordon, and given a new legislative set of powers.[11] Along with a host of lesser departmental committees, boards, and regulatory agencies, these major bodies moved the government into the complex era of wartime finance. Thus, the community of ex-academics was concentrated in those departments where the intellectual community had made inroads during the 1920s and 1930s – the Department of Finance and related agencies, the Bank of Canada and related agencies, and the Department of External Affairs. To this group might be added Leonard Brockington's Wartime Information Board and its coterie of academic psychologists.[12]

Each of these areas tended to hire a distinct type of person. Though all the civil service was dedicated to the common goal of winning the war, there were differences in attitude and background that could lead to confrontation between key elements of the bureaucracy. Typical of the cool relations that existed was Clifford Clark's half-serious, half-bantering reply to a string of complaints against the civil service. Surely, he concluded, the problem must lie with the dollar-a-year men around Howe and not with the permanent civil service.[13] The academic community had, in various ways, expounded a philosophy of the state that was at odds with the business community's view of how best Canada might be served. The two groups had clashed before, and now that they were wrapped tightly within the cocoon of bureaucracy there was every chance they would clash again. This would be especially likely if, as was inevitable, the focus shifted from winning the war to the shape of the post-war world.

The growing importance both of the civil service and of the intellectuals within it means that in the Second World War it is possible for the first time to talk in terms of a 'brain trust' in the sense that the term was used during the American New Deal – to describe a group of intellectuals with direct access to the levers of power. More appropriate for Canada, however, is the term favoured by Mackenzie King, the *intelligentsia*. It was not always a term of endearment. King remained cautious of this new elite and was constantly suspicious that it sought to reinforce its own power at the expense of the politicians whom it ostensibly served. Thus, for example, in 1942, when Alex Skelton recommended W.A. Mackintosh as a possible deputy minister, King commented that this was just one more example 'of the intelligentsia trying to run a government on their own lines.' Skelton's alternate suggestion of Brooke Claxton as a possible minister only confirmed King's opinion. It was, as he correctly perceived, another route to the same end.[14] However often King might complain about the cliquish nature of the intellectual community in Canada, the facts remain that it existed and that he realized just how central it had become to the running of government. King may have looked with reluctance on occasion to his braintrust, but look to it he did.

Those intellectuals who, in one form or another, had cast their lot with government knew that their role was important and that their influence was part of a larger tendency in modern government. Generally they seem to have accepted with relative equanimity not only the obvious fact that the state was much more involved in the lives of the public than ever before but also the more controversial point that this intervention was bound to alter the traditional liberties of Canadians. As early as 1937, Norman Rogers noted this point, arguing that the new activities of the state have 'blurred the traditional frontier between governmental authority and individual liberty.' Brooke Claxton went even further and accepted the decline of the legislature and the rise of bureaucratic power as flowing inevitably from the nature of the modern state. Government, he wrote in 1942, 'will become more and more a job of engineering.' In the process Parliament 'will be recognized as being an electoral college to record the vote at a general election.'[15]

Underlying such statements was an implicit denial of the traditional liberal assumption that concentrations of power and expertise posed potential dangers to political liberty. Those who clung to such assumptions were but the dying voices of another era.[16] The intellectual community of reformers in Canada, after all, had over the past gen-

eration argued that in modern society opportunity for the average citizen called for direct intervention rather than the reverse. By 1940 it
appeared as if their long battle was on the verge of being won. As the
Rowell-Sirois Report commented, North Americans seem 'unconsciously but inevitably' to have abandoned earlier assumptions about
rugged individualism in favour of greater state intervention.[17] The majority of the intellectual community, the needs of modern society, and
the public mood all dictated that the state continue to expand its role
and that the expert adviser would be central to that expansion.

In the various speeches, letters, and memoranda that deal with the
coming of the new state, the language is that of technocratic pragmatism rather than that of formal philosophic systematization such as
existed in the First World War. Indeed there is an almost studied indifference, even hostility, to traditional political philosophy. W.A.
Mackintosh made this explicit in his 1937 presidential address to the
Canadian Political Science Association. Economics, he maintained,
was a science and thus free from the distortions inherent in any set of
value judgments: 'Modern theoretical economics prescribes no policy
and enunciates no doctrine apart from the analysis of the particular
facts of a problem.' That scientific structure, however, was often weakened or destroyed by economists who 'confused' their own personal
views and their economic training. Those who would practise economics had to separate their own biases from their profession. The economist, such as Mackintosh himself, brought no ideology or philosophy
to government, only expertise. The very nature of the expert adviser,
he felt, demanded that personal views be left behind. 'Our philosophy,'
he commented, 'should always be ready to retreat before science.'[18]

This practice on the part of the new 'intelligentsia' to play down
political philosophy was not accidental. For two reasons philosophical
discussion was seen as a sterile occupation that would not promote
reform and might even hinder it. First, there was a strong belief that
the traditions of ideology and analysis handed down from the late
nineteenth century, with their focus on the industrial revolution, were
anachronistic in the new managerial state of the twentieth century.
Terms and forces like class, property ownership, and others associated
with the production process seemed less important as a new non-pro-
prietary managerial class, including the civil service, asserted its influence in the running of the economy. As economist B.S. Kierstead
wrote in 1940, 'It does not matter whether the planning be socialistic
or within the legal framework of private property. Indeed, the differ-

ences are becoming blurred.' Brooke Claxton was even more explicit in his vision of the future. 'By this time,' he wrote of the post-war world, 'we will probably have recognized that ownership of the means of production has come to mean practically nothing. What counts there is management and labour and their interests will come to be regarded as identical ... The difference between all the "isms" will be enormously reduced.'[19]

Shaping this new perspective was the fact that, for all their denial of class in the traditional sense, these writers reflected the views of the new 'managerial' middle class, especially that component of it drawn from the academic world. The rejection of philosophical categorization and debate seemed to them a rejection of dogmatism in favour of open debate and the pragmatic adoption of ideas, whatever their ideological source. In a less extreme form, then, Mackintosh's vision of the a-philosophical expert was typical of this group of activists and intellectuals. What counted was rationality, and strong attachment to a philosophical or ideological creed was all too likely to be the road to dogmatism.

Of course none of this should be taken to mean that Mackintosh, Claxton, Rogers, or the others had forsaken the search for an ethical basis on which to build the new state. The practitioners of the managerial state in Ottawa, as their correspondence clearly reveals, possessed strong political and social ideals. Rather, what it does indicate is a rejection of formal philosophy as obscurantist and in opposition to social scientific rationalism. As for ideology, it seems to have been viewed as a source of immense destructiveness in the modern world. The Russian revolution, the rise of Italian Fascism, and the ascension of Nazism in Germany all gave testimony to the ways in which ideology had, in recent years, served as an anti-democratic and anti-progressive instrument. Mackintosh warned in 1940 of the dangers of a frightened and insecure post-war world that might 'sacrifice both the individual and society to serve some dogma ... One sees a flood of self-seeking attempts to reconstruct the world in the interests of particular groups or schools of so-called thought. One sees a further abandonment of reason by carrying to even greater lengths than in the past two decades the programme of salvation by slogans or condemnation by branding.'[20] For people like Mackintosh, the rejection of philosophy was deliberate, part of a statement that reason rather than slogans would rule the modern state.

Accordingly, the hallowed concept of a 'planned state,' which had been a part of progressive rhetoric from before the First World War, underwent some changes. Plans, after all, could also become dogma. Thus, instead of being an ordered step toward the achievement of a specific social order, planning had become a way of governing, a part of the managerial concept. It was becoming, in the rhetoric of the technocratic class, an ongoing means of accommodating the state and society to ever-shifting historical circumstances. As R.A. Mackay, former Rowell-Sirois commissioner and 1944 president of the Canadian Political Science Asssociation, wrote, 'Human society never really is, it is always becoming.' Given this inability or unwillingness to define a final state of being, the aims of planning were becoming considerably more short run and variable. The process was taking over from the end, and planning was a means of minimizing the disruption of governing in an increasingly complex world.[21]

Most Canadians probably more or less accepted the positive image of the wartime state that was reflected in the writings of many of the bureaucrat-academics involved in it. Public grumbling over price controls, rationing, and higher taxes was mitigated by the belief that the cause was good and that the authoritarian aspects of government were but a temporary expedient to ensure victory. There was an element in the intellectual community, however, who, for various personal, philosophical, and partisan reasons, distrusted the Liberal government. For them the rise of government interventionism, the power of the bureaucracy, the decline of parliamentary authority, and the overwhelming majority that King received at the polls in 1940 all raised disturbing questions. What were the long-term implications of this relation between an assertive bureaucracy, a government with wartime powers, and an apparently complacent public? Once again a war to fight for freedom in Europe seemed to be dangerous to freedom at home. 'The temper of the Canadian people seems to be becoming more and more arbitrary,' Arthur Lower complained in 1941, 'and we are fast losing whatever tolerance and magnanimity we once possessed. Arbitrary arrest is gradually destroying our way of life, and no one seems to mind very much.'[22]

Such concerns were especially acute for those left outside the governing process. In particular, the CCF and the LSR had been thrown into considerable turmoil by the declaration of war. Most intellectuals in the CCF had long been resistant to any hint of British imperialism and had sought, apparently in vain, to separate Canadian foreign policy from that of Great Britain. Yet when war came, the implications for the party were uncertain and the principles involved contradictory. Canada was involved in another European war, but one against fascism, and the party found itself divided. J.S. Woodsworth's idealistic but lonely gesture of voting against the declaration of war did little to improve the situation. There were those who, like Graham Spry, had become more sympathetic to the British position and saw in the war the possibility of moving towards a socialist state of one form or another. However, there was Frank Scott's already mentioned warning that 'war is the handmaid of the reactionaries.' He was echoed by younger LSR supporter Kenneth McNaught, who, in 1942, expressed concern about 'revolution from the right.' Autocracy in war was to be followed by reaction in peace. 'Nothing matters but the victory – and a swift removal of all controls from industry when war ends.'[23]

The concerns within the party about the implications of the war accentuated the growing debate on the nature of the state. Historically the CCF and the League had stood dedicated to two related propositions. The first was that only an enlarged and efficiently managed state, run on socialist principles, could bring about the reforms necessary to ensure opportunity and equality in an industrial world. Increasing the power and functions of government was thus central to the position of the League and the party. The second was the importance of civil liberties in Canada. Partly on principle, partly because those on the left had been made acutely aware of the tendencies of many Canadians towards intolerance, and partly because of the academic tradition of open debate which influenced members of the LSR, civil liberties had occupied almost as much of the attention of some members as socialism itself. From a plank in the Regina Manifesto through fights against section 98 of the Criminal Code and against Duplessis's infamous Padlock law, the intellectuals in the LSR had demonstrated sensitivity to the possible abuses of power by the state.[24]

The potential paradox between a support for the enlargement of state powers and resistance to abuse of power by the state was not seen as a serious problem in the 1930s. The LSR believed that the basic problem was the control of the state by corrupt and selfish interests. With an assertion of national interests over those of big business and with a well-trained and disinterested bureaucracy drawn from the best minds of the nation, the state could safely be given power without its threatening civil liberties.[25] In other words, the LSR differed from traditional nineteenth-century liberalism in believing that concentration of power, if managed properly, did not have to lead to its abuse. The bureaucracy and the powerful state were to be a benign force for social betterment rather than an irresponsible purveyor of tyranny. In this the LSR was in tune with the intellectual network of reformers as a whole in the years before the war and presented a somewhat more ideological view of the sort of acceptance of state planning that was reflected from within the bureaucracy once the war began.

The experience of the first years of the war forced a re-examination of this whole question. In Ottawa a civil service was developing that in many ways reflected the LSR ideal. Many of the nation's most able intellectuals now were in government, including such supporters of the League as J.F. Parkinson, C.B. Macpherson, and Leonard Marsh. Yet the direction of the new state was, at best, uncertain. Power could be used to reform or to suppress. Frank Scott summed up the choices and, in doing so, the dilemma for many LSR members in a 1940 article in the *Canadian Forum*: 'The greater the number of social controls, the greater the danger of tyranny if they fall into the wrong hands; but the greater also is the opportunity of secure and ordered living if they are infused with a democratic purpose and made answerable to the democratic will.'[26] As of the first half of the war it remained unclear whether reform or tyranny was going to be the hallmark of this new state power.

The different sides of Scott's proposition were nicely depicted in an exchange of correspondence between Frank Underhill, Harry Cassidy, and Kenneth McNaught in late 1942 and early 1943. In the face of rising doubts about the direction of the LSR and the CCF both Underhill and Cassidy found themselves beginning to question the harder-line socialism of earlier party positions and looking instead to the gradual evolution of socialism through the intermediary step of a mixed economy. McNaught was disturbed with the idea, arguing that 'we cannot concede that a working arrangement with private enterprise, except in the case of very small competitive businesses, could lead to anything but a sabotaging of the whole idea of a planned economy.' For both Underhill and Cassidy, however, the difficulty in a rapid move to socialism, including large-scale nationalization of business, was that it raised serious problems in terms of the relation between power and freedom. 'I think that the evidence of recent years suggests very clearly,' wrote Cassidy, 'that there are great dangers in the concentration of political power no less than economic power. I am not clear as to how the survival of a genuine political democracy can be guaranteed when all economic power is under the control of the state.' Instead, Cassidy concluded, checks and balances, decentralization of power, and other measures might prove necessary to ensure the preservation of democracy in the modern state. Underhill revealed just how much the war was changing his views when he sided with Cassidy rather than McNaught. 'I am also worried, as Harry is, about the problem of freedom in a community in which the state has become the nearly universal employer and I'd just as lief have us approach the problem gradually.' The doubts expressed by Underhill and Cassidy were, of course, far from universal within LSR ranks, but they did reflect deep concerns. Henceforth the advocates of socialism would have to balance fear of a return to depression against anxiety about the autocratic tendencies of the state. The gradualism advocated by Underhill was, increasingly, to be the approach adopted by the CCF, though the exact reasons for the shift are complex.[27]

The war also had dramatic effects on members of the intellectual network within Conservative ranks and raised similar concerns to those posed within the LSR. For years, of course, men like Macdonnell and Finlayson had urged the causes of the new reformism upon their party. With Bennett's defeat in 1935, however, and his subsequent retirement in 1937, the party had been left without ideological or, for that matter, political direction. Then, with the war and the overwhelming 1940 victory of the Liberals, the Conservatives had to come to grips with the dilemma that confronted them or face extinction as an effective opposition.

In a series of articles in July 1942, J.M. Macdonnell attempted to go to the root of the problem and to chart a way out that would save both his party and, he believed, democracy in wartime Canada. The starting point for Macdonnell was, as with other intellectuals, the rapidly changing nature of the state in Canada. Those changes, in turn, reflected the paradox of modern war. 'We are fighting for freedom,' he noted, 'yet for the moment we have very little freedom.' As in the First World War, it was necessary in order to defeat totalitarian states 'to adopt many of their characteristics.' In particular, as the 1940 election revealed, party politics had largely collapsed in Canada as the citizenry sought to support the government in time of war. The government was increasingly ignoring Parliament, including its own back-benchers, in favour of bureaucrats. Management and control, rather than responsible government and freedom, were the watchwords in Ottawa. Even the most powerful politicians found themselves 'bound hand and foot' by the system they had created.

This might seem the prelude to the type of watchful anti-statism that had come to characterize elements of the Conservative party in recent years. For Macdonnell, however, such a position was unrealistic. The public had come to expect an active state, and any party that failed to comprehend this had no chance at gaining power. The new combination of the Liberal party and the burgeoning civil service seemed currently to reflect the wishes of the public.[28]

For both partisan and ideological reasons Macdonnell, unlike Claxton, could not accept a purely managerial system of government in which one party served as an electoral college for an ongoing bureaucracy. Rather the party system was 'crucial to freedom.' The only possible means of ensuring the continuation of freedom and of meaningful responsible government both during and after the war, therefore, was to ensure that the parties did not become so ideologically entrenched or polarized that the public would have no real choice because all alternatives to the present system would present too drastic a change. In this age of the bureaucratic state the party system was thus not irrelevant. Indeed, the Conservative party was, he felt, the only vehicle that offered the opportunity to break the chains of bureaucratic control without slavish acceptance of state socialism in even more ideological form. There was, however, a catch. The party had to frame a program that was 'dynamic as well as sound and sane.' For Macdonnell this meant inevitably an acceptance of the modern state rather than a rejection of it. As he concluded, the 1942 equivalent to John A. Macdonald's National Policy 'is a broad measure of social security.'[29]

Macdonnell's plea for a new course for the Conservative party reflected changing political currents. The Conservatives had sought success by returning their hero of the Frist World War, Arthur Meighen, as leader. That plan had proved delusory when he was defeated in a 1942 by-election. Now the question of leadership was surfacing once again, and Macdonnell and those who shared his views hoped that a new leader would also mark a change in party policy. To help prepare the ground for such a shift Macdonnell, Finlayson, and H.R. Milner of Edmonton, along with a number of others, were instrumental in arranging an unofficial discussion of policy at Port Hope in September 1942. This conference, reminiscent of the summer schools of the 1930s brought together the 'progressive' elements of the party in an effort to outflank the entrenched hierarchy and to force the party to accept many of the concepts of state intervention and planning that were common to both the CCF and, increasingly, the Liberal government in

Ottawa. For those who sought reform the conference was a resounding success. Improved labour relations, housing programs, unemployment insurance, improved old age pensions, and other social security meas-ures all received approval. A few months later the unofficial resolutions of the 'Port Hopefuls' were enshrined in a party platform and a former Progressive, John Bracken. The new leader would faithfully support the Port Hope program and came to depend on men like Finlayson and Macdonnell to a degree that seemed to indicate that the party had indeed departed from its old ways.[30]

Perhaps the most interesting thing about the shift of the Conservative party in 1942 was the people behind it. As one article in the wake of Port Hope pointed out, the new position reflected the ascendancy of a new generation. For the first time the same generation that had been so instrumental in shaping the LSR and in defining the new bureaucracy in Ottawa was at the centre of policy development for the Conserva-tives. The 'fundamental division in Canada today,' wrote Armour Mackay, is on the basis of age. Port Hope reflected the assertion by those born between 1890 and 1910 of their view of the modern world. Moreover, as the strong professional orientation and high educational attainments of the group indicate, the intellectual network that had existed since the late 1920s now had a powerful effect on all three national parties.[31]

Yet there was at least one well-known intellectual who was not moving towards an acceptance of technocratic liberalism and the im-portance of the intelligentsia in the governing process. Harold Innis had long taken a sceptical view of the pretensions of the new experts and their role in the aggrandized state. Through the 1930s he had expressed concerns that the development of the social sciences was being distorted by the hunt for quick and palatable solutions. This distortion and, ultimately, superficiality were masked by the growing faith that society was placing in the expert. The Second World War heightened these earlier concerns and made them so important to Innis that they fundamentally reshaped the direction of his research for the rest of his life.

In a very practical sense the effects of the war were likely to make Innis predisposed to criticism. As head of the largest social science department in the nation he had to face the myriad problems brought about by the rush of colleagues and graduate students into government service. Courses had to be readjusted, sections joined, new lecturers sought in an increasingly tight market, and work loads increased. Inevitably the time available for research and reading diminished accordingly.[32] For a man who believed that the university was essential to the scholarship of a nation it was not an encouraging time.

Also affecting Innis's views of the relation between the bureaucracy, the state, and society was his attitude toward the Rowell-Sirois Commission. When, in a survey by *Culture* magazine, Innis was asked whether his department supported the report's recommendations he exercised the prerogative of a headship to scrawl an emphatic 'No!!' in the margin. It summed up his unrelenting and almost single-handed campaign against a report on which so many of his friends and peers had worked. For Harold Innis to have detailed all his concerns about the report would have required a volume thicker than the report itself. Sloppiness in some of the supporting studies, unevenness in drafting, and numerous factual errors were all noted. More basic, however, was what the whole commission revealed about the emerging relation between the intellectual and government. Innis complained that the experts prevailed at the expense of the public in both the studies and conclusions of the commission. Individual Canadians were prevented by the commission's own rules from presenting briefs to it, and even where depositions were made they were overwhelmed by the sheer mass of material accumulated by the dozens of research studies. 'Research, like Mesopotamia, is a blessed word' and could be used to blind people to completely valid criticisms raised by non-specialists. A trend that had disturbed him from early in the Depression seemed to have reached new heights. 'Has the sovereignty of economists been finally established in Canada? Is this a further indication of the menace of economists in the decline of political alertness?'[33]

Even worse, the prestigious research studies masked the basic nature of the commission. The mandate of the commissioners and the premisses of its staff indicated that this had not been, according to Innis, an open-ended study of federal-provincial relations. Rather it was a vehicle towards the implementation of a political program that, at least in broad detail, had already been worked out. The massive studies of the economists were thus merely a cloak in which to dress some political moves aimed at the centralization of certain tax revenues and welfare systems.[34]

Many of the concerns that Innis expressed were simply reiterations of his own long-standing complaints. In his discussion of the use of data as a means of legitimizing essentially political actions, Innis was asking a question that would lead to a discussion on the basic problems of the relation between expert advisers in the service of the state and the nature of choice in the modern state. The growth of a powerful core of experts standing behind the federal government had sought, in the case of the commission, to assert a quasi-official view of the constitutional and economic evolution of Canada. That view, not surprisingly, fitted the preliminary aims and assumptions that lay behind the report. The conclusions of this same body were now being employed by many of the same people, now back in civil service postings, to seek a significant constitutional realignment of the Dominion. The public, Innis warned, should be aware of these relations and hesitate before blindly accepting the advice of the experts. The report's 'chief defect,' he warned, 'is its pretence at final thoroughness and the danger of supporting the dogmatic fallacy. It is almost necessary to write that there is no last word in the writing of economic or any other history except in the totalitarian states.'[35] Expert advice, if accepted without criticism by the public, could allow a series of changes that would forever reshape the Canadian nation into a more centralized and bureaucratized entity. The sovereignty of the economists would then be well on the way to being an irreversible fact.

Innis was concerned not merely with the Rowell-Sirois Report. It was part of a longer-term trend that seemed to be accelerating in the war. Innis began to fear that the rise of social scientific expertise within government was intimately tied to the decline of public watchfulness and the growth of arbitrary use of state power. There were already disturbing signs of what he termed the 'spiral of control,' which, if unchecked, could 'have no other result than a gradual movement toward a completely fascist system, nor can the operation of various controls be expected to be more efficient than the relative efficiency and wisdom of the people charged with the responsibility of administering them.' The level of that wisdom was questionable, given a growing number of incidents in which bureaucrats seemed to be usurping the proper role of the politicians by acting as propagandists for the policies they administered. Innis was critical, in particular, of the semi-autonomous nature of the Bank of Canada and agencies like the Wartime Prices and Trade Board. A favourite target of his criticism was Donald Gordon, who on more than one occasion went to the public to push a particular policy dispute. 'I thoroughly disapprove,' he wrote in 1943, 'of continual flagrant violation of [the] British tradition of anonymity in the Civil Service.' Canada's public service seemed increasingly unable to resist the tendency to what Innis termed 'bureaucratic exhibitionism.'[36]

These concerns led Innis to write perhaps his most significant piece of political comment. 'Decentralization and Democracy,' published in the August 1943 issue of the *Canadian Journal of Economics and Political Science*, was in many ways a typical Innis article. Concerned with the changes 'in types of power in the Atlantic basin following the discovery of America,' Innis runs through the history of Canada from the founding of New France. The prose is convoluted and obscure and the purpose of the article is in continual danger of being lost amid details on the fur trade, the American revolution, or other particulars of history. For Innis, however, the connections were clear. A system originally developed on the St Lawrence had expanded by the twentieth century to a size where the original forces tying the system together had become seriously weakened. 'Regionalization has brought complex problems for an economy developed in relation to the St. Lawrence.' In particular, the fragmentation of the nation had weakened or destroyed integrating political mechanisms such as a national two-party system. The CCF, Social Credit, and the Union nationale all testified to that fact. Into this national vacuum left by the declining party system had stepped the executive branch of government. The federal cabinet and especially its expert advisers had recently become more prominent. On this point Innis was in essential agreement with people like Claxton.

The problem was that, according to Innis, the trend had dangerous implications. 'A new civil service has emerged with much looser responsibilities to Ministers in charge of Departments. Ministers are able to evade responsibility by using the pronouncements of members of Civil Service as kites to test public opinion, or by throwing individuals to the wolves when the chase becomes too warm.' As the role of government altered, so too did that of the opposition. The declining importance of the legislative branch and the rising importance of 'expert' research left the opposition increasingly ineffective. The result was that the only real check on the national executive rested with the provincial governments. This is the key point that Innis was trying to make. A new balance had developed between the province and the Dominion that was the result of long-term, deeply rooted forces. 'The dangers of an obsolescent political structure cannot be avoided by patchwork solutions and plans of bureaucracies. Each region has its conditions of equilibrium in relation to the rest of Canada and to the rest of the world.' To tamper carelessly with the system, as Innis felt the Rowell-Sirois Report intended, was to enter into a dangerous area in which existing balances could be upset with unforeseen consequences. Certainly any further trend toward centralization would, rather than help the nation as a whole, benefit the central provinces at the expense of the outlying regions. 'Full employment,' he commented in enigmatic fashion, could become 'a racket on the part of the central provinces for getting and keeping what they can.'[37]

For all the complexity of prose, the article's basic message was straightforward. A series of historical changes had thrust the Dominion executive forward and had weakened traditional countervailing powers. In the process the bureaucracy, as both an adviser to and manipulator of the executive, had assumed an unprecedented influence in national policy formation. For Innis this was obviously dangerous, and the provinces, as the only meaningful source of opposition, were thus essential to preserving freedom in Canada. It was not so much that Innis was a strong provincialist. He did, after all, view the collapse of the old St Lawrence system with some regret. It was more that in current circumstances he felt he had to support the claims of the provinces against the growing federal presence. The growth of the bureaucracy in Ottawa may have been only a symptom of more basic changes, and its intentions were, undoubtedly, honourable. To Innis, however, it had become an internal threat to Canada rather than the means of entering a new and rational world of security and justice. Social scientists had simply misunderstood the nature of the problem facing Canada and had thereby added to it. Only an 'escape from the hocus-pocus of the economist' and a return to the much broader tenets of political philosophy, he concluded, would lead to a way out of the current situation.[38]

Innis had, by mid-war, gone much further than Underhill, Cassidy, or Macdonnell in developing his concerns about the nature of the state in the modern world. The basic point was the same, however. All were concerned that traditional values were being sacrificed in the name of the modern state. Concerns for individual liberty, responsible government, and the return of control to the average citizen ran through their writings. The more that traditional liberalism was replaced by a new interventionist and statist liberalism, the more those outside the apparatus of government began to focus on the issue. Harold Innis later summed up what was happening in a 1946 publication by citing with approval, of all people, Goldwin Smith: 'The opinions of the present writer are those of a Liberal of the old school as yet unconverted to state socialism.'[39] Whether state socialism was an appropriate term was debatable, but the fact that men both on the conservative and socialist side of the political spectrum were increasingly concerned with the direction of modern liberalism in the face of a growing bureaucracy reveals much about the nature of dissent within the intellectual community.

Traditionally liberalism had seen restrictions on state activity as central to modern freedom. In recent decades, however, that proposition had come under increasing challenge from intellectuals in Canada employing the counter-proposition that intervention by the state was essential to human security and opportunity. In a dialectic process the collapse of notions of the organic state in the wake of the First War seemed to make the need for traditional liberal anti-statism obsolete. The people rather than some semi-mystic 'state' would now reign supreme. It was not that simple, however, and the events leading to the Second World War made explicit the paradoxes that existed. Movements of mass popularity that reflected the democratic tenor of the century had created some frightening results when combined with the power of the modern state. As one writer noted, Fascism and Nazism could be described as democratic in the sense that they rested on broad popular movements; closer to home so too could Quebec's Padlock law. It was thus necessary, whatever the final conclusion, to ask some fundamental and essentially philosophical questions about the nature of government in Canada and of the relation between mass democracy, the role of the state, and liberal ideals.[40] For Innis especially, but also to a lesser degree with Macdonnell, Cassidy, and Underhill, the modern juggernaut of the state was increasingly something to be approached with caution. The great majority of the intellectual community, however, including those who had expressed such concerns, did not reject the modern state. It was just that they sensed the dilemma. Such awareness of the problems, however, raised a series of questions that could be resolved only by an act of faith in the state and in their ability as a class to manage that state. For the great majority of the intellectual community the risks and costs of being without interventionist policies and plans were greater than the risks and costs of having such intervention.

For all the changes that had taken place there were strong continuities with the progressivism of the First World War era. The supporters and detractors of the modern relation between the bureaucracy and the state were the direct intellectual descendants of men like Adam Shortt and James Mavor. In taking their respective positions they were emphasizing different aspects of the thought of those earlier advocates of expert reform. Men like Innis felt that amid the rush of planners to assume their position within the state apparatus the very firm ethical, religious, and philosophical context in which men like Shortt and Mavor grounded their advocacy of reform had been forgotten. Without such grounding, the purposes being sought in the proliferation of experts would eventually be lost and self-interest would take over. However, men like Mackintosh, though conscious of the need for ethical precepts on which to base planning for the future, stressed the concept of objective and detached expertise in the service of the state. Philosophical obsessions would only detract from the scientific pursuit of knowledge in the public arena. One position was an older viewpoint drawn from, and still propagated by, those within the university. The other view was that from the new pulpit of the intellectual, the civil service.

Related to this split in the view of the intellectual community was an increased specialization of subject matter and approach on the part of social scientists. By the 1940s the concept of social science as a unified discipline was giving way to a much more fragmented view. Economists, in particular, were detaching themselves from their colleagues by the Second World War, and as quantification spread throughout the discipline a new generation of specialists was spewing out articles and papers that were suitably erudite, replete with figures and graphs, and that dissected in some detail the sort of casual generalizations that had riddled the profession in earlier years. They were also completely technical in orientation and thus had none of the conscious philosophic precepts that Innis saw as essential. And they were unreadable by non-economist social scientists. At the same time, and partly in response to such specialization, other disciplines like sociology were beginning to assert a presence independent of the traditional field of political economy.[41]

The trend that had begun in the 1940s would continue through the next decades, but even by the middle of the war the close communications that had existed within a common social scientific community and educated public were in doubt. This challenged the basis on which the Canadian Political Science Association had been established by Skelton and Shortt back in 1913 and re-established by a coterie of active social scientists in the late 1920s. That organization had been based not just on higher degrees and technical knowledge but also on an attitude towards the investigation of public problems. Now that was being challenged and the organization was in the process of being transformed into a specialized professional society.

R.A. Mackay warned of the problems inherent in the changing nature of the social sciences in his 1944 presidential address to the association. There was, he said, considerable 'intellectual anarchy' in the social sciences at the moment, and those working in the field should be careful not to ignore the desirability of a broad synthesis of all the social sciences, along with philosophy and ethics: 'The social scientist must remember that he deals with a complex sensitive, living web of social relations, and that examination from one standpoint or any single thread or segment is only a partial and limited view of the whole. Indeed, in the social sciences all specialization is in a sense distortion, and as such intellectually dangerous unless corrected by examination from other standpoints.'[42] The trend, however, was irreversible. Canada was merely following the patterns established by the social sciences in other, and larger, nations.

The link between the fragmentation of the social sciences and the debate over the nature of the modern bureaucratic state is more immediate than might be imagined. For Mackay, like Innis, was concerned that the fragmentation of the broad conceptual framework of the social sciences into compartmentalized studies might threaten the value of the work being done at a time when that work was affecting public policy to an ever greater degree. Even more seriously, the goals sought were being separated from the studies undertaken. What, after all, aside from these goals, separated the social sciences in the allied countries from those in Germany or other axis nations? If there was no link between the expertise being developed and the purposes for which that development was taking place then the way was open, at least in theory, for the employment of scientific techniques in the assertion of abusive goals on the part of the state.

To move from the perceptions of what the war and the new bureaucracy might mean for Canada to the reality of the relation between the intelligentsia in the civil service and the government gives cause to wonder, at least initially, what all the debate was about. That bureaucracy, looked upon with such suspicion by some and such expectations by others, often seemed more the prisoner of circumstance than a new ruling elite in the process of transforming the state.

At first, it is true, the war did not deflect the advocates of reform from their various causes. Indeed, the war seemed to offer promise in overcoming at least one of the major obstacles to reform. It had given the federal government a set of emergency powers that meant that

Canada possessed a strong central government for the first time in years. As Frank Scott said two months after the war began, 'national planning, long urged in vain by progressive groups, is being undertaken on a vast scale. And the B.N.A. Act is no longer in the way.'[43] The hope was that these same war powers might be used to ensure that key reforms were implemented before old federal-provincial squabbles re-emerged in the post-war world.

In fact the war did encourage the passage of the most significant social security measures yet passed in Canada. Provincial opposition to unemployment insurance collapsed, and the way was thus cleared for the Dominion government to pass into law recommendations of, among others, such key bodies as the National Employment Commission and Rowell-Sirois Commission. Any federal objections to the scheme were reduced, if not eliminated altogether, by another result of the war – diminishing unemployment. Now the scheme would begin in a time when contributions would be able to accumulate. As King noted in his diary, it was a completely different situation than just a year or two earlier. 'The contribution will be easily paid during the years of prosperity and it could be two years before the benefits can be paid out under the Act.' Accordingly the bill was brought forward and, in the summer of 1940, became law.[44]

In addition, the government seemed to have learned from the experience of the First World War that consideration of the post-war world could not be left until the final days of the conflict. Within three months of the declaration of war a cabinet Committee on Demobilization and Rehabilitation was created to consider the problems associated with the assimilation of military personnel back into civilian life. Even earlier, on the advice of Clifford Clark, a co-ordinating group of senior civil servants, known as the Economic Advisory Committee (EAC), was struck to consider various economic problems resulting from the war effort. With a membership that included Clark, R.B. Bryce, Graham Towers, Norman Robertson, R.H. Coats, and, before long, W.A. Mackintosh, the committee had the potential to become the sort of super-bureaucratic planning group that Alex Skelton had been fond of proposing in the 1930s. Finally, the government decided that the Rowell-Sirois Report would be dealt with at a full-scale federal-provincial conference in January 1941. If successful, the conference would clear away permanently some of the major financial and constitutional difficulties which, in the minds of the intellectual community, hampered the development of a rational social security system. There were thus a number of promising developments early in the war, and it was just possible that reform currents established in the 1930s were being accelerated by the war situation.[45]

On closer examination it is apparent that this was not the case. The promising leads yielded few results. The Committee on Demobilization and Rehabilitation, and the advisory committees it spawned, remained narrowly focused on specific problems of demobilization. The broader implications of the problem, such as the general economic state of the nation, were not initially considered within the mandate of the committee at either the bureaucratic or political levels. The same unwillingness to look beyond immediate concerns appears to hold true for the first years of the Economic Advisory Committee. Specific and pressing issues, rather than the general shape of future policy, dominated the committee. Dairy boards, pork imports, copper requirements, and foreign exchange concerns, not social or economic reform, occupied the time of committee members. As W.A. Mackintosh commented in 1940, the committee 'had tended to become more of an inter-departmental committee called from time to time to deal with specific subjects.'[46]

The fate of the Rowell-Sirois Report was even less encouraging. It was not that the intellectual community in Canada did not push hard for action. On the Canadian Club circuit and in scholarly journals there were numerous arguments in favour of the report and its rapid implementation by the government. Indeed, writing on the report became such an industry that for a few issues CJEPS set aside a special section to list works on just that topic. Thus, for example, the February 1941 issue listed 16 recent publications on the report. The themes were familiar to anyone who had been observing discussions in the period since the commission was struck in 1937. Complex interdependence made the provisions of the BNA Act, at least as it had evolved over a century of court battles, obsolete. 'A unitary economy,' concluded J.A. Corry in early 1941, 'argues for a unitary state.' The Rowell-Sirois Report at least recognized the imperatives of unified action within a continuing federalism. Within the government both Alex and O.D. Skelton, as well as Clifford Clark, worked hard in the final weeks before the conference to convince King that he should push hard for implementation of the report.[47]

Within the cabinet, however, and especially in the case of King himself, there was a reluctance to push the report too hard. The problem in part was that the goals of the prime minister and his advisers

were quite different. Whereas King wanted some temporary understanding with the provinces in order to be able to plan war finances,
those committed to the Rowell-Sirois Report were, understandably,
loath to see the impetus of their investigations lost. For Alex Skelton,
perhaps the most ardent supporter of the plan, the war made implementation of the report all the more essential. 'Reforms that were
desirable yesterday,' he commented, 'are today essential.' The more
that Skelton and others pushed the report, however, the more cautious
King became. There were, the prime minister recorded, two forces that
were 'not the best' in their advice to him on this matter. 'These influences were two: (1) The Finance Department with the Bank of Canada
back of them, and the influence of Queen's University with its Orthodox money theories ... The other, the Manitoba Influence. Brockington, Pickersgill, etc., particularly as the report is largely a Dafoe report.'[48]

In this case bureaucratic enthusiasm had to give way to the prime
minister and the realities of federal-provincial relations. It was apparent from the opening of the conference on 14 January 1941 that Hepburn
of Ontario, Aberhart of Alberta, and Pattullo of British Columbia were
all determined to prevent the passage of the report's major recommendations. 'Is this the time to send a courier to bomb torn London?'
Hepburn asked in melodramatic fashion. Mackenzie King quickly abandoned the hopes of his public servants in the search for a compromise,
and the conference soon collapsed. King recorded that he was 'relieved
and happy' with the result. 'Had I gone the length of those financial
men and intelligentsia around me would have wished, saying that the
whole thing was to be taken or nothing. I would have played completely into the hands of Hepburn, Pattullo and Aberhart.' While King
may have been correct in his assessment, there is no doubt that the
collapse of a campaign for constitutional changes that dated back to
the mid-1930s was a bitter disappointment to men like Skelton and
Clark. The war was not to provide the opportunity for the greatest
reform stroke of them all, the constitutional adjustment necessary to
make other reforms possible.[49]

The collapse of the Dominion-provincial conference, King's growing
resistance to the 'impractical' ideas of the 'intelligentsia,' and the narrow focus of both the EAC and Demobilization and Rehabilitation committees provide a more meaningful pattern than the passage of the
isolated, though important, Unemployment Insurance Bill. Both the
government and the majority of the civil service were preoccupied with
winning the war. At the political level the reform influence that had

existed before the war was, if anything, declining. Norman Rogers had been transferred to Defence and then, in June 1940, killed in a tragic airplane accident while on his way to Toronto. Back-bench members of Parliament, like Claxton and Martin, consistently favoured reform but were not yet within the inner circles of policy formation. Perhaps the pessimists were right after all. The war might have deflected the long term goals of the civil service and have left major changes in the social and economic policies of the nation in greater doubt than they had been before September 1939.

Even as these various causes were going down to defeat, there was at least one corner of government where the pressures of early wartime did not lead to a loss of interest in reform. The Department of Pensions and National Health, under the energetic Minister from British Columbia, Ian Mackenzie, undertook an almost isolated campaign to convert the government to the support of various social security measures. Though Mackenzie's department was not to play the central role that he hoped it would, it was none the less significant in that by its very insistence on the importance of such issues, it eventually forced other elements of the civil service and cabinet to sit up and take notice.

The campaign of the department began in the autumn of 1939 with the cabinet shuffle that moved Rogers into National Defence. Mackenzie, the displaced minister, was given Pensions and National Health. In peacetime such a shuffle might have been considered a promotion for Mackenzie, but in wartime it was an obvious vote of non-confidence in the minister's ability to handle the newly important portfolio. Mackenzie, 49 years old, was a veteran of the First World War, well educated, and a member of both the generation and social class of such reformers as Claxton, Rogers, and the many civil servants who advocated social security measures. Moreover, as a member of the legislative assembly of British Columbia in the years after First World War, he had been exposed to the various reform ideas circulating through the province at the time. Finally, and not least important, Mackenzie's advocacy of reform in his new portfolio was a means by which he could enhance his own portfolio and demonstrate to King his importance as a colleague. At the same time Mackenzie does not seem to have had the direct social, educational, or professional ties that bound together so many other intellectual reformers in the country. Thus when he decided to embark on a campaign for social security he did so without the personal ties and support that might have helped in translating his ideas into policy.

One possible means by which Mackenzie could become involved in questions of reform came from a proposal that already existed within the Department of Pensions and National Health. Dr J.J. Haegerty, an assistant deputy minister in the department, had long been interested in the possibilities of public health insurance in Canada. Such ideas had been around for some time, but the Depression, with the resultant decrease in doctors' incomes, had made such a proposal at least tolerable in the eyes of the medical profession. Further, a study done for the Rowell-Sirois Commission by A.E. Grauer had stressed the importance of health in Canada. Thus by the time Mackenzie assumed the portfolio there had been a fair amount of preliminary discussion on the whole principle of health insurance. The minister's desire to find a specific direction for his reform enthusiasm and the growing interest of Heagerty in the whole matter meshed well. Within a few weeks of assuming the portfolio, Mackenzie was making speeches in favour of such a scheme as an integral part of the war effort. 'Is it too much to hope that, under the stimulus that war has given to our sense of social responsibility ... we may evolve a great constructive joint health programme on a broad national basis?' Within a few more months Mackenzie had commissioned Heagerty to investigate the question. By the time of the Dominion-provincial conference on the Rowell-Sirois Report, that investigation had been completed and the principle of health insurance adopted. Ian Mackenzie had found a cause to champion.[50]

Also shaping Mackenzie's interest in social security was his responsibility as chairman of the cabinet Committee on Demobilization and Rehabilitation. From that committee there sprang, in the spring of 1940, an advisory committee on the same subject. Thus Mackenzie was, from the time he assumed his new portfolio, faced with the implications of peace when most of his colleagues were still coming to grips with the war. Further, the more the advisory committee studied the whole matter and the more sub-committees it spawned, the more apparent it became that the scope of the investigation had to be widened. It was the only way in which the underlying issues of demobilization could be addressed. Thus in February 1941 Mackenzie got cabinet agreement to expand the mandate of the Committee on Demobilization and Rehabilitation to investigate the general problem of reconstruction.[51]

Soon after this, Mackenzie, with the assistance of Robert England, the secretary of the demobilization and rehabilitation advisory committee, began to pull together a number of individuals whose combination of intelligence, reputation, and connections would, he hoped, allow the issue of reconstruction in the broad sense to be brought forcefully before the government. It was an impressive group. Emerging eventually as chairman was Cyril James, the president of McGill University. Also on the committee were men who had for some time been interested in the issues of planning and reform: J.S. McLean of Canada Packers and R.C. Wallace, principal of Queen's. To these men was added Tom Moore, president of the Trades and Labour Congress, a former member of the National Employment Commission, and a man at one time offered a cabinet post by King. Completing the membership was Edouard Montpetit, the most senior and best-known French-Canadian economist. On 22 March, this still informal group met in Ottawa to discuss the whole problem of reconstruction. Within a few weeks the meetings had become more formalized with the membership remaining, aside from Montpetit, as it had been from the beginning. Finally, in September of that year, the cabinet gave formal recognition to Mackenzie's committee with the passage of an order in council creating the Advisory Committee on Reconstruction.[52]

Given the support of Mackenzie and the eventual blessing of the cabinet, the committee began the investigation of the rather awesome question of the nature of the post-war world. In the fashion of other government committees and task forces since at least Rowell-Sirois, a full-time appointment was made of a social scientist to co-ordinate activities of the part-time committee members, act as a general administrator, investigate the questions raised by the committee, and provide links with the permanent civil service. The man chosen for this task was Leonard Marsh, director of the School of Research at McGill. Marsh, born in England in 1905, had studied at the London School of Economics and worked with the well-known British social reformer Sir William Beveridge before joining the staff at McGill at the beginning of the Depression. As the head of a major social research body and as a member of the LSR, Marsh soon came into contact with various advocates of social reform in Canada. Indeed, he had been involved in the writing of the League's *Social Planning for Canada* and was therefore associated with one of the most ambitious attempts to chart the future of the Dominion.[53] Thus by the time he came to Ottawa to assist James he was both well known and had a good many ideas as to what was needed in Canada in terms of post-war social reform. The commission provided a vehicle by which those views might influence government directly. The challenge now was, therefore, not so much to devise the necessary programs as it was to convince first the committee and then the government that such changes were a necessary part of wartime planning.

It is a testimony to the interconnected nature of reform thought in Canada that Marsh and the committee found themselves in general agreement in spite of the considerable political differences that existed. From the beginning the committee seems to have worked on the basis of three general assumptions about reconstruction. The first was that there existed a close relation between a healthy economy, defined primarily in terms of full employment, and social security measures. The latter, it was believed, would pave the way to the former. Second, there was concern that the post-war period would bring considerable economic and social dislocation, as had occurred after the First World War. Third, these facts meant that, inevitably, the state and the bureaucracy would have to continue to exercise in the post-war world at least a portion of the powers they had assumed to handle the wartime emergency. 'Even though, as individuals, we may regret the passing of the older order of free trade, competion and capitalism,' commented one memo, probably written by Marsh, 'the democratic-capitalist order of society suggests that the attainment of reasonable economic security for the average individual will demand a large measure of coordination and governmental control.'[54]

Though such comments were hardly new, the blunt statement of the necessities of the new order reflects a major difficulty faced by the Advisory Committee on Reconstruction. It was, as its name suggests, an advisory committee designed to serve government by preparing it for possible policy requirements at the end of the war. To the degree that this was the committee's role it had to be politic, to avoid taking stands that might prove awkward for the government. Yet, given King's cautious attitude in 1941 to the whole question of the post-war world, such an approach would have allowed the committee practically no scope for anything but the most narrowly focused of studies. That was neither the commission's view of itself nor Mackenzie's intention for it. This led the committee members to emphasize the second role they had, as a lobby group on behalf of reconstruction planning. Hearings, appearances before parliamentary committees, and meetings on federal-provincial relations soon led James and his committee members into the position of advocates of a set of policies not yet approved by government. While this suited Mackenzie's purposes it also meant that, if the committee misjudged the governmental mood, it might come to be seen as a nuisance to be controlled. Thus there was nothing in the actual appointment of the committee that indicated the government was moving toward serious consideration of social security measures.

This was clearly revealed when Mackenzie and the committee began to come forward with various reform proposals. Thus, for example, when the minister began in the fall of 1941 to push his own particular interest in health insurance he found his cabinet colleagues somewhat reluctant. Mackenzie King, always a reformer in principle, agreed to let Mackenzie pursue the matter but raised concerns about potential costs. J.L. Ilsley, the minister of finance, was even more sceptical about the whole proposal. Moreover, Ilsley's correspondence on the subject was actually drafted for the most part by Clifford Clark, just as Mackenzie's was drafted by Heagerty. Behind the façade of ministerial correspondence two groups of civil servants were staking out their respective positions on the nature of social reform in the future. On the grounds of constitutionality, integration of social security plans, and other issues, the 'intelligentsia' in Finance seemed by late 1941 to be in opposition to the one group active in government in the development of reform proposals.[55]

Nor was it merely a question of health insurance. For when, in the autumn of 1942, the Advisory Commitee issued an interim report, the disagreements reappeared. In terms of the actual proposals put forward, the interim document was extremely modest. There were none of the sweeping changes advocated in some committee discussions or in public speeches by Mackenzie. The only substantive reform measure was a 'Construction Reserve Commission' that would assist and time the undertaking of public works along the well-known principles advocated by the senior Skelton more than thirty years earlier. The committee blundered, however, in the second part of the report. It recommended that a new portfolio be created to handle reconstruction. The clear implication was that many of the functions now scattered around the civil service and such temporary bodies as their own would be integrated into one department with, presumably, Mackenzie at its head. 'It is recommended that the Minister should have departmental responsibility for such economic aspects of the war effort as are included in the duties of the Wartime Prices and Trade Board, the supply functions of the Minister of Munitions and Supply ... Semi-independent Committees such as the Joint Economic Committee and the Committee on Reconstruction should report to him directly, and he should also have the power to set up other committees as in his opinion would contribute to the more effective utilization of the nation's economic resources for war or reconstruction.'[56] Such a department would have made the presiding minister one of the most powerful in government. It would also have cut a swath through such bodies as the Bank of Canada and the Department of Finance. Not surprisingly it aroused opposition from key areas of the civil service.

Particularly affected, should the recommendations be accepted, was that network of civil servants that, in the National Employment Commission, Rowell-Sirois Report, and other measures, had long advocated the more effective use of planning in government. War pressures had tended to keep them from abstract discussions of the post-war world, and the initiative had thus passed to Mackenzie's group. For some time, however, there had been a growing concern about this failure to look at the longer term. As early as the spring of 1940, Mackintosh had raised the question before the Economic Advisory Committee. Nothing concrete emerged from his comments at that time, but the issue had been renewed in June 1942, when Hume Wrong of External Affairs had expressed concern about the lack of involvement with reconstruction matters on the part of the permanent civil service. In July these concerns had been expressed directly to James by Wrong's superior, Norman Robertson. Robertson, James noted, seems to be 'thinking either of a reconstruction committee made up of permanent civil servants or of some cabinet appointments in this field.' Members of the permanent civil service, particularly the 'intelligentsia' in the Financial and External portfolios, were thus becoming aware of the need to look at reconstruction in a serious way before the advisory committee's interim report was released. The release of that report, with its implications for power relationships within the civil service, would force bodies like the Economic Advisory Committee to come to grips with the issue. Reconstruction was about to become a major topic in government circles.[57]

11

The triumph of
macro-economic management
1943-5

Until the autumn of 1942 Ian Mackenzie and those working under his direction had been almost isolated in their efforts to deal with reconstruction problems. The war was the dominant concern, and the Ottawa bureaucracy generally remained remote from such issues. Only with the Port Hope conference in September 1942 and the release of the interim report of the James' Advisory Committee on Reconstruction did this begin to change. Once the change began, however, it quickly gathered force, and within a few months reconstruction became a major topic in the nation. Lying immediately behind the rise of such interest was a complex series of interactions between the intellectual community in general, the 'intelligentsia' within the civil service, and the politicians who ultimately had to choose the direction that Canada would take. In the longer term the coming plans were also the product of a generation or more of discussion as to the needs of society and the role of the modern state.

At the bureaucratic level the catalyst was the interim report. For some time there had been growing concern about a group of outsiders, however well intentioned, assuming a dominant role in discussions of reconstruction. With the possible exception of Graham Towers, the EAC reflected this opinion that the issues raised by the Advisory Committee on Reconstruction were too central to be ignored by the individuals within the Bank of Canada and Department of Finance. This was revealed at a 10 November meeting when the EAC asserted its own position by refuting on a point-by-point basis the interim recommendations of the James and his committee. It was unlikely, they felt, that a new department to handle reconstruction was possible, given its broad sweep, nor was a minister without portfolio 'of first-rate ability' likely to be found. Rather than focus on the political levels, the EAC suggested that it would be necessary 'that the main work in preparation for post-war action would have to be done in the departments' – by the professionals in other words – and that the 'Economic Advisory Committee or some sub-committee of it should be the main agency responsible at the official level for the development of plans dealing with post-war questions.'[1]

The EAC did see the James Committee's report as important in one respect. It brought home the necessity of planning for reconstruction at a time when the EAC itself had become bogged down in the day-to-day details of running the war. In a report to the cabinet at the end of November, Clark and his committee stressed that while it rejected the specific proposals of the James Committee it accepted the importance of 'beginning at once to prepare specific governmental plans to deal with at least several of the major problems of the post-war period.' In a clear case of damning the James Committee with faint praise, it concluded that there was still a role for James to play. 'The Committee believes that an outside or non-departmental committee of the type of Committee on Reconstruction can perform valuable functions in assisting with the development and promotion of post-war plans.' That assistance was to be limited, however, for the report also asserted that 'planning must be the responsiblity of the government itself.'[2]

That planning fell to the Economic Advisory Committee. A.D.P. Heeney, clerk of the Privy Council, supported the idea that such activities should take place within the regular civil service and used his influence to ensure that such would be the case. He proposed to King that the EAC was the natural body to take on such matters and thereby curb the influence of the James Committee. With Heeney's powerful support, the EAC was able to get cabinet approval to begin the investigation of reconstruction. In January 1943 a new sub-committee of the EAC was established specifically to study the problem of reconstruction. Under the chairmanship of W.A. Mackintosh, this new committee would soon assume an importance that rivalled that of the EAC itself. Though the membership varied over time, the sub-committee's personnel reflected the importance of the new body. Aside from Mackintosh as chairman, the young Keynesian R.B. Bryce was present as secretary. From the Bank of Canada came two of the architects of the Rowell-Sirois Report, J.J. Deutsch and Alex Skelton. Also present were Heeney; a third Bank of Canada official, Louis Rasminsky; and, from the James Committee, Leonard Marsh. Even more than the EAC itself, therefore, the sub-committee reflected the influence of the new 'intelligentsia' in the civil service by the 1940s. Here were the pioneers of the campaign for a central bank, a member of the National Employment Commission, and key figures in the Rowell-Sirois investigation sitting together on the committee charged with post-war policy formation. The brain trust of which King so often complained had just assumed a central role in the shaping of the post-war world.[3]

The bureaucratic enthusiasm for reconstruction would mean little if the politicians remained uninterested. Such interest could not be assumed. At the time that the EAC began to look at reconstruction issues the inner circles of the Liberal government had shown little awareness of the problem. There were some long-standing allies, of course. Brooke Claxton, Paul Martin, and Ian Mackenzie consistently sought to remind their colleagues of the need for planning and reform. Except for Mackenzie, however, these men were backbenchers, and however bright their future, they carried limited weight in the party in 1942. If the expensive and complex policies being evolved by the James Committee and, soon, by Mackintosh's sub-committee were to have a chance of being adopted, the cabinet would have to be convinced of the importance of the problems. This meant, in reality, the conversion of Prime Minister Mackenzie King. 'At no time during the war years,' records Heeney, 'was there the slightest doubt that Mackenzie King was in fact and in law the head of the government and the master of his cabinet.'[4]

In the first couple of years of the war King paid little or no attention to problems of social security or post-war reform. Nor was he interested in 'reconstruction' except possibly in the narrowest sense of providing for a smooth demobilization process. When, shortly after its establishment, the James Committee compiled ministerial statements on reconstruction, only a very few and innocuous comments could be pulled from the often verbose speeches of the prime minister. It was not that King was oblivious to the need for reconstruction planning. He disliked hasty action, however, in part because of his naturally cautious manner, and in part because he distrusted the planners' faith in quick solutions. 'I myself, took strong issue with the attempt to do everything at once,' he wrote in 1941 of a proposal from Clark and Towers regarding wage and price controls. 'They seem to think that we can at one stroke, legislate to have prices kept where they are and wages, the same. I pointed out that an effort of that kind would probably result in such an upheaval of different classes, groups, that the government would find itself in an intolerable position. That we should all be made ridiculous in the end by trying to do by order-in-council something which the economic forces of the world would deny with impunity.' King had not completely severed his youthful roots. He remained enough of a Christian idealist, not to say politician, to believe that legislation could not precede human will.[5]

However, Mackenzie King had always thought of social reform as a primary purpose in his life. It was, after all, 'all set out in my Industry and Humanity,' he noted in January 1943.[6] It was not so much a matter of convincing King that social reform was important as it was of reminding him of that fact and of convincing him that a particular time and approach were appropriate to the needs of the nation and the Liberal party. To employ a loose analogy, it was more like reminding the wayward Christian of his duty to the church than a matter of converting the heathen.

In late 1942 several coincidences brought the pilgrim back to the fold, at least temporarily. Suddenly it seemed as if everywhere King turned the matter of reconstruction kept appearing. In the United Kingdom, Sir William Beveridge released his report on social insurance, advocating, among other things, health insurance, old age pensions, and children's allowances.[7] This in itself had little immediate impact on King. In fact, it would appear that he knew little or nothing about the report when in early December he visited Washington. Then, at dinner in the White House, Franklin Roosevelt raised the issue of the Beveridge Report and argued that this sort of social welfare program was the natural mission of the two North American leaders. King replied lamely that Canada already had much of the report in place. This was, however, only an awkward response by a man who found his knowledge of current social reform measures lacking. King found the conversation caused him to think once again of the issue. As he later reflected in his diary, 'What impressed me particularly was his desire that we should work together on the lines of social reform in which we had always been interested ... I felt a relief from the mere thought of dealing with social questions and reform, instead of the problem of war and destruction.'[8] Mackenzie King returned to Ottawa with a new interest in the currents of social change that were swirling through the nations of the Western alliance.

Not all the forces favouring reform were international. While King was visiting Roosevelt in Washington the Conservatives were actively courting John Bracken, the premier of Manitoba and a man more as-

sociated with Progressivism than Conservatism. At the party's convention in Winnipeg not only was Bracken elected leader but also the
platform adopted was drawn essentially from the reformist ideals of
the Port Hope conference. While King himself was not apparently worried by these events, they did bring home to several cabinet Ministers,
including Mackenzie, the point that unless the Liberals developed social policies of their own they could be outflanked by the Conservatives.
Mackenzie took the first opportunity to press on King the necessity of
action on reform. While accompanying the prime minister on a train
trip to Brockville in early January he played on King's reform instincts
and political sense to urge that the next election be run on the basis
of social reform. He also pressed into the prime minister's hand a summary of the Beveridge Report so that King might see what all the recent
fuss was about.[9]

These events and the growing public interest in reconstruction resulting from them would have led even the most reluctant politician
to recognize the necessity of seriously considering reconstruction measures. Mackenzie King was not, of course, a man who pictured himself
as a reluctant politician in matters of reform. Was he not the person
who had written some of Canada's most basic social welfare legislation?
Was he not the man who had pioneered investigation into labour problems? King, in other words, had a self-perception that dictated a certain
response to reform overtures, at least when it became apparent that
they could no longer be ignored. 'It looks as though I were to have the
privilege of completing the circle of federal social security measures
which, with the exception of the annuities bill, I was responsible for
beginning,' he commented in early 1943.[10]

One final event requires mentioning. In January 1943, as the cabinet
discussed social welfare measures, it also had to deal with a major steel
strike that threatened to upset war production. King, while determined
to end the strike, was dismayed by the extremely hard line taken around
the cabinet table by his colleagues. It awoke the spirit of the former
labour conciliator in him and highlighted in his own mind how he
stood apart as a man with sympathy for the common working man. In
a world full of reactionaries it was all the more important for the true
reformer to stand up and be counted.[11]

Of course there was a degree of self-deception in King's pious rhetoric
on reform. He was not, by the standards of the 1940s, a crusader for
change, and he had never advocated the sort of economic planning
that was inherent in bureaucratic reform policies. He was too old, too

cautious, and too much a student of human frailty to believe that technocratic reform was the key to the nation's future. Such reformism as he did possess was based on an ameliorative paternalism that came from an earlier time. However, the temporary bursts of enthusiasm, such as the one he had in January 1943, caused him to give his blessing for detailed reconstruction planning by those who really were committed. He also could, if courted in the proper manner, be won over to the reform cause and thus be a valuable ally.

King's support meant that reconstruction became a central issue in Ottawa through the winter and spring of 1943. In January the Speech from the Throne used language reminiscent of the American New Deal to promise 'freedom from fear and want' in the post-war world and called for 'a comprehensive national scheme of social insurance.' The same month Mackenzie brought forward his new health insurance proposal for approval in principle by the cabinet, and Mackintosh's subcommittee was formed. By March that committee would present an interim report to the cabinet. In the same month the Senate created a Committee on Economic Reconstruction and Social Security while the House created a Committee on Social Security. By May the committees were hearing testimony from Sir William Beveridge, whose visit to Ottawa served as an occasion for Canadian reformers to meet and discuss problems with one of the high priests in international reform circles. Even Mackenzie King was moved to remind Beveridge of the roots of Canadian reform by sending him a copy of – what else? – *Industry and Humanity*.[12]

The highlight of these months so far as the public was concerned was not the creation of Parliamentary committees, the Speech from the Throne, or the visit of Beveridge, but the release in March of the first comprehensive plan for social security emanating from Ottawa. Written by Leonard Marsh and presented to the Commons Committee on Reconstruction, the Report on Social Security for Canada was over 300 pages long and dealt with everything from unemployment assistance through job retraining and health insurance to children's allowances. Few documents in Canadian history had set out to provide such a detailed description of how social change might be implemented.[13]

However detailed the report, there is some question as to how much importance should be attached to it. Little of the report was original, and, as Marsh himself candidly admitted, the whole thing had been thrown together fairly quickly. Nor can it be said to have represented evolving government policy in any specific sense. By March 1943 the

James Committee was on the periphery of power, the central role having been assumed by the Economic Advisory Committee. Moreover, the Marsh Report was not even an official document of the James Committee, just the view of its director of research. As a cynical W.A. Mackintosh pointed out, 'the so-called Marsh Report did not emanate from any of the Government Departments and I am afraid it is likely to boomerang.'[14] Clearly the central place accorded it by historians has probably exaggerated its importance.

The report did, however, receive a great deal of attention. By the spring of 1943 Canadians were increasingly preoccupied with the post-war world. The tide of war was turning, and the day of victory now seemed much closer than even a few months earlier. Also, the public was far from immune to the currents of international social reform. Beveridge had received a considerable degree of attention in Canada, as had plans emanating from the National Resources Planning Board in the United States. At home the Progressive Conservatives and the CCF did their best to ensure that the public was reminded of the post-war issue. The result was that even before Marsh released his report, social reform was in the air in Canada. Indeed, the day before the Marsh Report was released, the Ontario legislature was discussing a study on post-war needs by the minister of education, an ex-academic and former colleague of Mackintosh, Duncan McArthur. Thus Leonard Marsh's report was opportune in its timing: a year earlier it would have been overshadowed by the concern about the war that was still not going well; a year later it would have been but one of many studies of similar problems. As it was, it generated a tremendous amount of publicity.[15]

Press coverage of the report was extensive. As might be expected, the *Canadian Forum* was enthusiastic, devoting a special section of its next several issues to it. More revealingly, several major urban dailies treated the report as somewhat of a landmark in the war. Lead headlines, full-column editorials, and voluminous background stories greeted Marsh's study from coast to coast. The *Winnipeg Free Press* was typical, if on the enthusiastic side, in its coverage. Aside from its looming banner headline on 16 March, 'Social Security Plan for Canada,' it devoted about one-third of the first page to the report, almost all of the third page, and a good part of the fourth. The next day there was further extensive coverage, and the entire editorial column was dedicated to the report and the challenge it posed for Canadians. 'Those who disagree with Mr. Marsh,' the paper warned, 'must make counter-propositions which will meet the situation.' Across the nation the story was more or less the same. Even the Conservative *Globe and Mail* termed the study a 'worthwhile document' that demanded serious consideration.[16]

The newspaper coverage points to the importance of the Marsh Report: it generated a tremendous degree of publicity in Canada. The public was thus oriented even more toward post-war concerns, and politicians, increasingly aware of the public tendency in this direction, knew that henceforth reconstruction would remain an issue of great importance. Marsh had not done much original nor had he developed a document that was likely, in its details, to reflect final government policy, but he had raised the stakes significantly.

The six months from the interim report of the James Committee through to the publication of the Marsh Report saw essentially a drawn out government equivalent to the Conservative's Port Hope conference. The civil servants who took up the cudgels in favour of reconstruction planning played the role of the Port Hopefuls and came from the same social and intellectual circles as their counterparts. By the end of March they had, like their Conservative colleagues, successfully asserted the importance of planning for the post-war period, and the government that they served seemed to be moving toward acceptance of their position. Also like Port Hope, however, the period produced nothing to indicate final and full acceptance by the party of either the welfare state or economic planning in the post-war world. Thus, for example, as late as September 1943 King cautioned Claxton that a series of pro-reform proposals emanating from the National Liberal Federation should be seen 'merely as some suggestions from the Advisory Council to the Government.'[17] What did exist by the spring of 1943 was a body of proposals that made it possible to understand something of what such acceptance entailed.

What fears and hopes underlay this flurry of government committee creation, bureaucratic infighting, and report-making? For the general public the concern was obviously of a future in which the government remained unable to cope with the wild fluctuations in the economy that seemed to mark the twentieth century. As a Wartime Information Board study reported, the populace seemed to face the post-war world with a feeling 'akin to dread.'[18] Something of this dread existed within the intellectual community, but its fear was countered by faith in its own ability, historical memories, and personal aspirations. The result was a peculiar mixture of anxiety and optimism that did much to shape the impulse for reconstruction planning.

For those who sought to demonstrate the need for reconstruction planning the primary argument was couched in historical terms. This is not surprising, for members of the intellectual community could look to the history of their own times as one of the best reasons why the government should become involved in detailed planning. The First World War provided a direct analogy. Then Canada had fought a modern industrial war while largely ignoring the shape of the post-war world, the problems of transition from wartime to peacetime production, or any of the other serious matters that demanded attention. J.A. Corry's comment that the nation fought the war in economic terms 'largely by laissez-faire methods' overstated the point, but it reflected the perceptions of the generation concerned with reconstruction after the Second World War. On the Canadian Club circuits, in scholarly journals, and elsewhere, Corry's basic position was restated by intellectual after intellectual. The years 1914-18 pointed to the fallacy of assuming that modern welfare could be fought without considering the dislocations on domestic social and economic structures.[19]

That dislocation was already apparent. Even more than in the First War, it was obvious that the economy, if left to its own devices, would not make a smooth transition to peace. 'In the last war the government was faced with the task of demobilizing some 300,000 soldiers and about 300,000 workers in munitions,' wrote Claxton in July 1943. 'Of those in the army 80% had come from the farms and a great proportion of them returned to the farms.' Even so, demobilization caused major problems. What would happen then at the end of the current war? 'Today the figure is close to two million and the great majority have special skills.' The message was clear. The government had to continue the planning it had developed for wartime into the post-war world. As Cyril James warned a House committee, reconstruction planning was necessary 'partly for the purpose of shaping the war pattern, where it is possible, as nearly as we may according to our ideas of post-war conditions; and partly for the purpose of recognizing the influence that each of these wartime activities, controls and regulations will have upon the post-war Canadian scene.'[20]

By 1943 economists inside and outside government felt they had a pretty clear idea as to how these wartime activities would affect the post-war world. Though there were some differences, the general conclusion was that the first months after the war would bring a great outpouring of consumer demand. Voluntary savings would be shifted to consumption, while the removal of certain forced savings measures would put money into the pockets of people seeking to make purchases postponed during the war. Such a consumer-led boom coming at a time when the effects of war production were still being felt in the economy could lead to two problems. The first was inflation, as an economy at full production was fuelled still further by consumer demand. The second was the inability of the market system to adjust quickly enough. The result would be a shortage of goods and hence further inflationary pressure.[21]

Such an inflationary boom would be temporary. As war production wound down and as thousands of soldiers were released from the armed forces, consumer demand was all too likely to give way to consumer uncertainty. If the servicemen could not be absorbed into industry and if industry did not make a rapid and large-scale investment to shift from war to peacetime production, there would be a rise in unemployment. The economy would then sink into recession. After all, only war production fuelled by state expenditures had lifted the economy out of the depression of the 1930s, and with the end of that production there was no certainty that depression would not return. If nothing was done, in other words, post-war boom could be followed by post-war bust. Once again, Cyril James summed it up: 'We are compelled therefore to look to the fact that there will *inevitably* be a post-war depression either immediately after the war or at the end of this brief period of prosperity.' R.H. Coats put it more drastically when he warned the EAC as early as 1940 that post-war unemployment could be the highest Canada had ever seen.[22]

What made such a prognosis especially disturbing was that by this time few economists retained much faith in the concept of the business cycle as a self-correcting mechanism. This, in turn, reflected a widely based trend among Canadian economists away from neo-classicism and toward the theories of Keynes. In government circles there were key individuals like R.B. Bryce whose intelligence and thoroughness gave him an increasingly central role as the war went on. As Secretary to both the EAC and its sub-committee on reconstruction he was in a position to further Keynesian theory in policy development. Also preaching the gospel of Keynes was A.F.W. Plumptre. He had worked under the British economist and promoted Keynesian views in his assessment of war finance. There were a good many others who, though not Keynesian, were increasingly sympathetic to his theories. Both

Alex Skelton and W.A. Mackintosh revealed such ideas in their numerous memos. W.C. Clark has been aptly described as an 'unacademic Keynesian' whose growing faith in government interventionism led him down an increasingly Keynesian path. Yet it would be unduly formalistic to see the development of thought on the post-war economy as primarily a conversion to Keynesian theory. For the public at large, for the politicians, and for many economists the central fact was not the *General Theory* but the clear lesson to be learned from the Depression. J.F. Parkinson summarized the situation in 1940 when he wrote that the 'experience of the last decade has shown the peoples of most capitalist democracies that a condition of under-employment is not self-correcting.'[23]

If the civil service 'intelligentsia' expressed a sense of anxiety about the post-war world, it also revealed a paradoxical optimism. There were two different reasons for this. The first was the changed perception of the civil service. In the First World War and afterwards, as W.L. Grant's efforts at civil service reform indicated, there was a strong feeling within the intellectual community that the civil service was riddled with patronage appointees possessing little merit and even less understanding of the problems of modern society. The expert who was so badly needed to deal with current problems was thereby largely excluded from an active role in policy formation. By the 1940s, of course, this had changed, and the intellectual community saw its own presence in government as making all the difference. The government apparatus was now competent, or at least competent where it counted. J.A. Corry reflected this commonly held view in a 1940 article on the First World War. In it he excused Borden's lack of planning by noting that the government 'lacked the trained civil service vital to such an undertaking. It lacked the scientific taxation system.' The intervening years, however, had brought significant changes: 'Fortunately the Dominion government is in a much better position to give sustained intelligent direction and to apply comprehensive control in this war than in the last one. The Canadian civil service may still leave a good deal to be desired but it is far stronger than it was twenty five years ago. After twenty years of growing government intervention in economic matters, such essential knowledge about the Canadian economy is available and numerous techniques of regulation have been worked out.'[24]

Corry's argument also points to the other factor creating confidence. Reconstruction planning had a precedent. It was, in many ways, merely an extension of the sort of planning undertaken for the running of the war. Modern warfare made certain demands upon nations, and the course of events in the Second World War indicated that those demands had been met by those involved in planning. As John Deutsch noted, in the First War the government had attempted to run the war without disrupting traditional approaches to finance. 'The government thought that heavy direct taxation would be a deterrent to expansion and private initiative which it had done so much to promote. Canada was a land of promise and that promise must not be destroyed by vexatious levies upon business and the individual.' By the Second War, however, there was a recognition that war 'calls for a reorientation of industrial effort entailing heavy investment of capital and extensive training of labour. This cannot be accomplished quickly without detailed planning, a high degree of centralized direction of economic forces, and effective coordination.' In order to accomplish this, a 'far greater proportion of the real goods needed to wage this war must be made available by taxation and a voluntary reduction in consumption through saving than was the case in 1914-1918.'[25]

Such beliefs gave heart to advocates of ongoing economic management. Deutsch was supported by another Bank of Canada official, Louis Rasminsky, who argued in a speech before the Winnipeg branch of the CIIA that the war provided a demonstration 'of what a determined state with a single objective can do to provide employment and raise the national output.' The most obvious example of this was probably the success of wage and price controls. Never before had such large-scale intervention in the market economy been undertaken in Canada, and never, in economic terms, had the government so directly impinged on the day-to-day lives of its citizens. Yet in spite of King's scepticism it had worked. Intelligent legislation backed, the economists would argue, by even more intelligent administration had allowed the government to dictate market conditions rather than have market conditions dictating to the government.[26]

What had worked so well in wartime could work just as well in the post-war period. The experts were proving on a daily basis that they were capable of managing the economy, and there was no reason why those management techniques could not be used to ensure that the gloomy scenario of boom and bust did not come to pass. For in its most simple terms the war had an important message about the running of the post-war economy. It was a practical laboratory of Keynesian theory which revealed, as A.F.W. Plumptre said, that 'government spending directly augments the income stream.'[27] If that spending was to be timed correctly and used most effectively, however, the planners would need sufficient resources, public acceptance of centralized planning, and, of course, political support. 'No one can foresee what will be the exact situation in Canada at the end of the war,' commented Alex Skelton. 'Of one thing only can we be certain: that imagination, courage, planning, organization, investment of means and energy, and national unity of purpose will be necessary on a scale comparable only with that necessary to win the war.'

Exactly how all this could be accomplished was more problematic. In the attempt to provide a solution, Canadian intellectuals poured out scores of proposals of varying quality over the next years as to the way in which reconstruction might be handled. In the *Canadian Journal of Economics and Political Science*, for example, more than 40 works on reconstruction were listed as 'recent publications' in 1943 alone.[28] Within the civil service a good deal of time not spent writing memoranda was spent preparing responses to public suggestions of varying quality for the signature of the minister.[29] From all this material it is possible, however, to discern at least a general framework which the more informed proposals for reconstruction had in common. Two major strategies – social security and the provision of jobs – appear and reappear in both government reports and those by experts, and often the not-so-expert, outside government.

The first strategy was a broadened commitment to social security, or social insurance as it was often termed. Such social insurance was seen as distinct from the sort of dole programs that had operated through the Depression. Those were condemned by the social reform experts of the 1940s as both demeaning to the recipient and inefficient in their use of public funds. Social insurance, in contrast, was portrayed as a system that would employ a set of objective standards with well-established criteria for use and thus a means of escaping the problems of the 1930s. As such, Leonard Marsh argued, it had to be developed as a comprehensive program rather than as a patchwork response to need. 'The demand for comprehensiveness,' he warned, 'is not a mere academic straining after perfection: it is one of the practical realities of economic and efficient operation.'[30]

It was difficult to translate the concept of comprehensive social insurance into a definitive set of proposals. Planners liked to talk in terms of a 'decent minimum,' to use Skelton's phrase, 'social minimum,' to use that of Marsh, or 'low-water mark,' to use that of Dr Weir of

Pensions and National Health. All these phrases envisaged a 'safety net,' below which no individual in Canada would be permitted to fall. Such proposals often remained vague, however, for, as both Mackintosh's and James' committees realized, 'in an internationally vulnerable and fluctuating economy as Canada's' was, it would be foolhardy to spell out that minimum. Nonetheless, those who wrote remained confident, even exuberant, in their belief that the concept of a social minimum remained viable and that its implementation would mean, again in the words of Marsh, 'the direct elimination of poverty.' Health insurance, old age pensions, unemployment insurance, and children's allowances were the main forms of social security designed to accomplish this end.[31]

As of 1943 the social security proposal that had been most fully developed was Ian Mackenzie's pet plan for health insurance. Since the early part of the war Mackenzie and Heagerty had continued to work to develop a scheme that would be acceptable to the public, the medical profession, and the provinces. In February 1942 the Advisory Committee on Health Insurance had been established to deal with the issue and to reinforce the expert support for the plan. By the end of the year the proposals were developed to the extent that Mackenzie was ready to present a report for both public and cabinet discussion.[32] Health insurance, if Mackenzie had his way, would be the first of the major social insurance programs after unemployment insurance to be implemented by the Dominion.

The enthusiasm within the Department of Pensions and National Health was not shared by all sectors of the civil service. Marsh, as might be expected, had endorsed the principle of health insurance in his report, but there was scepticism within the Department of Finance. As early as 1941 Mackintosh had revealed that he, at least, was distinctly cool to the idea.[33] That coolness remained in 1943 as Mackenzie sought to get approval for his proposal. Moreover, by this time the EAC was so central to government financial planning that backers of any scheme as important as health insurance could not afford to ignore the committee. Thus, in a reflection of new power relations within the government, Mackenzie, the cabinet minister, was to go before a committee of civil servants to plead his case. In January 1943 he met with the EAC and argued forcefully that though the specifics of other social programs were as yet incomplete, there was no reason not to implement health insurance as the first building-block in a social insurance program. 'Dr. Clark then stated,' as the dry minutes of the EAC record the event, 'that he belonged to the other school of thought that Mr. Mackenzie had mentioned – those who favoured a comprehensive Dominion scheme and a constitutional revision to make clear the Dominion's responsibility for such measures and to enable the Dominion to have the necessary freedom in its tax fields to finance it.' Clark was actively supported by Towers, and the committee as a whole decided not to support the Mackenzie proposal.[34] The minister of pensions and national health would have to press forward, if he dared, without the support of the financial experts within the civil service.

The next step came a few days later, when Mackenzie presented his plan to the cabinet. Once again it was not the ministers who took the lead but Heagerty on behalf of Pensions and National Health and Clark on behalf of Finance. King, while sentimentally in favour of such a plan, found Clark's warnings too serious to ignore. All that Mackenzie got was agreement to establish the already mentioned House Committee on Social Security to investigate the whole matter.[35] Though not officially dead, there was no doubt after this meeting that health insurance would have to await the development of the 'comprehensive' program that Clark had seen as necessary, if it was to come at all.

The three other major programs were less developed as of 1943. Old Age Pensions had been in existence in Canada for some time, but by the 1940s there were criticisms of them on three counts. The first was that they were based on need, partly for constitutional reasons, and were therefore demeaning to an element of the population who, almost by definition, should not have to be dealt with under the principles of less eligibility. The second criticism was that the age of 70, at which point the existing pensions came into force, was too elderly. The third complaint was that the size of the pension was too small to allow otherwise indigent elderly to live in even a minimum standard of decency. Indeed by July 1943 the government recognized the force of this latter complaint and raised monthly pensions to $25. These complaints had led Marsh to recommend that the first priority of any social security scheme should be to drop the qualifying age to 65 and to make the plan universal. There was also support both by Marsh and in Mackintosh's committee for some sort of contributory pension plan that would allow for much more substantial pensions for the aged. Indeed, when Mackenzie came forward with his health insurance scheme, Mackintosh countered, through Ilsley, that the reform of old age pensions should come first.[36]

There was also discussion of an overhaul of the recently instituted unemployment insurance scheme in order to expand its coverage and to supplement it with some form of 'unemployment assistance' for those who were without work for a longer term. Also suggested was a series of proposals to improve opportunities for employment through the use of employment exchanges, retraining, and other such measures. This was especially important given the expected dislocation of thousands of workers at war's end as munitions and other war-related industries shifted production. As the James Committee warned, 'this problem of speedy re-employment is of greater importance than all the questions of relief and social security, since the success of Canada's reconstruction policy will be realistically measured in terms of the number of useful jobs that it offers to the men and women who are seeking them.'[37]

The final major proposal was for some sort of children's allowance. In 1943, however, this remained one of the lowest priorities of the various social planning groups. Marsh saw it as the last of the four major proposals he would institute, while those involved in reconstruction planning at Finance do not seem even to have discussed the idea seriously at any time in the first half of the year.[38] As will be seen, other factors would have to alter before this particular scheme assumed any importance in the minds of planners.

In addition to these four major programs, there were numerous other suggestions raised by one committee or another, or by academics outside government. Greater government involvement in housing was urged by C.A. Curtis in a report that would lead to the passage of the 1944 National Housing Act.[39] Such reforms were an enthusiasm of Clifford Clark's, and he was instrumental in their development during the war. There were also special recommendations from various bodies for disability insurance, funeral assistance measures, designs to improve the position of women in the post-war world, and so forth. All of these, however, remained secondary to the major proposals and received less attention from politicians, civil servants, and the general public.

The second strategy for reconstruction focused on provision of as much employment as possible. If the economic pie could be made larger, then dependence on social security would thereby be lessened. In general terms, such proposals divided into two related categories, one international and one domestic. The former, as everyone recognized, was crucial for a nation like Canada that was so dependent on exports. Full employment in Canada, as the James Committee noted early in its deliberations, 'can only be attained through close and continuous collaboration between Canada and the other leading nations of the world.' W.A. Mackintosh stated the issue even more straight-forwardly when he asked how the war might affect the Canadian economy. 'The kind of world which will emerge after the war,' he replied, 'will have more effect on Canada's destiny than any changes that are taking place within Canada during the war.'[40]

This led Canadian civil servants into a series of endeavours on the international scene to ensure that the chaotic monetary situation of the 1930s did not recur and to help develop freer trade between nations. Officials in the Bank of Canada, External Affairs, and Finance, with various other agencies, were active in asserting the need for a planned and rational international system that would parallel their intentions for national economic management. Though, as Plumptre later wrote, the development of the post-war international monetary system was largely 'a tale of two cities,' London and Washington, Canadian civil servants played an important part in the discussions that went on through 1943 and 1944. Their participation in such conferences as the one at Bretton Woods in 1944, which created the International Monetary Fund, helped ensure that whatever the international economic difficulties of the post-war world, the monetary chaos of the 1930s would not return.[41]

The official meetings and memoranda were only part of the process. Having trained outside the country, the emerging mandarin class had developed a series of international friendships in graduate school. Those acquaintances had, like the Canadians, often gravitated to the growing civil services of the United States and Great Britain. There was thus a series of links at the official level between nations as well as within them. Individuals corresponded on a regular basis and, in many cases, brought their enthusiasm both for economic theory and for economic planning together in a series of informal discussions as to how goals of international stability and growth might best be achieved. Where there were no previous contacts, international meetings between like-minded experts, often about the same age and with similar beliefs in the importance of expertise, allowed such contacts to develop. There were also, of course, the continued ties between former teachers and pupils and the common theoretical basis that that often implied. 'Many thanks for sending me your paper on post-war economic relations,' wrote Keynes to Bryce in 1942. 'I am, as you might expect, in general sympathy with your main approach.'[42]

Common theoretical perspectives, friendship, and a keen sense that economic rationality must prevail thus created an international network of policy formation. Though obviously constrained by national perspectives and political imperatives, these ties did make the search for solutions to post-war problems somewhat easier. At least the participants all spoke the same language – that of the social scientist and confident technocrat. They also aroused suspicions, once again, on the part of Mackenzie King, who saw such international bureaucratic planners as all too ready to usurp functions properly within the sphere of the elected government. 'There is a great danger,' he commented, 'of members of the permanent service trying to frame policies and make members of the govt. their mouthpiece instead of members of govt. shaping policy and members of the civil service carrying it out. While we are fortunate in having a few good men in the public service, it would be a great misfortune if they should ever come to be a controlling bureaucracy as at times they threaten to become.'[43]

If the international scene was the most important for Canada's economic prosperity, the domestic was more immediate and more within the control of Canadian policy formation. Canadian reconstruction planners tended to agree that domestic economic management after the war would demand a continuation, for some period, of wartime controls. Canada simply could not expect to revert to the uncontrolled free-market system immediately upon the return of peace. 'It cannot be over-emphasized,' Skelton warned, 'that the extent to which the necessary controls are retained will determine the extent to which a full employment policy can be followed.'[44] These controls, in the minds of most experts, included wage and price controls, foreign exchange restrictions, and some rationing. They were the domestic equivalent of the international agreements needed to maintain stability in a potentially volatile period.

Controls, however, were only the first step. They provided government with the time to develop longer-term solutions. The question that then had to be faced was the degree to which the government should continue to intervene in the market-place after the transition was complete. What did reconstruction planning really mean? On one side stood a group of individuals, of whom C.D. Howe was the most prominent, for whom the process was a very specific one involving demobilization and the conversion of military to peacetime production. Controls might be necessary. Some social welfare might even be desirable. The objective, however, was the reassertion of as much 'normalcy' as possible within a relatively short time.[45] Reconstruction, then, was a transitional process, the interlude between war and peace.

For Howe, reconstruction should therefore rely on the strengthening of the private sector. That sector's investment in new enterprise and employment of workers would be crucial in determining the level of economic activity and therefore prosperity after the war. As the war approached a conclusion, Howe and his advisers would develop a series of proposals such as depreciation allowances and other tax incentives to encourage a rapid shift from wartime to peacetime production.

To a degree the James Committee also reflected this concern that the transition be handled in a manner that would allow private enterprise to return to normal operations. With members like J.S. McLean and Tom Moore, the Committee was oriented more toward the marketplace than many of the academically derived bodies in Ottawa. 'The immediate post-war period,' it warned, 'must not be regarded as the time for comprehensive social and political revolution.'[46] For this committee, social security measures, public works, and other government interventions would occur in the post-war period, but all were seen as ancillary to the primary task of restoring business. Neither the James Committee nor even Howe was an advocate of laissez-faire capitalism. Such a position had few powerful defenders by 1943, but Howe and James did maintain a relatively cautious approach about the benefits of direct government intervention in the economy.

Opposing this concept of reconstruction was a much more expansive, even symbolic, definition of the term. According to this view, reconstruction referred not only to the transition from war to peace but to the change from a traditional and outmoded 'laissez-faire' capitalism to a new, more humane and more efficient era in which capitalism was subordinated to social needs. The war was an opportunity, a catalyst, to bring about changes that had been shown desirable by numerous events from the early twentieth century on. War had demonstrated the revenue-gathering ability of the government, the willingness of the people to accept government intervention, and the potential of an enlarged civil service. The war had also given the Dominion a series of powers that abrogated long-standing constitutional barriers, at least temporarily.

The reconstruction process thus had to be planned with an eye to the transformation of Canada, or the opportunity, once lost, might be difficult to regain. It was a concept that was in many ways reminiscent of the 'new era' envisaged by First World War writers. This time, however, the new era was being defined less in moral and philosophical terms and more in material ones. A sound economy, controlled capitalism, and social security would mark the entry into the post-war world. As much of the debate on the nature of reconstruction took place within the supposedly non-political world of the civil service and within the confines, politically, of the governing party, the ideological implications of the different proposals tended not to be made explicit. Instead the issues were dealt with in terms of specific policy proposals, and in this area there were clashes.

Those who advocated a sweeping approach to reconstruction did so, at least in part, because of a strong distrust of both the capabilities and purposes of private enterprise. This was a reflection not so much of a hard-line ideology as of the growth of an intellectual community that had long believed that business had failed in both its economic and social responsibilities. 'To say that public enterprise can do it alone,' wrote Claxton, 'is to utter words which will strike unfriendly ears in all those who suffered through the 1930's.' For people like Claxton, Alex Skelton, and Leonard Marsh, it was foolish to cling to the belief that one could move toward a planned economy while pretending that all would remain within the old capitalist orbit. 'Even though, as individuals, we may regret that passing of the older order of free trade, competition and capitalism,' wrote Marsh in 1941, 'the available evidence concerning the impact of industrialism on a democratic-capitalist order of society suggests that the attainment of reasonable economic security for the average individual will demand a large measure of coordination and governmental control.'[47]

For those who took such a position, there was a need in the post-war world to focus primarily on direct government activity in the market-place. Social security measures would help, of course, but there were also plans for a sophisticated series of 'public investments.' Such investments would be employed on a scientific basis to counter negative forces within the private sector. When a local economy fell behind expected or desired employment and growth patterns, public investment would be used to build useful and required projects in an area and thus provide needed jobs. At the national level, a similar principle could be applied. 'Approached with imagination, and in a spirit of co-operative endeavour, it can become an inspiring national program for providing the equipment with which to win the peace.' All the grandiose phrases, however, could not hide the fact that there was little new in such ideas. What it came down to, after all, was the old concept of using public works as a counter-cyclical mechanism. R.B. Bryce sharply outlined the limitations of such a program when he commented that these 'look like the 1930's all over again.'[48]

Nevertheless, public investment proposals were a necessary first step toward an ongoing policy of economic management and were soon taken up by the EAC. Specifically, it proposed the creation of a National Development Board to handle public investment in the post-war period. This was, in turn, an extension of the suggestion of the James' Committee for a Construction Reserve Commission and reflected the widespread conviction that public works would be a part of any post-war policy.

Though hardly revolutionary, the National Development Board (NDB) had important implications. The proposal raised once again the assertions by the intellectual community that government would have to help direct the economy and that expert guidance would be needed for that direction. This was clearly revealed at a meeting of the EAC in March 1943, when Skelton and Mackintosh, the two main proponents of the idea, argued that the board's functions would demand 'additional high quality staff' if it was to function properly and that various constitutional obstacles would have to be overcome. Echoes of the experience on the Rowell-Sirois Commission and the National Employment Commission in the 1930s were apparent as they developed their thoughts. 'In the field of Social Services,' argued Skelton, 'the Dominion should have as a matter of principle jurisdiction over every scheme of contributory insurance, including health insurance.' Moreover, Dominion fiscal powers had to be adequate to the challenge implied in such activities. Grants-in-aid to the provinces, after all, resulted only in 'building up irresponsible provincial political machines.'[49]

The EAC saw the proposal as relatively modest and apparently expected little difficulty when it was forwarded to the cabinet War Committee. The EAC's confidence seemed rewarded when that committee approved it in principle in March 1943. That was followed in June by another suggestion by the Mackintosh Committee to the effect that all recommendations of the Department of Munitions and Supply be channeled through the EAC. Only if this were done could public investment be fully co-ordinated. Had both suggestions been approved they would have had important implications. The government's commitment to long-term involvement in public investment would have been confirmed and that investment would have been primarily under the direction of expert civil servants. In the process 'Howe and Co.' would have found their independence of action curtailed by a committee dominated by the Bank of Canada and the Department of Finance. The implications did not escape the notice of the formidable minister of munitions and supply. At the 11 June meeting of the War Cabinet,

Howe opposed the proposals, and they were rejected. Once more Mackintosh, Skelton, and the other members of the intelligentsia were thwarted by an element in the government that did not share their vision of the future. The opportunity to employ the reconstruction planning process to assert certain basic principles in the process of government and in the goals toward which that process was directed had not yet been carried.[50]

The defeat of the proposal for a National Development Board is important for three reasons. First, it illustrates the lack of certainty within the government as to the exact role it should play in the post-war period. Second, it reveals that for all the influence and power acquired by the intellectual community within the civil service, its power was still limited when faced by a determined and powerful political figure. Third, and most important, the defeat came at a time when the bureaucracy was already beginning to alter its focus on the problems of reconstruction. By destroying one possible avenue for the achievement of goals, the defeat of the NDB proposal may have assisted in the development of a new focus, one that would prove central to the development of the positive state in the post-war world.

Shaping reconstruction proposals to date was the historical and theoretical context in which the debate about the modern state had evolved from 1900 to 1940, an evolution that had left reform proposals bifurcated. One set of proposals was essentially an extension, as in the case of the National Development Board, of the nineteenth-century activities of the Canadian state as an active supporter of development. The other set of policies, which might be grouped under the heading of social security, was still viewed as an extension of ameliorative and religious concerns, albeit on a much more systematic basis. The former policies stressed efficiency and growth, though they were also obviously concerned with human welfare, and the latter stressed the plight of the poor and disadvantaged, though expecting that a well-cared-for society would also be an efficient one. Even as late as the Second World War, the two approaches remained essentially separate, if complementary. Social welfare proposals were primarily designed not for society as a whole but for those who 'fell through the cracks' of the modern industrial economy. In contrast, public works measures, taxation proposals, and international agreements were designed to work towards the general health of the economy rather than towards the benefit of a particularly needy segment.

By the 1940s the separation was anachronistic. The development of Keynesian theories of national income levels and other elements of consumer demand theory pointed to the essential unity of the two sets of proposals. The distribution of income, the level of aggregate demand for consumer goods, and other factors in modern economic theory meant that social welfare proposals had significant implications for the overall pattern of economic development. On occasion this was recognized by proponents of social welfare. Marsh, for example, reminded his readers that social security was a 'strategic factor in economic policy generally.' Even he, however, tended to emphasize the ameliorative aspects of his proposals: 'The social insurances, and even some straightforward disbursements like children's allowances are investments in morale and health, in greater family stability, and from both material and psychological viewpoints, in human productive efficiency.' The traditional separation thus remained. When Marsh released his report, several newspapers commented pointedly that while social security measures had benefits, 'work is more desirable than unemployment insurance.'[51]

This bifurcation created a dilemma for those who would make reconstruction something more than a short-term, transitional process. So long as public investment was seen primarily in terms of public works, however broadly defined, there were definite limits to what a capitalist government could do in the disbursement of funds without disrupting the private sector. This point was raised by several individuals through 1943 and 1944, but it was put perhaps most succinctly in a memo by Alex Skelton in November 1943: 'Granted the undesirability of a leaf-raking and monument building programme, the reaction of investors and of business to large scale government investment in competition with private industry is very likely to defeat the ends of the programme.' How much money could the government pump into a finite number of useful works without beginning to choke off private investment in the same areas? Public works, Skelton felt, would always be limited to the traditional areas of government activity, albeit timed to fluctuations in the economy. Otherwise government intervention could 'lead to a totalitarian economy and in the process produce a hybrid state which would be extremely unsatisfactory from both an economic and political viewpoint.'[52]

The problem was summed up in the last sentence. In effect the reformers were trying to create a hybrid state of sorts, rejecting both outright capitalism and yet denying the necessity of dismantling the market system in Canada. The Canadian Forum described the attitude of the planners and, it felt, of much of the public in sarcastic fashion. 'Yes, it would be nice to have some of that uncertainty removed from the process of making a living, and to be able to do some of the things we really want to do as we go along, instead of putting them off until we're just about ready to die of old age ... If these fellows who talk about a "planned economy" would only tell us what they really mean, show us how they propose to bring it about, and convince us that it can be done without abolishing individual initiative or making us all slaves of the state – why we'd kinda like a crack at it, and we'd be willing to turn in and help.'[53]

For the *Forum*, of course, the dilemma was no dilemma at all. Socialism, as advocated by the CCF, did not imply a loss of freedom, and a fully planned economy was not only possible but desirable. For those who advised Mackenzie King and the Liberals, however, it was necessary to find some means of resolving Skelton's problem without proposing a program so radical that it was bound to be unacceptable to the mainstream of the party. The answer came in a blending of social security and macro-economic proposals to concentrate on what Skelton termed the overall 'maintenance of purchasing power, leaving it to private industry to supply the demands of this purchasing power.' As the James Committee pointed out at about the same time as Skelton wrote his memo, one of the easiest ways of achieving a high level of consumer demand in the post-war world would be to provide social security measures. These would provide a 'systematic form of saving for contingencies.' The two traditions of reform were merging into one.[54]

There is a danger of either overstating the revolutionary nature of these proposals in late 1943 or, on the contrary, underestimating their significance. Such approaches were far from revolutionary theoretical insights. They were a part of the baggage of economic thought developed during the Depression, and similar ideas had been expressed during the first years of the war. Yet it does appear that only in 1943 did the concept of employing social security measures as a means of achieving a high and stable level of national income come to the fore. This was extremely important in that it shifted the focus of reconstruction planning and redefined the importance of social security. Economic planners were now provided with an alternate means of approaching the issue of direct government investment after the war. Bridges, docks, and public buildings would be useful, but their impact on the economy was dwarfed by the potential to be derived from massive government monetary injections directly to the consumer.

The growing acceptance of this position also marked the culmination of a long evolving relation between social work and economics. Earlier progressive reformism had emphasized social welfare as an ameliorative process central to the needs of the modern state. Social workers, sociologists, economists, and other social scientific professionals had, as has been argued, seen themselves as but differing parts of the same effort to drag a reluctant society into the twentieth century. This perception was reinforced by the institutional ties that had existed between the disciplines in their founding years within Canadian universities. That relation was symbolized in the inter-war years by men like MacIver and Urwick, at the University of Toronto, who held positions both in the Department of Political Economy and in the School of Social Work. Also, people like Cassidy and Marsh, while primarily involved in social work, had economic training.

As the disciplines developed, and especially as economics began to assert its own importance in the 1930s a new element of tension crept into the previously close relation. When, for example, social work expert Harry Cassidy went to the Political Economy department at Toronto in 1936 with a series of proposals for an institute of social science research, he found senior members of that department distinctly cool toward the whole endeavour. Significantly, they objected to the very philosophy of applied social work research, citing problems 'not only in connection with finance but with the possible difficulties which may arise through political complications.' Two years later the situation was reversed. When a number of social scientists sought Charlotte Whitton's support for the establishment of a Social Science Research Council she argued that it should be developed not along the academic lines suggested but as an applied art.[55] The interests and enthusiasms of the two disciplines had thus diverged somewhat in the years before the war.

By the 1940s there is little doubt that most economists saw the social worker's orientation toward the poor and disadvantaged as humane but as generally less scientific or helpful than what W.C. Clark termed a 'comprehensive' approach to the economy. Moreover, as social work was largely a provincial responsibility, the diverging disciplines had focused their attention on different levels of government. Thus when the Dominion began to turn its attention to reconstruction the social worker was without a strong presence. Other than Leonard Marsh no social worker occupied a central place in reconstruction planning in Ottawa. The profession was thus, if not irrelevant, at least peripheral for most of those who would shape post-war Dominion policy. Harry

Cassidy, among others, recognized and lamented the trend. 'Why oh Why oh Why hasn't somebody done something about it [social work planning] by this time,' he complained in late 1943. 'Why can't Mc-Intosh [sic] and Clark and James and Skelton and some of the high powered economists around Ottawa get the idea that social research facilities are needed in the field of the social services. I have the sad surmise that the economists think they can do this kind of job them-selves.'[56] He was probably right. The economic planners in Ottawa were rapidly coming to the conclusion that social welfare had to take second place to, and be planned as, an instrument of economic management.

This was clearly shown over the next months as the government finally moved to implement some reconstruction policies. Mackenzie King, whose ardour for social reform had cooled somewhat since the January 1943 Speech from the Throne, was given a sharp reminder of the imperative need to do something when, in August 1943, the Liberal government in Ontario was defeated by George Drew's Conservatives and, more ominously, the CCF became the official opposition. Hard on the heels of this defeat for Liberalism came four by-elections in which two CCF, one Bloc populaire, and one Communist MP were elected to the Dominion Parliament. All the seats had previously been Liberal. 'In my heart,' commented King, 'I am not sorry to see the mass of the people coming a little more into their own but I do regret that it is not the Liberal party that is winning the position for them. It should be and still can be that our people will learn their lesson in time.'[57] Politics thus reminded King of his duty, and reconstruction once again assumed a high priority at the political level. Rather surprisingly, the policy that dominated discussions over the next months was one that only a few months before Marsh had put at the bottom of his list – family allowances.

The idea of making some sort of payment from government on the basis of family size had a long history in a country like Canada, where under- rather than overpopulation had been the norm. When the bill came before Parliament in 1944 members would trace its origins as far back as nineteenth-century Quebec premier Honoré Mercier, who granted land to large families. In fact, if a loose definition of the principle is applied, origins can be found in the seventeenth century, when New France attempted to increase its population by offering cash bonuses for families with more than ten children.[58]

In more recent times, payments along this line had first seriously been discussed during the First World War. Concerns for families of soldiers overseas as well as the general wave of social reform that swept the nation during the war years led to a demand for things like mothers' allowances, widows' pensions, and other devices designed to assist the family unit. As early as 1915 Elizabeth Shortt of the National Council of Women supported the idea of both widows' and mothers' pensions. The next few years saw, as has been mentioned, various provinces institute acts of varying kinds.[59]

As the reform tide ebbed in the wake of the war, so too did the demand for such social measures. On occasion there were calls by individuals to look into some such scheme once again. In 1929 Quebec Liberal MP Joseph-Etienne Letellier and J.S. Woodsworth co-sponsored a resolution in favour of family allowances. Again, in 1936, when the Junior League of Manitoba recommended the measure, Woodsworth took the opportunity to raise the issue in the House.[60] In Quebec, Father Léon Lebel wrote various articles arguing in favour of family allowances and demonstrating their usefulness to the community.[61] Such proposals, however, do not alter the fact that family allowances were but one of the more exotic varieties of social reform in the pre-war years. Most schemes that had been passed by the provinces were limited in their application, either to widows with children or to indigent families. There is no indication that strong support existed for the extension of the principle. Before 1943 most social reformers would have agreed with Marsh that family allowances were low on their list of priorities.

In June 1943 this changed as officials at the Department of Finance started to look more favourably on family allowances. As has been argued, the relation between the defeat of the National Development Board scheme and the rise of family allowances may be more than mere coincidence. A re-evaluation of Finance strategy for government intervention in the post-war economy was necessary in the wake of the 11 June defeat of the proposal. Within two weeks memos within the department by R.B. Bryce were including family allowances as possible post-war measures. At the same time family allowances remained a controversial measure. The experts within the EAC found themselves seriously divided on the policy when it was brought before them. Though one member suggested that 'given a year to spread propaganda, one might secure widespread support of the proposal,' the committee was uncertain whether the policy was justifiable. In the end it could conclude only, as of early September, that 'it was evident that there was no unanimity of view in the Committee as to the desirability of recommending children's allowances.'[62]

At this point a second factor became important. The committee was also discussing labour relations in Canada in general and wage levels in particular. A report on the problem by Mr Justice McTague was due to go to the cabinet within a few weeks, and the economic advisers had to try to reconcile labour's concerns over deteriorating living standards with the maintenance of the successful wage-and-price control program. By late 1943 pressure was building to allow some deviation from wage control policies in order to improve some workers' incomes. Occasional strikes had already flared on the issue, and it looked as if the whole program might have to yield to these demands. The McTague Report, which recommended adjustment of sub-standard wages, would only increase the pressure. Children's allowances became a means by which the civil service felt it might preserve the policy. Cash payments could be provided to those workers who most acutely felt low wages – the ones with large families. Jack Pickersgill, who actively supported the EAC on this issue, summarized, probably in hyperbolic terms, the hopes for the policy when he commented that 'probably three-quarters of labour's real grievances on the score of wages could be removed by immediate establishment of children's allowances.'[63]

Several points need to be made about the push for family allowances. The first is that the new importance of the cause illustrates the argument made earlier that economic policies now dominated social welfare issues. For whether the primary consideration of the EAC was the preservation of wage stability or the maintenance of national income does not matter in this case. Both arguments illustrate the use of social welfare measures to support macro-economic policy. This view is reinforced by the nature of family allowances. For while civil service officials, in presenting the matter to the politicians, talked about rescuing a 'Milton or Pasteur' through the $5-a-month payments, the very characteristics that made family allowances so useful as wage control or, even more so, as income maintenance tended to make them relatively inefficient as social welfare. Except in the most general sense – that large poor families were likely to need more assistance than the childless poor – the policy was not framed on the basis of need. Indeed the universality proposal, necessary for reasons of constitutionality, meant that the wealthy as well as the poor received payment. Reliance was then put on the income tax system to recover at least a portion of such an inequitable use of public funds. As a social welfare measure, therefore, family allowances were a blunt instrument indeed.

The second point is that on two grounds, however, they were superb. First, the program was a simple and straightforward way of dispensing money to those who tended to be, proportionately, high consumers of income – people with children. The expense of the policy, estimated to be about a quarter-billion dollars a year, thereby ceased to be a negative factor and became instead an argument in its favour. These points were neatly summarized in a series of articles by Grant Dexter of the *Winnipeg Free Press*. Dexter's close ties to many senior officials in Finance and the Bank and the close parallel between his own pieces and their internal memoranda indicate that he was probably transmitting civil service views to the public as a means of smoothing the way for the program. His message was straightforward. 'The best way of maintaining full employment is to increase the incomes of those who earn least.' Given constitutional problems with means tests, problems of administration, and the desire to meet the needs of urban and rural communities alike, family allowances seemed the best answer: 'What the experts and the governments were searching for was a policy that would increase the incomes of the needier people and do so with the least injury to free enterprise.'[64]

The second of the two grounds was political. Mackenzie King was nervous about the public reaction when the issue of family allowances was first raised, and there were some concerns about the 'racial' aspects of the policy, given the high birth-rate in Quebec. In general terms, however, the great strength of family allowances was that, unlike complex depreciation measures, they did not have to be sold to either the politicians or the public purely on their benefits to the overall economy. They could become, quite simply, a motherhood issue. Clifford Clark was aware of these political possibilities, and when he brought the proposal before the cabinet in January 1944 he reminded the politicians that 'the state is merely all its citizens and that its health and soundness depends upon their physical and moral health, their education and training, and their productive efficiency.' Inadequate incomes resulted in 'disease and crime' as well as 'low morale and political instability.' These were passages that could have come directly from *Industry and Humanity*. Finally, in a sincere but none the less obviously political appeal, Clark noted: 'Children's allowances should bring the Dominion Government closer to the people of Canada.' These were difficult arguments to resist, and in what King termed 'one of the most impressive and significant' cabinet meeting he attended, only C.D. Howe resisted the appeal. The Liberal party decided to make family allowances the centre-piece of its post-war social security program.[65]

The third and final point to be made about family allowances is the degree to which they were throughout a measure from within the civil service. The politicians remained, with the exception of Mackenzie, sceptical about the proposal as it evolved, and the experts under Clark sought throughout to persuade them. In a highly revealing diary entry for the day on which the cabinet approved the measure, King notes that J.L. Ilsley, the minister of finance and the man supposedly recommending the policy, had little or no enthusiasm for it. Although the afternoon had been set aside specifically for a discussion of this major issue and some 17 members of the cabinet attended, Ilsley announced that he could stay only for a few minutes, being off to Toronto. King, a little taken aback, asked him if he did indeed recommend family allowances. In his reply the finance minister again revealed his lack of enthusiasm. 'He hesitated considerably,' wrote King, 'and then said: I suppose I should; indeed – I do – or words to that effect.' Having given the measure such a hearty endorsement, Ilsley then hastily turned the whole matter over to Clark who, to all intents and purposes, acted as the cabinet representative of Finance in the ensuing discussions. Grant Dexter appears to have been accurate when he commented that 'only the braintrust' fully understood these implications and it was they who made the family allowances the centre-piece of government policy.[66]

Family allowances were the particular solution of the 'intelligentsia' within the civil service to the problem of wage-and-price controls in the specific sense and the means of providing extra purchasing power within the economy in the longer term. Their establishment thus represented a considerable triumph for the concept of macro-economic management and reflected the growing influence of the expert within the government.

There was some opposition within the intellectual community. Most notably, Charlotte Whitton challenged the whole concept in a series of newspaper articles and in a later election pamphlet. The baby bonus, she argued, had little to do with social welfare, being essentially electioneering on the part of the politicians and fiscal management on the part of their advisers. 'Its mother was fiscal policy, its father political expediency: the respectability of social welfare considerations was summoned to act as godmother for reassurance to a restless public questioning both the circumstance and timing of the parenthood.' Rather than an indiscriminate subsidy, she continued, the government should have employed the vast sums of money that a baby bonus would consume in improving the social infrastructure on which families depend

– such as health and educational services. 'Far too much of the social thinking of today ascribes to economic need or pressure alone, too great responsibility for social maladjustment and individual inadequacy ... It cannot be assumed the child is secure just because there is income in the home.'[67]

Whitton's position was hardly surprising. She had made essentially the same argument in a more general challenge to the direction of social welfare policy in Canada in a 1943 pamphlet entitled *The Dawn of an Ampler Life*, commissioned by the Conservative party. Nor was she alone in her doubts about family allowances. J.A. Corry, though recognizing the consumption-maintenance role of the program, saw family allowances as potentially less useful than the sorts of things Whitton was talking about. Even W.A. Mackintosh admitted privately that he was 'somewhat on the fence' with regard to the program. What is significant is not that there was some doubt but that Whitton found so little support within the reform community. Even within the social work profession she could not claim strong support for her position. As for the Conservative party with which she was so closely associated, it would avoid voting against the bill when it came before Parliament.[68]

It was not that Whitton's objections were frivolous or, as some said, merely reactionary objections to state interventionism. They were, however, not suited to the temper of the times. Her view that individuals had to be guided in their actions as part of the state's responsibility was seen as excessively paternalistic. As Grant Dexter complained, her position 'takes a defeatist view of human nature.'[69] Further, her view that there was an unwarranted belief that money could resolve social problems was the product of an earlier age. The founding generation of modern reform in Canada, people like Adam Shortt and W.L. Grant, had possessed a conservative enough view of social relations to lament the 'cash nexus' and to believe that material improvement was important but secondary to moral and social improvement. Such views, however, had been swept away in the years after the First World War. Whitton had more in common with Robert Falconer than with W.C. Clark or Brooke Claxton. She remained a conservative idealist in an age of liberal technocracy. Ultimately her views carried little weight because her philosophical presuppositions no longer had any meaning to the majority of intellectual reformers or the politicians who took their advice.

The months from March 1943 through January 1944 were crucial in the shaping of the Dominion government's reconstruction plans. The passage of the ensuing policies into law was almost anti-climactic. In February 1944 the government moved to create the bureaucratic apparatus for the transition to the post-war world. The Department of Pensions and National Health, itself a product of the First War, was expanded and renamed the Department of Health and Welfare. The new name said much about the government's changing sense of its own role. Also created was the Department of Veteran's Affairs, reflecting the concern that had existed from the beginning of the war for the smooth handling of problems caused by military service. Finally, reflecting the tremendous importance that had come to be attached to reconstruction, a new Department of Reconstruction was established. In July the family allowances bill was put before Parliament and passed into law without any serious opposition to the principle of the bill.

It was not until March 1945, however, that a full statement of the new macro-economic approach to post-war policy was released. In a white paper released under the authority of the new Department of Reconstruction and written by W.A. Mackintosh, the accumulated wisdom of the war years was set forth.[70] Its contents revealed the degree to which the concept of the state's role in the post-war world had evolved since the writing of the Marsh Report only two years earlier. The fact that it was released under the authority of the new minister of reconstruction, C.D. Howe, also showed how the dominance of economic management had lessened, though not ended, the earlier disagreements between various parts of the government. The focus of the white paper was not social security as such but post-war markets, international trade, and the problems of private investment. In spite of its rather traditional adherence to the developmental role of the Dominion government, it was a product of the evolving values and theories of recent decades.

The white paper saw the post-war years as being, in their requirements, 'like the wartime mobilization program,' involving the continuation of direct government intervention in the market-place. Included in this governmental activity were such social welfare measures as the family allowance and unemployment insurance. By maintaining the public's confidence in its own financial security they were essential to the recovery of private peacetime industry. As such they would not be tax burdens in which the government used public money to assist the poorer members of society at the expense of the better-off. They would be, in a sense, self-generating. 'The supplementary effect which they will have on increasing or maintaining employment will ultimately be paid for, in substantial part, out of an increase in income.'[71] Social security and economic management had by now become two aspects of one plan in the minds of the Ottawa mandarinate.

The white paper revealed its attachment to the most recent expectations for social improvement in two other ways as well. First, as with so many other wartime writings, it took the position that reform was not so much a process of reaching a defined set of goals as it was an ongoing juggling act in which the experts rode herd on the economic forces of the day. The attainment of a positive post-war position, it noted, 'will require the effective working of a number of compatible policies, all directed to the same end, and each contributing to the success of the others.'[72] Also, it reflected the belief that such policies, given current knowledge, enabled government to challenge economic rhythms previously thought unalterable. The commitment to a 'high and stable level' of employment represented the acceptance in semi-official form by government of the possibilities of counter-cyclical economics. Having pledged itself to contain unemployment, the state would henceforth find itself increasingly held accountable for it in the future.

The expert had triumphed in Ottawa. Having managed the war with such success he had convinced the government that he could manage the post-war world as well. In the process the state was committed to a set of policies and expenditures unprecedented in Canadian history. The Liberal party went to the electorate in 1945 on a platform that was essentially drawn from the policies of the Department of Finance, the Bank of Canada, and pens of 'experts' across the nation. The message that the Liberals took to the voter was simple. As Brooke Claxton outlined to his own constituency, Liberals had to be re-elected in order to 'Finish the Job.'[73] The voters responded positively, and the actions of the mandarinate thus received their political justification.

Along with the triumph of the intellectual had come the triumph of the positive state, however far short it may have been from the ideals set forth in the writings of the past years. There was still one unanswered question, however, from the time of the Rowell-Sirois Report. How was this new interventionist state at the national level going to implement its vision of Canada within a federal constitutional framework designed in the nineteenth century? A positive state based on widespread social welfare and a managed economy would be able to emerge fully only if the provinces shared the intelligentsia's view of the future.

12

Epilogue

The Dominion-provincial
conference on reconstruction –
the limits of success

Though it might have seemed that Ottawa had assumed a great deal
of power during the war, there were those who were sceptical of what
it all meant. Frank Scott described the concern in a 1942 issue of the
Canadian Forum. 'Mr King,' he charged, 'by balancing a pyramid of
war controls upon the pinpoint of the War Measures Act, and by his
extensive use of temporary dollar a year men in key positions, has
carefully arranged for an immediate collapse of government intervention at the end of the war.'[1] Though Scott's accusations as to King's
intentions were probably unfair, his charge that Dominion power rested
on a pinpoint base was accurate.

Keenly aware of this were those members of the civil service who
sought to employ the reconstruction period to transform the role of the
state in Canada. Ever since the failure of the Dominion-provincial
conference of 1941, the haunting thought had existed that the great
opportunity for social change that currently existed would come to
little if, with the lapsing of emergency powers, the provinces were
successful in asserting their traditional jurisdictional claims upon the
Dominion. Reform and economic management would then have to
operate within the confines of a constitution that, as one social scientist
pointed out, did not even include the concept of public administration.
This was especially important in two key areas. First, the provincial
hold on social welfare programs under the BNA Act threatened to make
effective co-ordination of any recovery program impossible. Second,
even if the Dominion government were able, through generous grants-
in-aid, to convince the provinces to allow federal intrusion into social
services, without a rearrangement of fiscal powers Ottawa would not
have sufficient financial resources to meet the new demands. As early

as June 1943 Mackintosh warned Heeney of the 'serious obstacles which [the EAC] believes the present arrangements between the Dominion and the Provinces offer to the preparation of any adequate post-war measures.'[2]

Of all the civil servants, however, the man most sensitive to the issue was the one who had had so much to do with the Rowell-Sirois Report, Alex Skelton. Skelton, it is fair to say, had never had much sympathy with the provinces and like so many others saw the defence of provincial jurisdictions as a major obstacle to the implementation of the necessary rational management of the economy within a positive nationalist state. In memo after memo he argued that 'the Dominion must play all its cards and use its vast war-time powers, the present national unity of purpose and the great public anxiety for the future, to secure effective action.' At all costs the Dominion should not be forced to return to ad hoc policies of the Depression years. A new system had to be found to ensure 'adequate Dominion powers to regulate and assist private business' and 'to initiate and administer social insurance and other social security programs.'[3]

There was also growing concern among the provincial premiers about the implications of Dominion reconstruction planning for the post-war world. As federal policies unfolded in late 1943 and early 1944 it became increasingly apparent that the Dominion intended to maintain a presence in key areas of social and economic planning after the war. In January 1944 the new Conservative premier of Ontario, George Drew, wrote to King to warn him of what appeared to be an intrusion into areas of provincial jurisdiction under the protection of temporary war-time controls. The provinces, Drew realized, could do nothing about this for the moment, but his letter served notice that any continuation of such activities into the post-war era would face resistance.[4]

By early 1944, if not before, the government responded to these concerns by planning for a Dominion-provincial conference at the end of the war. Of course there had been conferences before, and little had come of them. This time, however, there was hope that the half-hearted efforts of 1941 would not be repeated. From 1943 on, reconstruction had been a subject of lively interest. Indeed, the federal government could claim, by the time the conference met, that it had won a mandate from the Canadian public on the issue of social reform and that this mandate could be implemented only if the provinces agreed to changes. All these factors led to the hope, as Mackintosh put it, that 'political opinion is now ripe for a real tackling of the problems involved.'[5]

When the delegations assembled in the Chamber of the House of Commons in August 1945 the social scientific experts within the Dominion civil service had a high profile. It was, after all, their meeting to a large degree. Alex Skelton was secretary to the conference and John Deutsch was his assistant. These two thus picked up where they had left off with the conclusion of the Rowell-Sirois discussions in 1941. There had been changes however. The 'Advisers' that the Dominion brought to the Conference reflected the tremendous growth of the economic community within the civil service through the war years. Mackintosh, Towers, Bryce, and Heeney were all present, as were Bank of Canada officials like J.E. Coyne, J.R. Beattie, and W.E. Scott. The new Department of Reconstruction sent, aside from Mackintosh, H.C. Goldenberg and O.J. Firestone. Background papers were written by people like James Coyne and M.C. Urquhart. It was an impressive array, including some of the best social scientific minds of the nation. The fact that they were all in the employment of the Dominion reveals a great deal about the evolving role of the expert in Canada. The growing influence of the intellectual community at the political level was also apparent by the time of the 1945 conference. Brooke Claxton had moved up from his parliamentary secretary's position to assume the new portfolio of National Health and Welfare while Paul Martin had become Secretary of State. Mackenzie King, for his part, had gained renewed faith in reconstruction with the convincing Liberal victory in the previous election. Not since Norman Rogers' death had the intellectual community had such strong support within the cabinet.[6]

The high profile of the intelligentsia at the conference table was paralleled by the careful preparation of the government. It was one of the best-documented Dominion-provincial conferences to date. Detailed background studies were prepared on each measure by the experts within the government, and a dazzling array of statistics, charts, tables, and graphs was brought to the aid of the Dominion's case. At the opening sessions of the conference itself, lengthy briefs were presented by relevant ministers in support of the various parts of what the federal civil servants involved saw as the comprehensive package necessary to develop a successful reconstruction program. Given the decision to read aloud the extended papers on these complex and often convoluted proposals, one has to admire the ability of those present to stay awake as pages of figures flowed around them.

For those who did manage to stay awake and alert during the long speeches, it became apparent that there were actually two agendas for the conference. The first was designed to try and find a means that would permit the ongoing development of the positive state in Canada under federal direction. Numerous proposals emanating from the discussions of the Marsh Report, the EAC, parliamentary committees, and other bodies were presented. In particular, health insurance, old age pension, and unemployment assistance proposals were laid out in some detail by the federal planners. If the provinces agreed to develop such plans along Dominion guidelines they would be subsidized from the federal treasury to amounts of 60 per cent, 50 per cent and 85 per cent, respectively.[7]

Though the specifics of some of the Dominion proposals were new, the general arguments presented were not. Rather, the conference takes on significance for the fact that the Dominion position represented the culmination of a long process of policy formation dating back to the National Employment Commission, the New Deal, and the Rowell-Sirois Report. The personnel arguing the case for the government, in turn, represented the group that had been most actively involved in many of these earlier discussions and that were the most committed to the implementation of this new role for the state. By 1945, however, these proposals were also clearly set within the context of macro-economic planning as it had developed in the latter half of the war. As Claxton argued to the assembly, 'a significant volume of social security payments, flowing into the consumer spending stream, will stabilize the economy of the country as a whole and work against a fall in income.'[8] Employment policy was thus closely related to the proposed social security measures.

The second agenda was fiscal and demanded immediate attention. The Dominion government had, under wartime tax agreements, monopolized the key fields of direct taxation. Now that the war was over, those fields could be invaded by the provinces. The Dominion, however, was unwilling to cede such valuable sources of funds. Items like income tax, which had been a relatively small part of government revenue in the 1930s were, by 1945, the source of about 40 per cent of Dominion government revenue.[9] Both Dominion and provincial governments feared the chaos that might result from uncontrolled double taxation in areas like income and corporate taxation.

The two agendas were closely related, and the hope of the Dominion planners was that they would be solved as one. For though taxation issues might be resolved independently of economic planning and social security proposals, the converse was not the case. If the Dominion were to assume the responsibility for whole new social programs it was, as minister of justice Louis St Laurent stated at the opening of the conference, 'essential that the federal treasury be in a position to carry these burdens.'[10] A taxation agreement might be possible without an agreement on all the proposals of the Dominion for social intervention, but the proposals for social intervention would be impossible if the provinces did not agree to leave the Dominion sufficient powers of taxation to ensure dominance of the national fiscal scene.

The conference documents leave a contradictory set of impressions as to the nature of what occurred. There is, on the one hand, no doubt that both the politicians and the civil service presented a sincere case and that the discussions around the table were thorough. The Dominion-provincial conference itself would drag on, with long intermissions, from August 1945 through May 1946. The formal record of the plenary discussions constitute more than 600 pages, and there were, in addition, a series of 'off the record' talks that probably equalled the plenary sessions for verbiage. The Dominion government, for its part, stated that it was flexible and willing to listen to the legitimate concerns of the provinces. Indeed, there were a number of changes made in the Dominion position as the conference proceeded. Add to this all the thorough background documents, and the impression is given of a real effort by men of good intention to bring about the necessary changes in Canadian social and economic institutions.

On the other hand, a close reading of the proceedings soon reveals a significant degree of repetitiveness and rhetoric. Much of what needed to be said had been said within the first few sessions. More than that, it could be seen from the opening day that the intentions of the federal politicians and civil servants for sweeping alteration of federal-provincial relationships were doomed to failure. George Drew, the premier of Ontario, and Maurice Duplessis of Quebec effectively laid the conference to rest in their opening statements. Six hundred pages of talk would not sway them from their basic position. This made all the rational analysis ineffective, for the point remained that the two largest provinces in Canada stood resolutely opposed to the plans of the Dominion. 'Centralization,' concluded the premier of Quebec, 'always leads to Hitlerism.' George Drew, for his part, had as one of his purposes at the Conference 'the bringing of some of the "Brains Trust" back to reality.'[11] When, after numerous meetings, the conference adjourned *sine die* without any agreement in May 1946, it is unlikely that anyone was surprised.

Of course Drew and especially Duplessis were viewed with something akin to contempt by the intellectual community in Ottawa, and the civil servants around the table must have been tempted to blame them for the failure that became inevitable from that opening day. Both were seen as the sort of reactionary, patronage-oriented politician whose attitudes proved just how necessary it was to wrest a degree of fiscal and social control from the provinces. Brooke Claxton, whose contempt for these premiers was never far below the surface, tangled with Drew on more than one occasion. The feeling was mutual, Drew at one point referring to Claxton as a 'bubbling spring of misinformation.' Such clashes were to a large degree the stuff of partisan politics. Drew, King charged, was interested only in the degree to which such a conference might help depose the Liberals in Ottawa. As for Maurice Duplessis, he had a good many reasons to wish to hurt the federal Liberal party. Other premiers, even if less rancorous or designing in their motives, saw such conferences as an opportunity to restate broad grievances concerning the economic and political structure of the nation. Obstructionism was thus, to a degree, at fault. Yet it is an insufficient explanation of what occurred.[12]

If obstructionism and partisanship were not sufficient, then a further explanation is provided by ideological differences. CCF premier T.C. Douglas of Saskatchewan argued that the vision of the positive state held by the Ottawa planners was too restricted to meet the demands of the new age. Only an acceptance of the necessity of broadly based state ownership would, he believed, resolve the problems Canada faced. At the opposite end of the scale, Maurice Duplessis of Quebec took a straightforward line of opposition to the interventionist direction of the Dominion. 'The issues of the conference,' he argued, 'are not racial issues; they are national issues; it is bureaucracy against democracy; parliamentary institutions and prerogatives against bureaucrats.' The presence of a significant coterie of French-Canadian civil servants within the central ranks of reconstruction planning would not have changed Duplessis's position, but their absence was made all the more noticeable by Quebec's hostility to the emergence of the new bureaucratic and technocratic state. Duplessis was not alone in his attitude, though he was the most ideologically explicit in his resistance. Drew was far from enthusiastic about the move toward planning, and Manning of Alberta had earlier protested the tendencies of Ottawa toward centralization and planning. 'The manner in which the whole situation is being developed,' he warned Charlotte Whitton, 'has for its purpose the rapid introduction of the Socialist State.'[13]

Yet even the addition of ideological disagreements to partisan ones cannot fully explain the failure of the reconstruction conference. For at the basis of the collapse of the conference was an insurmountable difference in perspective between Dominion and provincial jurisdictions that rested not on a clash of ideologies but on a consensus. Even where partisan and ideological differences were minimal, it was impossible for the provinces simply to hand over their responsibilities to the Dominion. This position was most clearly revealed in the position taken by Manitoba. Stuart Garson, the premier, was sympathetic to the aims of reconstruction planning and seems to have held no partisan or ideological grudges against the Dominion planners. Indeed, during the war he had corresponded regularly with W.A. Mackintosh who, in spite of his position as a Dominion official, acted as an unofficial adviser to the Manitoba premier. Moreover, as he commented a few months before the conference began, the difficulties of reconstruction were such that 'partisanship therefore is and will be a luxury which we should abandon during this critical period.'[14]

However sympathetic Garson might be, he could not accept any Dominion scheme that threatened his own government's capability to meet what were, after all, demands that the public was directing at the provinces as well as at the federal government. The very logic of the positive government acted as a stumbling block to Dominion policies. 'The present level of income and employment,' Garson reminded the conference, 'is the result of wartime spending. To maintain the total of peacetime spending by governments, businesses and citizens' was thus essential to the maintenance of high employment. Manitoba understood the implications of Keynes as well as Ottawa, and for those reasons had difficulty with the federal proposals: 'In the field of goverment a very substantial part of this increase must come under provincial jurisdiction, namely in education, health and public welfare, natural resources development, road building provincial public works. An increase in the standard of these services is therefore dependent in large measure upon the financial ability of the provinces to take care of these matters which fall under provincial jurisdiction. If the provinces lack financial capacity these provincial matters will not be handled adequately, and to this important extent the Canadian standard of living will not rise sufficiently, the national income will not be maintained, and there will be greater difficulty in maintaining adequate employment.'[15]

The Dominion confirmed the point raised by Garson when it was asked by the provinces whether it would assume 'full fiscal responsi-

bility for unemployment.' That, said King, was impossible. There were
too many areas of jurisdiction beyond the federal system that no degree
of economic management could control. The provinces would thus
have to undertake a share of the responsibility. Given that inescapable
fact, it was difficult to deny the argument that the provinces had to
have sufficient fiscal and constitutional resources to meet the responsibilities that would be placed upon them. In the end, in spite of the
extremely generous Dominion subsidies proffered in the name of health
insurance, old age pensions, and other matters, the only agreement to
flow immediately from the conference was a series of agreements to
allow the Dominion to 'rent' income taxes in order to avoid double
taxation.[16]

The Dominion-provincial conference of 1945-6 reveals both the degree to which the positive state had become accepted in Canada and
the limits to the influence of the intelligentsia. On the one hand, the
conference revealed that practically all Canadian governments had
accepted the importance of social services and the necessity of using
modern techniques of economic management to reduce the impact of
downturns in the business cycle. Equally important, there was widespread acceptance that in the effort to prevent unemployment it was
impossible to draw hard and fast lines between the public and private
sectors. Provincial governments as much as the federal government
were willing to use public investment as a means of ensuring economic
prosperity and, not incidentally, ensuring their own political survival.
Over the previous twenty years the dominant view as to the role of
government had changed drastically, and what had seemed extreme
now seemed commonplace.

On the other hand, if there was a new acceptance of the positive
state, though sometimes reluctant and occasionally resisted, the mandarins' view that the Dominion government should direct that planning
was rejected. It was, as it turned out, the Ottawa civil servants and
their academic colleagues who were isolated when it came to constitutional matters. For in spite of the prestige they had acquired and in
spite of their attempt to promote a planned and centralist view of
Canada, the positive state would emerge not by means of a rational,
efficient, and bureaucratically dominated Dominion government but
as a series of compromises between the demands of industrial society
and the public on one hand and the realities of a federal constitution
and regional divergence on the other. Harold Innis, who was as suspicious as ever of the designs of his social scientific colleagues, summed

it up in 1946. Across the land, he said, the social scientist 'can be seen carrying the fuel to Ottawa to make the flames of Nationalism burn more brightly. Or he is constantly devising schemes throughout the Provinces to thwart the human spirit and to fasten the chains more tightly.' In such a context the long-standing Canadian lament of disunity became a guarantor of freedom. 'Fortunately,' Innis concluded, 'we are sufficiently divided in regions, races and religion to resist his demand for centralization.'[17] Whatever one might think about his view of the social sciences, the results of the 1945-6 conference reveal that Innis was correct in his estimate of the nature of Canada. The social scientist had become a major force in the new managerial state that he had done so much to develop. At the same time the effects of the positive state would always be limited by the absence of a single overriding sense of priority, purpose, or authority to translate that interventionism into action.

Whatever the limits to its power, the intellectual community in Canada had tremendous success in the quest for a redefinition both of the role of the state and of its own place in it over the years 1900-45. It is fitting that this work should have begun with a debate in an academic journal on the morality of legislation and should end at a conference discussing a wide sweep of proposed government policy. In 1900 the university and government had operated in separate spheres, as befitted James Mavor's vision. The academic, when involved in public affairs, had acted as the detached moral force, arguing the philosophic principles on which government should proceed. Men like George M. Grant or Goldwin Smith typified the traditional academic role. The civil service and political parties, for their parts, saw little, if any, participation from highly trained intellectuals. By 1945 the separate spheres had become inalterably intertwined. The civil service depended on the expertise that the university could provide, and for men of advanced learning the government had become a prime alternative to university teaching. It had become a much more likely alternative than religious service.

Assessing the implications of the change that took place is a complex matter. More than twenty years after the end of the war, Frank Underhill was in Kingston to give the prestigious Brockington Lecture at Queen's University. It was a visit replete with symbolism. Underhill was one of the men most active in public causes within the intellectual community through the 1930s and 1940s. Leonard Brockington, after whom the lectures were named, was well known to members of the same intellectual community with which Underhill was so associated. Queen's, of course, may be seen as the birthplace of the vision of the activist intellectual. It had trained, in successive generations, Adam Shortt, O.D. Skelton, and W.A. Mackintosh. J.A. Corry was currently principal and introduced Underhill to the packed audience in Grant Hall. The message that Underhill gave was straightforward but in that setting, ironic. In search of a definition of the intellectual Underhill concluded, after various witty remarks, that 'the mark of an intellectual is that he is in search of truth rather than power.'

Were Underhill to maintain his definition too rigorously he would have to eliminate as intellectuals much of his own generation of scholars. Many of Underhill's most respected university colleagues had, after all, sought power from the time that they had begun to question the current state of Canadian society. The Queen's community, as much as any other, led the movement from the isolated search for truth in the ivory tower to the centres of national influence. For these intellectuals truth without influence was a sterile commodity in a world beset by turbulent and dangerous forces, unsound ideas, and potentially violent change. They thus sought, through such associations as the CPSA, the Civil Service Reform League, the Canadian Radio League, and then through the political parties and bureaucracy a great amount of power. Indeed, the one constant in the rapidly changing role of the intellectual was the belief in the relation between ideas and power. From Adam Shortt in 1913 through Graham Spry's 1920s articles in the *Canadian Nation* to Frank Underhill in the post-war world, the belief remained that 'the hope of our political salvation lies in the building up of this intellectual elite within our mass democracy.'[18]

By 1945 intellectuals had achieved significant success in their quest, though, of course, they would continue to grumble that neither politicians nor public paid sufficient attention to them. All three political parties had been influenced by them in significant ways, and in Ottawa 'Dr. Clark's boys' had established the golden age of the Ottawa mandarinate.[19] Along with this success had come an alteration of the nature of intellectual advice. Just as the social sciences had become specialized, so the role of the intellectual was seen in more specialized terms. The idea of the activist intellectual as a person charged with broad responsibility for defining social and ethical goals had been appropriate for an age in which intellectual training was intimately bound up with religious concepts. As society became more secular, however, this view had given way to a more precise but also more narrow concept of reform as material improvement. Intellectuals in public life were less interested in defining the principles of social improvement and more concerned with the means by which such improvement might be achieved. The process of reform had come to dominate discussion of its ultimate purpose.

Not everybody, not even every intellectual, was completely pleased with this. Gilbert Jackson joined with Harold Innis at the end of the war in doubting that the intellectual elite could deliver on its promises. Management of an economy as complex as Canada's to the degree implied in recent political and economic writings was, he warned, impossible. 'Wherever one turns ... one hears endless debate about the meaning of ensuring Full Employment. Much of the discussion is carried on, as if some up-to-date Moses, on some lonely Mt. Pisgah, looking out over the scientific landscape has recently descried for the first time the Promised Land.'[20]

For Jackson it was a case of misleading the public concerning the abilities of the economist. For Charlotte Whitton the implications were much more sinister. The effect of the war, she wrote to R.B. Bennett, was not merely to give intellectuals a role in an expanding state but to give a particular clique control of the levers of power. Integrity and meaningful debate were sacrificed in the process. Specifically, and in this she was correct, she saw close ties between the Canadian Club circuit, key politicians like Brooke Claxton, and the new role of the intellectual community in Ottawa. Concluding in melodramatic fashion, she warned that she had 'watched the same thing grow in Germany and Italy, steadily from 1926.'[21]

Whitton's comments were obviously alarmist and reflected the disgruntlement of one member of the social scientific community who found herself at odds with the new vision of social action. Yet her charges are important, for they raise a question about the relation of the intellectual network that had developed before the war and the Liberal party. Various writers have referred in terms almost as conspiratorial to the symbiosis that developed between the Liberal government and key civil servant intellectuals in the post-war years.[22] The issue of bias on the part of the civil service remains contentious, but it is difficult to argue that the Liberal governments of King and St Laurent did not have a special relation with their civil servant intellectuals. In a tradition that went back to Claxton and Rogers, key individuals continued to see the line between being a member of the intellectual community and an active Liberal as very fine. One key civil servant, former academic, and member of the External Affairs 'intelligentsia,' Lester Pearson, would go on to become leader of the Liberal party and prime minister. Jack Pickersgill, always more openly partisan than many of the intellectual community, easily moved from his quasi-political position in the Prime Minister's Office to the supposedly non-political position of clerk of the Privy Council and then back into politics, this time directly, as a Liberal member of Parliament and cabinet minister. From outside the civil service Frank Underhill would abandon his long stormy relationship with the CCF to become an active Liberal by the early 1950s. A community of interest was thus seen to exist between the goals and aspirations of key elements of the 'intelligentsia' and the Liberal party. In this at least Whitton and other critics of Liberal hegemony are correct.

Yet, as this work has tried to indicate, the tendency should not be viewed as some sort or preordained conspiracy designed to suborn the intellectual community and maintain the Liberals in power. What had occurred was much more subtle than Whitton imagined. Complex historical forces, not the design of a few men, brought about the situation to which Whitton so strenuously objected. Four key elements explain what did, in fact, occur in the relations between the intellectual community and the state in the years 1900-45. The first was a social, economic, and demographic revolution brought about by the rapid development of an industrial economy. The second was a change in the philosophical precepts by which the intellectual viewed the state. Third, there was, in response to these changes, the assertion by some in the intellectual community of their particular importance as professional experts in guiding Canadians through the intricacies of the twentieth century. Fourth, there were the particular political and economic events that channeled reform in certain directions and defined the details of the modern Canadian state.

Most basic of all was the economic and demographic revolution that occurred after 1896. Agriculture gave way to industry, and the self-employed farmer gave way to the industrial wage earner. Concomitant with this came the move from the small town and countryside to the large cities. The raw figures of the census are revealing enough. In 1891, the beginning of the decade in which many members of the active intellectual network of the inter-war years were born, less than 32 per cent of Canadians lived in urban centres. By 1941 that figure had increased to nearly 55 per cent. If, however, one defines the term *urban* more narrowly than the census, to exclude all towns and villages of 5000 people or less the figures become even more dramatic.[23] In that case, as late as 1901, only 25 per cent of Canadians would be designated as urban. By 1941 50 per cent would be. In 1901 only five Canadian cities had a population of more than 50,000. By 1941 there were sixteen such cities, and four had a population of more than 200,000. In contrast, in 1901 the largest city in Canada, Montreal, had numbered only 129,000.[24] The basic revolution that had taken place in Canada therefore was in where people lived and in how they earned their living.

These changes forced a fundamental reassessment of the presumptions and values on which theories of society, economy, and state had functioned in the nineteenth century. For the reformers of the time, and often those since, there has been a tendency to portray the debate as a clear-cut one between the forces of light and reason, that is advocates of the positive state, and those of reactionary darkness, the proponents of laissez-faire. Such a picture would be of limited use even for Great Britain, where a continuing class system encouraged polarization, or in the United States, where the myth of the individual was well entrenched. For Canada it is completely inappropriate. In fact, the Canadian intellectual scene was especially complex and must be pictured as a three-cornered debate. Traditional values of British Victorian liberalism competed with the dominant idealist philosophy of the late nineteenth century. Also present was a new interventionist liberalism that rested on a socio-mechanistic view of the state. What made the debate all the more confusing is that, in spite of Victorian liberals like Arnold Haultain or idealists like James Cappon, the philosophical lines were rarely neatly drawn. Intellectuals trained in the Canadian system in the years around 1900 were likely to have admiration for constitutional liberalism and philosophical idealism and, with the rise of the social sciences, faith in the empirical method. These contradictions rested uneasily within a community seeking a means to reform society while preserving it from the increasingly threatening movements of a working class that few of them understood. After the First World War, of course, modern technocratic liberalism assumed a dominant position within the intellectual community. Economic circumstances dictated that traditional laissez-faire liberalism be abandoned. The experience of the war dictated that the alternative could not be Hegelian idealism with all its implications for the state. With the rejection of Hegelian idealism as a formal system came the dismissal of formal philosophical precepts as the basis on which to approach social questions. Ultimately religion and philosophy yielded to the concepts of technique and management. The social and economic revolutions of the early twentieth century thus brought about a fundamental reorientation in the way in which man organized knowledge and approached problems.

Even with this very basic shift it would be dangerous to draw a line through the twentieth century and to place empirical technocrats on one side and philosophical idealists on the other. To do so would imply that all those intellectuals of the 1920s and 1930s could completely reject their own upbringing. Rather, the generations of the intellectual elite flowed into each other. Newton Rowell was an active supporter of Graham Spry, and O.D. Skelton was brought up in an educational system presided over by George Grant. Many of those who assumed positions of importance in the intellectual reform world of the 1930s were the children of strongly religious parents. The idealist influence, and the religious element that went with it in Canada, did not disappear overnight – or between generations. It is just that it fragmented after the First War and ceased as a formal system to dominate Canadian writings on the state. It remained, however, as a strong current, implicit rather than explicit, shaping the thinking of the generation of the 1930s and 1940s. Only gradually did the idealist sense fade in influence so that it may be possible, by the end of the Second War, to talk in terms of the completion of the process begun by the First – the destruction of the idealist impulse in Canadian life. Even as late as 1945, however, eddies and pools of the once all-powerful philosophical current were still visible.

It is only in light of these facts that Whitton's complaint can be set in context. In response to various changes a generational elite of intellectuals did actively seek to assert the importance of its ideas. By 1945 a particular group within that community had become tied to the state and was influential in its policy discussions. Yet what occurred by 1945 was far from preordained. The intellectual community was surprisingly multi-partisan through the 1930s. The CCF initially had the closest links between academics and politicians in the League for Social Reconstruction. The Conservative party under R.B. Bennett employed the technique of the summer school, brought Clifford Clark to Ottawa, and formed the Bank of Canada. The New Deal of 1935 was to a large degree the product not merely of electoral desperation but of the growing influence of men connected to the intellectual community like R.K. Finlayson and W.D. Herridge. Had the Conservatives retained power in 1935, there is every indication that for all of Bennett's discomfort with intellectuals, the influence of the concepts of planning, social security, and an expert civil service would have continued to develop.

Bennett did not win, however, and the Liberals came to power. To that point in time, it is fair to say, the Liberal party was perhaps the most cautious of all major parties about expanding the role of the state. It was, after all, the descendant of Laurier and Cartwright. Circumstance, the growing coterie of civil servants, and the presence of men like Rogers and then Claxton all dictated that change would come. Mackenzie King, who often seemed as distrustful of the intellectuals around him as did Bennett, nevertheless was ideologically 'vulnerable' to their arguments because he thought of himself as a reformer if not a planner. He was also realistic and sensed the importance of expert advice from men like Skelton and Clark. Thus, bit by bit, the Liberal party found itself the focus of attention from the bulk of the intellectual network. This process was assisted by the fact that the Liberals did not possess the authoritarian baggage that clung to Bennett Conservatism and because, unlike the CCF and the Conservatives, they were in power. In other words, as the work of Macdonnell, Finlayson, Scott, Underhill, and others indicates, the intellectual community was willing to give advice and support to any political party that was willing to listen to its ideas. All three parties were indeed influenced to a great degree by that advice between 1930 and 1945. It was the Liberal party, however, that, due to historical circumstance, provided the best opportunity to translate ideas into power. Partisan ties were initially secondary to the acceptance of the principle of modern interventionist reformism.

Whitton's disgruntlement with her intellectual peers and her charges of conspiracy were thus reactions to a major and basic shift in Canadian social and political values. The intellectual community, for its part, had been instrumental in the reshaping of those values, but it was also responding to the realities of the world in which it lived. In a sense, therefore, Whitton's complaint was not about the liaison between Liberalism and the intellectual community but about the values that now dominated in that intellectual community. Yet if those values reflected the broader currents of modern industrialism and industrial values, then Whitton was, perhaps reluctantly and certainly without being aware of it, being forced on to the same ground as another critic of modern academics, George Parkin Grant, when he lamented a few years later that there was no place for conservatism's organic view of society in the modern industrial era.[25]

As for the intellectuals who were a part of the government apparatus by 1945, they had reason to be optimistic. The state had adopted the interventionist attitude toward the economy and society that they and their predecessors had long advocated. Adam Shortt's vision of the expert civil service had been fulfilled, and they were at the centre of power in Canada. Moreover, they had confidence that the expectations of their predecessors had been met and that they had done much to adapt Canada to modern requirements while preserving the basic system of middle-class values that was a part of their own outlook. Yet while the state was permanently changed and while the highly trained expert was henceforth a fixture of the Canadian civil service, the tightly knit elite was a transitory phenomenon.[26] Paradoxically, it may have been that the vast expansion in both government and universities that was supported by the elite was instrumental in destroying the relations that so marked the inter-war years. The number of Canadians attending university expanded dramatically after the war, and as a result the close personal connections that characterized an earlier generation gave way to a much more complex series of separate and competing elites. Lobby groups, labour unions, provincial governments, and others would, within a generation of the Second World War, be able to bring views of social reform and planning to bear that used the same technocratic language and commanded the same prestige of expertise. Within the civil service itself, the very success of the Ottawa mandarins of the 1930s and 1940s ensured an ever-broadening base of university-educated civil servants, with little or no previous knowledge of each other, in an increasingly fragmented civil service.[27] It may have been, as well, that having established the basic practices of the modern state the elite became uncertain about where to go next. Post-war prosperity may have promoted conservatism and caution among a group that had always seen itself as a promoter of change and reform. Or perhaps the basic structures and purposes of the elite survived, albeit in transformed fashion, despite all these changes. Any precise understanding of what happened in the years after the war must await a great deal more study of an era that is just now becoming the subject of serious historical inquiry.

At the very least, however, age ensured the passing of the original activists from the scene. It was thus with the sense that an era had come to a close that a number of the surviving mandarins of the 1940s and 1950s got together over dinner in Ottawa in 1970 to discuss the golden age in which they had all participated. It was an impressive gathering. Graham Towers, Louis Rasminsky, and John Deutsch were there representing the founding generation of the Bank of Canada. W.A. Mackintosh and R.B. Bryce looked back to their days in Finance, while the presence of the retired prime minister Lester Pearson revealed the degree to which the intellectual community had become a part of politics in Canada. Fascinating stories, reminiscences, and a continued confidence in their role in developing modern Canada marked the evening. There was, however, one note of concern. John Deutsch ventured the notion that perhaps as a group they had become over-confident, expecting to manage an economy as complex as Canada's in such a way as to maintain at all times, in the words of the 1945 white paper, high and stable employment: 'There was a very large thought that those kinds of things could be done over what they now call the levers, and you could push the levers and very quickly get the economy to react and if you go off too much in one direction, you pull the lever back a bit, it adjusts itself, and you do that, and you keep nicely on this employment thing.' Deutsch was not alone in his doubts. After much banter and jocularity, the consensus of the group was that the successful management of the war and post-war period was partly good management, but also partly good luck. The experience of years had taught, again in the words of Deutsch, 'the limitations of this thing [economic planning].'[28] Recent events have only emphasized this point. Years of experience have shown that while the state had changed immeasurably since the turn of the century, the new experts who had come to play such an important role may have been good managers, but they were not magicians and their theories were not the key to the promised land. From the perspective of 1970, the distance between Innis and his mandarin acquaintances remained, but it was not as great as it once had been.

Note on sources

If there are two groups in society that are anything but reticent in putting their ideas down in writing they are intellectuals and bureaucrats. As this study is concerned with both, there were ample written records to provide the necessary material for the previous pages. Indeed, the main problem was the sheer volume of material on subjects as important as the proper role of the state in Canada, the problems of modern society, and the social changes thought necessary in response to these. Any attempt, therefore, to set out a full bibliography would be impracticable.

Generally this work relied about evenly on two types of sources. The first were the printed works, both the primary ones of the era and the secondary sources that relate to it. Articles in 'intellectual' journals like the *Queen's Quarterly*, *Canadian Journal of Economics and Political Science*, *Canadian Forum*, and numerous others constantly raised themes of relevance to the relation between the intellectual, reform, and the state. There were also scores of books, political tracts, records of conferences, and other monograph material consulted.

The secondary literature that relates to this subject, both about Canada and about other Western nations, is immense. Much, though far from all of it, appears in the notes, and I acknowledge some of the most helpful works in the preface. To go further than this and to try and list a 'select bibliography' of printed sources would face one with an impossible choice. Either valuable works would be left out, or the list would threaten to overwhelm the text. A rough (and probably incomplete) count of printed sources of a primary and secondary nature in my files indicates over a thousand titles.

The other major source was unprinted manuscript collections. The Public Archives of Canada, the Archives of Ontario, and the Provincial Archives of Alberta, university archives at Toronto, Queen's, Alberta, and the University of British Columbia, and the Archives of the Bank of Canada provided me access to the large and invaluable collections that helped me to understand the private thoughts behind the public announcements. All told, I studied more than thirty manuscript collections in whole or in part. At the Public Archives of Canada, I examined the papers of Brooke Claxton, Frank Underhill, Graham Spry, Charlotte Whitton, Ian Mackenzie, W.L. Grant, Newton Rowell, Adam Shortt, O.D. Skelton, J.S. Willison, Ian Mackenzie, William Lyon Mackenzie King, L.B. Pearson, R.B. Bennett, J.S. Woodsworth, Eugene Forsey, F.R. Scott, the Canadian Reconstruction Association, and the Canadian Political Science Association. The Public Archives was also essential because it is the repository of the public records of the Canadian government. Numerous collections were delved into in investigating the latter parts of this study. Some, as with the records of the Department of Finance, were crucial both because of the important policy and discussion papers that existed and because individuals like Mackintosh and Bryce maintained much of their personal correspondence within departmental files. Other collections were used in more specific fashion to investigate some issue that affected the departments concerned. Efficient archivists, or indexes produced by them, usually made it possible to find these specific details within the voluminous collections without much anguish. In addition, the Mackenzie King diaries, within the provenance of the Public Archives, have been made available on microfiche by University of Toronto Press and were a valuable asset in understanding the thought of the complex prime minister and intellectual whose career is so important to events in this study.

Across the street at the Bank of Canada, the papers of Graham Towers, of Louis Rasminsky, and of the Bank itself were made available to me. In Kingston, so much a centre of activist intellectuals in the years encompassed by this study, were the papers of W.A. Mackintosh, J.M. Macdonnell, and Norman Rogers. For Mackintosh and Rogers, of course, many papers were available in the departmental files at the Public Archives in Ottawa. At the University of Toronto, important collections exist in the papers of Harold Innis, H.M. Cassidy, and the university's Department of Political Economy. At the Ontario Archives are the Frank Beer papers. The W.S. Wallace papers at the University of Alberta and the premiers' papers at the Provincial Archives of Alberta provided details for specific aspects of the study. The Alan Plaunt papers in the Special Collections section of the University of British Columbia library were helpful in determining many of the ties that existed between intellectuals in the inter-war period. Robert Bryce provided an archival resource of another sort. His patience with my questions and his accounts of the personalities and issues within the bureaucracy of the 1930s and 1940s added material and understanding that would not have been retrievable from the written records. In addition, he was kind enough to furnish me with an early draft of a projected history of the Department of Finance.

Notes

ABBREVIATIONS

AO   Archives of Ontario, Toronto
BCA   Bank of Canada Archives, Ottawa
CAR   *Canadian Annual Review*
CHR   *Canadian Historical Review*
CJEPS   *Canadian Journal of Economics and Political Science*
CPSA   Canadian Political Science Association
JCS   *Journal of Canadian Studies*
PAC   Public Archives of Canada, Ottawa

PREFACE

1 *Canada Year Book*, 1921, 766; *Canadian Sessional Papers*, 1897, vol. 16a,
   vi. Note that the 5000 figure is drawn from the 1897 civil list and thus
   excludes certain types of temporary employees.
2 For 1945 see *Canada Year Book*, 1946, 889 and 1141. Comparisons between
   1896 and 1945 are, at best, approximate as the categories included
   altered over the intervening years. Allan Smith 'The Myth of the Self-
   Made Man in Canada, 1850-1914' *Canadian Historical Review* 49: 2 (June
   1978) 189-219
3 F.W. Gibson *Queen's University* II *1917-1961: To Serve and Yet Be Free*
   (Kingston and Montreal 1983) 136

CHAPTER ONE: A CITY OF PIGS

1 A.B. McKillop *A Disciplined Intelligence: Critical Inquiry and Canadian
   Thought in the Victorian Era* (Montreal 1979) 229

2 Andrew Haydon 'The Relations Between Legislation and Morality' *Queen's Quarterly* 7: 1 (July 1899)

3 On prohibition in this period see R.C. Brown and G.R. Cook *Canada: A Nation Transformed* (Toronto 1974) 22-5; Margaret Prang *Newton Rowell: Ontario Nationalist* (Toronto 1975) 32-4; Graham Decarie 'Something Old, Something New. Prohibition in Ontario in the 1890s,' in D. Swainson *Oliver Mowat's Ontario* (Toronto 1972).

4 Haydon 'The Relations between Legislation and Morality,' 1, 7, 19

5 Responses to Haydon in *Queen's Quarterly*: Adam Shortt 'Legislation and Morality' 8: 4 (April 1901) 354; G.M. Macdonell 'The Relations of Legislation and Morality' 7: 2 (1899) 304; W.S. Morden 'The Relations of Legislation to Morality' 8: 4 (April 1901) 346; Haydon 'Relations' 6.

6 Morden 'The Relation of Legislation to Morality' 343. McKillop *A Disciplined Intelligence* chaps 6-7; John Irving 'The Development of Philosophy in Central Canada,' *CHR* 31 (September 1950) and Leslie Armour and Elizabeth Trott *The Faces of Reason: An Essay on Philosophy and Culture in English Canada 1850-1950* (Waterloo 1981) contain the most detailed discussions of Canadian philosophy in this period.

7 Haydon 'The Relations between Legislation and Morality' 8; Morden 'Legislation and Morality' 331

8 Morden 'Legislation and Morality' 345-6

9 See Allan Smith 'The Myth of the Self-Made Man in English Canada, 1850-1914' *CHR* 59: 2 (June 1978). For the businessman's version of the myth see Michael Bliss *A Living Profit: Studies in the Social History of Canadian Business, 1883-1911* (Toronto 1974). Arnold Haultain 'Complaining of Our Tools' *The Canadian Magazine* 9: 3 (July 1897) 183-9, 184

10 Newton Rowell 'The Liquor Problem' *Proceedings of the Canadian Club, Toronto, for the year 1912-1913* 23-4

11 Adam Shortt 'The Influence of Daily Occupations and Surroundings on the Life of the People' *Sunday Afternoon Addresses* 3rd series (Kingston 1893).

12 The bibliography on universities in Canada is growing at a rapid rate. See, for example, Robin Harris *A History of Higher Education in Canada* (Toronto 1976); Hilda Neatby *Queen's University Vol 1 1841-1917: And Not to Yield* (Montreal 1978); S.B. Frost *McGill University: For the Advancement of Learning Vol 1 1801-1895* (Montreal 1980); W.L. Morton *One University: A History of the University of Manitoba* (Toronto 1957).

13 Harris *History of Higher Education* 137, 627.

14 The best discussion of the relation between scientific and religious

thought in Canada is contained in A.B. McKillop *A Disciplined Intelli-gence*. For citation on scientific method see David Noble *The Paradox of Progressive Thought* (Minneapolis 1958) 6.

15 Cited in S.E.D. Shortt *The Search for an Ideal: Six Intellectuals in an Age of Transition* (Toronto 1976) 99. The above comments on Shortt's background are also drawn from this work. Adam Shortt has received more attention than most pre-war academicians. See, aside from S.E.D. Shortt, Barry G. Ferguson 'The New Political Economy and Canadian Liberal Democratic Thought: Queen's University 1890-1925,' PhD thesis, York University, 1982; Bruce Bowden 'Adam Shortt' PhD thesis, University of Toronto, 1980. On early political economy within the Canadian university system see Morley Wickett 'The Study of Political Economy at Canadian Universities' *Ontario Sessional Papers*, 1898, No. 32. The 1888 date marks Shortt's appointment in political science. He had done some sessional lecturing before that.

16 David Legate *Stephen Leacock* (Toronto 1970) chaps 1-4 gives details of Leacock's youth; quotation is from p. 26.

17 Ian Drummond *Political Economy at the University of Toronto, 1888-1982* (Toronto 1983) 27

18 Armour and Trott *The Faces of Reason* 388-97

19 Mary O. Furner *Advocacy and Objectivity: A Crisis in the Professionali-zation of American Social Science* (Lexington 1975); Thomas Haskell *The Emergence of Professional Social Science: The American Social Sci-ence Association and the Crisis of Authority* (Urbana 1977)

20 See Haskell, *The Emergence of Professional Social Science* for the Ameri-can experience. See also Eric Roll *A History of Economic Thought* (London 1973) 368-424.

21 A.B. McKillop *A Disciplined Intelligence* 181 and passim

22 Arnold Haultain 'A Search for an Ideal' *The Canadian Magazine* 22: 5 (March 1904) 427-30

23 Carl Berger *The Sense of Power* 147-51; R.C. Brown and G.R. Cook *Canada: A Nation Transformed* (Toronto 1976) 65-8; Howard Palmer *Nativism in Alberta* (Toronto 1983)

24 George M. Grant 'Thanksgiving and Retrospect' *Queen's Quarterly* 9: 3 (January 1902) 231

25 Alfred Cambray 'Le socialisme, religion nouvelle' *Revue canadienne* 50 (1906) 384; on French Canada: Joseph Levitt *Henri Bourassa and the Golden Calf* (Ottawa 1969) chapter 7; H.J. Cody 'The Test of a True Democracy' *Proceedings* of the Canadian Club, Toronto, for the Year

1912-13, 242-9, 245; Arnold Haultain 'Complaining of Our Tools' 184; G.M. Macdonnell 'Legislation and Morality' 307; O.C.S. Wallace 'Conscience as a National Asset' *Empire Club Addresses, 1903-1904* 104-14, 109

26 Stephen Leacock *Arcadian Adventures of the Idle Rich* orig pub 1914 (Toronto 1969) 2, 104

27 Paul Craven *'An Impartial Umpire': Industrial Relations and the Canadian State 1900-1911* (Toronto 1980) 50. See also, for a related view, S.E.D. Shortt *Search for an Ideal* chap 7. I feel, however, that both Mavor and Adam Shortt were more influenced by idealism than does S.E.D. Shortt. Adam Shortt 'Recent Phases of Socialism' *Queen's Quarterly* 5: 1 (July 1899) 11. He expresses similar sentiments earlier in 'Some Observations on the Great North West' *Queen's Quarterly* 2: 2 (January 1895). Adam Shortt 'In Defence of Millionaires' *Canadian Magazine* 13: 6 (October 1899) 498

28 *Canada Year Book*, 1930, 386-7

29 Quotations from Thomas Haskell *The Emergence of Professional Social Science* 28-9, 14

30 William Robert Young 'The Countryside on the Defensive: Agricultural Ontario's Views of Rural Depopulation' MA thesis, University of British Columbia, 1973, 5; Reverend John Macdougall *Rural Life in Canada: Its Trends and Tasks* (Toronto 1913) 29; *Canada Year Book*, 1930, xxvi

31 *Canada Year Book*, 1930, 117-20

32 Macdougall's *Rural Life in Canada* was commissioned by the Board of Social Service and Evangelism of the Presbyterian Church of Canada. The Methodist Church commissioned, under the auspices of its Department of Temperance and Moral Reform, *Report of a Rural Survey of Agricultural, Educational, Social and Religious Life* (Toronto 1913-14). Social Service Congress, Ottawa *Report of Addresses and Proceedings* (Toronto 1914) 145. Public Archives of Canada *William Lyon Mackenzie King Papers* Series J1 Reel c-1912, King to O.D. Skelton, 13 February 1914

33 Adam Shortt 'The Social and the Economic Significance of the Movement from the Country to the City' *Addresses of the Canadian Club, Montreal 1912-13*, 66. See also William Young 'The Countryside on the Defensive' 85-6.

34 William Young 'The Countryside on the Defensive.' See also David C. Jones ' "We Can't Live on Air All the Time," Country Life and the Prairie Child' in P. Rooke and R. Schnell *Essays on Childhood History* (Calgary 1982) 185-203. James C. Marsh 'Holding our Own' *The Canadian Countryman* 11: 8 (3 May 1913), cited in Young 'The Countryside on the Defensive' 23. Social Services Congress *Report* 145

35 Macdougall *Rural Life in Canada* 57-61
36 McCarthy in Social Services Congress *Report* 122; Sir George Ross 'Depopulation of Rural Ontario' *Monetary Times Annual* (January 1913) 249; Introduction by James W. Robertson, 13, to Macdougall, *Rural Life in Canada*; J.C. Chapais 'Un probleme d'économie social' *Revue canadienne* 56 (1904) 116. See also tome 57 (1905) for a second article by Chapais on the same theme. Levitt *Henri Bourassa and the Golden Calf* 76; Adam Shortt 'Social and Economic Significance' 71
37 Shortt, Ross, and McCarthy were born in rural Ontario, and Chapais in a small village in Quebec. James Robertson and John Macdougall were both born in villages in Scotland.
38 Herbert Ames *The City below the Hill* Introduction by P.F.W. Rutherford, orig pub 1897 (Toronto 1972). William Lyon Mackenzie King *Report to the Honourable the Postmaster General of the Methods Adopted in Canada in the Carrying out of Government Clothing Contracts* (Ottawa 1898). C.A. Magrath 'The Civil Service' *University Magazine* 12: 2 (April 1913) 250
39 J.C. Cooper 'People and Affairs' *The Canadian Magazine* 22 (November 1913). For the controversy over the rejection rate in Great Britain see G.R. Searle *The Quest for National Efficiency* (Oxford 1971). W.L. Smith 'Overcrowding in the Cities' *The Farmer's Magazine* (December 1911), cited in Young 'The Countryside on the Defensive' 25
40 John Hay 'A General View of Socialistic Schemes' *Queen's Quarterly* 3: 4 (April 1896) 283; Adam Shortt 'The Influence of Daily Occupations' 65
41 The most complete study of the social gospel movement in Canada is Richard Allen *The Social Passion: Religion and Social Reform in Canada 1914-1928* (Toronto 1971); quotation from William Munroe 'The Church and the Social Crisis' *University Magazine* 8: 2 (April 1909) 343
42 Though published somewhat later, Salem Bland *The New Christianity* (1918) provides the best example of this sort of ideal of a change in outlook as the basis for social change.
43 One exception was O.D. Skelton *Socialism: A Critical Analysis* (Boston 1911). James Emery, 'The Problems of Industry and Labour' *Empire Club Addresses* 1906-1907; E.J. Kylie 'The Menace of Socialism' *Empire Club Addresses* 1908-1909, 122-3
44 Alfred Cambray 'Le socialisme, religion nouvelle' 396
45 Adam Shortt 'Recent Phases of Socialism' *Queen's Quarterly* 5: 1 (July 1897) 12-13. See also Shortt 'The Incorporation of Trades Unions' *Canadian Magazine* 20: 4 (February 1903) 361-3. John Hay 'A General View of Socialistic Schemes' 283

46 G. Macdonnell 'Legislation and Morality' 307
47 For a brief summary of Caldwell's argument see Armour and Trott *Faces of Reason* 299.
48 William Caldwell 'The Place of the Church in a Modern Life' *University Magazine* 7: 4 (December 1908), 657-76; William Caldwell 'Our Anxious Morality' *University Magazine* 10: 1 (February 1911) 164-81, 164; William Caldwell 'The Place of the Church' 663
49 William Caldwell *Pragmatism and Idealism* (London 1913) 163; William Caldwell 'Anxious Morality' 176; William Caldwell *Pragmatism and Idealism* 12
50 William Caldwell 'Our Anxious Morality' 181
51 Armour and Trott *Faces of Reason* 300

CHAPTER TWO: THE INTELLECTUAL AND THE STATE

1 The literature on this theme is vast. See, as examples, Joseph Hamburger *Intellectuals in Politics: John Stuart Mill and the Philosophic Radicals* (London 1965); Sidney Fine *Laissez-Faire and the General Welfare State 1845-1901* (Ann Arbor 1956); Richard Hofstadter *Social Darwinism in American Thought* (New York 1955); Elizabeth Wallace *Goldwin Smith, Victorian Liberal* (Toronto 1957); Walter Houghton *The Victorian Frame of Mind* (New Haven 1957); W.H. Greenleaf *The British Political Tradition vol 2* The Ideological Heritage (London 1983).
2 Leonard Krieger 'The Idea of the Welfare State in Europe and the United States' *Journal of the History of Ideas* 24 (October-December 1963), 553-68, 557
3 Edouard Montpetit, 'L'Economie politique,' *La Revue canadienne* 52 (1907) 165; Edouard Montpetit 'La Valeur scientifique de l'économie politique' *Revue canadienne* new series 10 (1912) 142
4 'L'économie politique' 267, 'La valeur scientifique' 142
5 Richard Allen *The Social Passion: Religion and Social Reform in Canada 1914-1928* (Toronto 1971). S.W. Dean 'The Church and the Slum' 132; C.W. Gordon 'The New State and the New Church' 194; see also Rose Henderson 'Mothers' Pensions,' all in Social Services Congress *Report of the Addresses and Proceedings* (Toronto 1914). A full account of the congress is given in Richard Allen *The Social Passion* 18-34.
6 Stephen Leacock *Elements of Political Science* (Boston 1907) 382. Gilbert Jackson 'Unemployment' *The Canadian Banker* 21: 3 (April 1914) 154-8. Canadian commentators: Andrew Drummond 'A Social Experiment' *Queen's Quarterly* 8: 1 (July 1900) 46-50; John Cooper 'People and

Affairs' *The Canadian Magazine* 20: 1 (November 1902) 83-6; M.D. Grant 'Old Age Pensions' *University Magazine* 8: 1 (February 1909) 148-58. The comparison also came up periodically in Parliament. See *Debates* of the House of Commons, 3 February 1908, 2425.

7 Maurice Hutton 'The Academic Mind in Politics,' *Proceedings of the Canadian Club, Toronto. For the year 1912-1913*, 250-61, O.D. Skelton 'Are We Drifting into Socialism' *Monetary Times Annual* January 1913, 50

8 O.D. Skelton *Socialism: A Critical Analysis* (Boston 1911) 310; quotation: Skelton 'Are We Drifting?' 52

9 John Willison *Wilfrid Laurier and the Liberal Party* vol. 1 (London 1903) 320-6. See also James Cappon 'Sir Wilfrid Laurier's Liberalism' *Queen's Quarterly* lli 3 (January 1904) 334-40 on Willison and Laurier's ideology.

10 *Debates*, House of Commons, 2 December 1907, 54. On Old Age Pensions see Kenneth Bryden *Old Age Pensions and Policy Making in Canada* (Montreal 1974). See also *Debates*, 3 February 1908, 2425.

11 *Debates* House of Commons, 10 March 1908, 4697

12 James Struthers 'No Fault of Their Own; Unemployment and the Canadian Welfare State 1914-1941' PhD thesis, University of Toronto, 1979, 8; Dennis Guest *The Emergence of Social Security in Canada* (Vancouver 1980) 1-2

13 Paul Craven '*An Impartial Umpire': Industrial Relations and the Canadian State* (Toronto 1980) 6

14 On King's labour relation policies see ibid; on Graham: Mackenzie King Diaries, Microfiche (Transcript Version), University of Toronto Press (henceforth King Diary), 2 December 1908. King would reappoint Graham to the cabinet in the 1920s. On King's idealism see Craven 'An Impartial Umpire' chap. 2. On social control: *Debates*, House of Commons, 12 April 1910, 6861

15 See, as examples, *Debates*, House of Commons 27 June 1900, 8390-430; 7 July 1900, 9377. See also R. Macgregor Dawson *William Lyon Mackenzie King 1874-1923* (Toronto 1958), 97-115 on King's work under the Conciliation Act.

16 *Annual Report of the Department of Labour*, 1903, 58. On the Industrial Disputes Investigation Act see Dawson *Mackenzie King* 133-7; Craven '*An Impartial Umpire*' chap 9

17 Annual Report of the Department of Labour, 1906-7, 50; King Diary 11 December 1909, December 13, 1909; *Debates*, House of Commons, 12 April 1910, 6862, 6863, 6868

18 Robert Stamp *The Schools of Ontario 1876-1976* (Toronto 1982), chaps 3

and 4 and his 'Technical Education, the National Policy and Federal-
Provincial Relations in Canadian Education, 1899-1919,' *CHR* 52: 4 (Sep-
tember 1971); *Debates,* House of Commons, 6 December 1909, 1064;
King Diary, 6 December 1909

19 Craven *'An Impartial Umpire'* 318-52 details these negotiations. His view
of King's role is, however, somewhat different than what follows here.

20 PAC, William Lyon Mackenzie King Papers, Series J1, Reel C-1912, Laurier
to King, 11 August 1910; King to Laurier, 16 August 1910

21 *Canada Sessional Papers,* 16a for the year 1900 and 30 for the year 1911;
*Report of the Royal Commission on Dominion-Provincial Relations,
Canada: 1867-1939* (Ottawa 1940) 82. On Ontario Hydro see V. Nelles *The
Politics of Development* (Toronto 1974). The Ontario Hydro experiment
was popular among intellectuals, at least as they are represented in
their writings in journals.

22 'People and Affairs' *The Canadian Magazine* 26: 6 (April 1906) 594;
Andrew Macphail 'Consequences and Penalties' *University Magazine* 13:
2 (April 1914) 174-5

23 Stephen Leacock *Arcadian Adventures* 143, 157

24 Andrew Macphail 'Why the Conservatives Failed' *University Magazine* 7:
4 (December 1908), 537-8

25 W. Swanson 'Independence in Canadian Politics' *Queen's Quarterly* 18: 1
(July 1910); A.W. Andrews 'Political Corruption and Its Cure' in Social
Services Congress. *Report of Addresses and Proceedings* (Ottawa 1914) 283

26 S.F. Wise and R.C. Brown *Canada Views the United States* (Toronto
1967); Andrew Macphail 'Certain Varieties of the Apple of Sodom' *University Magazine* 10: 1 (February 1911) 41-2. On Hutton see S.E.D.
Shortt *Search for an Ideal: Six Intellectuals in an Age of Transition*
(Toronto 1976) 86-7

27 Barry Ferguson 'The New Political Economy and Canadian Liberal
Democratic Thought: Queen's University 1890-1925' PhD thesis, York Uni-
versity, 1982, 86, has citation on Shortt. W.L. Grant Papers, Skelton to
Grant, 12 February 1904; O.D. Skelton 'The Referendum' *University
Magazine* 12: 2 (April 1913), 197-214

28 *Mackenzie King Papers* J1, Reel C-1916, Skelton to King, 24 September
1911; King to Skelton, 30 September 1911; PAC, W.L. Grant Papers, vol 10,
Grant to Edmund Walker, undated 1911. See also W.L. Grant 'Current
Events' *Queen's Quarterly* 19: 2 (December 1911) 170-1.

29 *Canada Sessional Papers,* 1913, 57a: 'Sir George Murray's Report on the
Organization of the Civil Service of Canada'

30 PAC Sir John Willison Papers, vol 39, Sifton to Willison, 7 February 1901.

For details of Sifton's patronage policies see D.J. Hall, *Clifford Sifton: The Young Napoleon* (Vancouver 1981); Pierre Berton *The Promised Land* (Toronto 1984).

31 Goldwin Smith *Canada and the Canadian Question* (Toronto 1891); J.S. Willison 'Civil Service Reform in Canada' *Addresses of the Empire Club of Toronto, 1907-1908*, 131. See also John Cooper 'Wisconsin's Civil Service' *Canadian Magazine* 26: 6 (April 1906); C.A. Magrath 'The Civil Service' *University Magazine* 12: 2 (April 1913). For similar concerns about corruption and patronage at the municipal level see P. Rutherford *Saving the Canadian City: The First Phase 1880-1920* (Toronto 1974) part 4. Whether patronage was actually a major source of inefficiency is, of course, a separate issue. See J.E. Hodgetts, William McLoskey, Reginald Whitaker, and V. Seymour Wilson *The Biography of an Institution: The Civil Service Commission of Canada* (Montreal 1972), 18-19.

32 Adam Shortt. Letter to the Editor, *Canadian Magazine* 27 (1906)

33 Skelton 'The Referendum' 207; Errol Bouchette 'La necessité d'une politique industrielle et ce qu'elle devrait être' *Revue Canadienne* 49 (1905)

34 W.W. Swanson 'Independence in Politics' 58; Andrew Macphail 'Certain Varieties of the Apples of Sodom' 46; Andrew Macphail 'Why the Conservatives Failed' 530

35 Thomas Haskell *The Emergence of Professional Social Science* 47

CHAPTER THREE: THE SOCIAL SCIENCES

1 James Emery 'Problems of Industry and Labour' *Empire Club Addresses*, for 1906-1907, 33. Emery would later clash with one of Canada's more famous political economists, William Lyon Mackenzie King; see P. Craven, *'Impartial Umpire': Industrial Relations and the Canadian State* (Toronto 1980) 4-5.

2 Stephen Leacock 'Apology of a Professor' in Alan Bowker ed. *The Social Criticism of Stephen Leacock* (Toronto 1973) 35; A.W. Flux 'Is the Study of Political Economy Helpful to Bankers in Their Daily Occupation?' *Canadian Banker* 10:1 (October 1902) 8; W.W. Swanson 'Canadian Bank Inspection' Queen's University, *Bulletins* of the Departments of History and Economic Science, No. 4 (July 1912)

3 James Mavor 'The Relation of Economic Study to Public and Private Charity' *Annals of the American Academy of Political and Social Science* 4 (1893-4), 35-7

4 On early urban reform movements in Canada see P. Rutherford 'Tomor-

row's Metropolis: The Urban Reform Movement in Canada' Canadian
Historical Association *Papers* (1971) 203-24. The following couple of
paragraphs are drawn from this excellent summary. See also for a parallel
movement Walter Van Nus 'The Fate of City Beautiful Thought in
Canada, 1893-1930' in G. Stelter and A.F.J. Artibise eds *The Canadian
City* (Toronto 1977).

5 Herbert Ames *The City below the Hill* was published in 1897 and described
conditions in Montreal. C.S. Clarke *Toronto the Good* was published in
1898 and emphasized the social more than the physical evils of the
city. On the child welfare movement see Andrew Jones and Leonard
Rutman *In the Children's Aid: J.J. Kelso and Child Welfare in Ontario*
(Toronto 1981).

6 A.H. Sinclair 'Municipal Monopolies and Their Management' in P.
Rutherford ed. *Saving the Canadian City* (Toronto 1974) 25-6

7 John Weaver 'Order and Efficiency: Samuel Morley Wickett and the
Urban Progressive Movement in Toronto, 1900-1915' *Ontario History* 69
(1977)

8 See S. Morley Wickett 'City Government by Commission' *An Address
before the Canadian Club of Hamilton, 1912* (Toronto n.d.); 'The Movement for Civic Reform' *Industrial Canada* 7 (December 1906); 'The
Problem of City Government' *Empire Club Addresses for 1907-1908.*

9 S. Morley Wickett 'City Government in Canada' *Political Science Quarterly* 15 (1900) 240, 241, 109; John Weaver 'Order and Efficiency' 224-6

10 W.B. Munro 'Should Canadian Cities Adopt Municipal Government?'
Queen's University, *Bulletin* of the Departments of History and Economic
Science, No. 6 (January 1913) 9. Frank Underhill 'Commission Govern-
ment in Cities' (1910-11), reprinted in P. Rutherford *Saving the Canadian
City* 333-4. See also in the same volume W.F. Burditt 'Civic Efficiency
and Social Welfare in Planning of Land' (1917).

11 S. Morley Wickett 'Problems of City Government' 114. See also PAC,
Willison Papers, Wickett to John Willison, 27 May 1913, cited in Weaver
'Order and Efficiency' 224. Frank Underhill 'Commission Government
in Cities' 333-4

12 O.D. Skelton 'Current Events' *Queen's Quarterly* 16: 3 (January 1909)
290; W.B. Munro 'Should Canadian Cities Adopt Commission Government?', see also 'Boards of Control and Commission Government in Canadian Cities' *Proceedings of the Canadian Political Science Association*
1 (1913). Munro's basic argument was paralleled by T.C. Allum 'Government by Commission' *Monetary Times* 7 January 1911.

13 C. Ray Smith and David R. Witty 'Conservation, Resources, and Environment' *Plan Canada* 2: 1 (1970) 2: 3 (1972); D.J. Hall *Clifford Sifton The*

Lonely Eminence 1901-1929 (Vancouver 1985) vol. 2, chap 11. On the conservation movement in Canada generally see Janet Foster *Working for Wildlife: The Beginnings of Preservation in Canada* (Toronto 1978).

14 Hall *Sifton 2*, 253-4

15 Paul Adolphus Bator 'Saving Lives on the Wholesale Plan: Public Health Reform in the City of Toronto 1900 to 1930' PhD thesis, University of Toronto, 1979, 16. P.H. Bryce 'Measures for the Improvement and Maintenance of the Public Health' *Annual Report of the Commission of Conservation* (Ottawa 1910)

16 Charles Hodgetts 'Unsanitary Housing' *Annual Report of the Commission of Conservation*, 1911, 67. G. Frank Beer 'A Plea for City Planning Organization' *Annual Report of the Commission of Conservation*, 1914, 113

17 Lorna Hurl 'The Toronto Housing Company, 1912-1923: The Pitfalls of Painless Philanthropy' *Canadian Historical Review* 65: 1 (March 1984)

18 PAC Willison Papers, vol 3, Willison to Beer, 23 January 1913

19 Ibid, Beer to Willison, undated 1913. AO, Frank Beer Papers, Box 1, Beer to Sifton, 19 November 1913. See also Beer to Edmund Osler, 31 October 1913. *Annual Report of the Commission of Conservation*, 1915. On Thomas Adams see John David Hulchanski 'Thomas Adams: A Biographical and Bibliographical Guide' *Papers on Planning and Design* (Department of Urban and Regional Planning) no. 15 (Toronto 1978) and Alan H. Armstrong 'Thomas Adams and the Commission of Conservation' in L.O. Gertier ed. *Planning the Canadian Environment* (Montreal 1968) 17-35.

20 PAC Willison Papers, vol. 1, folder 4, contains the correspondence between Adams and Willison leading to the formation of the Civic Improvement League. The League, unfortunately, seems to have left no records.

21 Commission of Conservation. Civic Improvement League of Canada *Report of a Preliminary Conference Held under the Auspices of the Commission of Conservation at Ottawa* (Ottawa 1916)

22 *Annual Report of the Commission of Conservation*, 1919, 102

23 Civic Improvement League *Report of a Preliminary Conference* 25. See also 11 for comment by Adams and 4 for Sifton's remarks at the opening of the conference.

24 PAC Willison Papers, vol. 1, Adams to Willison, 19 April 1917

25 Civic Improvement League *Report of a Preliminary Conference* 17

26 On the American Social Science Association see Thomas Haskell *The Emergence of Professional Social Science. The American Social Science Association and the Nineteenth Century Council of Authority* (Urbana 1977)

27 R.B. Bryce 'William Clifford Clark' *CJEPS* 19 (1953) 414. W.A. Mackintosh

'William Clifford Clark: A Personal Memoir' *Queen's Quarterly* 60 (spring 1953) 6. Robin Harris *History of Higher Education in Canada* (Toronto 1976) 243

28 S. Morley Wickett 'Commercial Education at Universities' *Canadian Magazine* 17: 6 (October 1901). See also J.E. Le Rossignol 'Economics in the High School' *Canadian Magazine* 18: 1 (May 1901) 68-73

29 Stephen Leacock 'The University and Business' *University Magazine* 12: 4 (December 1913), 544-5

30 On the formation of the CPSA and the initial program see PAC, Adam Shortt Papers, vol 58, Skelton to Shortt, 14 June 1913, 1 August 1913, 16 October 1913.

31 PAO, Frank Beer Papers, Box 1, Skelton to Beer, 20 June 1913. PAO, Adam Shortt Papers, Skelton to Shortt, 5 November 1913

32 Adam Shortt 'Aims of the Political Science Association' *Proceedings of the Canadian Political Science Association* 1 (1913) 9-19 contains analogy to surgeons. Adam Shortt 'Some Aspects of the Social Life of Canada' *Canadian Magazine* 2 (May 1897) 9-10 contains analogy to architects. See B. Ferguson 'The New Political Economy' 74-90 for a detailed discussion of Shortt's views on the nature of political economy.

33 Edouard Montpetit 'Le mouvement économique, l'économie politique est elle une science ennuyeuse et abstrait?' *Revue canadienne* new series 9 (1912) 146, 150. See also Montpetit 'L'économie politique' *Revue canadienne* 52 (1907). Paul Cook *Academicians in Government: From Roosevelt to Roosevelt* (New York 1982) chap 3

34 Cook *Academicians*, 48-9; he is citing Frederick C. Howe. Charles McCarthy *The Wisconsin Idea* (New York 1912). Richard Van Hise 'What the University Can Do for the State' *Proceedings of the Canadian Club Toronto* 1913-1914. For an earlier comment on the system see John Cooper's editorial remarks in *Canadian Magazine* 26: 6 (April 1906) 607-8.

35 Harold Innis 'Economics for Demos' *University of Toronto Quarterly* 3: 3 (November 1933) 395; Harry Johnson 'The Social Sciences in an Age of Opulence' *CJEPS* 32: 4 (November 1966)

36 PAC Mackenzie King Papers, J1, Reel C1909, Grant to King, 6 February 1910. Ibid, Reel C-1916, Skelton to King, 24 September 1911

37 Ibid, Reel C-1914, King to Coats, 14 August 1911. The work had a high degree of political orientation, given the proximity of the 1911 election. See Reel C-1916, Skelton to King, 9 August 1911.

38 Ibid., Reel C-1904, Shortt to F. Haultain, undated; Shortt to King, 4 January 1905. Department of Labour, *Annual Report*, 1911

39 *Canadian Magazine* 26 (March 1906) 495. PAC, Willison Papers, vol 37, Shortt to Willison, 10 January 1905

40 *Statutes of Canada*, 1908, chap 15. See criticisms by Borden, *Debates*, House of Commons, 25 June 1908, 11392.

41 J.E. Hodgetts, William McCloskey, Reginald Whitaker, and V.S. Wilson *The Biography of an Institution: The Civil Service Commission of Canada* (Montreal 1972) 28-41 summarizes Shortt's activities as commissioner. Barry Ferguson 'The New Political Economy' 225

42 PAC Borden Papers, vol. 265, 'Memorandum Respecting R.M. Dawson's Work on the Civil Service.' For the Murray Report see *Canada Sessional Papers*, 1913, No. 57a. For Shortt's views, see Memorandum from Shortt to Borden 30 August 1913 in Borden Papers, vol. 229.

43 Speech before the 'People's Forum' cited in Ottawa *Citizen* 15 February 1915

44 *Debates*, House of Commons, 25 February 1915, 471. For Shortt's views see PAC W.L. Grant Papers, vol 9, Shortt to Grant, 18 March 1915. PAC Shortt Papers, vol 58, Grant to Shortt, 27 February 1915; see also Skelton to Shortt, 3 March 1915; Swanson to Shortt, 5 March 1915; George Wrong to Shortt, 19 March 1915. PAC Borden Papers, vol 282, Willison to Borden, 17 August 1914

45 R. MacGregor Dawson *William Lyon Mackenzie King* vol 1, 92-3

46 Cited in Carl Berger *The Writing of Canadian History: Aspects of English Canadian Historical Writing in Canada* (Toronto 1976) 24

47 James Struthers *No Fault of Their Own: Unemployment and the Canadian Welfare State* (Toronto 1983) 14 for citation on White. See also Frank Beer 'National Ideas in Industry' in J.O. Miller ed *The New Era in Canada* (Toronto 1917) 162. PAC Willison Papers, vol 2, Willison to Borden, 17 August 1914. AO, Beer Papers, vol 1, Beer to W.J. Hanna, 17 September 1913

48 Province of Ontario *Report of the Ontario Commission on Unemployment* Ontario Sessional Paper No. 55, 1916, 1-4. On MacMurchy see Paul Bator 'Saving Lives on the Wholesale Plan' 33-4. PAC Willison Papers, vol 13, Beer to Willison, 23 July 1915; 7 September 1915; 8 October 1915

49 Gilbert Jackson 'Unemployment' *Canadian Banker* 21: 3 (April 1914) 15

50 *Report of the Ontario Commission on Unemployment* 11, 9, 10

51 Ibid, 11, 15

52 On unemployment insurance see ibid, part 1, chap 4. On pre-planned public works, see 28; on immigration, see 50; on unemployment bureaux, see 41-4.

53 There were those who looked to a more imaginative use of taxation and other measures to make fiscal policy an effective tool in combatting recession. See O.D. Skelton 'Current Events' *Queen's Quarterly* 16: 3 (January 1909) and 16: 4 (April 1909).

54 Sidney Fine *Laissez-Faire and the General Welfare State* (Ann Arbor 1956) chap 3
55 The term *urban* progressivism is used with emphasis. The powerful rural progressive movement raises separate, though related, issues.
56 The works on American populism and progressivism are many. For a general overview see David Noble *The Paradox of Progressive Thought* (Minneapolis 1957); Arthur A. Ekirch jr *Progressivism in America* (New York 1974) On the sense of crisis that prompted and shaped Progressivism see Robert Wiebe *The Search for Order 1877-1920* (New York 1967). On public health see Heather Anne MacDougall 'Health Is Wealth, The Development of Public Health Activity in Toronto, 1834-1890' PhD thesis, University of Toronto, 1981.
57 Charles Forcey *The Crossroads of Liberalism* (New York 1961)

CHAPTER FOUR: STATISM AND DEMOCRACY

1 G.M. Wrong 'Why Germany Is at War' *Addresses of the Canadian Club* Toronto, for the year 1914-1915, 32
2 John English *The Decline of Politics. The Conservatives and the Party System 1901-1920* (Toronto 1976) chaps 6 and 3-4
3 Stephen Leacock *The Unsolved Riddle of Social Justice* (London 1920) 6
4 University of Toronto *Roll of Service 1914-1918* (Toronto 1921) xiv. Barbara Wilson *Ontario and the First World War* (Toronto 1977) cv; A.G. Bedford *The University of Winnipeg: A History of the Founding Colleges* (Toronto 1976) 121-2; Maureen Aytenfisu 'The University of Alberta: Objectives, Structure and Role 1908-1928' MA thesis, University of Alberta, 1982, 183. McGill University *The McGill Honour Roll, 1914-1918* (Montreal n.d.) lists both the students who joined the service and those who were killed in the war. Bedford *The University of Winnipeg* 123
5 On Grant's sentiments at the outbreak of the war see W.L. Grant 'Current Events' *Queen's Quarterly* 22:2 (October 1914) 219-31. For a brief summary of his career see the obituary in *CHR* 16: 1 (March 1935) 94-5.
6 University of Toronto *Roll of Service* xvii. Andrew Macphail *Official History of the Canadian Forces in the Great War: The Medical Services* (Ottawa 1925). Ralph Connor *The Sky Pilot in No Man's Land* (Toronto 1919)
7 Charles Gordon 'Stripped to the Skin' *Addresses Delivered before the Canadian Club, Ottawa 1916-1917* 154. For two good examples of this see Willison's Toronto *News* and J.W. Dafoe's *Winnipeg Free Press*. One of the best studies of the impact on the war on man's perceptions is Paul

Fussell's *The Great War and Modern Memory* (New York 1975). For
Canada, Michael Bliss 'The Methodist Church and World War I' *CHR*
49:3 (September 1968) 213-33 gives a sense of the war mentality of at
least one section of Canadian society. A full-length study of the impact
of war on Canadian thought still needs to be written.

8 'Public Meeting to Inaugurate the Canadian Patriotic Fund Campaign,
Address by Mr. N.W. Rowell' *Addresses Delivered before the Canadian
Club, Ottawa, 1916-1917* 180. Herbert Stewart 'The Prussian Spirit' *Addresses Delivered before the Canadian Club of Ottawa, 1915-1916* 73

9 R.C. Smith 'The Gospel of Force' *Addresses of the Canadian Club, Toronto
1914-1915* 217. J.W.A. Hickson 'German and Other Theorizing and the
Present Crisis' *University Magazine* 14: 3 (October 1915) 330; see also A.S.
Ferguson 'Neitzsche and German Culture' *University Magazine* 14: 2
(April 1915) 218-28; Robert Falconer *The German Tragedy and Its Meaning for Canada* (Toronto 1915) part 3, 'Fundamental Causes of the
Tragedy'; G.M. Wrong's 'Why Germany Is at War' 31

10 J.O. Miller 'The Better Government of Our Cities' in his *The New Era in
Canada* (Toronto 1917) 360

11 Robert Borden 'Address' *Addresses of the Canadian Club, Toronto, 1914-
1915,* 88

12 Adam Shortt 'War and Economics' *Proceedings* of the Canadian Club,
Montreal, 1914-1915, 315. Stephen Leacock 'Our National Organization for
War' in Miller ed. *The New Era in Canada* 411 and Marjorie Macmurchy
'Women and the Nation' in the same work

13 Clifford Sifton 'The Foundation of the New Era' in Miller *The New Era in
Canada* emphasizes civil service and electoral reform. John English
Decline of Politics 121

14 Francis Mills Turner 'Our Great National Waste. The First of Three
Articles on the New Conservation' *Canadian Magazine* 46:1 (November
1915). See also parts 2 and 3 in ibid. 46:2 and 3.

15 Adam Shortt 'War and Economics' 313-14

16 John Macgillivray 'What Makes Germany Formidable' *Queen's Quarterly*
18 (1910-1911) 65. On the British enthusiasm for German efficiency
before the war see G.R. Searle *The Quest for National Efficiency: A Study
in British Politics and Political Thought* (Oxford 1971) 54 and passim.

17 G.M. Wrong 'Why Germany Is at War' 28. Francis Turner 'Our Great
National Waste, Part 1' 3

18 S.T. Wood 'After the War, What?' *The Canadian Magazine* 47:3 (July
1916) 180. O.D. Skelton 'Current Events, - Financing the War' *Queen's
Quarterly* 25:2 (October 1917) 214

19 PAC W.L. Grant Papers, vol. 6, John Macnaughton to Grant, 29 October 1910. Ibid. vol 9, Skelton to Grant, 19 March 1917. PAC O.D. Skelton Papers, unpublished draft article, 'Linking East and West' (undated, probably 1915)

20 R.C. Brown and G.R. Cook *Canada 1896-1921. A Nation Transformed* (Toronto 1976) chap 15. Gerald Hallowell *Prohibition in Ontario* (Ottawa 1972) 7

21 For an example of contemporary views see Thomas L. Jarrott 'The Problem of the Disabled Soldier' *University Magazine* 16: 2 (April 1917). For a good account of government response to the growing problem of disabled soldiers see Desmond Morton ' "The Noblest and Best": Retraining Canada's War Disabled, 1915-1923' 16 (3 and 4) (autumn and winter 1981) 75-85. Frank Beer 'National Ideals in Industry' in J.O. Miller ed *The New Era in Canada* 178, 188-9

22 Stephen Leacock *Unsolved Riddle* 119-20

23 Recruiting sermon of the Reverend W.T. Herridge, Ottawa 27 June 1915, cited in B. Wilson *Ontario and the First World War, 1914-1918: A Collection of Documents* (Toronto 1977)

24 Robert Falconer *The German Tragedy*. On Bland see A.B. McKillop 'John Watson and the Idealist Legacy' *Canadian Literature* 83 (winter 1979). On Tory see M. Aytenfisu 'The University of Alberta, 1908-1928' MA thesis, University of Alberta, 1982, 207-8. The proposal that idealism was the dominant philosophy of Canadian social thought does not imply that it was unanimously accepted. O.D. Skelton, to give one example, revealed little attachment to idealism even before the war.

25 Cited in Frederick W. Gibson *Queen's University vol. 2 1917-1961* (Kingston 1983) 11

26 John Watson *The State in Peace and War* (London 1918) 9, 56, 48

27 Ibid, 87, 120, 158

28 Ibid, 112, 213

29 Ibid, 246, 110

30 Ibid, 203, 229

31 Robert Falconer *German Tragedy* 35. John Watson *State in Peace and War* 171. Falconer, *German Tragedy*, 38, 64-5

32 Falconer, *German Tragedy* 89

33 'Public Meeting to Inaugurate the Canadian Patriotic Fund Campaign, Address by Thomas White' *Addresses Delivered before the Canadian Club, Ottawa, 1916-1917*, 171. On the Canadian Patriotic League see P.H. Morris *The Canadian Patriotic Fund; A Record of the Activities from 1914-1919* (Ottawa, n.d.)

34 John English *Decline of Politics* 110. R.C. Brown and G.R. Cook *Canada: 1896-1914: A Nation Transformed* 213. O.D. Skelton 'Current Events' *Queen's Quarterly* 26: 1 (July 1918) 128

35 PAC Andrew Macphail Papers, vol. 1, Diary, 13 January 1916

36 For an example see AO, Frank Beer Papers, Beer to C.A. Magrath, 15 April 1916. Beer's nephew was killed. He was also a friend of Edward Kylie. See Magrath to Beer, 18 May 1916. John MacNeill, 'The YMCA and the Higher Patriotism' *Proceedings of the Canadian Club, Toronto, 1918-1919*, 3-4

37 Falconer *German Tragedy* 6-7, 9

38 John Watson *The State in Peace and War* 231

39 J.O. Miller 'Introduction' in *The New Era in Canada* 6. Both English and Brown and Cook make the point that the Union government was interested in reform as well as in conscription. PAC Willison Papers, vol 4, Willison to Borden, 22 July 1917

40 PAC W.L. Grant Papers, vol 9, Skelton to Grant, 13 August 1917. PAC Laurier Papers, Reel C-908, Skelton to Laurier, 18 February 1916, 25 July 1916; Reel C-913, Skelton to Laurier, 30 May 1917. See, for example, Grant Papers, Skelton to Grant, 13 August 1917; Laurier Papers, Reel C-913, Skelton to Laurier, 7 August 1917.

41 Arthur Darby 'The Individual and the State' *University Magazine* 17: 4 (December 1918) 488, 490-1

42 Adam Shortt Papers, vol 58, Grant to Shortt, 25 June 1915

43 'The Super-State and the Mere Politician' *Canadian Banker* 27: 1 (October 1919) 20. Woodsworth cited in K. McNaught *A Prophet in Politics: A Biography of J.S. Woodsworth* (Toronto 1959) 83-4

44 See M. Bliss *A Canadian Millionaire: The Life and Times of Sir Joseph Flavelle Bart* (Toronto 1978).

45 Annual Report, Commission of Conservation for 1919. PAC, Adam Shortt Papers, vol 58, Skelton to Shortt, 18 February 1915, 3 March 1915. Richard Allen *The Social Passion* chap 3

46 W.L. Grant Papers, vol 2, Cappon to Grant, 9 September 1919. See also Cappon 'Current Events' *Queen's Quarterly* 25: 3 (January 1918). Andrew Macphail Papers, vol. 1, diaries, 29 April 1918

47 PAC, James Shaver Woodsworth Papers, vol 2, W. Lashley Hall to Woodsworth, 15 July 1918

48 William Lyon Mackenzie King *Industry and Humanity* orig pub 1918, 114. W.W. Swanson 'Canadian Labour as Affected by the War' *The Canadian Magazine* 50: 5 (March 1918) 418. Richard Allen *The Social Passion*, chap 3

49 Salem Bland *The New Christianity*. King *Industry and Humanity* 225. Stephen Leacock *Unsolved Riddle* 76. King *Industry and Humanity* 225. Leacock *Unsolved Riddle* 128

50 Leslie Armour and Elizabeth Trott *The Faces of Reason: An Essay on Philosophy and Culture in English Canada 1850-1950* (Waterloo 1981) 434. For Brett's work in philosophy and psychology see his *The History of Psychology* 3 vols (London 1912-21).

51 G.S. Brett 'The Revolt against Reason: A Contribution to the History of Thought' *Transactions of the Royal Society of Canada* series 3 vol 13 (1919) 16

52 Ibid

53 Ibid, 17

CHAPTER FIVE: THE SOCIAL SCIENCES

1 Randolph Carlyle 'Social Service and the State' *The Canadian Magazine* 52: 6 (April 1919) 1049. R.C. Henders 'Post-War Constructive Period from a Western Viewpoint' *Addresses of the Empire Club for 1919*, 291-302, 296

2 Gerald Hallowell *Prohibition in Ontario* (Ottawa 1972) 71-2. For a good example of this type of moral concern see 'The New Order: W.E. Raney and the Politics of "Uplift" ' in Peter Oliver *Public and Private Persons* (Toronto 1975). The writings of moral uplift in the decade were voluminous. See, as examples, W.E. Raney 'The Way to Social and Industrial Peace' *The Canadian Magazine* 53: 1 (May 1919) 3-7; 'Prohibition in Canada' *Social Welfare* 2: 6 (May 1920), or practically any issue of the *Christian Guardian*.

3 Veronica Strong-Boag 'Wages for Housework: Mothers' Allowances and the Beginnings of Social Security in Canada *JCS* 14: 1 (spring 1979) 25; Denis Guest *The Emergence of Social Security in Canada* (Vancouver 1980) 58

4 Stephen Leacock was by far the best-known anti-prohibitionist among social scientists. See Leacock 'The Tyranny of Prohibition' in *Living Age* 2 August 1919. This is reprinted in Alan Bowker ed *The Social Criticism of Stephen Leacock* (Toronto 1973) 61-9. Mackenzie King Diaries, 18 April 1921. John Herd Thompson with Allen Seager *Canada 1922-1939: Decades of Discord* (Toronto 1985) 66-8

5 Some were obviously hostile. See Stephen Leacock 'The Woman Question' (1915) in Bowker *Social Criticism* 61-9. Thompson *Canada 1927-1939*, 774

6 PAC, Canadian Reconstruction Association Papers 'Minutes of the Executive Committee, December 9, 1918'
7 Tom Traves *The State and Enterprise: Canadian Manufacturers and the Federal Government 1917-1931* (Toronto 1979) chap 2
8 Ibid, chap 4
9 R.M. MacIver 'The New Social Order' *Social Welfare* 1: 7 (April 1919). PAC, Willison Papers, vol 3, Willison to Beer, 23 July 1918. See also John Willison 'From Month to Month' *Canadian Magazine* 53: 3 (July 1919) 257 and *Montreal Star* 18 August 1923: editorial by Willison entitled 'Lack of Leadership.'
10 Skelton was probably the most sympathetic to the farmers' movements; see PAC Laurier Papers, Reel C-918, Skelton to Laurier, 25 November 1918 enclosure. See also Barry Ferguson 'The New Political Economy' 328-30. ODS 'Current Events' *Queen's Quarterly* 27: 1 (July 1919) 121; 'Current Events' 29: 2 (December 1921) 199-205. Even the avowedly reformist *Social Welfare* was critical of the tactics of the strikers in Winnipeg. See 'The Winnipeg Strike and Its Significance,' 1: 11 (1 August 1919).
11 C.A. Eaton 'Democracy or Bolshevism' *Empire Club Speeches* 1919, 237. On the American 'red scare' see R.K. Murray *Red Scare* (New York 1955). Gilbert Jackson 'What the Public Needs' *Canadian Forum* 1: 2 (November 1920); O.D. Skelton 'Current Events' *Queen's Quarterly* 27: 3 (January 1920) terms the red scare 'panicky Prussianism,' 320.
12 Stephen Leacock 'The Proper Limitations of State Interference' *Empire Club Speeches* 1924, 115. 'Month to Month' *Willison's Monthly* 1: 10 (March 1926). David Hall *Clifford Sifton*, vol 2, (Vancouver 1984) 336
13 William Lyon Mackenzie King 'Four Parties to Industry' *Empire Club Speeches*, 1919, 167
14 See, as examples, T.R. Robinson 'Old Age Pensions' *Social Welfare* 6: 2 (November 1923). H.R. Kemp 'The Old Age Pension Plan in Canada,' in ibid 11: 2 (November 1928).
15 Exceptions can always be found, of course. What is interesting about the 1920s is how relatively few exceptions there are. Even such committed 'reform' journals as the *Canadian Forum* remained fairly tame through most of the decade. Denis Guest *The Emergence of Social Security in Canada* (Vancouver 1980) 70 also makes this point about progressivism, arguing that the split between 'professionalism' and 'zeal' weakened social reform in the 1920s
16 J.A. Calder 'Repatriation and Employment' *Proceedings of the Canadian Club*, Toronto, 1918-1919, 175. R.M. MacIver 'Vicious Circles and Others'

Proceedings of the Canadian Club, Toronto, 1918-1919, 211. Hall, *Clifford Sifton* vol 2, 294

17 Mackenzie King Diaries, 17 September 1918. See R.M. Dawson *William Lyon Mackenzie King* vol 1, 1894-1923 (Toronto 1958) chaps 10-11 for the details of the months leading up to the assumption of the leadership.

18 Ross Harkness *J.E. Atkinson of the Star* (Toronto 1963) 116. PAC Mackenzie King Papers, J1, Reel C-1925, Atkinson to King, 16 March 1916, King to Atkinson, 18 March 1916. PAC, Mackenzie King Papers, J1, Reel C-1939, Skelton to King, 8 August 1919. See also C-1940, G.M. Wrong to King, 10 August 1919; C-1943, Andrew Macphail to King, 17 February 1920.

19 Ibid, Reel C-1951, C.B. Sissions to King, 7 December 1921

20 'Back to Economic Sanity' *Canadian Banker* 27: 3 (April 1920) 167. William Lyon Mackenzie King 'Four Parties to Industry' 165. J.A. Walker 'The Legal Minimum Wage' *Canadian Magazine* 55: 1 (May 1920)

21 William Lyon Mackenzie King *Industry and Humanity* (Toronto 1973) orig pub 1914, 72. T.R. Robinson, 'Unemployment Insurance' *Social Welfare* 5: 1 (October 1922)

22 See for example Gilbert Jackson 'After the War – The Future of the Doctor' *Canadian Forum* 1: 11 (August 1921). F.N. Stapleford 'The Contribution of Social Work to Social Progress' *Social Welfare* 8: 8 (June-July 1926) 190

23 R.M. MacIver *As a Tale Is Told: The Autobiography of R.M. MacIver* (Chicago 1968): note that MacIver was exposed to idealism at Oxford under Bosanquet. R.M. MacIver *Community: A Sociological Study* (London 1917)

24 R.M. MacIver *The Modern State* (London 1926) 4. R.M. MacIver 'Personality and the Suprapersonal' *Philosophical Review* 24: 5 (September 1915) 505

25 MacIver *The Modern State* 219, 161-2, 11. For a direct comparison see John Watson *The State in Peace and War* 212

26 MacIver, *The Modern State* 12

27 Ibid 9, 491. MacIver *Community* provides a detailed discussion of the concept of association and of its importance to society.

28 MacIver *The Modern State* Preface

29 Ibid, 460

30 Ibid, 185-6, 311-12

31 MacIver was distinctly hostile to morality legislation. See ibid, 174. His self-conscious secularism was matched by a strong personal anti-puritanism. See *As the Tale Is Told* 86-7. Indeed, it is tempting to see both his sexually active lifestyle and his view of church and state as a revolt

against a strict Presbyterian upbringing in his native Scotland. MacIver *Modern State* Preface

32 B. Ferguson 'The New Political Economy' 406-10 argues for this new liberalism in the work of the Political Economy department at Queen's. The presence of Skelton, Mackintosh, and, soon afterward, Norman Rogers means that, in this specific instance, Liberalism and liberalism are more directly equated than in the broader context of the social sciences.

33 Perhaps the most articulate advocate of an older-style liberalism was J.W. Dafoe of the *Free Press*.

34 R.M. MacIver 'The Phantom Public' *Canadian Forum* 6: 67 (April 1926) 211; see also B.K. Sandwell 'The Need for Followers' *Canadian Club of Toronto*, 1924-25. Ira Mackay 'Educational Preparedness' *The Canadian Magazine* 52: 4 (February 1919) 812

35 *Contributions to Canadian Economics* vol 2, 1929, 6

36 On the founding of the CHA see L.G. Thomas 'Associations and Communications' *Canadian Historical Papers* 1973 and C. Berger *The Writing of Canadian History* (Toronto 1976); on the CHR see J.M.S. Careless 'Fifty Years with the Beaver Patrol' *CHR* 50 48-71. K.W. Taylor's calculations, cited in Robin Harris *History of Higher Education in Canada* (Toronto 1976) 388

37 *Universities Year Book*, 1931. Staff from year 1930. R.M. MacIver *As a Tale Is Told* 96 notes that he thought of himself primarily as a sociologist and left the University of Toronto in part because he did not have the opportunity to introduce the discipline there. McGill probably had the most advanced sociology program. See Harry H. Hiller *Society and Change: S.D. Clark and the Development of Canadian Sociology* (Toronto 1982) 40-1. By the late 1920s several political economy departments had either split into economics and political science or, at the very least, distinguished between political scientists and economists in terms of course assignments. See, for example, calendars of the University of Alberta from 1921 to 1929. Robin Harris *History of Higher Education in Canada* 249

38 Various aspects of the growth of professional social work have been studied. See Veronica Strong-Boag 'Intruders in the Nursery: Childcare Professionals Reshape the Years One to Five' in Joy Parr ed, *Childhood and Family in Canadian History* (Toronto 1982); James Pitsula 'The Emergence of Social Work in Toronto' *JCS* 14: 1 (spring 1979).

39 C.A. Dawson 'Social Work as a National Institution' *Social Welfare* (July 1928) 226. J.A. Dale 'Social Work's Coming of Age' *Social Welfare* 9: 3 (December 1926). See also C.A. Dawson's call for such a body in 'A

Canadian National Conference of Social and Health Work' in 6: 10 (July 1924). Dawson 'Social Work as a National Institution' 226

40 *Social Welfare*, 2: 9 (June 1920) has a description of a course offered by the Social Services department at the University of Toronto.

41 See, as examples of social engineering, Ruth Hill 'The Social Case Work Method' Ibid, 2: 10 (July 1920) and CASC editorial 'Is Social Work Inspiration Declining?' 11: 1 (October 1928); J.A. Dale 'The Training of Social Workers' 6: 10 (July 1924) puts somewhat more stress on a general education. Peter Bryce 'Recent Constructive Elements in Social Welfare' ibid, 2: 10 (July 1920). See also J.H.T. Falk 'The Future of Social Work in Canada' *Dalhousie Review* 1 (July 1921) and PAC, Charlotte Whitton Papers, vol 19, talk entitled 'Dependency and Organized Relief Work' (undated).

42 Editorial *Social Welfare* 9: 3 (December 1926) and especially the column 'Are YMCA Workers Eligible?' Peter Bryce 'Recent Constructive Elements in Child Welfare' *Social Welfare* 2: 10 (July 1920) F.N. Stapleford 'The Contribution of Social Work to Social Progress' ibid, 8: 10 (July 1960) 19

43 PAC Willison Papers, vol 17, Grant to Willison, 22 July 1918. See also Skelton Papers, draft manuscript, 'Mobilizing Our Resources' Mackenzie King Papers, J1, Reel C-2289, W.L. Grant to King, 5 May 1926.

44 PAC, W.L. Grant Papers, vol 2, Grant to G.S. Campbell, 17 March 1924

45 Ibid, vol 4, Grierson to Grant, July 1924.

46 The full story of these relations is beyond the scope of this study. The Grant Papers, however, provide a fairly clear idea of the work being done. See Grant's correspondence with William Foran, Horace Britain, A.P. Grierson, and William Roche.

47 J.A. Hodgetts et al *Biography of an Institution* 66-8. W.L. Grant Papers, vol 10, Grant to Willison, 7 November 1925

48 Mackenzie King Papers, J4, vol 61 'Report of the Committee of Deputy Ministers on Civil Service Matters, December, 1922'

49 R.M. Dawson *The Civil Service of Canada* (London 1929) 252

50 Ibid, 257, 256. Both Grant and Shortt generally accepted Dawson's interpretation. See W.L. Grant Papers, vol 1, Grant to C.H. Bland, 5 January 1934; Shortt to Grant, 16 March 1923. One person who did not accept Dawson's argument was R.L. Borden. See Borden Papers, vol 265, Borden to A.K. Maclean, 17 February 1931.

51 Mackenzie King Diary, 13 October 1919 (dined with Adam Shortt), 16 October 1919 (honorary degree from Queen's, various social contacts), 18 October 1919 (attends lecture by Thomas Adams), 27 October 1920 (visit with Swanson at Saskatoon), 19 May 1921 (dinner with Haydon

and Skelton). References to correspondence between King and various social scientists in this period appear elsewhere in notes.

52 Mackenzie King Diary, 21 January 1922; King Papers, J1, Reel C-2249,
King to Skelton, 22 October 1922

53 J.L. Granatstein *The Ottawa Men: The Civil Service Mandarins 1935-1957*
(Toronto 1982) 39

54 A great deal has been written on and by this generation of External
Affairs men. See J.L. Granatstein *A Man of Influence: Norman Robertson
and Canadian Statecraft* (Toronto 1981); H.L. Keenleyside *Hammer
the Golden Day: Memoirs of Hugh Keenleyside* vol 1 (Toronto 1981); L.B.
Pearson *Mike: The Memoirs of L.B. Pearson* vol 1 (Toronto 1972).

55 On Rogers' search for a position see Queen's University, Norman Rogers
Papers, Box 1, King to Rogers, 29 December 1925; Under-Secretary of
State to Rogers, 7 June 1926; H.W. Rogers to Norman Rogers, 14 January
1927. For a general overview of Rogers's career see John R. Rowell 'An
Intellectual in Politics: Norman Rogers as an Intellectual and Minister of
Labour, 1929-1939' MA, Queen's University, 1978.

56 PAC, Mackenzie King Papers, J1, Reel C-2247, King to Montpetit, 20
February 1922; Montpetit to King, 22 February 1922.

57 Ibid, J1, Reel C-2263, Coats to King, 22 February 1924

58 R.H. Coats 'The Wealth of Canada and Other Nations' *Canadian Banker*
27: 1 (October 1918) 80-6

59 See obituary for James Mavor in *Transactions of the Royal Society of
Canada* series 3, Proceedings for 1926, xiii-xiv. Carl Berger *The Writing of
Canadian History* 28-9 discusses Shortt's devotion to purely historical
matters in the 1920s. S.E.D. Shortt *The Search for an Ideal* 147. PAC Willi-
son Papers, vol 3, Beer to Willison, 9 September 1924. 'From Month to
Month' *Willison's Monthly* 1: 4 (September 1925); 1: 10 (March 1926). See
John Thompson *Decades of Discord* 59-62.

60 J.S. Woodsworth Papers, vol 2, E.A. Partridge to Woodsworth, 31 August
1922. 'FHU' 'O Canada' *Canadian Forum* 9: 104 (May 1929) 269

CHAPTER SIX: THE FORMATION OF A NEW REFORM ELITE

1 PAC Brooke Claxton Papers, vol 19, Claxton to T.W.L. Macdermott, 10
October 1935. Ibid, Claxton to J.M. Macdonnell, 18 September 1936

2 Michiel Horn *The League for Social Reconstruction: Intellectual Origins
of the Democratic Left in Canada 1930-1942* (Toronto 1980); J.L. Granatstein *The Ottawa Men: Civil Service Mandarins 1935-1957* (Toronto 1982)

3 Mary Vipond 'National Consciousness in English-Speaking Canada in

the 1920's: Seven Studies' PhD thesis, University of Toronto, 1974, 539. This thesis, though focusing on nationalism rather than the state, is invaluable in identifying the elite that formed in these years. Nationalist enthusiasm, as will be argued, was closely linked to social and economic reform.

4 J.L. Granatstein *Ottawa Men* 7-8. In 1927-8, for example, there were 106,663 students enrolled in Grade 8 compared to only 9,667 in Grade 12. That same year there were 5,700 university degrees conferred. *Canada Year Book*, 1930, 912, 925.

5 Michiel Horn *The League for Social Reconstruction* 13-14. Queen's University, Norman Rogers Papers, H.W. Rogers to Norman Rogers, 30 July 1927; Walter Murray to Rogers, 6 July 1927; O.D. Skelton to Rogers, 29 April 1931 give a flavour of Rogers's views of university and civil service. For biographical details see John R. Rowell 'An Intellectual in Politics' MA thesis, Queen's University, 1978

6 Fyfe cited in F. Gibson *Queen's University* vol 2: *To Serve and Yet be Free* (Montreal 1983) 136. Carl Berger *The Writing of Canadian History* (Toronto 1976) 83

7 Michiel Horn 'Academics and Canadian Social and Economic Policy' *JCS* 13: 4 (winter 1978-9) 3-10; 'Free Speech within the Law: The Letter of Sixty-Eight Toronto Professors, 1931' *Ontario History* 72: 1 (March, 1980) deals with the debate over the role of the academic as does C. Berger *The Writing of Canadian History*, especially the chapter on Underhill. See, for an example of fears about political bias, University of Toronto Archives, Papers of the Department of Political Economy, Box 1, Helen Reid to Harold Innis, 9 November 1938, concerning Henry Laureys's retirement.

8 University of British Columbia, Special Collections, Alan Plaunt papers, Box 2, Drew to Plaunt, 18 April 1939. PAC Frank Underhill Papers, R.A. MacKay to Underhill, 17 April 1939; D.A. MacGibbon to Underhill, 9 January 1941. See also letters from B.S. Kierstead, 15 April 1939 and A.R.M. Lower, 16 April 1939. Berger *The Writing of Canadian History* 83

9 The information in this paragraph is drawn from various sources. See *Who's Who in Canada* for the relevant years, J.L. Granatstein *The Ottawa Men* chap 1 for the civil servants, Michiel Horn *League for Social Reconstruction* for members of the LSR. Obituaries provided background of individuals, though to list them in detail would take up too much space.

10 For an example of specifically Christian social reform in the 1930s see R.B.Y. Scott and Gregory Vlastos *Toward the Christian Revolution* (Chicago 1936). Note the presence of essays by LSR members like Forsey,

King Gordon, and Eric Havelock. J.A. Corry *Memoirs of J.A. Corry: My Life and Work, a Happy Partnership* (Kingston 1981) 108. For an example of the inimitable McQueen style see Claxton Papers, vol 20, McQueen to Claxton, July 1937. In a few short paragraphs he manages to insult many of New York's ethnic groups as well as a couple of prominent academics.

11 Vincent Bladen *Bladen on Bladen: Memoirs of a Political Economist* (Toronto 1978) 8-9. Whitton's early style is shown in her various printed pieces in *Social Work* and in her various lectures, the notes to which exist in PAC Charlotte Whitton Papers, vol 19. Arthur Lower *My First Seventy Five Years* (Toronto 1967) 25. Obituary to McQueen by D.A. MacGibbon CJEPS 7: 2 (May 1941) 278

12 Harris *History of Higher Education in Canada* (Toronto 1976) 629; *Canada Year Book,* 1930, 931. *Census of Canada,* 1931, vol 1, Table 83

13 Whitton Papers, vol 3, gives a good impression of the concern for classmates and relatives in the war. L.B. Pearson *Mike: The Memoirs of the Rt. Honourable Lester B. Pearson* vol. 1 (Toronto 1974) 36. Claxton Papers, vol 18, Claxton to Uncle Fred, 20 November 1920

14 Census of Canada, 1931, vol 1, Table 83; 1941, vol 6, Table 6

15 Cassidy was born in 1900 and attended the University of British Columbia and Brookings before joining the staff of the University of Toronto in 1929. In 1934 he became director of social welfare for the province of British Columbia.

16 Norman Robertson and Harry Cassidy both attended Brookings, though Robertson also went to Oxford. University of Toronto political economist and future civil servant A.F.W. Plumptre went to Cambridge. See G.L. Granatstein *A Man of Influence: Norman A. Robertson and Canadian Statecraft,* 1929-1968 (Toronto 1981) chap 1. D. G. Creighton *Harold Adams Innis: Portrait of a Scholar* (Toronto 1957) 40-8 discusses Innis's experiences at Chicago.

17 Charles Ritchie *An Appetite for Life: The Education of a Young Diarist 1924-1927* (Toronto 1977) recounts one Canadian's experiences. See, for example, Underhill's reaction as cited in Carl Berger *The Writing of Canadian History* 57-8. Bladen *Bladen on Bladen* 9

18 PAC, Graham Spry Papers, vol 13, Spry to Arnold Heeney, 26 August 1923. See also vol 2, Spry to his father, Christmas 1922. At the time the Spry papers were researched they were in the process of being organized by the PAC. My thanks to the Archives for allowing me to look at them in this state. The position of the citations within the papers may have since changed.

19 Underhill received a Flavelle scholarship; Berger *The Writing of Canadian History* 57. Pickersgill received an IODE: Granatstein *The Ottawa Men* 209.

20 PAC, Spry Papers, vol 13, Spry to Woodsworth, 15 July 1923. See, on the various connections, PAC Spry papers, vol 2, 13; M. Vipond 'National Consciousness in English Speaking Canada in the 1920's: Seven Studies' PhD thesis, University of Toronto, 1974; Berger *The Writing of Canadian History*; Granatstein *The Ottawa Men.*

21 University of Toronto Archives, Harold Innis Papers, Correspondence, Innis to M.Q. Innis, 7 June 1933

22 CPSA *Annual Reports* 1930 indicate that Montpetit and Laureys were the only francophone academics on the executive.

23 Harris *History of Higher Education* 398

24 Linda Kealey *A Not Unreasonable Claim* (Toronto 1979)

25 Nancy Woloch *Women and the American Experience* (New York 1984) 387

26 PAC, Papers of the CPSA, vol 1, F.A. Knox to Cudmore, 7 October 1931. Executive lists drawn from CPSA *Proceedings* 1930-5. The statement of aims was printed at the beginning of each issue.

27 *Canadian Forum* 11 (July 1931) 366

28 Papers in CPSA *Proceedings* 1931. Queen's University Archives, Norman Rogers Papers, Box 1, Scott to Rogers, 9 November 1932

29 Allen George Mills 'The Canadian Forum 1920-1934 PhD thesis, University of Western Ontario, 1976, 47-8, preface

30 Mary Vipond 'National Consciousness' chap 4. The CAR in the later 1920s provides lists of 'Important National Organizations.' These examples are drawn from the 1926-7 number. Vipond 'National Consciousness' 264. University of British Columbia, Plaunt Papers, Box 1, Claxton to Plaunt, 30 October 1935

31 Editorial *The Canadian Nation* 1: 3 (December 1928) 18

32 D.J. Hesperger 'The League of Nations Society in Canada during the 1930's' MA thesis, University of Regina, 1978, 32-4. Granatstein *The Ottawa Men* 13 indicates how important the CIIA was to those members of the intellectual community who went into the civil service.

33 For a general view of the period see G.R. Cook *The Politics of John W. Dafoe and the Free Press* (Toronto 1963) chaps 7 and 8. On Canadian culture in the 1920's see Peter Mellen *The Group of Seven* (Toronto 1970); Mary Vipond 'National Consciousness.' On the rift, see, for example, E.J. Tarr 'National Character' *The Canadian Nation* (December 1928).

34 Mary Vipond 'National Consciousness' chap 4 and the *Canadian Nation*

provide the general background information on the Canadian Clubs and their revival. See lists of executive and speakers given each year in *Addresses of the Canadian Club of Toronto* for the relevant years.

35 *Canadian Nation* (December 1928)

36 Ibid (February 1929) 'Public Opinion' 11-12. First cited sentence from Graham Spry 'Canadian Problems and the Canadian Club' *Addresses of the Canadian Club*, Toronto, 1927, 334. Citation from 'The Canadian Club Job' *Canadian Nation* (December 1928) 20. See also R.M. MacIver 'The Phantom Public' *Canadian Forum* 6: 67 (April 1926) 210-12.

37 See Spry Papers, vol 13, Spry to Laurie, 7 October 1929. Granatstein *The Ottawa Men* 13. *Canadian Nation* (December 1928)

38 *Canadian Nation* (April 1929) 18

39 The best summary of the work of the Aird Commission is F.W. Peers *The Politics of Canadian Broadcasting – 1920 to 1951* (Toronto 1969) chap 3. For the brief report of the commission see Canada *Royal Commission on Radio Broadcasting* (Ottawa 1929).

40 *Financial Post* 10 October 1929, cited in Peers *Politics of Canadian Broadcasting* 52

41 On the League, see F.W. Peers *Politics of Canadian Broadcasting*, chap 4; Margaret Prang 'The Origins of Public Broadcasting in Canada' *CHR* 46: 1 (March 1965); J.E. O'Brien 'A History of the Canadian Radio League, 1930-1936' PhD thesis, University of California, 1964. Citation from Graham Spry 'The Origins of Public Broadcasting in Canada: A Comment' *CHR* 46: 2 (June 1965) 138

42 University of British Columbia, Plaunt Papers, Box 1, Atkinson to Plaunt, 30 December 1930; Box 2, Dafoe to Plaunt, 30 June 1931; Finlayson to Plaunt, 2 January 1931; 22 January 1931; 12 February 1931. See also Peers *Politics of Canadian Broadcasting* 65.

43 PAC Claxton Papers, vol 1, 'Minutes of a Meeting of the Publication Committee' 3 July 1930

44 Ibid vol 5, Claxton to Spry, autumn 1930. Ibid, Claxton to Spry 15 December 1930; see also Claxton to Spry, 12 December 1930. Ibid, Claxton to Gladstone Murray, 14 May 1932 and 10 January 1933, for his later views on the League. On the legal battles see Peers *The Politics of Canadian Broadcasting* 69-72.

CHAPTER SEVEN: MOVING INTO THE INNER COUNCILS

1 O.D. Skelton *Our Generation: Its Gains and Losses* (Chicago 1938) 95

2 King's first reference in his diaries to serious economic problems in his

diary does not come until 30 March 1930, and then only in reference
to western Canada. A good summary of the nation's slide into depression
is given by A.E. Safarian *The Canadian Economy in the Great Depression*
(Toronto 1959). PAC, W.L. Grant Papers, vol 6, Grant to the Marquis of
Lothian, 4 May 1931

3 *Canadian Forum* 11: 122 (November 1930) 51. FHU 'O Canada' in ibid 12:
135 (December 1931) 93. PAC Graham Spry Papers, vol 13, Spry to unknown, 31 October 1927

4 J.M. Simpson 'Industrialism and the Future' *Queen's Quarterly* 40: 4
(winter 1930)

5 PAC, Frank Underhill Papers, vol 3, S.D. Clark to Underhill, 8 April 1933
and 8 June 1933. PAC, Frank Scott Papers, vol 23, Scott to 'My Future
Self' 16 February 1933. King Diaries, 15 April 1931

6 See, for example, PAC, Brooke Claxton Papers, vol 20, Claxton to Arnold
Toynbee, 30 December 1938; Underhill Papers, Clark to Underhill, 22
July 1935. *Canadian Forum* 16: 190 (November 1936) 'Quebec's Iron Heel'
4. Queen's University Archives, Norman Rogers Papers, Box 2, Skelton
to Rogers, 26 October 1935. J. King Gordon 'The Political Task' in R.B.Y.
Scott and Gregory Vlastos eds *Towards the Christian Revolution* (Chicago 1936) 146

7 This argument was so common as to be practically a necessity in talking
about the future of Canada. As examples in the first years of the Depression, see the discussion on Canadian economic history in *CPSA Proceedings* (1931) 204; F.J. Westcott 'Government Interference in Industry:
Necessity or Menace?' *Canadian Banker* 29: 3 (April 1932); A.F.W.
Plumptre 'Expert Opinions upon Problems of Today' *Canadian Banker* 40:
1 (October 1932); A. Brady 'The State and Economic Life in Canada'
University of Toronto Quarterly 2: 4 (July 1933).

8 Edgar McInnes 'Consider the Politician' *Canadian Forum* 11: 122 (November 1930)

9 D.A. MacGibbon 'Economics and the Social Order,' *CJEPS* 2: 1 (February
1936) 72. *Canadian Forum* 12: 135 (December 1931) 93

10 The definitive history of the LSR is Michiel Horn *The League for Social
Reconstruction: The Intellectual Origins of the Democratic Left in
Canada 1930-1942* (Toronto 1980). T.W.L. MacDermott 'Radical Thinking
in Canada' *Canadian Forum* 12: 133 (October 1931). Underhill Papers,
vol 7, Underhill to Rogers, 18 January 1932

11 Underhill Papers, vol 8, Scott to Underhill, undated. See also Horn *The
League for Social Reconstruction* 37-9. Rogers Papers, Box 1, Rogers
to Underhill, 18 January 1932

12 Stephen Leacock 'What Is Left of Adam Smith?' *CJEPS* 1: 1 (February 1935). See also Leacock's Introduction in R.B. Bennett 'The Premier Speaks to the People' (Ottawa 1935).

13 H.A. Innis 'The Penetrative Powers of the Price System' *CJEPS* 4: 3 (May 1935) 286. H.A. Innis 'The Role of Intelligence: Some Further Notes' *CJEPS* 1: 2 (May 1935) 286.

14 Gordon Hewart *The New Despotism* (London 1929); J.A. Corry *My Life and Work: A Happy Partnership* (Kingston 1981) 63-4; J.A. Corry 'Administrative Law in Canada' CPSA *Proceedings* (1932), 190-207; 'Administrative Law and the Interpretation of Statutes' *University of Toronto Law Journal* 1: 2 (1936) 286-9. For a similar view see A.B. Harvey 'Tendencies in Legislation' *Queen's Quarterly* 38: 4 (autumn 1931).

15 University of Toronto Archives, Political Economy Papers, vol 8a, Mac-Gibbon to Innis, 31 January 1936. Ibid, Box 8, A.L. Macdonald to Innis, 25 May 1934.

16 Ibid, vol 1, Biss to Innis, 10 June 1935. Ibid, Biss to Innis, 20 August 1935. Ibid, Biss to Innis, 20 August 1935, 6 September 1935

17 O.D. Skelton 'Fifty Years of Political and Economic Science in Canada' Royal Society of Canada *Fifty Years Retrospect* (n.p. 1932)

18 *Canadian Forum* 12: 133 (October 1931) 4

19 Underhill Papers, vol 6, Underhill to Macdonnell, 22 September 1935. Ibid, Maclean to Underhill 23 September 1935

20 Ibid, vol 4, Forsey to Underhill, 19 September 1939; Underhill to Forsey, 20 October 1939

21 PAC, Eugene Forsey Papers, vol 4, contains the Meighen-Forsey correspondence. PAC, Underhill Papers, vol 4, Forsey to Underhill, 2 November 1940. Christina McCall-Newman *Grits: An Intimate Portrait of the Liberal Party* (Toronto 1982) 22-3. Rogers Papers, Box 2, Scott to Rogers, 16 October 1935

22 *Report of the Royal Commission of Provincial Economic Enquiry* (Halifax 1934) vol 1. PAC, R.B. Bennett Papers, Box 593, Innis to Bennett, 17 October 1932, 26 October 1932.

23 F.J. Westcott 'Government Interference in Industry: Necessity or Menace?' *Canadian Banker* 29: 3 (April 1932) 346. Duncan McArthur 'Public Affairs' *Queen's Quarterly* 41: 2 (summer 1934) 258

24 As with the 1920s, it was in religious reform circles that the concept seemed to survive. See, for example, John Line 'The Philosophical Background' 22-3 in Scott and Vlastos *Towards the Christian Revolution*.

25 Copy of Regina Manifesto reprinted in K. McNaught *A Prophet in Politics: A Biography of J.S. Woodsworth* (Toronto 1959) 321-30

26 Introduction to reprint of League for Social Reconstruction *Social Planning for Canada* xviii. The introduction is signed by F.R. Scott, Leonard Marsh, Graham Spry, J. King Gordon, E.A. Forsey, and J.F. Parkinson. *Canadian Forum* 11: 126 (March 1931) 203

27 Frank Underhill 'Bentham and Benthamism' *Queen's Quarterly* 39: 4 (November 1932) 660, 663, 666

28 Rogers Papers, Box 2, Scott to Rogers, 16 October 1935

29 Claxton Papers, vol 19, Claxton to Alice Massey, 7 April 1933

30 Ibid, vol 18, Claxton to Finlayson, 22 July 1930; Claxton to Herridge, 21 July 1930. See, for example, ibid, Claxton to Lindsey, 1 October 1934.

31 Ibid, vol 18, Claxton to Finlayson, 24 April 1931. Ibid, vol 20, Claxton to Tarr, 24 April 1931. Michiel Horn *The League for Social Reconstruction* 21-2

32 Claxton Papers, vol 19, Claxton to Lindsey, 21 January 1929; 3 February 1929. Ibid, Claxton to Alice Massey, 17 April 1933

33 Ibid, Claxton to Alice Massey, 17 April 1933. Ibid, Claxton to Gladstone Murray, 10 January 1933

34 Ibid, Claxton to Leif Egeland, 2 March 1935; vol 19, Claxton to Michael Lubbock, 12 November 1935

35 R. Whittaker *The Government Party*, chap 2

36 A traditional interpretation of the CCF has argued that farmers, militant unions, and intellectuals comprised the three groups forming the CCF in the early 1930s. See K. McNaught *A Prophet in Politics* 255 and passim. A more recent work challenges only the meaningfulness of worker support for the CCF in its formative years; see Bryan Palmer *Working Class Experience: The Rise and Reconstitution of Canadian Labour, 1800-1980* (Toronto 1983) 215.

37 *Canadian Problems as Seen by Twenty Outstanding Men of Canada* (Toronto 1933)

38 Granatstein *The Ottawa Men* 44-9

39 This was related to the author by R.B. Bryce who, in turn, heard it from Clark.

40 PAC, R. Finlayson Papers, 'Life With R.B.: That Man Bennett' 255. Claxton Papers, vol 18, Claxton to Herridge, 26 December 1934

41 PAC, R. Finlayson Papers, 'Life with R.B.,' 261

42 See, for example, PAC J.W. Dafoe Papers, M-75, Dafoe to Borden, 7 September 1929; Dafoe to Rowell, 24 August 1931; 19 June 1931, 27 October 1933; R.C. Brown *Robert Laird Borden: A Biography* vol 2 (Toronto 1980) 202; Margaret Prang *Newton Rowell: Ontario Nationalist* (Toronto 1975) 378. As these biographies indicate, the main point of connection

with the intellectual community was through international affairs
and bodies like the CIIA and the League of Nations Society.

43 Mackenzie King Diary, 9 August 1931, provides the chain of connections
in full. Massey, however, did not accept the hint and was called into
a stormy meeting with Bennett. See Vincent Massey *What's Past Is Prologue: The Memoirs of Vincent Massey* 172-7 (Toronto 1963). J.W. Dafoe
Papers, Reel M-75, J.M. Macdonnell to Dafoe, 12 August 1930. W.L.
Grant Papers, vol 6, Grant to Massey, 16 June 1931

44 Claxton Papers, vol 19, Macdonnell to Claxton, 5 December 1930

45 Ibid, Claxton to Lindsey, 1 October 1934

46 See, for example, A.B. Balcolm 'Why All Tariffs Are Evil' *Dalhousie
Review* 4: 4 (January 1925) 477-84.

47 Mackenzie King Diary, 2 March 1932: 'I think what I have in Industry
and Humanity is exactly in the right lines and that I can make a
real contribution.'

48 Ibid, 29 July 1930. See, for example, Rogers Papers, Box 2, King to Rogers,
20 May 1935, concerning a paper by C.A. Curtis. See King Diary, 27
June 1932, for one of various references to Rogers's 'acceptance' of spirit-
ualism. Mackenzie King Diary, 14 June 1932

49 Whittaker *The Government Party* 25, 33-5

50 Dafoe Papers, M-75, Massey to Dafoe, February 2, 1932.

51 Mackenzie King Diary, August 1931. See Claude Bissell *The Young
Vincent Massey* (Toronto 1981) chap 9 for details on relations with King.

52 The influence of Alice Massey remains somewhat circumstantial, as customs of the age dictated that the wife take a position secondary to her
husband. The numerous references to her presence, comments, and
suggestions, however, suggest that she was as much involved in the ques-
tion of policy as was Vincent. See, as examples, the cited reference to
Alice Massey in Hugh Keenlyside *The Memoirs of H.L. Keenlyside* vol 1.
Hammer the Golden Day (Toronto 1981) 402-3; Claude Bissell *The
Young Vincent Massey* 204; Mackenzie King Diary, 14 August 1931, 24
August 1931, 30 May 1932; Brooke Claxton Papers, Claxton to Alice
Massey, 7 April 1933. Bissell *The Young Vincent Massey* 204; Mackenzie
King Diary, 31 October 1932

53 Mackenzie King Diary, 14 August 1931; 24 August 1931. Bissell *Young
Vincent Massey* 208-9

54 Dafoe Papers, M-75, Dafoe to Dexter, 10 February 1932; Massey to Dafoe,
2 February 1932; Mackenzie King Diary, 6 January 1932. Bruce Hutchison
The Far Side of the Street (Toronto 1976) 167-71.

55 Hutchison *The Far Side* 198-9; James Gray *Troublemaker* (Toronto 1978) 135-6
56 On the Batterwood meeting, see the Dafoe Papers, M-75, Dafoe to Rowell, 30 September 1932; Dafoe to Harry Sifton, 29 August 1932, and Memorandum, 'Basis for Discussion at Massey's, September 7 1932.'
57 Mackenzie King Diary, 8 September 1932
58 Rogers Papers, Box 1, Massey to Rogers, 6 October 1932; Bissell *Young Vincent Massey* 212-13. See, as an example of linkage, Ralston's comment after one such meeting cited in R. Whittaker *The Government Party* 40.
59 Mackenzie King Diary, 9 February 1933
60 Dafoe Papers, M-75, Dafoe to King, 15 June 1933
61 *Winnipeg Free Press* 1 April 1933
62 Mackenzie King Diary, 19 March 1933 and 31 March 1933
63 On the summer school, see Mackenzie King Diary, 7-9 September 1933. R. Whittaker *The Government Party* 41
64 Vincent Massey *What's Past Is Prologue* 213, 212. Vincent Massey 'The Approach to the Problem: An Introduction' *The Liberal Way* (Toronto 1933) 4-5
65 Massey 'The Approach' 4-5

CHAPTER EIGHT: THE NEW MILLENNIALISTS

1 A variation of this chapter was published in the *Canadian Historical Review* under the title 'Economic Thought in the 1930's, The Prelude to Keynesianism' 66: 3 (Sept. 1985) 344-77.
2 The best study of the changing nature of the civil service is J.L. Granatstein *The Ottawa Men: The Civil Service Mandarins, 1935-1957* (Toronto 1982).
3 Mackenzie King Diary, 28 July 1932. Stephen Leacock *Hellements of Hickonomics in Hiccoughs of Verse Done in Our Social Planning Mill* (New York 1936) 84
4 H.A. Innis 'The Teaching of Economic History in Canada' *Contributions to Canadian Economics* vol 2, 58
5 Ian Drummond *History of the Political Economy Department at the University of Toronto* (Toronto 1983) 21. Queen's University Archives, W.A. Mackintosh Papers, Mackintosh to Skelton, 1 June 1925; Mackintosh to Principal Taylor, 30 June 1925. Skelton was furious at the failure of the principal to appoint Mackintosh, commenting that 'after wrecking the English Department it has been felt it would be invidious not to wreck the Economics Department also'; Skelton to Mackintosh, 9 June 1925. Carl Berger *The Writing of Canadian History* (Toronto 1976) chap 5

6 Barry Ferguson 'The New Political Economy and Canadian Liberal
  Democratic Thought: Queen's University 1900-1925' PhD thesis, York University, 1982, chap 8 argues that the interest in the West was part of a
  long-standing tradition at Queen's and an attempt to discover the roots of
  modern democracy. On frontier regions, see W.C. Clark 'The Country
  Elevator in the Canadian West' *Queen's Quarterly* 24: 1 (July 1916); W.A.
  Mackintosh 'The Canadian Wheat Pools' Queen's University *Bulletin of
  the Department of History and Political Science*, No. 51 (November 1925)
  and *Agricultural Co-operation in Western Canada* (Toronto 1924); H.
  Michell 'Profit Sharing and Producers' Co-operation in Canada' Queen's
  University *Bulletin of the Departments of History and Political and
  Economic Science* No. 26 (January 1918). D.A. MacGibbon, 'Economic
  Factors Affecting the Settlement of the Prairie Provinces' *Pioneer Settlement* (1932). P.C. Armstrong *Wheat* (Toronto 1930). On settlement
  series, see Ferguson, 'The New Political Economy,' 329.
7 Perhaps the best known of these studies was Harold Innis, *A History of
  the Canadian Pacific Railway* (London 1923), but see also as examples
  James Mavor *Niagara in Politics, a Critical Account of the Ontario
  Hydro-Electric Commission* (New York 1925); W.T. Jackman *The Economics of Transportation* (Toronto 1926); Eugene Forsey, 'Economic and
  Social Aspects of the Nova Scotia Coal Industry' McGill University
  Economic Studies, No. 5. Good bibliographies of publications in these
  years may be obtained in the volumes of the *Canadian Historical Review*,
  beginning in 1922, and the University of Toronto publications *Contributions to Canadian Economics*, running from 1928 to 1933. Eric Roll, *A
  History of Economic Thought* (London 1973), 303-11
8 J.W. Dafoe Papers, M-75, Coats to Dafoe, 7 March 1932
9 Robert Lekachman *The Age of Keynes* (New York 1966) 78-81. D.A.
  MacGibbon *An Introduction to Economics for Canadian Readers* (Toronto
  1924). The 1935 edition showed the impact of the Depression and included a section on the business cycle. It is also relevant to apply the
  comments on Carver and Hansen to Canada as that work was a standard
  textbook in Canadian universities. See Drummond, *Political Economy*.
  E.J. Hanson *The Department of Economics of the University of Alberta:
  A History* (Edmonton 1983) 15 indicates that no Canadian textbooks
  were used at the University of Alberta in sample years during the 1920s.
  A.F.W. Plumptre and A.E. Gilroy 'Review of Economics Texts' *Contributions to Canadian Economics* 7 (1934) 124. Robert Lekachman *The Age
  of Keynes* 81
10 For one of the earliest statements of the staple theory in Canadian
  history see W.A. Mackintosh 'Economic Factors in Canadian History'

CHR 4: 1 (March 1923) 12-25. See also, for more recent comments on the staple theory, Mel Watkins 'A Staple Theory of Economic Growth' *CJEPS* 29: 2 (May 1963) 141-58.

11 See, on this theme, Thomas Haskell *The Emergence of Professional Social Science: The American Social Science Association and the Crisis of Authority* (Urbana 1977).

12 PAC, Charlotte Whitton Papers, vol. 19, ms entitled 'Dependency and Organized Relief Work.' Grace Towers 'Is Poverty an Economic Ill?' *Social Welfare* 9: 7 (April 1927). Bryce Stewart 'The Problem of Unemployment' Ibid, 3: 8 (March 1921)

13 F.W. Learnmouth 'Social Effects of Unemployment' Ibid, 4: 5 (1 February 1922)

14 James Struthers, 'No Fault of Their Own: Unemployment and the Canadian Welfare State, 1914-1941' PhD thesis, University of Toronto, 1979, 131. See PAC, Brooke Claxton papers, vol 18, P.H. Gordon to Claxton, 2 November 1931, 5 November 1931, for attitudes on the collapse of the West. Note also James Struthers 'No Fault of Their Own' 208 for the impact of Gideon Robertson's tour through Palliser's triangle. For a general assessment of the problems of the West during the Depression see W.A. Mackintosh *The Economic Problems of the Prairie Provinces* (Toronto 1935). *Canadian Forum* 16 (May 1936) 20

15 H.A. Innis 'The Penetrative Powers of the Price System' *CJEPS* 4: 3 (August 1938) 318

16 W.W. Swanson *Depression and the Way Out* (Toronto 1931) 141. University of Toronto Archives, H.A. Innis Papers, vol 1, G. Britnell to Innis, 27 September 1937. H. Innis 'Government Ownership and the Canadian Scene' in *Canadian Problems as Seen by Twenty Outstanding Men of Canada* (Toronto 1933) 73

17 For good examples of this see Michael Stewart *Keynes and After* (London 1972) and Robert Lekachman *The Age of Keynes* (New York 1966).

18 PAC, J.W. Dafoe papers, M-76, Dafoe to Harry Sifton, 11 January 1934

19 See D.A. MacGibbon 'Economics and the Social Order' *CJEPS* 2: 1 (February 1936). In this sense, what was occurring in Canada fits Thomas Kuhn's paradigm on changes in scientific theory. See his *The Structure of Scientific Revolutions* (Chicago, 1970). See also Don Patinkin *Anticipations of the General Theory* (Chicago 1982).

20 Alfred Marshall *Principles of Economics* 8th ed (London 1930) viii

21 W.C. Clark 'Business Cycles and the Depression of 1920-1' Queen's University *Bulletin of the Departments of History and Political and Economic Science*, No. 40 (August 1921). The classic description of the

business cycle written in the inter-war period comes in Wesley Mitchell *Business Cycles: The Problem and Its Setting* (New York 1927).

22 Alfred Marshall, *Money, Credit and Commerce* (London 1923) book IV
23 Ibid, 47
24 On King's idealism, see Paul Craven *"An Impartial Umpire": Industrial Relations and the Canadian State 1900-1911* (Toronto 1980) chaps 2-3. Sidney Fine *Laissez Faire and the General Welfare State: A Study of Conflict in American Thought* (Ann Arbor 1965) 48-9. The closest example in Canada would be the elder James Mavor, but his idealism always moderated his laissez-faire. On accommodation, see for example, S.J. Maclean 'Social Amelioration and University Settlement' *Canadian Magazine* 8: 6 (April 1897); Adam Shortt 'Current Events' *Queen's Quarterly* 7: 3 (January 1904); James Mavor 'The Relation of Economic Study to Public and Private Charity' *Annals* of the American Academy of Political and Social Science 4 (1893-4).
25 O.D. Skelton 'Current Events' *Queen's Quarterly* 16: 4 (April 1909). See for example Bryce Stewart 'The Problem of Unemployment' *Social Welfare* 3: 8 (March 1921); J.B. Alexander 'Business Depressions' *Canadian Banker* 34: 4 (July 1927) 444-8.
26 E.S. Bates *Planned Nationalism: Canada's Effort* (Toronto 1935); W.C. Clark 'Current Events' *Queen's Quarterly* 38: 4 (autumn 1931); Gilbert Jackson 'The World in Which the Central Bank will Work' in Innis and Plumptre *The Canadian Economy and Its Problems* (Toronto 1934); Bank of Nova Scotia *Monthly Review* (March 1934)
27 J.A. Aikin *Economic Power for Canada* (Toronto 1930) 32-9; W.W. Swanson *Depression and the Way Out* (Toronto 1931) 3-8, 14. E.S. Bates *A Planned Nationalism* 87. Gilbert Jackson *An Economist's Confession of Faith* (Toronto 1935) 29, 33-34
28 Harold Innis 'Economics for Demos' *University of Toronto Quarterly* 3: 3 (November 1933) 392
29 'Central Banking and Business Recovery' *Canadian Banker* 38: 4 (July 1931)
30 H. Michell 'Monetary Reconstruction' *CJEPS* 8: 3 (August 1942). W.C. Clark 'The Flight from the Gold Standard' *Queen's Quarterly* 38: 4 (autumn 1931) 762. See also Queen's University Archives, Norman Rogers Papers, Box 1, Steven Cartwright to Rogers, 19 January 1933, attached memorandum.
31 B.K. Sandwell 'The Plague of the Amateur Economists' *Canadian Banker* 39: 3 (April 1932) 340. In terms of the quantity theory of money developed by American Irving Fisher in the years before the Depression,

M(money) × V (velocity with which money changes hands) = P (prices) × T (level of transactions). Since P increased, either T had to decrease proportionately or M and/or V increase proportionately. The implication is that in the 1920s V increased, but that in the longer term the quantity of money was insufficient and the velocity of transactions unstable. In 1929 both P and T began to decline. Jackson *An Economist's Confession of Faith* 34

32 H.A. Innis 'The Penetrative Powers of the Price System' *CJEPS* 4: 3 (August 1938). See also his introduction to Innis and Plumptre *The Canadian Economy and Its Problems* (Toronto 1934).

33 W.B. Hurd 'The Dilemma of Mass Production' *Canadian Banker* 39: 2 (January 1932) 193. Stephen Leacock 'What is Left of Adam Smith?' *CJEPS* 1: 1 (February 1935). Conservative Party 'The Premier Speaks to the People' (Ottawa, 1935). A copy is available in PAC, Ian Mackenzie Papers, vol 42.

34 Hurd 'The Dilemma of Mass Production' 197. Innis, in a variant on this theme, argued that expanding economies had encouraged firms and nations to assume high levels of debts. Those debts represented fixed costs which prevented the price system from making the necessary adjustments to restore equilibrium; Innis 'The Penetrative Powers of the Price System.'

35 For a good expression of the orthodox position see Bank of Canada Archives, Graham Towers Papers, Memorandum No. 17, June 1936.

36 R.C. MacIvor *Canadian Monetary, Banking and Fiscal Development* (Toronto 1958) 101. Linda Grayson 'The Formation of the Bank of Canada' PhD thesis, University of Toronto, 1974), 7, 10. R.C. Brown *Robert Laird Borden, A Biography* (Toronto 1977) vol 1, 200, notes that White was the choice of the Toronto group headed by Sifton, Edmund Walker, and Willison. See also English *The Decline of Politics* 52.

37 MacIvor *Monetary, Banking and Fiscal Development* 102-3. *Statutes of Canada* Finance Act of 1914, chap 3

38 A.F.W. Plumptre 'Canadian Monetary Policy' in Innis and Plumptre *The Canadian Economy and Its Problems* 165. Queen's University Department of Political Science and Economics 'The Proposal for a Central Bank' *Queen's Quarterly* 40: 3 (August 1933) 434, 439

39 Queen's 'Proposal' 425

40 Royal Commission on Banking and Currency *Proceedings* (Macmillan Commission), vol 3, (Ottawa, n.d.) 1053.

41 There were, of course, some bankers in favour of a central bank and some economists against it. *Mackenzie King Diary*, 30 September 1932; PAC, King Papers, J4, vol 52, file 303, contains the report by Curtis to

the Liberal party which recommended a central bank. See also C.A. Curtis 'Credit Control in Canada' CPSA *Proceedings* (1930) as one of many published pieces by Curtis supporting a central bank. Clark supported a central bank as far back as the early 1920s, when he did some work for W.C. Good on the idea. See Grayson 'The Formation of the Bank of Canada' 53.

42 On Clark's influence on the appointment of Plumptre see Grayson 'The Formation' 145. My thanks to R.B. Bryce, who notes that the mood of the CPSA was, by this time, overwhelmingly in favour of the bank. Bryce, in turn, was told this by Clark. On the Liberal study groups, see Queen's University, Norman Rogers Papers, Box 1, Steven Cartwright to Rogers, 7 October 1932, 19 January 1933. Plumptre was less than neutral even after he took the position, writing an anonymous article for the *Financial Post* challenging the testimony of the bankers. See article by 'Economist' in the *Financial Post* 16 December 1933. A marginal note by Clark in PAC, RG 19, Department of Finance Records, vol 3974 identifies the author as Plumptre.

43 MacMillan Commission *Proceedings* vol 1, 101, testimony of J.A. Macleod

44 For a breakdown of commission testimony see A.F.W. Plumptre 'The Evidence Presented to the Canadian Macmillan Commission' *CJEPS* 2: 1 (February 1936). Macmillan Commission *Proceedings* vol 3, 2554-2575. Ironically, Montpetit was later recommended for the position of deputy governor of the Bank. See PAC, R.B. Bennett Papers, M-962, J.A. Barrette to Bennett, 4 December 1934. Macmillan Commission *Proceedings* vol 3, 1357-95.

45 *Report of the Royal Commission on Banking and Currency* (Ottawa 1933) 59, 85-9, 95-7

46 PAC, Bennett Papers, vol 95, Clark to Bennett, 27 January 1934

47 Ian Drummond *The Floating Pound and Sterling Area 1931-1939* (Cambridge 1981) 60. Granatstein *The Ottawa Men* 52-3

48 Queen's 'Proposal' 426. BCA Graham Towers Papers, Memorandum No. 17, June 1936. Thomas Courchene 'The Interaction between Economic Theory and Bank of Canada Policy' in David C. Smith ed *Economic Policy Advising in Canada* (Montreal 1981). There are, however, indications that the Bank was a little more activist than Courchene argues. See BCA, Graham Towers Papers, Memorandum No. 177, re letter from Alvin Hansen to Stuart Garson, 31 August 1938.

49 Lekachman *The Age of Keynes* 69-76

50 Gilbert Jackson *An Economist's Confession of Faith* 46-7. B.K. Sandwell 'One Good Thing about Private Ownership' *Canadian Banker* 39: 1

(October 1931). D.C. MacGregor 'Outline of the Position of Public Finance' in Innis and Plumptre eds *The Canadian Economy and Its Problems* 57. Jackson *Economist's Confession of Faith* 51. Struthers *No Fault of Their Own* 62

51 See W.C. Clark 'What's Wrong with Us' *The Institute Bulletin* the journal of the Professional Institute of the Public Service, vol 10 (December 1931). A copy is available in Department of Finance Records, vol 3993.

52 The League for Social Reconstruction *Social Planning for Canada* 125, 195

53 Francis Hankin and T.W.L. MacDermott *Recovery by Control: A Diagnosis of the Relations between Government and Business in Canada* (Toronto 1933), 272. PAC, Claxton Papers, vol 18, Claxton to Finlayson, 24 September 1934

54 K.W. Taylor 'A Summary' in H. Innis and A.F.W. Plumptre *The Canadian Economy and Its Problems* 185. See appendix 3 for the participants in the conference.

CHAPTER NINE: THE PROBLEM OF NATIONAL UNITY

1 H.B. Neatby *William Lyon Mackenzie King: The Prism of Unity* (Toronto 1976) vol 3, 93. Norman Rogers saw the constitutional problem as especially important. See PAC, Mackenzie King Papers, J1, 210, Rogers to King, 19 January 1935. See also Claxton's prediction of reform legislation and the difficulties it would meet in constitutional terms; Claxton Papers, vol 18, Claxton to Kenneth Lindsey, 1 October 1934.

2 PAC, Underhill Papers, vol 4, Forsey to Underhill, 30 March 1933. Eugene Forsey 'Clerical Fascism in Quebec' *Canadian Forum* 17: 197 (June 1937) 90. Forsey was on the executive of the Montreal branch of the Civil Liberties League and thus aware of the proclivities of the Duplessis government. See University of British Columbia, Special Collections, Plaunt Papers, Box 1, John Camsell to Plaunt, 14 September 1938. PAC, Claxton Papers, vol 20, Claxton to Toynbee, 30 December 1938. Skelton cited in Neatby *Mackenzie King* vol 3, 187. Underhill cited from *Canadian Forum* 11: 129 (June 1931) 333

3 See, for an early analysis of this fact, H.M. Cassidy *Unemployment and Relief in Ontario 1929-1932* (Toronto n.d.) 211-12.

4 Nova Scotia Royal Commission on the Economy. Submitted to the Rowell-Sirois Commission as a study. See also Norman Rogers 'The Crisis of Federal Finance' *Canadian Forum* 15: 170 (November 1934). J.M. Cassidy *Unemployment and Relief in Ontario 1929-1932* (Toronto n.d.).

5 Claxton Papers, vol 6, Rogers to Claxton, 28 September 1929. See also in the same volume the file 'Constitutional Amendment – Proposals for.'

6 On excessive provincial power, see for example Norman Rogers 'The Constitutional Impasse' *Queen's Quarterly* 41: 4 (winter 1934) 475-86; 'Government by the Dead' *Canadian Forum* 12: 134 (November 1931); 'One Path of Reform' *Canadian Forum* 15: 171 (December 1934) as examples. For Claxton see 'Social Reform and the Constitution' *CJEPS* 1: 3 (August 1935) 409-35; 'Amendment to the BNA Act' McGill *Daily News* (supplement) (June 1929); see also Norman Rogers Papers, King to Rogers, 25 February 1933 and Claxton Papers, vol 18, Claxton to Herridge, 31 July 1930.

7 'F.H.U.' 'O Canada' *Canadian Forum* 11: 129 (June 1931) 332. Montreal Gazette 15 December 1934

8 University of Toronto Archives, Political Economy Papers, Box 8, Plumptre to Innis, undated (1935).

9 Ibid. Lower to Innis, 26 January 1935. See also W.C. Kierstead to Innis, undated (1935).

10 Claxton Papers, vol 18, Claxton to Herridge, 26 December 1934. For this line of argument see Grant Dexter 'Commerce and the Canadian Constitution' *Queen's Quarterly* 39: 2 (May 1932) 259; Norman Rogers 'One Path of Reform' *Canadian Forum* 15: 171 (December 1934). Norman Rogers Papers, Rogers to Cassidy, 1 August 1935

11 Frank Scott 'Strengthening Confederation' memorandum for the Association of Canadian Clubs (undated, early 1930s). A copy is available in Brooke Claxton Papers, vol 10.

12 Claxton Papers, vol 18, Claxton to Herridge, 26 December 1934. James Struthers *No Fault of Their Own* 140. James Struthers 'Prelude to Depression: The Federal Government and Unemployment, 1928-1929' *CHR* 58: 3 (September 1977)

13 See Report of the Royal Commission on Dominion-Provincial Relations Book 3, tables 57, 58, 59 for statistics on the evolution of the municipal debt load in Canada.

14 *Statutes of Canada*, 1930, chap 1. Report on Dominion-Provincial Relations Book II, 20, and Book I, 162

15 Mackenzie King Diary, 22 October 1935. Ibid, 10 March 1936.

16 See ibid, for 9 and 13 December 1935. See also Neatby *William Lyon Mackenzie King* vol. 3, 142-8; N. Hillmer and I. Drummond 'A Shaft of Baltic Pine: Negotiating the Anglo-American Trade Agreements of 1938' paper presented to Canadian Historical Association, Ottawa, 1982.

17 PAC, Ian Mackenzie Papers, vol 40, File G-44, memorandum entitled 'Dominion-Provincial Conference – November 19, 1935: 1st organizational Meeting.' King Diary, 18 October 1935. Ibid, 10 March 1936
18 Canada *Proceedings of the Dominion-Provincial Conference of 1935* Appendix A2. Neatby *Mackenzie King* vol 3, 155
19 J.R. Rowell 'An Intellectual in Politics: Norman Rogers as an Intellectual and Minister of Labour' MA thesis, Queen's University, 1978, 117-21, 129-36
20 King Diary, 23 March 1936
21 The most detailed summary of the work of the National Employment Commission is contained in Struthers *No Fault of Their Own* 141-74.
22 *Canadian Forum* 16: 184 (May 1936) 3. Struthers *No Fault of Their Own* 143-4
23 Queen's University, W.A. Mackintosh Papers, File 'Alleviation of Distress,' pt 2. The memorandum was probably written by Charlotte Whitton.
24 Canada, Department of Labour, National Employment Commission *Interim Report* (Ottawa 1937) 10, 19. Neatby *Mackenzie King* vol 3, 247. See also King Diary, 20, 21 December 1937. Canada, Department of Labour *Final Report of the National Employment Commission* (Ottawa 1938). Note Mary Sutherland's minority report on 45-51.
25 King Diary, 3 January 1936. See, for example, Arthur Purvis 'Obligations of Government toward Social Security' *Child and Family Welfare* 13: 3 (September 1937).
26 King Diary, 3 January 1936
27 On Skelton, see J.L. Granatstein *The Ottawa Men: The Civil Service Mandarins 1935-57* (Toronto 1983) 59-60.
28 BCA, Research Department File 2b-400, memo of 4 January 1936, 'Provincial Debt Conversion and Loan Proposals' and file 2b-500, memo of 8 January 1936. My thanks to David Fransen for bringing these to my attention.
29 Ibid, 2b-500, 8 January 1936
30 PAC, Records of the Department of Finance, vol 3896, File P-1-10-1, Clark to Finlayson, 5 January 1935. BCA Research Department, File 2b-400, memo of 21 January 1936, 'The National Finance Council.' Canada, *Proceedings of the Dominion-Provincial Conference of 1935* Appendix A2, 'Report of the Sub-Conference on Financial Matters'
31 BCA, Research Department, File 2b-400, memo of 8 January 1936. Ibid, memo of 21 January 1936
32 Ibid, memo of 21 January 1936

33 Ibid, 2b-400, 1 February 1936
34 PAC, RG 47, vol 62, File C-1-5-1, memorandum by H.C. Goldenberg, 'Control of Public Debts in Canada.' Ibid, file of meeting of 9-13 December 1935, Clark to Dunning, 5 December 1935
35 LSR, *Social Planning for Canada* 345, 370-1. Brooke Claxton 'Social Reform and the Constitution' and W.A. Carrothers 'The Problems of the Canadian Federation,' both in *CJEPS* 1: 1, 3 (August 1935) 409-35 and 1, 1 (February 1935) 26-40. A.W. Ling, 'Centralization of Our Governments' *Canadian Banker* 43: 1 (October 1935). Norman Rogers 'The Political Principle of Federalism' *CJEPS* 1: 2 (May 1935)
36 BCA, Research Department, File 2b-170, A.E. Grauer, 'The Distribution of Taxing Powers in Canada' 30 August 1936. Records of the Department of Finance, E2C, vol 22, File 101-85-15, memorandum by 'ASk': 'The Case for a Royal Commission Enquiry on Provincial Finances.'
37 *Canadian Forum* 16: 194 (March 1937) 6
38 BCA, Research Department, File 2b-500, J.C. Osborne, 'Memorandum on Provincial Finances,' March 1936
39 BCA, Osborne to Lefeaux, 24 February 1937. *Debates*, House of Commons, 16 February 1937, 921-2. PAC, Newton Rowell Papers, vol 89, Rowell to Aunt Mary, 1 August 1937
40 G.F. Henderson *Federal Royal Commissions in Canada* (Toronto 1967) 134. Instead, Alberta presented its case in a separate publication, *The Case for Alberta* (Edmonton 1937). In all but the formalities this was another submission on the provincial position in Confederation.
41 PAC, Records of the Department of Finance, vol 22, W.C. Clark, 'Royal Commission on the Economic Basis of Confederation,' 12 December 1936
42 A.E. Grauer *Public Assistance and Social Assistance* appendix 6 to the Rowell-Sirois Report (Ottawa 1939); Brooke Claxton *Legislative Expedients and Devices Adopted by the Dominion and Provinces* Appendix 8 (Ottawa 1939); H.C. Goldenberg 'Municipal Finance in Canada' mimeographed study for commission; Donald Creighton *British North America at Confederation* (Ottawa 1939)
43 Report on Dominion-Provincial Relations, vol 2, 41.
44 Ibid, 27. Final Report of the National Employment Commission, 35. Report on Dominion-Provincial Relations, vol. 2, 28
45 Report on Dominion-Provincial Relations 83.
46 Ibid, 276. Larry Pratt 'The State and Province-Building: Alberta's Development Strategy' in Leo Panitch ed *The Canadian State: Political Economy and Political Power* (Toronto 1977) 133-62
47 Report on Dominion-Provincial Relations vol 2, 84

48 Ibid, vol 1, 13

49 F.R. Scott 'The Royal Commission on Dominion-Provincial Relations' *University of Toronto Quarterly* 7: 2 (January 1938) 145. *Winnipeg Free Press* 30 April 1938. 'Confederation Clinic' was the title of a column by McGeachy that appeared regularly during the hearings. *Financial Post* 10 April 1938

50 J.C. Dent *The Last Forty Years* vol 3 (Toronto 1881); A.W. Tilby *British North America 1763-1867* (London 1911); William Kingsford *The History of Canada* (London 1898). Of course new historical interpretations tend not to appear overnight, and it is possible to see the roots of the thinking of the 1930s in the work of the earlier generation of political economists. See, for example, *Canada and Its Provinces* vol 5. Adam Shortt 'Economic History, 1840-1867' 185-242; Edward Kylie 'Constitutional Development, 1840-1867' 105-157; Duncan McArthur 'History of Public Finance, 1840-1867' 165-80. See also Reginald Trotter *Canadian Federation* (London 1924). Carl Berger *The Writing of Canadian History* (Toronto 1976), chaps 3-4

51 Claxton 'Amendment to the B.N.A. Act' 8

52 F.R. Scott 'Strengthening Confederation'

53 P.E. Corbett 'The British North American Act and Our Crippled Constitution' *Canadian Banker* 45: 2 (January 1938) 159. Scott 'Strengthening Confederation' 22

54 Report ... Dominion-Provincial Relations vol 1, 29. See generally 21-30. See also W.A. Mackintosh *The Economic Background of Dominion-Provincial Relations* Appendix III of the commission (Ottawa 1939), and D.G. Creighton *British North America at Confederation.*

55 Report on Dominion-Provincial Relations vol 1, 215

56 Scott 'Strengthening Confederation' 12

57 P.E. Corbett 'The British North America Act' 163. Claxton 'Amendment to the B.N.A. Act' 8-9. Report on Dominion-Provincial Relations vol 1, 32

58 O.D. Skelton 'General Economic History, 1867-1912' in Adam Shortt and Arthur Doughty *Canada and Its Provinces* vol 9, *Industrial Expansion* I (Toronto 1914). Report on Dominion-Provincial Relations vol 1, 79.

59 Report on Dominion-Provincial Relations vol 1, 112

60 W.A. Carrothers 'Problems of the Canadian Federation' *CJEPS* 1: 1 (February 1935) 26. J.W. Dafoe 'Canadian Problems of Government' *CJEPS* 5: 3 (August 1939) 291. J.A. Corry *The Growth of Government Activities since Confederation* (Ottawa 1939) 2

61 Report on Dominion-Provincial Relations vol 43; emphasis mine

62 Ibid, 84; vol 2, 15, 17

63 Brooke Claxton 'Amendment to the BNA Act' 3-4; Scott 'Strengthening
   Confederation' 5; Rogers 'The Constitutional Impasse' *Queen's Quarterly*
   41: 4 (winter 1934)
64 Corry 'Growth of Government Activities' 3. J.A. Corry *Memoirs* 23-5
65 Scott 'Strengthening Confederation' 22

CHAPTER TEN: BUREAUCRACY, WAR, AND REFORM

 1 University of British Columbia, Alan Plaunt Papers, Box 2, Arthur Lower
   to Plaunt, 24 December 1938, Box 3, Carlton Mcnaught to Plaunt, 25
   January 1939. C.P. Stacey *Canada and the Age of Conflict* vol 2 (Toronto
   1981) 235-6. PAC, Frank Underhill Papers, vol 7, Pickersgill to Underhill, 9
   October 1939. University of Toronto Archives, Harold Innis Papers, Box
   1, C.R. Fay to Innis, 14 November 1939
 2 F.R. Scott 'Parliament Should Decide' *Canadian Forum* 19 (January 1940)
   313. Plaunt Papers, Box 2, Lower to Plaunt, 21 September 1939
 3 On 1939 budget, see PAC, Records of the Department of Finance, vol 3444,
   Monteith Douglas to Bryce, 14 September 1939; Bryce to Walter Salant,
   12 October 1939. See also John H. Thompson *Canada 1922-1939: Decades
   of Discord* (Toronto 1985) 302. On difficulties of reform see King Diary,
   10 May 1940, 27 May 1940. On Rogers and McLarty, see Paul Martin
   A Very Public Life vol 1. *Far from Home* (Ottawa 1983) 159, 215.
 4 On effects of Duplessis's departure, see J.L. Granatstein *Canada's War:
   The Politics of the Mackenzie King Government 1939-1945* (Toronto
   1975) 173-74. B.S. Kierstead 'The Effects of the War on the Concept of
   National Interest' *CJEPS* 8: 2 (May 1942) 207
 5 *Canada Year Book*, 1946, 1141
 6 Personal movements have been gleaned from various sources. The best
   single source is the 'Current Topics' column of *CJEPS*.
 7 Innis Papers, Box 2, G.V. Ferguson to Innis, 30 September 1942
 8 On Dining Club, see records of the Department of Finance, 3583, Marsh
   to Mackintosh, 12 February 1942. The most detailed and easily read
   description of the social connections of the Ottawa mandarinate is Granatstein *The Ottawa Men* chap 1.
 9 Innis Papers, Box 2, Brebner to Innis, 18 September 1942
10 On first group, C.P. Stacey, *Arms, Men and Government: The War Policies
   of Canada, 1939-1945* (Ottawa 1970) 125-9; on second group, Robert
   Bothwell and W. Kilbourn *C.D. Howe: A Biography* (Toronto 1979) chaps
   10-11. See also J. de N. Kennedy *A History of the Department of Munitions and Supply* (Ottawa 1950).

11 Granatstein *Canada's War* 175, 179
12 William Young 'Academics and Social Scientists versus the Press: The Policies of the Bureau of Public Information and the Wartime Information Board, 1939-1945' CHA *Historical Papers* 1978, 217-40
13 PAC, Records of the Department of Finance, vol 3445, File – R.B. Bryce, 1943-44. Clark's comment on Bryce to Clark, 8 April 1943
14 King Diary, 18 November 1942
15 Queen's University Archives, Norman Rogers Papers, Box 4, File – Speeches, 'Founder's Day Address, University of Manitoba, 21 October 1937. PAC, Brooke Claxton Papers, vol 18, Claxton to R.A. McEachren, 10 November 1942
16 As an example see W.H. Moore *The Definite National Purpose* (Toronto 1933). Moore was a Liberal MP 1926-30 and 1935-40. He was often critical of King for allowing the traditional philosophy of the Liberal party to be eroded by new ideas of state interventionism.
17 Report on Dominion-Provincial Relations, Book 1, 210
18 W.A. Mackintosh 'An Economist Looks at Economics' *CJEPS* 3: 3 (August 1937), 311, 316. The following paragraphs are also drawn from other speeches, comments, etc in the late 1930s and early 1940s. See, as examples, R.C. Wallace 'Planning for Canada' Presidential Address, *Transactions of the Royal Society of Canada*, Series 3, vol 35, 1941; B.S. Kierstead 'The Effects of the War on the Concept of National Interest' *CJEPS* 8: 2 (May 1942); R.J. Deachman 'The Twilight of the Personal Devil' unpublished manuscript, Rasminsky Papers, BCA; W.C. Clark 'Financial Administration of the Government of Canada' *CJEPS* 4: 3 (August 1938); J.A. Corry 'The Fusion of Government and Business' *CJEPS* 2: 3 (August 1936); W.A. Mackintosh Papers, Box 4, File 100, 'Social Security in Canada.' Also revealing, of course, is the Rowell-Sirois Report and its various studies.
19 B.S. Kierstead 'The Sirois Report. An Evaluation' *Public Affairs* 4: 1 (August 1940) 6. PAC, Claxton Papers, vol 18, Claxton to McEachren, 10 November 1942.
20 Queen's University Archives, Mackintosh Papers, Box 8, File 20, 'The Post-War World,' 6
21 R.A. Mackay 'The Nature and Function of the Social Sciences' *CJEPS* 10: 3 (August 1944) 281. For a good example of this sort of attitude towards planning see Grant Dexter 'Oscar Douglas Skelton' *Queen's Quarterly* 48: 1 (spring 1941) 6.
22 PAC, Underhill Papers, vol 5, Lower to Underhill, 15 October 1941
23 On the CCF and the war see Horn *League for Social Reconstruction*

(Toronto 1980) 156-64. F.R. Scott 'How Canada Entered the War' *Canadian Forum* 19 (February 1940) 344-6. Underhill Papers, vol 8, Spry to Underhill, 28 June 1939. Ibid, vol 6, McNaught to Underhill, 28 December 1942.

24 Horn *League for Social Reconstruction* 45, 137. See also 'Democracy in Danger' *Canadian Forum* 37 (March 1938) 403 on the Padlock Law.

25 LSR *Social Planning for Canada* chap 11

26 F.R. Scott 'Social Planning and the War' *Canadian Forum* 20 (August 1940) 139

27 Underhill Papers, vol 6, McNaught to Underhill, 5 May 1943. Ibid, Cassidy to McNaught, 27 April 1943. ibid, Underhill to McNaught, 7 May 1943

28 J.M. Macdonnell 'Can We Return to Freedom?' *Saturday Night* 57 (July 11, 1942) and 'A Conservative Party Is Essential in Canada' in ibid, 52 (18 July 1942)

29 Macdonnell 'The Conservatives and the New National Policy' Ibid, 57 (25 July 1942). Macdonnell's view of the importance of party closely mirrored that of his political adversary, Frank Underhill. See the latter's 'The Canadian Party System in Transition' *CJEPS* 9: 3 (August 1943).

30 J.L. Granatstein *The Politics of Survival* (Toronto 1967) 133-4. John Kendle *John Bracken: A Political Biography* (Toronto 1979) 199-201.

31 Armour Mackay 'The Men of 1914-1918 Begin to Take Over' *Saturday Night* 58 (2 January 1943)

32 University of Toronto Archives, Innis Papers, Box 1, W.J. Waines to Innis, 4 June 1941; M. Timlin to Innis, 31 January 1942; J. Thompson to Innis, 26 September 1942; A.F.W. Plumptre to Innis, 16 September 1941. Records of the Department of Finance, vol 3550, Bladen to Mackintosh, 2 June 1941

33 PAC, Records of the Department of Finance, Walter Bedard to Innis, 10 June 1941. See also Papers of the Department of Political Economy, Box 1, Alex Skelton to Innis, 5 June 1939. Harold Innis 'The Rowell-Sirois Report' *CJEPS* 5: 4 (November 1940) 563, 565. Similar concerns were raised about the relation between the expert and the average citizen by F.E. Dessauer 'The Party System and the New Economic Policies' *CJEPS* 9: 2 (May 1943) 139-49.

34 Innis 'The Rowell-Sirois Report,' 563-4

35 Ibid, 564

36 Innis Papers, Box 1, 'Meeting of Policy Group in Toronto, 14th of October 1941' Ibid, Box 2, R.W. Thomson to Innis, 26 April 1942; Graham Towers to Innis, 18 April 1941. See also *CJEPS* 7: 1 (February 1941) 92-4, for obituary of Glazebrook which raises similar concerns. Innis Papers, Box

3, Stephen Leacock to Innis, 20 August 1943; the comments by Innis are handwritten on the back.

37 Harold Innis 'Decentralization and Democracy' *CJEPS* 9: 3 (August 1943) 327-8, 329

38 Ibid, 329-30. See also his obituary of E.J. Urwick, *CJEPS* 9: 2 (May 1945) 265-8.

39 Harold Innis ed *Political Economy in the Modern State* (Toronto 1946) xvii

40 H.N. Fieldhouse 'Dictatorship and Democracy' *Queen's Quarterly* 47: 2 (summer 1940) 163-4

41 See as examples of technical writing in *CJEPS*: M.W. Reder 'Inter-Temporal Relations of Demand and Supply within the Firm' 7:1 (February 1941) 25-38; B.S. Kirkstead 'A Note on Equilibrium in Process' 9: 2 (May 1943) 55-68; Benjamin Higgins 'Post-War Tax Policy' 9: 4 (November 1943) 408-28; H.G. Littler 'A Pure Theory of Money' 10: 4 (November 1944) 422-47; on sociology: C.A. Dawson 'Sociology as a Specialized Science' and C.W.M. Hart 'Some Obstacles to a Scientific Sociology' in 5 (May 1940) 153-86. See also Social Science Research Council *First Annual Report*, 1941, 17.

42 R.A. Mackay 'The Nature and Function of the Social Sciences' *CJEPS* 10: 3 (August 1944) 284

43 F.R. Scott 'The Constitution and the War' *Canadian Forum* 19 (November 1939) 243

44 King Diary, 5 January 1940. Struthers *No Fault of Their Own* 202-3

45 Granatstein *Canada's War* 254. On the formation of the EAC see PC 2698, 14 September 1939, and King Diary, 12 September 1939.

46 *Debates*, House of Commons, 6 December 1940. Statement by Ian Mackenzie, 781-6, gives a good summary of the work of the Committee on Demobilization and Rehabilitation. PAC Records of the Department of Finance, vol 3538, File – Economic Advisory Committee, 'Quarterly Reports to the Prime Minister on the Work of the Advisory Committee for 1940'; vol 4660, 'Minutes of the Economic Advisory Committee' 12 March 1940

47 *CJEPS* 7: 2 (February 1941) 144-5. J.A. Corry 'The Crisis in Federalism' *Canadian Banker* 48: 2 (January 1941) 157. Corry was prolific in his support of the report. See his 'The Report of the Royal Commission on Dominion-Provincial Relations' Parts I and II *Canadian Banker* 47: 2 (July 1940) 386-99 and 48: 1 (October 1940) 22-33; 'Speech before the Canadian Club of Ottawa.' See also 'The Sirois Report. A Discussion of Some Aspects' *Canadian Forum* 20 (November 1940) with pieces by Underhill,

R.F. Leggett, and Dorothy Steeves 233-7; B.S. Kirkstead 'The Sirois Re-
port. An Evaluation' *Public Affairs* 4: 1 (August 1940) 1-7. R.S. Lambert
Our Other War Aim: The Social Services as Mirrored in the Sirois Report
(Toronto 1941).

48 Records of the Department of Finance, vol 337, Alex Skelton, 'The Sirois
Report and the War.' King Diary, 14 January 1941

49 Hepburn cited in David Fransen, 'Unscrewing the Inscrutable: Mandarins
and Federal-Provincial Reform' unpublished CHA paper, 1983, 14; King:
King Diary, 15 January 1941

50 On the involvement of Pensions and National Health with the idea of
health insurance, see R. Bothwell, 'The Health of the Common People' in
J. English and J.O. Stubbs ed *Widening the Debate* (Toronto 1978) 191-
220. PAC Ian Mackenzie Papers, vol 41, File G25B, 'Ministerial Statements
on Social Security since the Outbreak of the War,' speech to the Health
League of Canada, 15 January 1940. Bothwell 'Health of the Common
People' 196

51 PC 1218, 17 February 1941

52 Ian Mackenzie Papers, vol 61, File 527-64, Robert England to Mackenzie,
10 March 1941; Mackenzie to James, 20 February 1941. PC 6874, 9 September 1941

53 Horn *League for Social Reconstruction* 67

54 Records of the Department of Finance, vol 3583, File R-09 'Memorandum
– Committee on Reconstruction.' See also Cyril James 'Basic Problems
of Reconstruction' (statement before parliamentary committee on Reconstruction and Re-establishment, 14, 19 May 1942) Mackenzie Papers,
vol 62, File 527-64 (5).

55 Mackenzie Papers, vol 79, File 567-27, Mackenzie to King, 22 September
1941. King to Mackenzie, 24 September 1941. Ibid, Ilsley to Mackenzie, 28
November 1941, Mackenzie to Ilsley, 9 December 1941.

56 Advisory Committee on Reconstruction 'Interim Report Regarding Certain
Aspects of Government Machinery for Planning of Reconstruction Policies' 6-7. A copy is to be found in Ibid, vol 62.

57 Records of the Department of Finance, vol 4660, EAC Minutes, 12 March
1940. Mackenzie Papers, vol 62, File 527-64 (4a), James to Mackenzie, 6
July 1942.

CHAPTER ELEVEN: THE TRIUMPH OF MACRO-ECONOMIC MANAGEMENT

1 PAC, Records of the Department of Finance, 4660, Minutes of the EAC, 10
November 1942

2 PAC, Mackenzie Papers, vol 62, File G-27-64-6, 'Report of the Economic Advisory Committee on the Reconstruction Committee's Recommendations regarding Ministerial Responsibility for Reconstruction Planning' 30 November 1942.

3 J.L. Granatstein *The Ottawa Men: The Civil Service Mandarins 1939-1957* (Toronto 1983) 161-2; my thanks as well to David Fransen for his comments on bureaucratic infighting. Records of Department of Finance, 4660, 187-EAC-I, Heeney to Clark, 26 December 1942. PC 608, 23 January 1943. Records of Department of Finance, 3447, EAC sub-committee meeting of 19 March 1943

4 A.D.P. Heeney *The Things That Are Caesar's: The Memoirs of a Public Servant* (Toronto 1972) 58

5 Mackenzie Papers, vol 41, File G25b, 'Ministerial Statements on Social Security Since the Outbreak of War.' King Diary, 3 October 1941

6 King Diary, 10 January 1943. See also 7 January 1943, 24 January 1943.

7 Sir William Beveridge *Social Insurance and Allied Services* (London 1942)

8 King Diary, 5 December 1942

9 J.L. Granatstein *The Politics of Survival: The Conservative Party of Canada 1939-1945* (Toronto 1967) 141-50. Mackenzie Papers, vol 79, File 567-27, Mackenzie to C. Campbell, 14 December 1942. King Diary, 5 January 1943. For a summary of the Beveridge Report see Finance Records, 3583, File 3, 'Reference Summary of the Beveridge Report on Social Security.'

10 King Diary, 17 January 1943

11 Ibid

12 *Debates*, 24 January 1943, 2. A copy of this report is contained in the King Papers, J4, vol 425. Mackenzie Papers, vol 55, File 520-88, Mackenzie to Beveridge, 13 May 1943. King Diary, 24 May 1943

13 Leonard Marsh *Social Security for Canada* orig pub 1943 (Toronto 1975)

14 Records of the Department of Finance, 4600, File 187-EAC-I, Mackintosh to Gordon, 23 March 1943

15 On general interest in social reform, see 'The Beveridge Report' *Canadian Forum* 22, (January 1943) 291-2; 'Wanted: A Post-War Plan' ibid, (February 1943) 317-18; Watson Thompson 'Public Affairs – Thoughts on Post-War Reconstruction' *Queen's Quarterly* 50: 1 (spring 1943); Harry Cassidy *Social Security and Reconstruction in Canada* (Toronto 1943); Alexander Brady 'Reconstruction in Canada: A Note on Policies and Plans' *CJEPS* 8: 3 (August 1942). On McArthur's speech, see *Globe and Mail*, 16 March 1943.

16 'Planning Post-War Canada' *Canadian Forum* 23 (May, June, July, August

1943). *Winnipeg Free Press* 16 March 1943, 1, 3, 4. Ibid, 17 March 1943,
6. Other newspapers surveyed include the *Edmonton Journal, Toronto
Star, Montreal Gazette,* and Vancouver *Sun. Globe and Mail* 17 March
1943, 6.

17 Cited in Whitaker *The Government Party* 151

18 Granatstein *Canada's War* 251

19 J.A. Corry 'Some Aspects of Canada's War Effort' *Queen's Quarterly* 47: 3
(autumn 1940) 357. See, as examples, J.A. Corry 'The Growth of Government Activities in Canada, 1914-1921.' CHA *Annual Report* 1940, 63-73;
John Deutsch 'War, Finance and the Canadian Economy' *CJEPS* 6: 4
(November 1940) 525-42; C.A. Curtis 'Public Affairs – The War Economy
and the Budget' *Queen's Quarterly* 48: 2 (summer 1941) 173-85.

20 Records of the Department of Finance, 3452, File 'Post-War Planning.'
The speech 'North African Victory' was drafted by Claxton for King.
Mackenzie Papers, vol 62, File 527-64(5), 'Basic Problems of
Reconstruction'

21 This and the following paragraph represent the arguments of the following
sources, among others: Records of the Department of Finance, 3446, File
'Post-War Planning'; Memorandum by A. Skelton, 'Constitutional Problems of Post-War Policy'; B.H. Higgins 'The War and Post-War Cycle
in Canada 1914-1923,' in ibid 3563, File E-05; O.J. Firestone 'Post-War
Residential Construction' *The Canadian Banker* 50 (1943) 119-27; F.A.
Knox, 'Post-War Employment Problems' Ibid, 49 (July 1942) 409-22.

22 James 'Basic Problems of Reconstruction' 4. See also records of the Department of Finance, 3450, Memorandum by R.B. Bryce concerning
'Refund of 20% Fraction of Excess Profits Tax.' 12 June 1942, and Stuart
Jamieson 'Business Plans the Post-War' *Canadian Forum* 24 (July 1944) 60-
2; Albert Rose 'Post-War Consumption Program' in ibid (November
1944), 177-8. Records of the Department of Finance, 4660, Minutes of the
EAC Meeting of 12 March 1940

23 See as examples Violet Anderson 'Foreword' vii in her *Canada and the
World Tomorrow* (Toronto 1944); B.S. Kierstead 'Theoretical Advance and
Economic Equilibria' *CJEPS* 9: 1 (February 1943); Mabel Timlin *Keyne-
sian Economics* (Toronto 1942). Granatstein *The Ottawa Men* 256-8.
A.F.W. Plumptre *Mobilizing Canada's Resources for War* (Toronto 1941);
Plumptre's influence was, however, limited by his posting in Washington
during much of this period. BCA, Louis Rasminsky Papers, 76-976-4-12,
'Informal Transcript of Dinner Conversation, November 1970 at Cercle
Universitaire,' 26; the comment is attributed to Rasminsky. J.F. Parkinson
'Some Problems of War Finance' *CJEPS* 6: 3 (August 1940) 415

24 J.A. Corry 'Public Affairs – Some Aspects of Canada's War Effort' *Queen's Quarterly* 47: 3 (autumn 1940)

25 Deutsch 'War Finance and the Canadian Economy' 527, 537

26 Rasminsky Papers, LB 76-966-4, 'Notes for a Lecture to the Winnipeg Branch of the Institute of International Affairs,' 13. See, for a good commentary on the public mood, John English 'Canada's Road to 1945' *JCS* 15, 3 and 4 (fall 1981-winter 1982) 102.

27 Plumptre 'An Approach to War Finance' 2

28 *CJEPS* 9: 1 (February 1943) 137; 2 (May 1943) 287; 3 (August 1943) 445; 4 (November 1943) 626

29 See, for example, Records of the Department of Finance, 3996, I. Price to Ralston, 27 November 1939; Ralston to I. Price, 28 March 1940; Clark to A.J. Hills, 8 December 1942; R.B. Bryce to Mackintosh, 2 April 1942.

30 Leonard Marsh *Report on Social Security* 51. See also Harry Cassidy *Social Security and Reconstruction in Canada* (Toronto 1943).

31 Records of the Department of Finance, 3446, File 'Post-War Planning,' Memorandum by Skelton, 22 April 1943, 'Constitutional Problems of Post-War Policy,' 5; Leonard Marsh *Report on Social Security* 30; Weir 'The Meaning of Social Security' in Mackenzie Papers, vol 72, File G-25-12. Skelton 'Constitutional Problems' 5. Marsh *Report on Social Security* 30

32 Bothwell 'Health of the Common People' 200-1

33 Records of the Department of Finance, 3580, Mackintosh to Ilsley, 21 November 1941

34 Ibid, 4660, Minutes of the EAC Meeting of 16 January 1943

35 King Diary, 22 January 1943

36 K. Bryden *Old Age Pensions and Policy Making in Canada* (Montreal 1974) 94. Marsh *Report on Social Security* 163-7. Bothwell 'Health of the Common People' 199

37 Advisory Committee on Reconstruction *Final Report* 24 September 1943, 27. A copy is available in Records of the Department of Finance, 3976, File E-3-0. The report was later printed by the government.

38 Marsh *Report on Social Security* 196-208 gives his ideas on childrens' allowances. His comment on their low priority is reported in the *Winnipeg Free Press* 16 March 1943, 4.

39 Dennis Guest *The Emergence of Social Security in Canada* (Vancouver 1980) 127

40 Records of the Department of Finance, 3585, 'Minutes of the Advisory Committee Meeting of December 4, 1941. Ibid, 3561, File D14, Mackintosh to Leonard Brockington, 30 November 1940

41 A.F.W. Plumptre *Three Decades of Decision, Canada and the World*

Monetary System, 1944-1975 (Toronto 1977) 38. See ibid, and also Keith Acheson, J.F. Chant, and Martin Prachowny *Bretton Woods Revisited* (Toronto 1972), especially the article by Rasminsky, Mackintosh, Plumptre, and Deutsch, 'Canadian Views' 34-48.

42 Records of the Department of Finance, 3445, Bryce to George Luxton, 13 February 1942. Note also that Frank Coe, once of the University of Toronto, was actively involved in the Department of Treasury policy formation in the United States. Plumptre 'Canadian Views' in Acheson et al *Bretton Woods Revisited* 41. Records of the Department of Finance, 3445, Keynes to Bryce, 11 April 1942

43 King Diary, 2 June 1943

44 Skelton 'Constitutional Problems of Post-War Policy' 3

45 Robert Bothwell and William Kilbourn *C.D. Howe: A Biography* (Toronto 1979) 181-2

46 Advisory Committee on Reconstruction *Final Report* 11

47 'North African Victory' 23. Records of the Department of Finance, 3583, File R-09, 'Committee on Reconstruction'

48 Records of the Department of Finance, 3562, File E01, Committee on Reconstruction, 'The Organization of a Public Works Program.' Bryce's words are a marginal comment on 'North African Victory' 34.

49 Records of the Department of Finance, 3447, 'Meeting of Sub-Committee of March 29, 1943'

50 Ibid, 'Meeting of June 3, 1943.' King Diary, 11 June 1943

51 For a good example of this see H.M. Cassidy *Social Security and Reconstruction in Canada* 11, 135. Marsh *Report on Social Security* 16, 273. *Globe and Mail* 17 March 1943, 6

52 BCA, Research Department File 3b-172, Memorandum, 'Post-War Problems' 3 November 1943, 1

53 *Canadian Forum* 2 (March 1943) 'Revolution or Patching' 341

54 Skelton, 'Post-War Problems' 2. Advisory Committee on Reconstruction *Final Report* 40

55 University of Toronto Archives, Department of Political Economy Papers, Box 1, E.J. Urwick to Cassidy, 25 September 1936. See also H.M. Cassidy 'A Canadian Institute of Social Economic Research' in ibid. Ibid, Whitton to R.H. Coats, 30 September 1938

56 PAC, Whitton Papers, vol 4, Cassidy to Whitton, 28 December 1943. See also in the same volume Cassidy to King, 10 December 1943.

57 King Diary, 9 August 1943

58 *Debates*, House of Commons, 26 July 1944, 5434 (J.E. d'Anjou). Diamond 'New France'

59 Veronica Strong-Boag *The Parliament of Women: The National Council*

of the Women of Canada 1893-1929 (Ottawa 1976) 297. Dennis Guest, *The Emergence of Social Security in Canada* 49-61. See also J.L. Cohen *Mothers' Allowance Legislation in Canada* (Toronto 1927).

60 *Debates*, House of Commons, 11 February 1936, 105-6. My thanks to Shirley Ayer for obtaining these references.

61 Leon Lebel 'Les allocations familiales et les hommes d'affaires' *Actualité économique* 9: 3 (June 1933)

62 BCA, Research Department Files, Untitled Memo by Bryce, 21 June 1943. Records of the Department of Finance, 3448, Minutes of the EAC, 8 September 1943. See also 4664, 187-EAC-62, Walter Woods to Bryce, 24 September 1943.

63 Granatstein *Canada's War* 279, 267

64 Grant Dexter *Family Allowances* 2, 6

65 King Diary, 1 October 1943. Mackenzie Papers, vol 72, File G25-1, 'Children's Allowances.' King Diary, 13 January 1944

66 King Diary, January 13, 1944. Dexter *Family Allowances* 8

67 Charlotte Whitton *Baby Bonuses, Dollars or Sense?* (Toronto 1945) 5, 27, 33

68 Records of the Department of Finance, 4660, File 187-EAC-1, Corry to Mackintosh, 1 March 1944. Ibid, Mackintosh to Corry, 28 March 1944. Whitton Papers, vol 4, Cassidy to Whitton, 28 December 1943. Guest *Emergence of Social Security* 133

69 Dexter *Family Allowances* 14

70 On the background to the White Paper, see Bothwell and Kilbourn *C.D. Howe* 192-4.

71 Canada, Department of Reconstruction *White Paper on Employment and Income with Special Reference to the Initial Period of Reconstruction* (Ottawa 1945) 13

72 Ibid 1.

73 Granatstein *Canada's War* 450

CHAPTER TWELVE: EPILOGUE

1 Frank Scott 'Confederation: An Assessment' *Canadian Forum* 22 (July 1942), 105-6

2 J.R. Mallory 'Changing Techniques of Canadian Government' *Public Affairs* 7: 2 (winter 1944) 112. PAC, Records of the Department of Finance, 3976, File E-3-0, Mackintosh to Heeney, 8 June 1943

3 BCA, Research Department File, 3b-172 Memorandum 'Dominion Post-War

Policy,' 3 April 1943. Records of the Department of Finance, 3542, Alex Skelton 'Approach to Post-War Planning 11,' 10 June 1943. See also 3447, Minutes of the EAC of 24 March 1943.

4 Drew to King, 6 January 1944; cited in Canada *Dominion-Provincial Conference on Reconstruction*, Session of 2 May 1946, 431. For the details of Drew's position at the conference see Marc J. Gotleib 'George Drew and the Dominion-Provincial Conference on Reconstruction of 1945-6' *CHR* 66 (March 1985) 27-47.

5 Records of the Department of Finance, 4660, File 187 EAC-1, Mackintosh to Corry, 28 March 1944

6 Canada *Proceedings of the Dominion-Provincial Conference on Reconstruction* 6-10 August 1945, vii-viii

7 *Dominion-Provincial Conference* Session of 25 April 1946, 386-7

8 *Dominion-Provincial Conference* 6 August 1945, Plenary Session, 85

9 *Canada Year Book*, 1946, 886

10 *Dominion-Provincial Conference* 6 August 1945, 57

11 *Dominion-Provincial Conference*, First Plenary Session, 6 August 1945, 21. Gotleib 'George Drew and the Dominion-Provincial Conference' 42

12 *Dominion-Provincial Conference*, Plenary Session of 30 April 1946, 431. King Diary, 22 July 1944

13 *Dominion-Provincial Conference* Session of 8 January 1946, 257. Ibid, Session of 30 April 1946, 530. Gotleib 'George Drew and the Dominion-Provincial Conference' 34. PAC, Charlotte Whitton Papers, vol 4, Manning to Whitton, 10 March 1945. See also Provincial Archives of Alberta, Premiers' Papers, File 1200, Manning to Patullo, 16 July 1945.

14 Records of the Department of Finance, 3563, File G-00A contains the Mackintosh-Garson correspondence. Whitton Papers, vol 4, Garson to Whitton, 29 March 1945

15 *Dominion-Provincial Conference* Plenary Session of 26 January 1946, 324-5

16 Ibid, Session of 5 April 1946, 338. The rental agreements came out of the Dominion's June 1946 budget, and the steps leading to the negotiations are contained in ibid, Appendix C3.

17 Harold Innis *Political Economy in the Modern State* (Toronto 1946) Preface, xii

18 Frank Underhill 'The University and Politics' (1959) in his *In Search of Canadian Liberalism* (Toronto 1960) 269

19 John Porter *The Vertical Mosaic: An Analysis of Social Class and Power in Canada* (Toronto 1965) 425-30

20 Gilbert Jackson 'More Facts in the Case' Mimeographed copy of a speech. A copy is available in the Records of the Department of Finance, 3569, File J-00.

21 Whitton Papers, vol 4, Whitton to Bennett, 14 August 1946

22 Donald Creighton *The Forked Road, Canada 1939-1957* (Toronto 1976) 93-4, 159-60, 234; John Diefenbaker *One Canada* vol 2 (Toronto 1976) 53-4; G.P. Grant *Lament for a Nation: The Defeat of Canadian Nationalism* (Toronto 1965) 9

23 The crucial distinction between small villages, intimately tied to the rural community around them, and larger communities has long been recognized. See Charles J. Galpin *The Social Anatomy of a Rural Community* (Madison 1915).

24 Canada Year Book, 1930, 118-19, 1946, 110-13

25 Grant *Lament for a Nation*

26 See on this with regard to the Ottawa mandarinate, Granatstein *The Ottawa Men* chap 9.

27 Ibid, 254

28 BCA, Rasminsky Papers, 'Informal Transcript of a Dinner Conversation, November 1970, 13-14

Index